Angular Intervie… Questions and Answers

A developer's guide to interview success from Angular 2 to 20

2nd Edition

Anil Singh

www.bpbonline.com

Second Revised and Updated Edition 2026

First Edition 2018

ISBN: 978-93-65899-528

To View Complete BPB Publications Catalogue Scan the QR Code:

www.bpbonline.com

Dedicated to

This book is dedicated to all the passionate learners, aspiring developers, and seasoned professionals who strive to grow, innovate, and make a difference through technology.

To my family and mentors—thank you for your unwavering support, encouragement, and belief in my journey. Your guidance has been the foundation of my success. In moments of doubt, your faith reminded me why I started, and in moments of triumph,your presence made it meaningful.

To the global developer community—may this book serve as a stepping stone in your path to mastering Angular and achieving your career goals. May it inspire confidence, spark curiosity, and remind you that every challenge you overcome is a testament to your resilience and passion.

About the Author

Anil Singh is a seasoned solution architect with over 15+ years of experience in the software industry, currently working with a leading U.S. MNC. His expertise spans enterprise architecture, cloud solutions, and full-stack development, with a strong focus on modern web technologies.

Anil holds a B.Sc. in mathematics, a **master of computer applications** (**MCA**), and is a **Microsoft Certified Professional** (**MCP**). His academic foundation and professional journey have equipped him with a deep understanding of both theoretical and practical aspects of software engineering.

He is the author of the book Angular Interview Questions and Answers, a comprehensive guide designed for students, software engineers, tech leaders, and architects. The book distills years of hands-on experience and technical insight into a practical resource for mastering Angular and excelling in technical interviews.

Anil is also the founder of Code-Sample.com, a popular platform where he shares tutorials, code snippets, and architectural best practices to help developers grow their skills and stay current with industry trends.

Whether you are preparing for an interview or looking to deepen your understanding of Angular, Anil's work offers clarity, relevance, and actionable knowledge.

About the Reviewers

- **Akash Chourasia** is an IT professional with over 8 years of experience, specializing in frontend development, particularly with Angular. He has a strong background in building scalable, high-performance web applications, and is passionate about using modern frontend frameworks to create seamless user experiences.

  Akash is dedicated to best practices in UI/UX design, clean code, and performance optimization. He enjoys exploring new technologies, sharing knowledge with the community, and reading up on the latest trends in software development.

- **Chandrani Mukherjee** is a senior enterprise architect at Mphasis, where she designs AI applications that enhance productivity and reduce latency. Since 2024, she has also mentored interns and colleagues while representing the company at technology forums and events. Her expertise spans Python, LangChain, generative AI, vector databases, and large language models, including Google Gemini and AWS Bedrock LLAMA.

  Before joining Mphasis, Chandrani worked as an AI full-stack architect at McKesson in 2024 and as a data analytics and AI consultant at First Abu Dhabi Bank from 2022 to 2023. She previously contributed as an application and data engineer at Etisalat (2018–2022), a platform security developer with OSN (2018), a senior software engineer at Hewlett-Packard Enterprise (2016–2017), and a systems engineer at Tata Consultancy Services (2011–2016).

  Chandrani earned her B.Tech. in information technology from Netaji Subhash Engineering College and an MSc in machine learning and AI from Liverpool John Moores University. She also holds certifications in generative AI fundamentals.

  A senior member of the Society of Women Engineers, Chandrani actively promotes women's advancement in technology. Recognized with an Award for Excellence, she aspires to grow into leadership roles while continuing to contribute research and thought leadership in AI.

- **Neha Bhargava** is a full-stack engineer with over 10 years of experience building scalable web applications and developer tools. She has deep expertise in modern frontend frameworks, including Angular and React, and works extensively across backend systems using Node.js and cloud platforms. Her focus areas include performance optimization, developer experience, and clean architecture.

  Neha is passionate about creating tools and experiences that help developers build faster and more confidently. She has led multiple cross-functional projects aimed at simplifying complex workflows and improving integration experiences. As a technical reviewer, she brings a sharp eye for clarity, accuracy, and practical relevance. Outside of work, she mentors engineers and actively contributes to the developer community.

Acknowledgement

Writing this book has been a journey of reflection, learning, and growth, and it would not have been possible without the support of many incredible people.

First and foremost, I would like to thank my family for their endless patience, love, and encouragement. Your belief in me gave me the strength to keep going, even during the most challenging moments.

To my mentors and colleagues, thank you for sharing your wisdom, challenging my thinking, and inspiring me to strive for excellence. Your insights and feedback have been instrumental in shaping the content and direction of this book.

A special thanks to the developer community—your questions, discussions, and shared knowledge have been a constant source of inspiration. This book is a reflection of the collaborative spirit that drives our industry forward.

To the readers, learners, and professionals who pick up this book—thank you for trusting me to be a part of your journey. I hope this book serves as a valuable resource in your preparation and growth.

Lastly, I am grateful to the team at Code-Sample.com and everyone who contributed directly or indirectly to this project. Your support made this vision a reality.

Preface

In the dynamic world of software development, staying current with frameworks like Angular is more than a technical requirement; it is a gateway to building scalable, efficient, and modern web applications. Angular has become a cornerstone in front-end development, and with its growing adoption, the demand for skilled Angular developers continues to rise.

Over the course of my 15+ years in the software industry, I have had the opportunity to work with diverse technologies, lead architectural initiatives, and mentor developers across various stages of their careers. One consistent challenge I have observed is the pressure professionals face when preparing for technical interviews—especially when trying to quickly review and consolidate their knowledge. This book was created to address that challenge.

This book is designed as a practical, easy-to-navigate guide for students, software engineers, tech leaders, and software architects. Whether you are preparing for your first interview or brushing up before a senior-level discussion, this book offers a structured way to review key Angular concepts, understand common interview patterns, and build confidence.

Each question is crafted to reflect real-world scenarios and interview expectations. The answers are concise yet comprehensive, aiming to not only help you recall information but also understand the reasoning behind it. The goal is to make your preparation efficient, insightful, and empowering.

Also, this book introduces AI-enabled concepts and practices that are becoming increasingly relevant in modern development workflows, helping you stay ahead in a rapidly evolving tech landscape.

I also want this book to serve as a reminder: interviews are not just about technical correctness; they are about clarity, communication, and confidence. With the right preparation and mindset, you can turn every interview into an opportunity to showcase your skills and passion.

Thank you for choosing this book as part of your journey. I hope it becomes a valuable companion in your growth as a developer.

Chapter 1: The Basic Concepts of Angular - Explores the essential concepts of Angular, laying the foundation for building dynamic web applications. You will learn about Angular's core architecture, including modules, components, and templates, and how they work together to create a seamless user experience. We will introduce TypeScript, which powers Angular with statically typed and advanced tooling. It will guide you through the installation and setup of Angular using the Angular **Command Line Interface** (**CLI**) and explain how Angular's modules and components help structure your application.

Chapter 2: Concepts of Components - Explores the fundamental concept of components in Angular, which serve as the building blocks of any Angular application. Components encapsulate UI elements, manage data, and define application behavior, making Angular a powerful framework for developing dynamic and interactive web applications.

Chapter 3: Concepts of Template - Looks into Angular templates, the declarative HTML-based syntax that defines the structure and behavior of the user interface. You will learn how to use interpolation, property binding, and event binding to create dynamic views, and how structural directives help control rendering logic.

Chapter 4: Concepts of Directives - Angular directives allow developers to extend HTML with custom behavior. This chapter explains built-in directives such as ngClass, ngStyle, and ngModel, and guides you through creating custom directives to encapsulate reusable logic and manipulate the DOM efficiently.

Chapter 5: Concepts of Signals- Shows how signals enable fine-grained reactivity, automatically tracking dependencies and updating the UI with precision. The chapter also explores computed signals, which derive values from other signals, and effects, which react to signal changes without cluttering component logic.

Chapter 6: Concepts of Dependency Injection - Covers providers, injectors, and hierarchical DI, showing how services are injected into components and other services to promote loose coupling.

Chapter 7: Concepts of Routing - Explains how to configure routes, use route parameters, and implement guards to control access based on user roles or authentication status. You will also learn how to leverage lazy loading to split your application into smaller modules, improving load time and scalability. It covers nested routes, route resolvers, and dynamic navigation, helping you build complex, multi-view applications with clean and maintainable routing logic.

Chapter 8: Concepts of Forms – Compares template-driven and reactive forms, explores form validation, dynamic form controls, and best practices for managing user input and form state.

Chapter 9: Concepts of HTTP Client - Introduces Angular's HttpClient module, demonstrating how to perform CRUD operations, handle errors, use interceptors, and work with observables for asynchronous data.

Chapter 10: Concepts of SSR and Hybrid Rendering - Introduces Angular Universal, the official tool for SSR, and explains how it enables pre-rendering of pages on the server before sending them to the browser. You will also explore hydration strategies, which allow client-side interactivity to take over after server-rendered content is loaded seamlessly. The chapter discusses partial hydration, deferred loading, and how to balance rendering between server and client for optimal user experience.

Chapter 11: Concepts of Pipes - Covers built-in pipes like date, currency, and async, and shows how to create custom pipes for advanced formatting and filtering.

Chapter 12: Concepts of NgModules - Explains how to define root and feature modules, manage imports and exports, and use shared modules to promote code reuse and maintainability. However, it is important to note that in the latest versions of Angular, the framework has introduced standalone components and optional NgModules, offering a more streamlined and flexible approach to application architecture. While NgModules are still supported, developers are encouraged to explore these newer patterns for simpler and more modern Angular development.

Chapter 13: Concepts of Internationalization - Introduces Angular's i18n capabilities, including translation files, locale data, and tools for managing multilingual content and formatting.

Chapter 14: Angular Security - Discusses common vulnerabilities like XSS and CSRF, Angular's built-in protections, and best practices for authentication, authorization, and secure data handling.

Chapter 15: RxJS Concepts with Angular - Introduces observables, Subjects, and key operators like map, filter, and switchMap, showing how they simplify complex workflows. You will learn how RxJS integrates with Angular's forms, HTTP client, and component lifecycle to build responsive, scalable applications.

Chapter 16: AI Experimental Features - Explores cutting-edge features such as predictive UI behavior, where interfaces adapt intelligently to user actions, and smart data handling, which leverages AI to optimize data flow and decision-making. You will also discover tools that offer automated code suggestions, error prediction, and performance tuning, helping developers write cleaner, faster code with less effort.

Chapter 17: Compiler and Build Tools - Covers **ahead-of-time** (AOT) compilation, Webpack, Vite, and build configurations that streamline deployment and improve load times.

Chapter 18: Developer Tools - Introduces Angular DevTools, CLI utilities, and browser extensions that help developers inspect component trees, monitor performance, and troubleshoot issues.

Chapter 19: Angular Best Practices - Shares best practices for architecture, naming conventions, folder structure, performance optimization, and maintainability to ensure long-term success.

Chapter 20: Angular Testing - Covers unit testing with Jasmine, end-to-end testing with Protractor or Cypress, mocking dependencies, and strategies for achieving high test coverage.

Chapter 21: Angular Material - Explores layout systems, responsive design, accessibility features, and how to build visually appealing interfaces with minimal effort.

Code Bundle and Coloured Images

Please follow the link to download the
Code Bundle and the *Coloured Images* of the book:

https://rebrand.ly/b7e401

The code bundle for the book is also hosted on GitHub at **https://github.com/bpbpublications/Angular-Interview-Questions-and-Answers-2nd-Edition**. In case there's an update to the code, it will be updated on the existing GitHub repository.

We have code bundles from our rich catalogue of books and videos available at https://github.com/bpbpublications. Check them out!

Errata

We take immense pride in our work at BPB Publications and follow best practices to ensure the accuracy of our content to provide with an indulging reading experience to our subscribers. Our readers are our mirrors, and we use their inputs to reflect and improve upon human errors, if any, that may have occurred during the publishing processes involved. To let us maintain the quality and help us reach out to any readers who might be having difficulties due to any unforeseen errors, please write to us at: errata@bpbonline.com

Your support, suggestions and feedbacks are highly appreciated by the BPB Publications' Family.

Piracy

If you come across any illegal copies of our works in any form on the internet, we would be grateful if you would provide us with the location address or website name. Please contact us at business@bpbonline.com with a link to the material.

If you are interested in becoming an author

If there is a topic that you have expertise in, and you are interested in either writing or contributing to a book, please visit www.bpbonline.com. We have worked with thousands of developers and tech professionals, just like you, to help them share their insights with the global tech community. You can make a general application, apply for a specific hot topic that we are recruiting an author for, or submit your own idea.

Reviews

Please leave a review. Once you have read and used this book, why not leave a review on the site that you purchased it from? Potential readers can then see and use your unbiased opinion to make purchase decisions. We at BPB can understand what you think about our products, and our authors can see your feedback on their book. Thank you!

For more information about BPB, please visit www.bpbonline.com.

Join our Discord space

Join our Discord workspace for latest updates, offers, tech happenings around the world, new releases, and sessions with the authors:

https://discord.bpbonline.com

Table of Contents

CHAPTER 1
The Basic Concepts of Angular

Introduction

In this chapter, we will explore the essential concepts of Angular, laying the foundation for building dynamic web applications. You will learn about Angular's core architecture, including modules, components, and templates, and how they work together to create a seamless user experience. We will introduce TypeScript, which powers Angular with a statically typed language and advanced tooling.

Additionally, this chapter will guide you through the installation and setup of Angular using the Angular **Command Line Interface** (**CLI**) and explain how Angular's modules and components help structure your application. By the end of this chapter, you will have a comprehensive understanding of Angular's basic concepts and be prepared to explore more advanced topics in Angular, such as routing, state management, and testing, in the upcoming chapters.

Structure

This chapter covers the following topics:

- High-level architecture of Angular applications
- Basic Angular
- Installation of Angular
- Basic TypeScript
- Angular architecture

Objectives

The primary objective of this chapter is to offer a comprehensive introduction to Angular, a widely adopted framework for building dynamic, modern web applications. You will begin by understanding what Angular is and why it stands out as a preferred choice for developers worldwide. We will walk you through installing Angular using the Angular CLI and setting up your first project. Alongside, you will be introduced to TypeScript, the language that powers Angular, highlighting its key features, such as statically typed and object-oriented programming benefits. This chapter also explores Angular's architecture, including core building blocks like modules, components, templates, and services, and how they collaborate to form a functional application. Furthermore, you will gain insights into the structure of an Angular project, learning the purpose and organization of essential files and directories. By the end of this chapter, you will have a strong grasp of Angular's fundamental concepts, setting the stage for deeper exploration in the upcoming chapters.

High-level architecture of Angular applications

The following figure illustrates the high-level architecture of an Angular application, showcasing how its core building blocks, such as components, modules, services, and routing, interact within the framework:

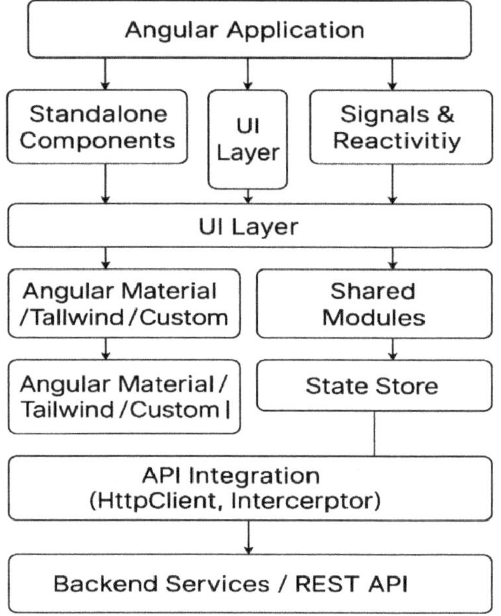

***Figure 1.1**: Architecture of Angular application*

Basic Angular

Question 1: What is Angular?

Answer: Angular is a powerful and versatile framework for building modern web applications. It provides a structured, scalable, and high-performance development environment. Some of its key features include:

- **Component-based architecture**: Promotes modularity and reusability by organizing the UI into cohesive, independent components.
- **Data binding**: Enables dynamic interaction between the component logic and the user interface.
- **Dependency injection (DI)**: Simplifies service management and promotes clean, testable code.
- **Routing**: Facilitates navigation and the creation of single-page applications with multiple views.

It is a TypeScript-based, open-source web application framework developed by *Google*. It is designed to build dynamic **single-page applications (SPAs)** with a component-based architecture. Angular offers a complete solution for developing scalable applications by providing built-in support for features like DI, data binding, routing, form management, and HTTP services. Its ecosystem includes the Angular CLI, which simplifies project setup, scaffolding, testing, and deployment.

Consider an example. When you run the following command, Angular CLI creates a new project with a standard file structure:

```
ng new my-angular-app
```

In Angular versions prior to v14, this command generated a root module (AppModule) and a root component (AppComponent), along with configurations for TypeScript, Webpack, and other tooling.

However, starting with Angular 14, and more prominently from Angular 17 onward, Angular introduced standalone components. By Angular 19, standalone components became the default, and creating a root module (AppModule) is no longer necessary unless explicitly specified.

Now, the project scaffold includes a standalone root component instead of a module-based setup. This shift simplifies Angular's architecture and aligns it more closely with modern frontend trends, making it easier for developers to start building applications without boilerplate module declarations.

It remains one of the most popular frameworks for front-end development. As of 2025, the latest stable version has been released, which introduces several of the following enhancements:

- **Incremental hydration**: Improves server-side rendering by allowing parts of the page to be hydrated incrementally, enhancing performance.
- **Route-level render mode**: Provides more granular control over how routes are rendered, allowing for optimized loading strategies.
- **Linked signals**: Introduces a new reactive programming model, enabling more efficient state management and data flow.
- **Event replay**: Enhances debugging capabilities by allowing developers to replay events in the application, aiding in troubleshooting.
- **Enhanced server-side rendering (SSR) with incremental hydration**: Angular 19 introduces incremental hydration, allowing parts of the page to be hydrated incrementally, enhancing performance. This approach enables faster initial page loads and smoother interactions by progressively activating server-rendered content on the client side.
- **Modernizing code with language service**: Improves the development experience by providing better code suggestions and error checking through the Angular Language Service.
- **Hot module replacement (HMR)**: Allows faster development cycles by enabling modules to be replaced without a full page reload.
- **Simplified management of micro frontend architectures**: Angular 19 simplifies the management of micro frontend architectures, allowing more efficient integration and development workflows. This enhancement facilitates the creation of scalable and maintainable applications by promoting modular development practices.
- **Standalone components by default**: A standalone component can exist without being part of any NgModule. Typically, in Angular prior to version 19, every component, directive, and pipe had to be declared inside an NgModule before it could be used. Standalone components eliminate the need for this structure and make the development process more flexible. The following are the benefits of standalone components:
  - **Reduced boilerplate code**: You no longer need to declare components in an NgModule to use them in other parts of the application.
  - **Improved flexibility**: Components, directives, and pipes can be used more independently, especially in smaller applications or micro-frontend architectures.
  - **Easier testing**: Standalone components can be tested individually without worrying about module dependencies.
  - **Cleaner and simpler application structure**: Developers can write cleaner code and structure smaller applications more easily.

  Above Angular 18, there is no need for the standalone as true declaration of the components is naturally standalone.

Example of a simple Angular component: The following is a basic example of an Angular component:

```
import { Component } from '@angular/core';
@Component({
  selector: 'app-root',
  template: `
    <h1>{{ title }}</h1>
    <button (click)="changeTitle()">Change Title</button>
  `,
  styleUrls: ['./app.component.css']
})
export class AppComponent {
  title = 'Hello, Angular 19!';
  changeTitle() {
    this.title = 'Title Changed!';
  }
}
```

In the preceding example, the **`AppComponent`** class defines a title property and a **`changeTitle()`** method. The component's template binds the title property to an **`<h1>`** element using **interpolation** (**`{{ title }}`**), and sets up a **click event binding** (**`(click)="changeTitle()"`**) on a button to invoke the method.

This demonstrates Angular's declarative approach to building user interfaces, where the view is automatically updated when the underlying data (model) changes. It also highlights two of Angular's core binding techniques: interpolation for displaying data and event binding for responding to user interactions.

Question 2: What are the main advantages of using Angular?

Answer: Angular's advantages include the following:

- **Modularity**: Code is organized into modules (NgModules) that group related functionality. Thus, it is easy to maintain and scale applications.
- **Component-based architecture**: **User interface** (**UI**) elements are encapsulated as components, making them reusable and testable.
- **Two-way data binding**: Synchronizes the model and view, reducing boilerplate code.
- **DI**: Improves modularity and makes components easier to test by providing required services.
- **Built-in tools**: Angular CLI, RxJS integration, and AOT compilation improve developer productivity and performance.
- **Seamless integration**: Works well with RxJS, Firebase, GraphQL.
- **Improved performance**: Faster rendering and change detection. Optimized change detection, lazy loading, AOT compilation
- **Better DI**: More efficient service management.
- **Enhanced forms application programming interface (API)**: Improved form handling and validation.
- **Angular signals**: A new way to manage reactive state.
- **Strong community support**: Backed by *Google* with frequent updates.
- **Security**: Built-in protections against **cross-site scripting** (**XSS**)

For example: Using DI, you can inject a service into a component without manually instantiating it by running the following code:

```
@Injectable({ providedIn: 'root' })
export class DataService {
  getData() {
    return [1, 2, 3];
  }
}
@Component({
  selector: 'app-numbers',
  template: `<div *ngFor="let num of numbers">{{ num }}</div>`
})
export class NumbersComponent implements OnInit {
  numbers: number[];
  constructor(private dataService: DataService) {}  // Dependency injected
  ngOnInit() {
    // Angular automatically calls ngOnInit when the component is initialized.
    // It is typically used to perform initialization logic like fetching data.
    this.numbers = this.dataService.getData();
  }
}
```

Question 3: What are standalone components in Angular?

Answer: Standalone components allow you to create Angular components without needing an NgModule.

Consider the following example:

```
import { Component } from '@angular/core';
@Component({
  selector: 'app-root',
  standalone: true,
  template: `<h1>Hello Angular!</h1>`,
})
export class AppComponent {}
```

Note: **The standalone: true property marks the component as a standalone component, meaning it does not need to be declared within an NgModule. This simplifies the application structure and is the recommended approach starting from Angular 17 and above.**

Installation of Angular

Question 4: How do you install Angular?

Answer: You can get started with Angular quickly with online starters or locally with your terminal. If you are starting a new project, you will most likely want to create a local project so that you can use tooling such as Git.

The following prerequisites must be met before installing Angular on your device:

- **Node.js**: V18.19.1 or later (compatible with Angular 19 and above).
- **Text editor**: Visual Studio Code is recommended.
- **Terminal**: Required for running Angular CLI commands.

- **Development tool**: To improve your development workflow, Angular Language Service is recommended.

The following is the step-by-step installation guide for the latest version of Angular:

1. **Install Node.js and npm**: Angular requires Node.js and **Node Package Manager (npm)**. To check if Node.js is installed, open a terminal and run the following:

   ```
   node -v
   npm -v
   ```

   If they are installed, you will see the version numbers on your screen.

   To install or update Node.js, perform the following:

   a. Download and install the **long-term support** (**LTS**) version from the official website of Node.js (**https://nodejs.org/en**).

   b. Restart the terminal after installation.

2. **Install Angular CLI**: Angular CLI helps in creating and managing Angular projects. To install and verify the installation, perform the following:

   a. Install Angular CLI globally by running the command:

   ```
   npm install -g @angular/cli
   ```

   b. Verify Angular CLI installation by running the following command, which displays the installed versions of the Angular CLI, Angular packages, and your development environment:

   ```
   ng version
   ```

3. **Create a new Angular project**: Once the CLI is installed, you can create a new Angular project by using the command:

   ```
   ng new my-angular-app
   ```

   Replace `my-angular-app` with your project name.

   It will prompt you to select additional options like routing and styling preferences (CSS, SCSS, etc.).

4. **Navigate to the project folder**: Run the command `cd my-angular-app`.

5. **Serve the Angular application**: To start a local development server, run the command:

   ```
   ng serve
   ```

   The default server runs at **http://localhost:4200/**. Open this URL in a web browser to view your Angular application.

6. **Upgrade to the latest Angular version**: This ensures compatibility with the newest features, performance improvements, and security updates.

   If Angular new version is released and you want to upgrade your project, run:

   ```
   ng update @angular/cli @angular/core
   ```

   This will update your Angular CLI and core packages to the latest version.

7. **Build the project for production**: To build an optimized version of your application for deployment, run:

   ```
   ng build --configuration=production
   ```

   This generates the `dist/` folder, containing the optimized production-ready files.

The following are optional steps you can perform:

1. **Installing additional dependencies**: For example, if your project needs Angular Material, run:

   ```
   ng add @angular/material
   ```

2. **Enabling standalone components**: If you are using standalone components instead of NgModule, ensure your component is marked with:

```
import { Component } from '@angular/core';
@Component({
  selector: 'app-root',
  standalone: true,
  templateUrl: './app.component.html',
  styleUrls: ['./app.component.css']
})
export class AppComponent {
  title = 'my-angular-app';
}
```

Question 5: How do you check the installed Angular version?

Answer: To check the version, run the command `ng version`. This will display the Angular CLI version and project dependencies.

Question 6: What is the difference between ng serve and ng build?

Answer: `ng serve` runs the application in development mode with live reloading. On the other hand, `ng build` creates an optimized production build inside the `dist/` folder.

Basic TypeScript

Question 7: What is TypeScript, and why is it used in Angular?

Answer: TypeScript is a superset of JavaScript that adds static typing, classes, interfaces, and other features. TypeScript compiles into standard JavaScript that is compatible with all browsers. Angular uses TypeScript because its static typing and advanced tooling (such as IntelliSense, compile time checking, and refactoring support) improve code maintainability and catch errors early during development.

TypeScript is used in Angular because it provides the following:

- **Static typing**: Helps catch errors at compile-time rather than runtime.
- **Better code maintainability**: Interfaces, classes, and strong typing improve code structure.
- **Object-oriented programming (OOP) features**: Supports classes, interfaces, and inheritance, making Angular more structured.
- **Improved tooling and IDE support**: It has features like autocompletion, refactoring, and IntelliSense.
- **ES6+ features**: TypeScript supports modern JavaScript features, making Angular development easier.

An example of a simple TypeScript class is as follows:

```
export class Person {
  constructor(public name: string, public age: number) {}
  greet(): string {
    return `Hello, my name is ${this.name}`;
  }
}
```

In Angular, you write components, services, and modules in TypeScript for a better developer experience.

Question 8: What are the key features of TypeScript that benefit Angular?

Answer: The following are some key TypeScript features that benefit Angular:

- **Interfaces**: Helps define object structures for better code consistency.
- **Strong typing**: Reduces runtime errors by enforcing variable types.
- **Decorators**: Used to define Angular components, services, and directives.
- **Classes and inheritance**: Supports OOP concepts.
- **Generics**: Allows reusable, type-safe functions and classes.
- **Modules and namespaces**: Helps organize code and avoid naming conflicts.

Question 9: **What are decorators in TypeScript, and how are they used in Angular?**

Answer: Decorators are special TypeScript functions used to modify classes, properties, or methods. In Angular, decorators are used for defining components, services, and directives.

For example:

```
import { Component } from '@angular/core';
@Component({
  selector: 'app-example',
  template: `<h1>Hello, Angular!</h1>`,
  styleUrls: ['./example.component.css']
})
export class ExampleComponent {}
```

Here, **`@Component`** is a decorator that marks **`ExampleComponent`** as an Angular component.

Question 10: **Can we use JavaScript instead of TypeScript in Angular?**

Answer: Technically, yes. However, Angular is built with TypeScript, and using JavaScript would mean losing the following:

- Type safety
- Decorators (like **`@Component`**, **`@Injectable`**)
- Better code organization (interfaces, modules)
- Enhanced development experience (**integrated development environment** (**IDE**) support, autocompletion)

For these reasons, TypeScript is the recommended language for Angular applications.

Question 11: **How does TypeScript improve performance in Angular applications?**

Answer: TypeScript improves performance in Angular applications by doing the following:

- **Compile-time error checking**: Detects issues before execution, reducing runtime crashes.
- **Code optimization**: Helps generate efficient JavaScript for better performance.
- **Predictable code execution**: Static typing ensures fewer unexpected errors.
- **Tree-shaking and dead code elimination**: Removes unused code, making the final bundle smaller.

Question 12: **What is the difference between TypeScript and JavaScript in Angular?**

Answer: TypeScript and JavaScript have the following differences, especially in the context of Angular development:

- **Typing**: TypeScript uses **static typing**, meaning variable types are defined at compile time, which helps catch errors early. JavaScript, on the other hand, is **dynamically typed**, where types are determined at runtime, making debugging harder.

- **OOP support**: TypeScript has built-in support for classes, interfaces, and inheritance, making it easier to write structured and maintainable code. JavaScript provides limited OOP support, relying mostly on prototypes.
- **Error detection**: TypeScript detects errors at compile-time, preventing many common bugs before execution. JavaScript detects errors only at runtime, which can lead to unexpected crashes.
- **ES6+ features**: TypeScript includes modern JavaScript features like arrow functions, async/await, and destructuring, even before they are natively supported in browsers. JavaScript often requires transpilers like Babel to use newer features.
- **Angular support**: TypeScript is officially used in Angular, leveraging decorators like `@Component` and `@Injectable`. While JavaScript can technically be used, it lacks support for these features, making Angular development less efficient.

In summary, TypeScript is preferred for Angular development due to its strong typing, better tooling, error prevention, and enhanced OOP capabilities, whereas JavaScript is more prone to runtime errors and lacks many advanced features required for large-scale applications.

Question 13: What is Angular used for?

Answer: Angular is a TypeScript-based front-end framework used for building SPAs and **progressive web applications (PWAs)**. It provides a component-based architecture, enabling developers to build scalable, maintainable, and modular applications.

The following are a few example use cases:

- **Enterprise web apps**: Large-scale business applications like dashboards (e.g., banking applications).
- **PWAs**: Web apps that behave like mobile apps (e.g., Twitter Lite).
- **E-commerce applications**: Online stores with dynamic product listings (e.g., Amazon, Flipkart).
- **Content management systems (CMS)**: Platforms like *WordPress* alternatives built using Angular.

Question 14: What is the difference between Angular and other frontend frameworks like React or Vue?

Answer: Angular is a full-fledged front-end framework developed by Google, while React and Vue are primarily libraries for building user interfaces. The key difference lies in their architecture, approach to state management, and learning curve, shown as follows:

- **Angular** is built using TypeScript and follows a component-based architecture with built-in DI, form validation, and routing. It provides everything required to develop a large-scale enterprise application without needing external libraries.
- **React**, developed by *Facebook*, is a UI library that focuses on building components using **JavaScript (JSX)**. It requires third-party libraries for features like routing and state management (e.g., React Router, Redux). React is more flexible but requires additional setup for a complete application.
- **Vue.js** is a progressive framework that is lightweight and easy to integrate. It allows developers to adopt its features gradually, making it beginner-friendly. Vue's templating syntax is similar to Angular's but simpler, and it provides built-in state management through Vuex.

The following are some use cases:

- Use **Angular** when building large-scale applications requiring built-in routing, DI, and form handling.
- Use **React** if you need a lightweight UI library with flexible state management.
- Use **Vue.js** for a simpler, faster development experience with minimal configuration.

In summary, Angular is a structured, opinionated framework best suited for large, complex applications, whereas React and Vue offer more flexibility and simplicity, making them popular for smaller, fast-paced projects. Here is a side-by-side visual comparison of the architectures of React and Vue to help you understand their core building blocks and design philosophies:

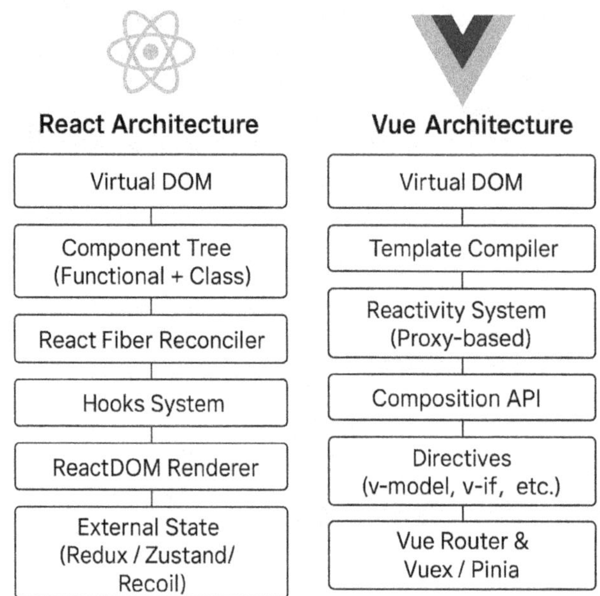

Figure 1.2: Architecture of React and Vue

Angular architecture

Question 15: What is the architecture of an Angular application?

Answer: Angular follows a modular architecture consisting of the following:

- **Modules (NgModule)**: Defines a cohesive block of functionality (e.g., `AppModule`).
- **Components**: UI building blocks with a template, logic, and styling.
- **Templates**: Define HTML structure using Angular directives and bindings.
- **Directives**: Modify the behavior of DOM elements (`ngIf`, `ngFor`).
- **Services and DI**: Reusable business logic and data management.
- **Routing**: Enables navigation across different views (`RouterModule`).
- **Pipes**: Format and transform data (e.g., date, currency).

For example:

```
@Component({
  selector: 'app-hello',
  template: `<h1>Hello, {{ name }}</h1>`,
})
export class HelloComponent {
  name = 'Angular';
}
```

Question 16: What is the role of Angular CLI?

Answer: Angular CLI simplifies project setup, development, and maintenance. It provides commands for the following:

- **Create a new project**: `ng new my-angular-app`
- **Serve the application**: `ng serve`
- **Generate a new component**: `ng generate component my-component`

- **Build the project for production**: `ng build --configuration=production`

Angular CLI automates tasks like compiling TypeScript, optimizing assets, and running tests.

Question 17: **What is the purpose of package.json in an Angular project?**

Answer: The **`package.json`** file contains metadata and dependencies for the Angular project. It contains the following key sections:

- **dependencies**: Lists required packages (e.g., **`@angular/core`**).
- **devDependencies**: Lists development-only packages (e.g., **`karma`**, **`typescript`**).
- **scripts**: Defines custom commands (**`ng serve`**, **`ng test`**).

For example (package.json snippet):

```
{
  "dependencies": {
    "@angular/core": "^20.0.0",
    "rxjs": "^7.8.0"
  },
  "devDependencies": {
    "typescript": "^5.0.0"
  },
  "scripts": {
    "start": "ng serve",
    "build": "ng build"
  }
}
```

Question 18: **What is the purpose of angular.json in an Angular project?**

Answer: The **`angular.json`** file configures the Angular workspace, including the following:

- Project settings (entry files, output directory).
- Build configurations (development, production).
- Optimization options.

For example (angular.json snippet):

```
{
  "projects": {
    "my-angular-app": {
      "architect": {
        "build": {
          "options": {
            "outputPath": "dist/my-angular-app"
          }
        }
      }
    }
  }
}
```

Question 19: How does Angular handle updates and versioning?

Answer: Angular follows semantic versioning (**MAJOR.MINOR.PATCH**), with new releases every six months.

Use ng update to upgrade dependencies with the following command:

```
ng update @angular/cli @angular/core
```

Breaking changes only occur in major versions. LTS is provided for enterprise projects.

Question 20: What are some common Angular build errors, and how do you troubleshoot them?

Answer: The following are some common Angular build errors with their solutions:

- **Module not found**

  Error: `Cannot find module @angular/core`

  Solution: Run **`npm install`** to restore dependencies.

- **Typescript compilation error**

  Error: `Type 'string' is not assignable to type 'number'`

  Solution: Ensure proper type assignments.

- **Port already in use**

  Error: `Port 4200 is already in use`

  Solution: Use a different port: **`ng serve --port 4300`**.

Question 21: What are monorepos, and how can Angular support them?

Answer: A monorepo is a single repository that contains multiple projects (e.g., frontend, backend, shared libraries). Angular supports monorepos using Nx or Lerna.

Let us consider an example. A monorepo containing an Angular app and a shared library can be created using the following command:

```
ng generate library shared
```

Question 22: What are polyfills in Angular, and why are they needed?

Answer: Polyfills allow Angular applications to support older browsers (e.g., IE11). It is defined in **`src/polyfills.ts`**.

For example, to enable ES6 support in older browsers, run the command:

```
import 'core-js/es6';
```

Question 23: What is the purpose of the main.ts file in an Angular application?

Answer: The **`main.ts`** file is the entry point of an Angular application. It bootstraps the root module (**`AppModule`**).

For example (main.ts):

```
import { platformBrowserDynamic } from '@angular/platform-browser-dynamic';
import { AppModule } from './app/app.module';
platformBrowserDynamic().bootstrapModule(AppModule);
```

Question 24: How does Angular handle browser compatibility?

Answer: Angular uses polyfills for older browsers and supports progressive enhancement for modern features. Additionally, it uses AOT compilation for optimized performance.

Question 25: What is the Angular workspace structure?

Answer: An Angular workspace contains the following:

- **src/**: Source code (components, modules).

- **angular.json**: Project configuration.
- **package.json**: Dependencies.
- **node_modules/**: Installed packages.

Question 26: **What is the purpose of the app.module.ts file in Angular?**

Answer: The **app.module.ts** file is the root module of an Angular application, where all the essential configurations, components, directives, and services are declared and imported. It is responsible for bootstrapping the application by defining the root component.

The following is the structure of **app.module.ts**:

```
import { NgModule } from '@angular/core';
import { BrowserModule } from '@angular/platform-browser';
import { AppComponent } from './app.component';
@NgModule({
  declarations: [AppComponent], // Declaring components, directives, and pipes
  imports: [BrowserModule], // Importing required Angular modules
  providers: [], // Defining services for dependency injection
  bootstrap: [AppComponent] // Defining the root component for bootstrapping
})
export class AppModule { }
```

The **app.module.ts** file has the following key roles:

- Declares components, directives, and pipes.
- Imports other Angular modules (e.g., FormsModule, HttpClientModule).
- Provides services for DI.
- Defines the entry component (bootstrap component).

With standalone components in Angular 17+, NgModule is now optional for new applications, but it is still used in existing projects.

Question 27: **What is prerendering in Angular, and how does it improve performance?**

Answer: Prerendering in Angular is an SSR technique where static HTML is generated at build time for pages that do not require dynamic content. It has the following benefits:

- Faster initial load time for users.
- **Search engine optimization** (**SEO**) friendly, as search engines can index pre-rendered pages.
- Better performance on slow networks.

Example using Angular Universal and prerendering:

1. To enable prerendering, install Angular Universal using the following command:

   ```
   ng add @angular/ssr
   ```

2. Configure prerendering in **angular.json** by running the following:

   ```
   "configurations": {
     "production": {
       "prerender": true
     }
   }
   ```

3. Run the prerender command:

   ```
   ng run my-app:prerender
   ```

This will generate static HTML files for each route, improving performance and SEO.

Question 28: What is a multi-project workspace in Angular, and how is it structured?

Answer: A multi-project workspace allows multiple Angular applications and libraries to exist within a single workspace, making it ideal for monorepos.

The following is the structure of a multi-project workspace:

```
my-workspace/
|— projects/
|   ├— app1/
|   ├— app2/
|   ├— shared-lib/
|— angular.json
|— package.json
|— tsconfig.json
```

To create a multi-project workspace, run the following:

```
ng new my-workspace --create-application=false
cd my-workspace
ng generate application app1
ng generate application app2
ng generate library shared-lib
```

This helps in code reuse, faster builds, and better project organization.

Question 29: What is lazy loading in Angular, and how does it work?

Answer: Lazy loading is a design pattern that loads feature modules only when they are needed, rather than at the initial application load. This improves performance by reducing the initial bundle size and speeding up the app's loading time.

Example of lazy loading: Here is a breakdown of the steps involved:

1. **Create a feature module**:

   ```
   ng generate module feature --route=feature --module=app.module
   ```

2. **Define routes in the app module**:

   ```
   const routes: Routes = [
     { path: 'feature', loadChildren: () => import('./feature/feature.module').then(m =>
   m.FeatureModule) }
   ];
   ```

3. **Create a feature component**:

   ```
   ng generate component feature/feature-component
   ```

4. **Define routes inside the feature module**:

   ```
   import { NgModule } from '@angular/core';
   import { RouterModule, Routes } from '@angular/router';
   import { FeatureComponent } from './feature.component';
   const routes: Routes = [{ path: '', component: FeatureComponent }];
   @NgModule({
   ```

```
  imports: [RouterModule.forChild(routes)],
  exports: [RouterModule]
})
export class FeatureRoutingModule { }
```

5. **Import the routing module in the feature module**:

```
import { NgModule } from '@angular/core';
import { CommonModule } from '@angular/common';
import { FeatureRoutingModule } from './feature-routing.module';
import { FeatureComponent } from './feature.component';
@NgModule({
  declarations: [FeatureComponent],
  imports: [CommonModule, FeatureRoutingModule]
})
export class FeatureModule { }
```

Now, the **`FeatureModule`** will only be loaded when the user navigates to '/feature', reducing the initial bundle size and improving app performance.

Question 30: **What is the difference between eager loading and lazy loading in Angular?**

Answer: **Eager loading** ensures that all modules are loaded when the application starts, regardless of whether they are used immediately. This method is commonly applied to core modules, such as the **`AppModule`**, which must be readily available for the application to function properly. Below are its key advantages and drawbacks:

The key advantages of eager loading are as follows:

- Faster navigation after the initial load since all modules are preloaded and readily available.
- Simpler setup as modules are loaded upfront, eliminating the need for dynamic loading configurations.

The following are the key drawbacks of eager loading:

- Slower initial load time since all modules are bundled together, increasing startup time.
- Higher memory consumption due to loading unused modules, which may impact performance.

Lazy loading loads modules only when they are requested, enhancing the application's startup time. It is commonly used for feature modules that are not required immediately after the application loads. The following are some of the key advantages and potential drawbacks of using lazy loading:

- Improved initial load time since modules are loaded only when needed.
- Better performance for large applications by reducing the initial bundle size.

Key drawbacks of lazy loading are:

- Navigation might be slower for the first use of a lazy loaded module since it needs to be fetched.
- More complex setup due to configuring routes for lazy loading.

In summary, eager loading is better for essential modules that need to be available immediately, while lazy loading optimizes performance by loading less critical modules on demand.

Question 31: **What is change detection in Angular, and how does it work?**

Answer: Change detection is the process by which Angular detects and updates the UI when the state of a component changes. The following are the types of change detection:

- **Default change detection**: It checks the entire component tree.

Example of default change detection: Here is a breakdown of the steps involved:

1. **Create a parent component (app.component.ts)**:

    ```
    import { Component } from '@angular/core';
    @Component({
      selector: 'app-root',
      template: `  <h1>Counter: {{ counter }}</h1>
        <button (click)="increment()">Increment</button>
        <app-child [message]="message"></app-child> `
    })
    export class AppComponent {
      counter = 0;
      message = 'Hello from Parent';
      increment() {
        this.counter++;
      }
    }
    ```

2. **Create a child component (child.component.ts)**:

    ```
    import { Component, Input } from '@angular/core';
    @Component({
      selector: 'app-child',
      template: `<p>Child Component Message: {{ message }}</p>`
    })
    export class ChildComponent {
      @Input() message!: string;
      ngDoCheck() {
        console.log('Change detection triggered in ChildComponent');
      }
    }
    ```

The preceding example performs the following points:

- Clicking the **`increment`** button updates the counter in the parent component.
- Even though the message input property in **`ChildComponent`** has not changed, Angular still triggers **change detection** in the child component because the default strategy checks the entire component tree.
- The **`ngDoCheck()`** lifecycle hook logs to the console whenever the child component undergoes change detection. Angular triggers change detection in the child component because its inputs are bound to the parent component. Even if the input values have not changed, Angular's default change detection strategy still checks the entire component tree, including child components.

This approach ensures the UI remains in sync with the application state but may lead to performance issues for large applications.

- **OnPush strategy**: It checks only when input properties change.

  Example of OnPush change detection:

```
import { Component, ChangeDetectionStrategy, Input } from '@angular/core';
```

```
@Component({
  selector: 'app-child',
  template: `<p>{{ data }}</p>`,
  changeDetection: ChangeDetectionStrategy.OnPush
})
export class ChildComponent {
  @Input() data!: string;
}
```

This approach optimizes performance by reducing unnecessary UI updates.

Question 32: How does Angular handle HTTP requests?

Answer: Angular provides **`HttpClientModule`** for making HTTP requests.

For example, to fetch data, complete the following steps:

1. Import **`HttpClientModule`** in **`app.module.ts`** using the following:

```
import { HttpClientModule } from '@angular/common/http';
@NgModule({
  imports: [HttpClientModule]
})
export class AppModule { }
```

2. Use **`HttpClient`** in a service by running the following:

```
import { HttpClient } from '@angular/common/http';
@Injectable({ providedIn: 'root' })
export class DataService {
  constructor(private http: HttpClient) {}
  fetchData() {
    return this.http.get('https://api.example.com/data');
  }
}
```

Question 33: What is the role of Angular interceptors in HTTP requests?

Answer: Interceptors allow modifying both HTTP requests and responses globally. They can be used to handle tasks such as authentication, logging, error handling, or transforming request and response data before it reaches the server or the application. Key capabilities of Angular HTTP Interceptors are as follows:

- **Modify requests globally**:
  - Add custom headers (e.g., authentication tokens, content type).
  - Modify request bodies before sending to the server.
  - Attach query parameters or credentials.
- **Handle responses**:
  - Catch and handle HTTP errors globally.
  - Log responses for auditing or debugging.
  - Transform response data before it reaches the component or service.

- **Authentication and authorization**:
    - Automatically attach JWT or OAuth tokens to requests.
    - Redirect to login if an unauthorized (401) error is encountered.
- **Centralized error handling**:
    - Handle common errors like 400, 401, 500, etc., in one place.
    - Show global error messages or notifications.
- **Loading indicators or spinners**:
    - Track and manage the start and completion of HTTP requests.

An example of adding an auth token is shown as follows:

```
import { HttpInterceptor, HttpRequest, HttpHandler } from '@angular/common/http';
@Injectable()
export class AuthInterceptor implements HttpInterceptor {
  intercept(req: HttpRequest<any>, next: HttpHandler) {
    const cloned = req.clone({
      headers: req.headers.set('Authorization', 'Bearer token')
    });
    return next.handle(cloned);
  }
}
```

Then, register the interceptor in providers by running the following:

```
providers: [{ provide: HTTP_INTERCEPTORS, useClass: AuthInterceptor, multi: true }]
```

The HTTP interceptors (**HTTP_INTERCEPTORS**) are powerful tools in Angular that:

- Allow centralized control of all HTTP traffic.
- Reduce redundancy in request/response handling.
- Improve consistency, security, and maintainability.

They are essential for building enterprise-grade Angular applications where cross-cutting concerns like auth and error handling must be managed efficiently.

Question 34: How does Angular handle animations, and what is the @angular/animations module used for?

Answer: Angular provides a built-in animation module (**@angular/animations**) to create smooth transitions.

For example, for a fade-in animation, run the following code:

```
import { trigger, state, style, transition, animate } from '@angular/animations';
@Component({
  selector: 'app-box',
  template: `<div [@fadeIn]>Hello</div>`,
  animations: [
    trigger('fadeIn', [
      state('void', style({ opacity: 0 })),
      transition(':enter', [animate('500ms ease-in', style({ opacity: 1 }))])
    ])
```

```
  ]
})
export class BoxComponent {}
```

Note: **In addition to this basic fade-in effect, Angular provides powerful animation APIs such as `trigger()`, `state()`, `transition()`, and `animate()` to define complex animations. These animations can be dynamically controlled based on component state, application logic, or user interactions, enabling the creation of highly interactive and visually engaging UIs with smooth transitions.**

The following are the benefits of Angular animations:

- **Improved user experience (UX)**: Animations enhance the smoothness of UI transitions, providing visual feedback and guiding users through interactions.
- **Performance optimization**: Animations use CSS for **graphics processing unit** (**GPU**) acceleration, improving rendering performance and reducing memory usage.
- **Declarative syntax**: Angular's animation API is simple to use, reducing complexity while allowing smooth integration with UI states.
- **Reusability**: Animations can be reused across components, ensuring consistency and reducing code duplication.
- **Responsive UI**: Angular enables conditionally triggered animations based on application state or user interactions.
- **Accessibility**: Animations can be customized for users with reduced motion preferences, enhancing accessibility.
- **Custom animations**: Angular supports advanced custom animations, providing control over keyframes, timing, and easing functions.
- **Cross-platform consistency**: Animations work consistently across browsers and devices, offering a smooth experience on mobile and desktop platforms.

In essence, Angular animations enhance UI interactivity and performance while ensuring simplicity, reusability, and accessibility.

Conclusion

In this chapter, we covered the foundational concepts of Angular, including the essential tools and structures that make Angular a powerful framework for building web applications. We explored the basics of Angular, components, and TypeScript, along with their benefits. By now, you should be equipped with the fundamental knowledge of Angular's architecture, enabling you to develop more complex applications.

In the next chapter, we will explore components, one of the most important aspects of Angular. You will learn how to create, configure, and manage components, which are the building blocks of your Angular applications. We will also explore component lifecycle hooks, templates, and styling, along with best practices for using and organizing components effectively.

Join our Discord space

Join our Discord workspace for latest updates, offers, tech happenings around the world, new releases, and sessions with the authors:

https://discord.bpbonline.com

Chapter 2
Concepts of Components

Introduction

This chapter explores the fundamental concept of components in Angular, which serve as the building blocks of any Angular application. Components encapsulate UI elements, manage data, and define application behavior, making Angular a powerful framework for developing dynamic and interactive web applications.

Components promote modularity, reusability, and maintainability in web applications. By structuring an application with well-defined components, developers can create scalable solutions that are easier to manage and extend. Understanding how components work, their lifecycle, and how they interact with one another is essential for writing efficient Angular applications.

By the end of this chapter, readers will gain a deep understanding of Angular components, including their structure, lifecycle hooks, data-binding techniques, and communication methods. This knowledge will enable developers to design well-structured applications while following best practices to enhance performance and maintainability.

Structure

This chapter covers the following topics:

- Basic questions
- Intermediate questions
- Advanced questions
- Performance optimization and best practices

Objectives

By the end of this chapter, you will have a strong understanding of the role and importance of components in Angular applications, enabling you to build modular and scalable user interfaces. You will learn about the structure of an Angular component, including its templates, styles, and logic, and explore different types of data binding that facilitate dynamic interactions within an application. Additionally, this chapter will guide you through the component lifecycle, explaining how lifecycle hooks help manage component behavior efficiently.

You will also gain insights into component communication by implementing input and output properties, event emitters, and service-based interaction. A dedicated section will focus on standalone components, highlighting their advantages and how they eliminate the need for NgModules, simplifying Angular development. Finally, you will explore best practices for designing reusable, maintainable, and performance-optimized components, ensuring that your applications are both scalable and efficient.

Basic questions

Question 1: What is a component in Angular?

Answer: A component is the fundamental building block of an Angular application. It controls a part of the UI and consists of the following:

- An HTML template (defines the view)
- A TypeScript class (defines logic)
- A CSS file (defines styles)

Each component is a TypeScript class decorated with **`@Component`**, which provides metadata such as the selector, template, and styles.

Example:

```
import { Component } from '@angular/core';
@Component({
  selector: 'app-hello-world',
  template: `<h1>Hello, {{ name }}!</h1>`,
  styles: ['h1 { color: blue; }']
})
export class HelloWorldComponent {
  name: string = 'Angular';
}
```

Here, **`HelloWorldComponent`** is an Angular component that displays **`Hello, Angular!`** in blue.

Question 2: How do you create a component in Angular?

Answer: You can create a component in Angular using the Angular CLI or manually.

To create a component using Angular CLI, which is the recommended approach, run the following command in the terminal:

```
ng generate component component-name
```

or

```
ng g c component-name
```

This will generate the following:

- **`component-name.component.ts`** (TypeScript logic)
- **`component-name.component.html`** (template)
- **`component-name.component.css`** (styles)
- **`component-name.component.spec.ts`** (unit test file)

To create a component manually, complete the following steps:

1. Create a new **.ts** file and define a class decorated with **@Component**.
2. Specify the selector, template, and styles.
3. Declare the component inside a module (**app.module.ts** or a feature module).

Example:

```
import { Component } from '@angular/core';
@Component({
  selector: 'app-manual-component',
  template: `<p>Manually created component</p>`,
  styles: ['p { color: green; }']
})
export class ManualComponent {}
```

Add the component to **app.module.ts**, shown as follows:

```
import { NgModule } from '@angular/core';
import { BrowserModule } from '@angular/platform-browser';
import { AppComponent } from './app.component';
import { ManualComponent } from './manual-component.component';
@NgModule({
  declarations: [AppComponent, ManualComponent],
  imports: [BrowserModule],
  bootstrap: [AppComponent]
})
export class AppModule {}
```

Question 3: What are the main building blocks of an Angular component?

Answer: An Angular component consists of three key building blocks, which are as follows:

- **Template (HTML)**: Defines the structure and layout of the UI.
- **Class (TypeScript)**: Contains logic, properties, and methods.
- **Metadata (@Component decorator)**: Provides Angular with configuration settings.

Example:

```
import { Component } from '@angular/core';
@Component({
  selector: 'app-example',
  template: `<h2>{{ message }}</h2><button (click)="changeMessage()">Click me</button>`,
  styles: ['h2 { font-size: 20px; }']
})
export class ExampleComponent {
  message: string = 'Hello, Angular!';
  changeMessage() {
    this.message = 'Button Clicked!';
  }
}
```

In an Angular component, the structure consists of a template, a class, and metadata, each serving a specific role, shown as follows:

- The template (template) displays the message and a button.
- The class (**ExampleComponent**) defines the message and a method **changeMessage()**.
- The metadata **(@Component)** provides the selector, template, and styles.

Question 4: What is the purpose of the @Component decorator?

Answer: The **@Component** decorator is a function that provides metadata to Angular about how to create and use a component. It helps Angular do the following:

- Identify the component using the selector.
- Associate an HTML template and styles.
- Handle encapsulation and lifecycle.

Without **@Component**, Angular cannot recognize a class as a component.

Example:

```
import { Component } from '@angular/core';
@Component({
  selector: 'app-demo',
  template: `<h3>This is a demo component</h3>`,
  styles: ['h3 { color: red; }']
})
export class DemoComponent {}
```

Here, **@Component** tells Angular the following things:

- The component's selector is **app-demo**.
- It has a template **<h3>...</h3>**.
- It applies the style color: **red;**.

In standalone components, it does the following:

- Specifies the component selector (**selector**).
- Declares the component as **standalone: true**.
- Links to the template and styles.
- Allows importing dependencies directly inside the component.

Example: Use the following code for a standalone component with dependency importing:

```
import { Component } from '@angular/core';
import { CommonModule } from '@angular/common';
@Component({
  selector: 'app-message',
  standalone: true,
  imports: [CommonModule],
  template: `<h3 *ngIf="showMessage">Hello, Standalone Component!</h3>`,
  styles: ['h3 { color: red; }']
})
export class MessageComponent {
  showMessage: boolean = true;
```

```
}
```

Here, `@Component` does the following:

- Declares the component as **standalone**.
- Uses `imports: [CommonModule]` to enable Angular directives like `*ngIf`.

Question 5: What are the essential properties of the @Component decorator?

Answer: The `@Component` decorator in Angular provides several essential properties that define the behaviors and configuration of a component. The following are its key properties:

- **selector**: Defines the HTML tag that represents the component. For example, if `selector: 'app-example'`, you can use `<app-example></app-example>` in templates.
- **standalone**: Marks the component as a standalone component. Setting standalone: true allows the component to work independently without being part of an NgModule.
- **template**: Specifies the inline HTML template for the component. Example: `template: '<p>Hello Angular</p>'`.
- **templateUrl**: Instead of inline HTML, this property links to an external HTML file. Example: `templateUrl: './example.component.html'`.
- **styles**: Defines inline CSS styles specific to the component. Example: `styles: ['h1 { color: blue; }']`.
- **styleUrls**: References an external CSS file for styling the component. Example: `styleUrls: ['./example.component.css']`.
- **imports**: Allows importing other standalone components, directives, or Angular modules directly inside the component. Example: `imports: [CommonModule]` enables built-in Angular directives like `ngIf` and `ngFor`.

These properties define how the component is structured, displayed, and interacts with other parts of the application.

Example:

```
import { Component } from '@angular/core';
import { CommonModule } from '@angular/common';
@Component({
  selector: 'app-product',
  standalone: true,
  templateUrl: './product.component.html',
  styleUrls: ['./product.component.css'],
  imports: [CommonModule]
})
export class ProductComponent {}
```

This tells Angular to perform the following actions:

- Use `<app-product>` as the component tag.
- Load `product.component.html` as its template.
- Apply styles from `product.component.css`.
- Import `CommonModule` for directives like `ngIf` and `ngFor`.

Intermediate questions

Question 6: What are standalone components in Angular (introduced in Angular 14)?

Answer: Standalone components were introduced in Angular 14 to simplify component-based architecture by removing the need for NgModules.

The following are the key features of standalone components:

- Can be used without being declared in an NgModule.
- Uses **`standalone: true`** in the **`@Component`** decorator.
- Allows direct imports of other standalone components, directives, and modules.
- Improves modularity and tree-shaking, reducing bundle size.

Example of a standalone component:

```
import { Component } from '@angular/core';
@Component({
  selector: 'app-hello-world',
  standalone: true,
  template: `<h1>Hello, Standalone Component!</h1>`,
  styles: ['h1 { color: blue; }']
})
export class HelloWorldComponent {}
```

This component does not need to be declared inside an NgModule.

Question 7: How do you create a standalone component?

Answer: There are two ways to create a standalone component: first, using Angular CLI, and second, manually.

To create a standalone component using Angular CLI, which is the recommended approach, run the following command:

```
ng generate component component-name -standalone
```

or

```
ng g c component-name -standalone
```

This generates a standalone component with the required files.

Follow these steps to manually create a standalone component:

1. Create a TypeScript file for the component.
2. Add **`standalone: true`** inside **`@Component`**.
3. Import required modules or standalone components inside imports.

Example:

```
import { Component } from '@angular/core';
import { CommonModule } from '@angular/common';
@Component({
  selector: 'app-example',
  standalone: true,
  imports: [CommonModule], // Importing Angular directives like *ngIf, *ngFor
  template: `<p>Standalone Component Example</p>`,
```

```
  styles: ['p { color: green; }']
})
export class ExampleComponent {}
```

Question 8: What is the difference between standalone components and traditional components?

Answer: Standalone components do not require an NgModule and can directly import dependencies like components, directives, and pipes, reducing boilerplate and improving modularity, tree shaking, and lazy loading. They are ideal for micro-frontends and modern Angular applications. In contrast, traditional components must be declared within an NgModule, where dependencies are managed at the module level. This ensures better organization for large-scale applications but introduces additional complexity.

The following are the key features of standalone components:

- No need for NgModule declarations.
- Uses **`standalone: true`**.
- Can be bootstrapped directly in **`main.ts`**.
- More modular and improves tree-shaking.

The following are the key features of traditional components:

- Must be declared inside an NgModule.
- Cannot work independently.
- Requires imports through modules.

Question 9: How do you bootstrap a standalone component without using NgModule?

Answer: Instead of bootstrapping a module, you bootstrap a standalone component directly in **`main.ts`**.

For example (main.ts):

```
import { bootstrapApplication } from '@angular/platform-browser';
import { HelloWorldComponent } from './hello-world.component';
bootstrapApplication(HelloWorldComponent);
```

This eliminates the need for AppModule.

Question 10: What is the difference between a component and a directive?

Answer: A component is a UI-driven building block in Angular with a template, styles, and logic, defining how a part of the application looks and behaves. It is created using **`@Component`**.

A directive is a behavior-modifying feature that enhances elements, components, or attributes without having a separate UI. It is created using **`@Directive`**.

The key differences between a component and a directive are as follows:

- **Component**: Has a template, styles, and logic user interface (UI representation).

  Example of a component:

  ```
  import { Component } from '@angular/core';
  @Component({
    selector: 'app-example',
    standalone: true,
    template: `<h1>{{ message }}</h1> <button (click)="changeMessage()">Click Me</
  button>`
  })
  export class ExampleComponent {
    message = 'Hello, Angular!';
  ```

```
  changeMessage() { this.message = 'You clicked the button!'; }
}
```

This standalone component displays a message and updates it when the button is clicked.

- **Directive**: Enhances the behavior of existing elements but does not have a UI.

  Example of a directive:

```
import { Directive, ElementRef, Renderer2 } from '@angular/core';
@Directive({
  selector: '[appHighlight]'
})
export class HighlightDirective {
  constructor(private el: ElementRef, private renderer: Renderer2) {
    this.renderer.setStyle(this.el.nativeElement, 'color', 'red');
  }
}
```

  This directive changes the text color to red when applied to an element.

Question 11: How do you pass data between parent and child components?

Answer: To pass data between parent and child components, complete the following steps:

1. Use **`@Input()`** for data transfer from parent to child.
2. Use **`@Output()`** with **`EventEmitter`** for data transfer from child to parent.

Parent to child (@Input()): Use **`@Input()`** in the child component to receive data from the parent.

- **@Input()**: Parent sends data to child (**`[property]="value"`**).

  Example: Child component (child.component.ts)

```
import { Component, Input } from '@angular/core';
@Component({
  selector: 'app-child',
  standalone: true,
  template: `<h3>Message from Parent: {{ message }}</h3>`,
})
export class ChildComponent {
  @Input() message!: string;  // Receiving data from parent
}
```

  Parent component (parent.component.ts)

```
import { Component } from '@angular/core';
import { ChildComponent } from './child.component';
@Component({
  selector: 'app-parent',
  standalone: true,
  imports: [ChildComponent],
  template: `<app-child [message]="parentMessage"></app-child>`,
})
export class ParentComponent {
```

```
    parentMessage = 'Hello from Parent!';
  }
```

Child to parent (@Output()): Use **`@Output()`** and **`EventEmitter`** in the child component to send data to the parent.

- **@Output()**: Child sends data to parent (**`(event)="method($event)"`**).

  Example: **Child component (child.component.ts)**

  ```
  import { Component, Output, EventEmitter } from '@angular/core';
  @Component({
    selector: 'app-child',
    standalone: true,
    template: `<button (click)="sendMessage()">Send to Parent</button>`,
  })
  export class ChildComponent {
    @Output() messageEvent = new EventEmitter<string>();
    sendMessage() {
      this.messageEvent.emit('Hello Parent!');
    }
  }
  ```

  Parent component (parent.component.ts)

  ```
  import { Component } from '@angular/core';
  import { ChildComponent } from './child.component';
  @Component({
    selector: 'app-parent',
    standalone: true,
    imports: [ChildComponent],
    template: `
      <app-child (messageEvent)="receiveMessage($event)"></app-child>
      <p>Message from Child: {{ childMessage }}</p>
    `,
  })
  export class ParentComponent {
    childMessage = '';
    receiveMessage(message: string) {
      this.childMessage = message;
    }
  }
  ```

Question 12: What are input and output properties in Angular components?

Answer: In Angular, **`@Input()`** and **`@Output()`** decorators are used for parent-child component communication, shown as follows:

- **@Input()**: Allows a parent component to pass data to a child component.
- **@Output()**: Allows a child component to send data or events back to the parent component using **`EventEmitter`**.

This enables efficient communication between parent and child components in Angular applications.

For example, refer to the examples in *Answer 11*.

Question 13: How do you use @Input() and @Output() decorators?

Answer: In Angular, the `@Input()` and `@Output()` decorators facilitate communication between parent and child components. They are used in the following manner:

- **@Input()**: Parent sends data to child (`[property]="value"`).
- **@Output()**: Child sends data to parent (`(event)="method($event)"`).

For example, refer to the examples in *Answer 11*.

Question 14: How do you implement event binding between components?

Answer: Event binding is done using `@Output()` and `(event)="method($event)"` syntax as shown in the examples in *Answer 11*.

Question 15: What is ViewEncapsulation in Angular?

Answer: ViewEncapsulation controls how styles from a component affect or are affected by other components.

Question 16: What are the different types of ViewEncapsulation strategies?

Answer: In Angular, ViewEncapsulation determines how styles are applied to components and whether they affect other components. Angular provides three encapsulation strategies, which are as follows:

- **Emulated (Default)**: Styles are scoped to the component.
- **ShadowDOM**: Uses native ShadowDOM for complete isolation.
- **None**: Styles are applied globally without any encapsulation, meaning they can affect other components.

Each strategy controls how styles are scoped and applied within an Angular application.

Example:

```
import { Component, ViewEncapsulation } from '@angular/core';
@Component({
  selector: 'app-example',
  standalone: true,
  template: `<h1>Hello</h1>`,
  styles: ['h1 { color: red; }'],
  encapsulation: ViewEncapsulation.Emulated // Default
})
export class ExampleComponent {}
```

Question 17: How does Angular handle styles inside a component?

Answer: Styles inside styles or styleUrls are scoped based on ViewEncapsulation.

Question 18: What is ng-content, and how is it used in Angular?

Answer: The ng-content is an Angular directive used for content projection, which allows a parent component to pass content inside a child component's template. This is useful for creating reusable and flexible components.

Instead of defining static content in a child component, ng-content acts as a placeholder for dynamic content provided by the parent.

The ng-content directive in Angular enhances component flexibility and reusability by enabling content projection. Here is why it is beneficial:

- Helps reusability by allowing different content inside a single component.
- Provides flexibility by letting the parent define the content dynamically.
- Eliminates the need for `@Input()` when projecting complex templates.

- Helps in creating flexible and reusable components.

These features make Angular components highly customizable and dynamic.

Question 19: How do you use content projection in Angular?

Answer: Content projection in Angular enables a parent component to pass dynamic content into a child component using **<ng-content>**, enhancing flexibility and reusability. Key aspects include:

- Default projection using **<ng-content>**.
- Multi-slot projection with **<ng-content select="[attribute]">**.
- Supports dynamic content, making components more reusable and adaptable.

An example of content projection with multiple slots is given as follows:

1. Create a standalone child component (**card.component.ts**). This component will accept title, body, and footer content using **<ng-content>**, shown as follows:

```
import { Component } from '@angular/core';
@Component({
  selector: 'app-card',
  standalone: true,
  template: `
    <div class="card">
      <header><ng-content select="[card-title]"></ng-content></header>
      <section><ng-content></ng-content></section>
      <footer><ng-content select="[card-footer]"></ng-content></footer>
    </div>
  `,
  styles: [`
    .card { border: 1px solid #ccc; padding: 10px; border-radius: 5px; width: 300px;
}
    header { font-weight: bold; color: #007bff; }
    footer { font-size: 0.9rem; color: gray; text-align: right; }
  `]
})
export class CardComponent {}
```

2. Use the card component in a parent component (**parent.component.ts**). The parent injects content into different slots, shown as follows:

```
import { Component } from '@angular/core';
import { CardComponent } from './card.component';
@Component({
  selector: 'app-parent',
  standalone: true,
  imports: [CardComponent],
  template: `
    <app-card>
      <h3 card-title>Angular Card</h3>
      <p>This is the main content inside the card.</p>
```

```
        <small card-footer>Updated: Today</small>
      </app-card>
    `,
})
export class ParentComponent {}
```

Advanced questions

Question 20: What is the lifecycle of an Angular component?

Answer: The lifecycle of an Angular component consists of different phases from creation to destruction. Angular provides lifecycle hooks to execute logic at different stages.

The following are the component lifecycle phases:

1. **Creation phase**: The component is initialized.
2. **Change detection phase**: Detects data-bound property changes.
3. **Rendering phase**: Updates the view based on detected changes.
4. **Destruction phase**: Cleans up resources when the component is removed.

The following figure illustrates the lifecycle of an Angular component, from creation to destruction, highlighting each lifecycle hook in order:

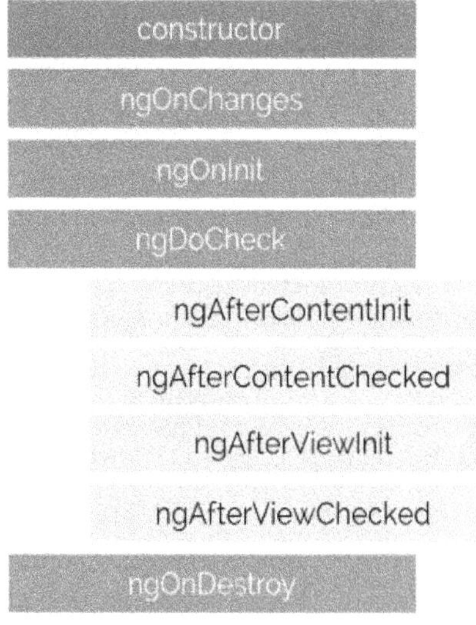

***Figure 2.1**: Angular component lifecycle hook*

The following is the full breakdown of the component lifecycle phases, including the constructor:

1. **Creation phase (initialization)**: The component is initialized, dependencies are injected, and **`ngOnInit()`** runs after the first change detection. Key aspects include:
   - The component instance is created.
   - The constructor is called to initialize properties.
   - Dependency injection occurs.
   - **`ngOnInit()`** is executed after the first change detection.
2. **Change detection phase**: Angular detects changes in data-bound properties and triggers hooks like **`ngOnChanges()`** and **`ngDoCheck()`**. Key aspects include:

- Angular detects changes in data-bound properties.
- Lifecycle hooks like `ngOnChanges()` and `ngDoCheck()` are triggered.

3. **Rendering phase (view update)**: The component's view updates based on detected changes, with hooks like `ngAfterViewInit()` and `ngAfterViewChecked()`. Key aspects include:
   - The component's view is updated based on detected changes.
   - Hooks like `ngAfterViewInit()` and `ngAfterViewChecked()` run for child views.
4. **Destruction phase (cleanup)**: The component is removed from the DOM, and `ngOnDestroy()` cleans up resources such as event listeners and subscriptions. Key aspects include:
   - When the component is about to be removed from the DOM.
   - `ngOnDestroy()` is called to clean up resources like subscriptions and event listeners.

Question 21: Can you explain all the Angular lifecycle hooks?

Answer: Angular provides the following lifecycle hooks that allow developers to hook into the component's lifecycle:

- **ngOnChanges()**: Called when an input property changes.
- **ngOnInit()**: Called once after component initialization.
- **ngDoCheck()**: Called during every change detection run.
- **ngAfterContentInit()**: Called after `<ng-content>` content is projected.
- **ngAfterContentChecked()**: Called every time projected content changes.
- **ngAfterViewInit()**: Called after the component view is initialized.
- **ngAfterViewChecked()**: Called every time the component view is checked.
- **ngOnDestroy()**: Called just before Angular destroys the component.

Question 22: What is ngOnInit(), and when should it be used?

Answer: `ngOnInit()` is called once after the component has been initialized. It is commonly used for the following:

- Fetching data from APIs.
- Initializing variables.
- Setting up subscriptions.

For example:

```
import { Component, OnInit } from '@angular/core';
@Component({
  selector: 'app-example',
  standalone: true,
  template: `<p>{{message}}</p>`
})
export class ExampleComponent implements OnInit {
  message = '';
  ngOnInit() {
    this.message = 'Component Initialized!';
  }
}
```

Question 23: How does ngOnChanges() work in Angular?

Answer: **`ngOnChanges()`** is called when any **`@Input()`** property changes. It receives a **`SimpleChanges`** object that contains the previous and current values.

For example:

```
import { Component, Input, OnChanges, SimpleChanges } from '@angular/core';
@Component({
  selector: 'app-child',
  standalone: true,
  template: `<p>Value: {{ value }}</p>`
})
export class ChildComponent implements OnChanges {
  @Input() value!: string;
  ngOnChanges(changes: SimpleChanges) {
    console.log('Previous:', changes['value'].previousValue);
    console.log('Current:', changes['value'].currentValue);
  }
}
```

Question 24: What is ngDoCheck(), and how is it different from ngOnChanges()?

Answer: In Angular, **`ngOnChanges()`** and **`ngDoCheck()`** are lifecycle hooks used for detecting changes, but they function differently. Key differences are outlined as follows:

- **`ngOnChanges()`** only detects changes to **`@Input()`** properties.
- **`ngDoCheck()`** runs on every change detection cycle, even if no **`@Input()`** property changed, allowing for custom change detection logic.

For example:

```
ngDoCheck() {
  console.log('Change Detection running!');
}
```

Note: **Use it carefully, as it can impact performance.**

Question 25: How does Angular optimize component rendering?

Answer: Angular optimizes component rendering by efficiently detecting and updating only the necessary parts of the application. Refer to the following list for some key optimization techniques:

- Uses change detection to update only changed components.
- Uses OnPush strategy to optimize performance.
- Uses **`*TrackBy in ngFor`** to prevent unnecessary DOM updates.
- Uses lazy loading to load components only when needed, reducing the initial load time.

Question 26: What is the difference between OnPush and Default change detection strategy?

Answer: Angular provides two change detection strategies, Default and OnPush, each determining how and when components are checked for updates. The key differences are as follows:

- **Default (CheckAlways)**: Re-evaluates the component and its children whenever data changes.
- **OnPush**: Updates the component only when an **`@Input()`** property changes or an event is triggered inside the component, improving performance by reducing unnecessary checks.

For example:

```
import { ChangeDetectionStrategy, Component } from '@angular/core';
@Component({
  selector: 'app-child',
  standalone: true,
  template: `<p>{{value}}</p>`,
  changeDetection: ChangeDetectionStrategy.OnPush
})
export class ChildComponent {
  @Input() value!: string;
}
```

Question 27: How do you use the change detection strategy in Angular?

Answer: By setting **`ChangeDetectionStrategy.OnPush`** in a component's metadata. Angular provides two change detection strategies:

- **Default (ChangeDetectionStrategy.Default)**:
  - Runs change detection on the entire component tree when any data changes.
  - Triggers on any event, async call, or property change.
  - Can be inefficient for large applications.
- **OnPush (ChangeDetectionStrategy.OnPush)**:
  - Runs change detection only when:
    - An **`@Input()`** property gets a new object reference.
    - A user event occurs inside the component.
    - **`ChangeDetectorRef.markForCheck()`** or **`detectChanges()`** is called manually.
  - Improves performance by reducing unnecessary checks.

An example of using OnPush is shown as follows:

```
import { Component, ChangeDetectionStrategy, Input } from '@angular/core';
@Component({
  selector: 'app-onpush',
  template: `<p>{{ user.name }}</p>`,
  changeDetection: ChangeDetectionStrategy.OnPush
})
export class OnPushComponent {
  @Input() user!: { name: string };
}
```

When using the OnPush change detection strategy, Angular optimizes performance by only checking for updates under specific conditions. Key behaviors include:

- Will not detect changes if **user.name** is modified directly, as OnPush does not track object property mutations.
- Will detect changes if a new object is assigned to the user, triggering change detection:

```
this.user = {name: 'Updated Name'}; // Change detection runs
```

The OnPush change detection strategy is beneficial in scenarios where performance optimization is crucial. It is best used in the following cases:

- When working with immutable data, ensure changes are detected only when a new object reference is assigned.
- When optimizing performance in large applications by reducing unnecessary change detection cycles.
- When changes are triggered only through new object references or component events, preventing unnecessary re-evaluations.

Question 28: How do you manually trigger change detection in Angular?

Answer: In Angular, change detection typically runs automatically, but there are cases where it needs to be triggered manually. This can be done using **ChangeDetectorRef** in the following ways:

- **Use ChangeDetectorRef.detectChanges()**: Forces an immediate change detection cycle to update the view:

```
import { ChangeDetectorRef } from '@angular/core';
constructor(private cdr: ChangeDetectorRef) {}
this.cdr.detectChanges();
```

- **Use ChangeDetectorRef**: It forces an update and marks the component for change detection, ensuring updates:

```
constructor(private cd: ChangeDetectorRef) {}
updateManually() {
  this.cd.markForCheck(); // Marks component for change detection
}
```

Question 29: What is the difference between component-level and module-level providers?

Answer: In Angular, services can be provided at different levels, impacting their scope, instance sharing, and memory usage. The two main types of service providers are as follows:

- **Module-level providers (providedIn: 'root')**: When a service is provided at the module level (typically using **providedIn: 'root'**), it acts as a singleton, meaning a single instance is shared across the entire application. These services are globally accessible, ensuring efficient memory usage and consistent state management throughout the app. It works in the following manner:
    - The service is provided in the root injector (**@Injectable({ providedIn: 'root' })**), making it available throughout the app.
    - A single instance of the service is created and shared among all components that inject it. For example:

```
import { Injectable } from '@angular/core';
@Injectable({
  providedIn: 'root' // Available across the entire app
})
export class LoggerService {
  log(message: string) {
    console.log(message);
```

```
    }
  }
```

- Any component using **LoggerService** will receive the same instance.
- **Alternative**: Adding to **providers** in a module

  Instead of **providedIn: 'root'**, we can add the service to the providers array of a module.

```
import { NgModule } from '@angular/core';
import { CommonModule } from '@angular/common';
import { LoggerService } from './logger.service';
@NgModule({
  imports: [CommonModule],
  providers: [LoggerService] // Service available for this module
})
export class SharedModule {}
```

- The service is now scoped only to **SharedModule** instead of the entire app.

The following are the advantages of module-level providers:

- Shared singleton instance across the app.
- Efficient memory usage as it does not create multiple instances.
- Automatically tree-shaken (removes unused services in production).

- **Component-level providers (providers in @Component)**: When a service is provided in a component's providers array, a new instance is created each time the component is instantiated. It works in the following manner:
  - Each component (and its child components) gets its own separate instance of the service.
  - Not shared with other components outside its component tree. For example:

```
import { Component } from '@angular/core';
import { LoggerService } from '../logger.service';
@Component({
  selector: 'app-child',
  template: `<p>Child Component</p>`,
  providers: [LoggerService] // Creates a new instance for this component
})
export class ChildComponent {
  constructor(private logger: LoggerService) {
    this.logger.log('Child Component Logger Instance');
  }
}
```

  - Every instance of **ChildComponent** gets a new **LoggerService** instance.
  - Parent components do not share this instance. Consider the following example of a nested component:

```
@Component({
  selector: 'app-parent',
  template: `<app-child></app-child>`
```

```
})
export class ParentComponent {}
```

- If multiple **ChildComponent** instances exist, each gets its own **LoggerService** instance, but they will not share data.

The following are the advantages of component-level providers:

- **Encapsulation**: Keeps service instances isolated to a component.
- **Memory optimization**: Only creates instances when the component is used.
- **Useful for stateful services**: Each component can manage its own state independently.

Question 30: How do you implement lazy loading for components?

Answer: Lazy loading components in Angular improves performance by loading them only when needed instead of during the initial application load. It is recommended for standalone components to implement lazy loading by using **loadComponent()** with standalone components, shown as follows:

```
import { Component, ViewChild, ViewContainerRef } from '@angular/core';
import { LazyComponent } from './lazy.component';
@Component({
  selector: 'app-parent',
  standalone: true,
  template: `<button (click)="loadLazy()">Load Lazy</button><ng-container #container></ng-container>`
})
export class ParentComponent {
  @ViewChild('container', { read: ViewContainerRef }) container!: ViewContainerRef;
  async loadLazy() {
    const { LazyComponent } = await import('./lazy.component');
    this.container.createComponent(LazyComponent);
  }
}
```

Question 31: How do you implement lazy loading with standalone components?

Answer: As shown in *Answer 30* and *Answer 6*, lazy loading with standalone components is achieved using **loadComponent()** dynamically to load components only when needed.

Question 32: How do you use dependency injection (DI) in Angular components?

Answer: DI in Angular allows components to receive services and dependencies without manually creating instances. It works in three steps:

1. **Provide the service**
    - Define the service using **@Injectable({ providedIn: 'root' })** for a global singleton.
    - Alternatively, provide it at the module or component level using providers: [].
2. **Inject the service**
    - Use constructor injection in the component's constructor.
    - Angular's DI system automatically provides the required service instance.
3. **Use the service**
    - Call methods or access properties from the injected service within the component.

Using DI in Angular components has the following benefits:

- **Reusability**: Services can be shared across multiple components.
- **Decoupling**: Components do not need to manually instantiate dependencies.
- **Testability**: Easier to mock dependencies for unit testing.
- **Scalability**: Helps manage complex applications efficiently.

Use **`@Injectable()`** for services and inject them into components, shown as follows:

```
import { Injectable } from '@angular/core';
@Injectable({ providedIn: 'root' })
export class MyService {
  getData() { return 'Service Data'; }
}
@Component({ selector: 'app-test', standalone: true, template: `{{data}}` })
export class TestComponent {
  constructor(private myService: MyService) {}
  data = this.myService.getData();
}
```

Question 33: How can you share data between sibling components?

Answer: Sibling components (components at the same level) do not have a direct relationship, so data must be shared using external mechanisms.

In Angular, data sharing between components can be achieved through various approaches, depending on the application's complexity and requirements. Common methods include:

- **Using a shared service with Subject or BehaviorSubject**: Create a service with **`Subject`** or **`BehaviorSubject`** to store and update shared data. Both components subscribe to the observable to receive updates.
- **Using a parent component as a mediator**: Pass data from one child to the parent via an event (**`@Output()`**), then send it to the other child via **`@Input()`**.
- **Using Angular signals (Angular 16+)**: Define a reactive signal in a shared service, and both siblings can read or update it.
- **Using a state management library (e.g., NgRx, Akita, NgXS)**: Useful for complex applications requiring centralized state management.

The best approach for sharing data depends on the application's needs:

- **For simple communication**, a parent component can mediate data between child components.
- **For frequent updates**, a service with **`BehaviorSubject`** ensures real-time data sharing.
- **For large-scale applications**, a state management library like NgRx provides a structured and scalable solution.

For example, use a shared service with **`Subject`** or **`BehaviorSubject`**, shown as follows:

```
@Injectable({ providedIn: 'root' })
export class DataService {
  private dataSubject = new BehaviorSubject<string>('');
  data$ = this.dataSubject.asObservable();
  updateData(data: string) {
    this.dataSubject.next(data);
```

```
  }
}
```

Sibling components subscribe to **data$** and update data via **updateData()**.

Performance optimization and best practices

Question 34: How do you optimize Angular component performance?

Answer: To optimize Angular component performance, ensure the following best practices:

- Use OnPush change detection.
- Use **trackBy** in ***ngFor**.
- Implement lazy loading for modules and components.
- Use debouncing and throttling for event handling.
- Avoid unnecessary bindings in the template.
- Use web workers for heavy computations.

Question 35: What is trackBy in Angular, and why is it used?

Answer: In Angular, **trackBy** is used in ***ngFor** to optimize rendering performance by tracking unique identifiers instead of recreating elements. It helps Angular identify and track items in a list when the data changes.

By default, Angular tracks list items by their index. This means if the list changes, Angular re-renders all items, even if only one has changed.

The **trackBy** function in Angular is used to optimize rendering performance when working with lists:

- Improves performance by preventing unnecessary DOM re-renders by tracking items uniquely.
- Enhances efficiency by updating only changed or newly added items instead of re-rendering the entire list.
- Reduces flickering by preventing UI glitches when lists update dynamically.

The **trackBy** function works by assigning a unique identifier to each item in a list, helping Angular optimize change detection, shown as follows:

- It provides a distinct key (such as an ID) for each item.
- Angular uses this identifier to detect changes and update only the necessary elements.
- Implementing **trackBy** is a best practice for efficiently managing dynamic or large lists.

For example:

```
@Component({ selector: 'app-list', standalone: true, template: `
  <div *ngFor="let item of items; trackBy: trackById">{{ item.name }}</div>
`})
export class ListComponent {
  items = [{ id: 1, name: 'Item 1' }, { id: 2, name: 'Item 2' }];
  trackById(index: number, item: any) { return item.id; }
}
```

Question 36: How do you handle large lists efficiently in Angular?

Answer: Handling large lists efficiently in Angular is essential for performance optimization. Several techniques can help manage large datasets effectively, some of which are as follows:

- Use virtual scrolling with **CdkVirtualScrollViewport**.

- Use pagination to load data incrementally.
- Use **trackBy** to prevent re-rendering unchanged items.
- Avoid loading all data at once.

Question 37: What are signals in Angular (Angular 16+), and how do they impact component state management?

Answer: Signals are a new reactive primitive in Angular 16+ that replace RxJS for state management.

For example:

```
import { signal } from '@angular/core';
const count = signal(0);
count.set(5);
```

Question 38: How do signals improve reactivity compared to RxJS?

Answer: Signals improve reactivity in Angular by providing a more efficient and straightforward way to manage state compared to RxJS in the following manner:

- Synchronous and immutable, ensuring predictable state updates.
- No need for subscriptions or manual unsubscribe handling, reducing complexity.
- More performant for local state management, as they avoid the overhead of RxJS observables.

Question 39: What are some best practices for writing efficient Angular components?

Answer: Writing efficient Angular components ensures better performance, maintainability, and scalability. The following list outlines the key best practices:

- Use standalone components.
- Use **ChangeDetectionStrategy.OnPush**.
- Minimize DOM manipulations.
- Optimize performance with **trackBy**, lazy loading, and caching.

Question 40: What are the control flow directives (@if, @for, @switch) introduced in Angular 17?

Answer: In Angular 17, new control flow directives (**@if**, **@for**, and **@switch**) were introduced to enhance template syntax and improve performance. These directives replace structural directives like ***ngIf**, ***ngFor**, and ***ngSwitch** with a more efficient and readable approach.

Angular 17 introduces the following new syntax-based control flow directives, replacing traditional structural directives for improved readability and performance:

- **@if** replaces ***ngIf**, offering a cleaner syntax for conditional rendering.

  For example: **@if** is a more efficient replacement for ***ngIf**, allowing conditional rendering:

  ```
  @if (isLoggedIn) {
    <p>Welcome back!</p>
  } @else {
    <p>Please log in.</p>
  }
  ```

- **@for** replaces ***ngFor**, optimizing list iteration and change detection.

  For example: Optimized iteration over lists, replacing ***ngFor** and improving performance:

  ```
  @for (item of items; track item.id) {
    <div>{{ item.name }}</div>
  ```

```
}
```

- **`@switch`** replaces **`*ngSwitch`**, simplifying multiple condition handling.

  For example: A streamlined version of **`*ngSwitch`**, offering a cleaner syntax for multiple conditions.

  ```
  @switch (status) {
    @case ('active') { <p>Active</p> }
    @case ('inactive') { <p>Inactive</p> }
    @default { <p>Unknown</p> }
  }
  ```

These new directives improve readability and performance by reducing boilerplate and optimizing DOM updates.

41. How do deferred views (@defer) improve performance?

Answer: **`@defer`** is an Angular feature (introduced in Angular 17) that delays rendering of a component or template until a specific condition is met. It is useful for improving performance by loading heavy or less critical content only when needed.

The **`@defer`** directive in Angular enhances performance by delaying the rendering of non-critical content, leading to faster load times and better resource management. The improvements are as follows:

- **Reduces initial load time**: Large components, images, or lists are not rendered immediately, making the initial page load faster.
- **Efficient resource usage**: Browser memory and processing power are utilized only when necessary, reducing unnecessary computations.
- **Optimized change detection**: Deferred content is excluded from Angular's change detection cycle until it is rendered, improving app responsiveness.
- **Improves UX**: Ensures smooth performance by prioritizing critical content while loading secondary elements later.

The **`@defer`** directive is ideal for optimizing performance by delaying the rendering of non-critical content until needed. It is particularly beneficial in the following cases:

- Loading lazy content (e.g., below-the-fold images, sidebars).
- Rendering dynamic components only when required.
- Delaying non-essential data fetching (e.g., charts, analytics dashboards).

Using **`@defer`** strategically ensures better performance and responsiveness in Angular applications. Additionally, it delays rendering of non-essential components until needed. It allows you to delay rendering specific content until needed, improving performance and efficiency.

The syntax of the **`@defer`** directive is as follows:

```
@defer {
  <div>Loaded later!</div>
}
```

Consider the following example with a placeholder, a loading indicator, and error handling:

```
<!-- Trigger for Deferred Content -->
<button (click)="loadData()">Load User Data</button>
<!-- Defer Block with Multiple Features -->
@defer (when dataLoaded)
  <p>Welcome, {{ user.name }}!</p>
@placeholder
```

```
  <p>Loading user data...</p>
@loading
  <p><span class="spinner"></span> Fetching details...</p>
@error (let error)
  <p>Error loading data: {{ error.message }}</p>
@end
```

The following is an explanation of the features used in the preceding code:

- **@defer (when condition)**: Loads content only when the condition is true.
- **@placeholder**: A static placeholder displayed before loading starts.
- **@loading**: Dynamic loading indicator shown while fetching data.
- **@error**: Handles and displays errors if the content fails to load.

Question 42: What is the difference between @if and ngIf?

Answer: `@if` is the modern replacement for `*ngIf`, offering better performance and syntax consistency.

Question 43: How does @for differ from ngFor?

Answer: `@for` is more optimized and integrates `trackBy` by default.

44. What is DI in Angular?

Answer: DI provides services to components dynamically using `@Injectable()`. DI in Angular is a design pattern that automatically provides dependencies (such as services) to components, directives, and other parts of the application.

The following are the key features of DI in Angular:

- **Inversion of control (IoC)**: Components do not create dependencies; they receive them.
- **Singleton services**: A single instance of a service is shared across the app.
- **Scoped providers**: Services can be provided at different levels (root, module, or component).
- **Improves testability**: Easier to mock and replace dependencies in unit testing.

DI in Angular simplifies code management by improving reusability, maintainability, and modularity. It also enhances performance by efficiently handling shared service instances.

- Enhances code reusability and maintainability.
- Decouples components and services for better modularity.
- Optimizes performance by sharing instances efficiently.

Question 45: How do you provide a service at the component level?

Answer: Use the providers array inside the `@Component` decorator, shown as follows:

```
@Component({ selector: 'app-test', standalone: true, providers: [MyService] })
export class TestComponent {
  constructor(private myService: MyService) {}
}
```

Question 46: How does dependency injection work with standalone components?

Answer: Standalone components directly inject services without NgModule.

Question 47: What is the difference between providedIn: 'root' and providedIn: 'any'?

Answer: The `providedIn` property in Angular determines how a service is provided and instantiated across the application. The key differences are as follows:

- **providedIn**: **'root'**: Single instance shared across the app.
- **providedIn**: **'any'**: New instance per lazy loaded module.

Question 48: How do you create and use a service worker for PWA components?

Answer: To use the Angular PWA package, run the following command:

```
ng add @angular/pwa
```

This generates a **`service-worker.js`** file for caching.

Question 49: What is the purpose of component providers, and how do they differ from module providers?

Answer: Component providers and module providers define how services are instantiated and shared within an Angular application. The key differences are as follows:

- **Component providers**: Service instance is created per component.
- **Module providers**: Service instance is shared across the module.

Question 50: What are multi-providers in Angular dependency injection?

Answer: Multi-providers in Angular allow multiple instances of a service to be provided under the same token, instead of overriding the previous one. This is useful when multiple services or values need to be injected for a single dependency token.

Multi-providers enhance flexibility in dependency injection by allowing multiple service implementations to coexist under a single injection token. This approach supports extensibility and modular system design.

- **Allows multiple implementations**: Different providers can be registered under the same injection token.
- **Does not override previous providers**: All instances are collected into an array and injected together.
- **Useful for extensible and modular systems**: Enables plugins, event handlers, or custom logging mechanisms.

Multi-providers offer a flexible approach to dependency injection, allowing multiple implementations under a single token. They enhance modularity and extensibility in various scenarios.

- Supports multiple strategies for handling a dependency.
- Helps in extending functionality dynamically without modifying existing code.
- Useful in scenarios like custom logging, event handling, and middleware patterns.
- Allows multiple implementations of the same token.

Here is how you can implement multi-providers in Angular step-by-step:

1. Define an injection token using the following code:

   ```
   import { InjectionToken } from '@angular/core';
   export const LOGGER_SERVICES = new InjectionToken<string[]>('LOGGER_SERVICES', {
     providedIn: 'root',
     factory: () => []
   });
   ```

2. Use **`InjectionToken`** to define a custom token for multi-providers, shown as follows:

   ```
   const TOKEN = new InjectionToken<string[]>('TOKEN');
   @NgModule({
     providers: [{ provide: TOKEN, useValue: ['value1'], multi: true }]
   })
   export class AppModule {}
   ```

3. Provide multiple services under the same token by registering multiple services using the **multi: true** option in **app.module.ts**, shown as follows:

```
import { NgModule } from '@angular/core';
import { LOGGER_SERVICES } from './logger.token';
@NgModule({
  providers: [
    { provide: LOGGER_SERVICES, useValue: 'Console Logger', multi: true },
    { provide: LOGGER_SERVICES, useValue: 'File Logger', multi: true },
    { provide: LOGGER_SERVICES, useValue: 'Remote Logger', multi: true }
  ]
})
export class AppModule {}
```

4. To inject and use multi-providers in a component, run the following code:

```
import { Component, Inject } from '@angular/core';
import { LOGGER_SERVICES } from './logger.token';
@Component({
  selector: 'app-logger',
  template: `<p>Check console for logger services.</p>`
})
export class LoggerComponent {
  constructor(@Inject(LOGGER_SERVICES) private loggers: string[]) {
    console.log('Registered Loggers:', this.loggers);
  }
}
```

This setup allows multiple services to be provided under a single token, ensuring flexibility and extensibility in your Angular application.

Output in console:

```
Registered Loggers: ["Console Logger", "File Logger", "Remote Logger"]
```

Conclusion

This chapter explored Angular components, the building blocks of an Angular application. We covered how components interact using @Input() and @Output() decorators, how Angular optimizes change detection using strategies like OnPush, and the importance of trackBy for handling large lists efficiently. We also learnt about lazy loading, content projection, and how DI helps manage services effectively at different scopes (module, component, and multi-provider levels). Additionally, we discussed control flow directives and also standalone components introduced in Angular 20, such as @if, @for, and @switch, along with performance optimizations like @defer for lazy rendering of non-critical elements.

In the next chapter, we will look at Angular templates, focusing on how to structure component views effectively. You will learn about template syntax, data binding techniques (interpolation, property binding, event binding, and two-way binding), built-in directives, and template reference variables. These concepts will enable you to create dynamic and interactive user interfaces efficiently.

Join our Discord space

Join our Discord workspace for latest updates, offers, tech happenings around the world, new releases, and sessions with the authors:

https://discord.bpbonline.com

Chapter 3
Concepts of Template

Introduction

In this chapter, we will explore the core concepts and advanced features of Angular templates, which are essential for building dynamic and interactive user interfaces. Templates in Angular are the views that define the structure of the UI, and they play a critical role in bridging the data from the component with the presentation layer. This chapter will cover the basic concepts, enhancements, and features of Angular templates, as well as best practices to ensure performance optimization. You will also learn how templates in standalone components work and how Angular handles **server-side rendering** (**SSR**) and hydration, which are crucial for improving app performance. By the end of this chapter, you will have a thorough understanding of Angular templates and how to use them efficiently to build scalable and high-performing Angular applications.

Structure

This chapter covers the following topics:

- Basic concepts of Angular templates
- Angular template enhancements and features
- Template syntax and performance optimization
- Template features in standalone components
- SSR and hydration in Angular templates
- Template best practices and common mistakes

Objectives

By the end of this chapter, you will understand the basic and advanced features of Angular templates. You will be able to optimize your templates for better performance and understand how to use templates in standalone components and SSR. The chapter will also equip you with best practices for writing clean, efficient templates and help you avoid common mistakes that can lead to poor performance or maintainability issues. With the knowledge gained in this chapter, you will be well-prepared to build highly interactive and optimized Angular applications.

Basic concepts of Angular template

Question 1: What is a template in Angular, and how is it different from a component?

Answer: A **template** in Angular is the HTML structure that defines how a component should be rendered. It contains Angular directives, bindings, and expressions. A **component** is a combination of a template and logic written in TypeScript.

For example:

```
@Component({
  selector: 'app-example',
  standalone: true,
  template: `<h1>Hello, {{ name }}!</h1>`
})
export class ExampleComponent {
  name = 'Angular';
}
```

Question 2: What are Angular template expressions, and how do they work?

Answer: Template expressions evaluate logic inside double curly brackets ({{ }}). They are used to bind values dynamically within the template.

For example:

```
<p>The total price is: {{ price * quantity }}</p>
```

Question 3: What are template reference variables, and how can they be used?

Answer: Template reference variables (**#var**) provide access to **Document Object Model** (**DOM**) elements or component instances in templates.

For example:

```
<input #username type="text">
<button (click)="log(username.value)">Log Username</button>
```

Question 4: What are Angular structural directives (*ngIf, ngFor, ngSwitch*)?

Answer: In Angular, structural directives are used to modify the structure of the DOM by adding or removing elements based on specific conditions. These directives play a crucial role in dynamically rendering content in the template. The three commonly used structural directives are as follows:

- ***ngIf**: Conditionally renders elements.
- ***ngFor**: Iterates over a list.
- ***ngSwitch**: Displays one out of multiple elements based on a condition.

Recent versions of the Angular framework introduced a new control flow syntax using **`@if`**, **`@for`**, and **`@switch`**, which can replace the traditional **`*ngIf`** and **`*ngFor`** in templates. This change improves readability and performance.

Example of @if:

- **Old *ngIf:** `<div *ngIf="condition">Content</div>`
- **New @if:** `@if (condition) { <div>Content</div> }`

Example of @for:

- **Old *ngFor:** `<li *ngFor="let item of items">{{ item }}</li>`
- **New @for:** `@for (item of items; track item) { <li>{{ item }}</li> }`

Example of @switch:

```
<div>
  @switch (userRole) {
    @case ('admin') {
      <p>Welcome, Administrator!</p>
    }
    @case ('editor') {
      <p>Hello, Editor!</p>
    }
    @case ('viewer') {
      <p>Hi, Viewer!</p>
    }
    @default {
      <p>Unknown role. Please contact support.</p>
    }
  }
</div>
```

The **`@switch`** version is more concise and aligns with modern JavaScript control flow patterns.

Question 5: What is data binding, and what are the types of data binding in Angular templates?

Answer: Data binding is the mechanism to synchronize data between the component and the view. The following are the types of data binding:

- **Interpolation ({{}})**: Displays values.
- **Property binding ([property])**: Sets properties dynamically.
- **Event binding ((event))**: Listens to user interactions.
- **Two-way binding ([(ngModel)])**: Syncs data between the UI and component.

A detailed explanation of the types of data binding in Angular, along with examples and a step-by-step breakdown of the preceding points, is as follows:

1. **Interpolation ({{}})**: Used to display component properties inside the template. For example:

   HTML code:

   ```
   <p>Welcome, {{ username }}!</p>
   ```

   TypeScript code:

   ```
   username = 'Anil Singh';
   ```

2. **Property binding ([property])**: Property binding in Angular (`[property]`) binds a component's property to a DOM property of an HTML element, not to its attribute. While attributes and properties can appear similar, Angular operates directly on the DOM, which ensures dynamic updates in the UI.

   In the following example, **`[src]`** binds to the src DOM property of the **`<img>`** element, not the HTML src attribute. This distinction matters because DOM properties reflect the current state, whereas attributes reflect only the initial values.

   HTML code:

   ```
   <!-- HTML Template -->
   <img [src]="imageUrl" alt="Profile Picture">
   ```

TypeScript code:

```
// TypeScript Component
imageUrl = 'https://code-sample.com/profile.jpg';
```

3. **Event binding ((event))**: Listens for user events like clicks, inputs, etc. For example:

   HTML code:

```
<button (click)="sayHello()">Click Me</button>
```

   TypeScript code:

```
sayHello() {
  alert('Hello, Anil!');
}
```

4. **Two-way binding ([(ngModel)])**: Syncs data between the input field and the component property.

   Beyond one-way property binding, Angular also supports two-way data binding using the `[(ngModel)]` syntax. This is primarily used in template-driven forms and synchronizes data in both directions between form elements and component properties.

   Use cases of `[(ngModel)]` are as follows:

   - Capturing user input in real-time.
   - Building prefilled or editable form fields.
   - Implementing live feedback or instant validation.
   - Keeping the UI and component state in tight sync without boilerplate code.

   Consider an example. To use `[(ngModel)]`, make sure to import the `FormsModule` in your module:

```
import { FormsModule } from '@angular/forms';
```

   HTML code:

```
<input [(ngModel)]="name" placeholder="Enter name">
<p>Your name is: {{ name }}</p>
```

   TypeScript code:

```
name = '';
```

   With `[(ngModel)]`, any changes the user makes in the input field will immediately update the username property in the component, and any programmatic update to username will reflect in the input field.

Question 6: **How does property binding ([property]) work in Angular templates?**

Answer: Property binding in Angular sets DOM element properties dynamically using square bracket syntax `[property]`. It allows values from the component class to be passed directly into HTML elements in the template, enabling dynamic rendering and updates. This mechanism interacts with the DOM's property (not just the HTML attribute), allowing real-time synchronization of state.

Refer to the example in *Answer 5*, which demonstrates property binding.

Question 7: **What is event binding ((event)) in Angular templates?**

Answer: Event binding listens for user actions like clicks or key presses.

Refer to the example in *Answer 5*, which demonstrates event binding.

Question 8: **What is two-way data binding ([(ngModel)]), and when should it be used?**

Answer: Two-way binding syncs data between input fields and component properties.

Refer to the example in *Answer 5*, which demonstrates two-way data binding.

Question 9: What is ng-template, and how does it work?

Answer: **`ng-template`** is an Angular structural directive used to define reusable template content that is not rendered by default. Instead, it acts as a blueprint that Angular can instantiate dynamically when needed.

ng-template is a powerful tool in Angular to optimize performance, improve reusability, and dynamically render UI elements.

The following are the key features of **`ng-template`**:

- **Lazy rendering**: Content inside **`ng-template`** is not rendered until explicitly referenced.
- **Used with structural directives**: Commonly used with **`*ngIf`**, **`*ngFor`**, **`ngSwitch`**, and **`ngTemplateOutlet`**.
- **Encapsulated and reusable**: Can be referenced multiple times in the same component.

Example of the use of ng-template:

```
<ng-template #message>
  <p>This is a reusable template.</p>
</ng-template>
<button (click)="showMessage(message)">Show</button>
```

Example to pass data to the ng-template using the let variable:

Let us break this down with an example for better understanding:

1. **Define the reusable template with a let variable**:

   ```
   <ng-template #messageTemplate let-name="data">
     <p>Hello, {{ name }}!</p>
   </ng-template>
   ```

2. **Render the template with different data**:

   ```
   <ng-container *ngTemplateOutlet="messageTemplate; context: { data: 'Anil' }"></ng-container>
   <ng-container *ngTemplateOutlet="messageTemplate; context: { data: 'AKS' }"></ng-container>
   ```

The **`<ng-template>`** element in Angular serves several key purposes, enabling flexible and efficient template management. It is commonly used in the following scenarios:

- **Delaying content rendering**: To defer the display of content until a condition is met, such as with **`*ngIf`**, which only renders the template when the condition evaluates to true.
- **Creating reusable content**: To define reusable blocks of HTML that can be rendered multiple times with different data using the **`*ngTemplateOutlet`** directive, promoting **Don't Repeat Yourself** (**DRY**) principles.
- **Conditionally rendering UI elements**: To dynamically show or hide parts of the UI based on runtime logic, offering a way to structure conditional templates cleanly.

Question 10: What is ng-container, and how does it differ from ng-template?

Answer: ng-container is an Angular element that does not render in the DOM but allows grouping multiple elements without affecting the structure of the HTML.

- **`ng-container`** is a logical grouping element that does not render in the DOM.
- **`ng-template`** defines content that is not displayed until explicitly used.

The following are the key features of **`ng-container`**:

- **Does not generate an extra DOM element**: It acts as a wrapper without adding a **`<div>`** or another tag.
- **Used with structural directives**: It works with **`*ngIf`**, **`*ngFor`**, etc., without altering the HTML structure.

- **Improves readability and maintainability**: It groups elements without unnecessary wrapper tags.

In Angular 19 and 20, **ng-container** for logic blocks has been deprecated, and is replaced by **@if** and **@defer**.

Let us consider the following example of using **ng-container** with ***ngIf**:

HTML code:

```
<ng-container *ngIf="isLoggedIn">
  <p>Welcome, User!</p>
  <button (click)="logout()">Logout</button>
</ng-container>
```

TypeScript code:

```
isLoggedIn = true;
logout() {
  this.isLoggedIn = false;
}
```

In Angular, choosing between **<ng-container>** and **<ng-template>** depends on their distinct roles. **<ng-container>** is ideal for grouping elements without introducing an extra DOM wrapper, while **<ng-template>** is best suited for defining content that needs to be conditionally rendered or loaded lazily.

The following are the key differences between **ng-container** and **ng-template**:

- **Rendering in the DOM**
  - **ng-container** renders its content in the DOM but does not add an extra wrapper element.
  - **ng-template** does not render its content until explicitly used with **ngTemplateOutlet**.
- **Usage**
  - **ng-container** is used to group multiple elements without affecting the HTML structure.
  - **ng-template** is used for defining reusable content that can be conditionally or dynamically rendered.
- **Interaction with structural directives**
  - **ng-container** can be used directly with ***ngIf**, ***ngFor**, and other structural directives.
  - **ng-template** requires **ngTemplateOutlet** or another directive to be rendered dynamically.
- **Dynamic content rendering**
  - **ng-container** immediately renders its child elements.
  - **ng-template** delays rendering until it is explicitly referenced.
- **Reusability**
  - **ng-container** cannot be referenced and reused elsewhere in the template.
  - **ng-template** can be referenced multiple times using **ngTemplateOutlet**, making it highly reusable.

Question 11: How does content projection () work in Angular templates?

Answer: Content projection allows components to accept dynamic content from their parent components and display it inside a predefined slot using the **<ng-content>** directive.

The following are the key features of content projection:

- Passes external content into a component.
- Uses **<ng-content>** as a placeholder for projected content.
- Supports multiple projection slots using select attributes.

Let us consider an example.

HTML code:

```
<!-- Parent Component -->
<app-card>
  <p>This content is projected!</p>
</app-card>
```

TypeScript code:

```
<!-- Child Component -->
@Component({
  selector: 'app-card',
  template: `<div class="card"><ng-content></ng-content></div>`
})
export class CardComponent {}
```

The process works as follows:

1. **`<ng-content>`** within the app-card component serves as a placeholder.
2. The **`<p>`** element provided inside **`<app-card>`** is projected into the placeholder.

Angular template enhancements and features

Question 12: What is the @let syntax introduced in Angular 18.1, and how does it enhance templates?

Answer: The **`@let`** syntax in Angular 18.1 is a control flow directive that simplifies variable declarations within templates, replacing the older **`*ngIf`** as or let syntax inside **`*ngFor`**.

The **`@let`** syntax introduced in Angular 18.1 is part of Angular's new built-in control flow syntax. It allows developers to declare standalone template variables more clearly and concisely, improving template readability and reducing the need for extra **`*ngIf`** as or awkward let bindings in structural directives.

Consider the following example:

```
@let fullName = user.firstName + ' ' + user.lastName;
<p>Hello, {{ fullName }}!</p>
```

In this example, **`@let`** declares a local variable **`fullName`** that can be reused throughout the template, just like a component property. This makes it easier to avoid repeated expressions and simplifies complex templates.

While **`@let`** enhances template logic, it does not replace:

- **`*ngIf="condition as alias"`**, which is used to conditionally render content and create a scoped alias.
- Let item of items in **`*ngFor`**, which is used to iterate over collections.

These are structural context bindings, whereas **`@let`** is a pure variable declaration mechanism.

Use with <ng-container>: **`<ng-container>`** is still useful and relevant when you need a logical grouping of DOM elements without rendering extra HTML. The **`@let`** syntax can be used inside **`<ng-container>`** to define variables structurally, without affecting the rendered output.

Example with <ng-container>:

```
<ng-container @let fullName = user.firstName + ' ' + user.lastName>
  <p>Hello, {{ fullName }}</p>
</ng-container>
```

Consider another example of using **`@let`** for cleaner code.

HTML code:

```
@let user = { name: 'Anil Singh', age: 30 };
<p>Name: {{ user.name }}</p>
<p>Age: {{ user.age }}</p>
```

It enhances the templates in the following manner:

- It removes the need for **<ng-container>** when using **`*ngIf`**.
- It improves template readability and expressiveness.
- It minimizes boilerplate code.

Question 13: What is @defer in Angular 18+, and how does it improve template rendering?

Answer: **`@defer`** is a new control flow directive that enables lazy rendering of template sections, improving performance by loading content only when needed.

Consider an example of using **`@defer`**.

HTML code:

```
@defer (on viewport)
  <p>Loaded when visible in the viewport</p>
@end
```

The benefits are as follows:

- Delays rendering until a condition is met (e.g., visibility, interaction).
- Reduces initial load time by deferring unnecessary DOM updates.
- Works well with SSR and hydration.

Question 14: What improvements were made to *ngIf, ngFor, and ngSwitch in Angular 19?

Answer: Angular 19 enhanced these directives with improved reactivity, better syntax, and more efficient change detection. The following are the key enhancements made:

- **Reactive template updates:** **`*ngIf`** now tracks changes more efficiently without rechecking unnecessary values.
- **Better loop performance:** **`*ngFor`** optimizes iteration performance, reducing memory overhead.
- **Enhanced ngSwitch:** More performant and supports more dynamic conditions.

Consider an example of optimized ngFor in Angular 19.

HTML code:

```
<ul>
  @for (item of items; track item.id) {
    <li>{{ item.name }}</li>
  }
</ul>
```

Using track item.id ensures Angular efficiently updates only changed elements.

Question 15: How does Angular 19 optimize template parsing and rendering speed?

Answer: Angular 19 includes the following:

- Faster template parsing using precompiled **Abstract Syntax Tree** (**AST**).
- Better hydration and incremental updates.
- Optimized change detection, reducing unnecessary DOM updates.

Consider an example of faster template compilation.

HTML code:

```
@let message = "Welcome to Angular!";
<p>{{ message }}</p>
```

Since Angular 19 pre-parses and compiles templates more efficiently, it results in faster initial render times.

Question 16: How does Angular 19+ improve hydration support for SSR template rendering?

Answer: Angular 19+ enhances hydration support for SSR template rendering in the following ways:

- **Improved stateful hydration:** It keeps client-server state aligned.
- **Partial hydration:** It loads only interacted components.

Consider an example of hydration-friendly template.

HTML code:

```
@defer (on interaction)
  <p>This section is hydrated only when clicked.</p>
@end
```

This improves SEO and first-paint performance.

Question 17: What are template block directives in Angular 19, and how do they simplify development?

Answer: Angular 19 introduces template block directives such as the following:

- `@if`
- `@for`
- `@switch`
- `@defer`

These are easier to read than `*ngIf` or `*ngFor`.

Consider an example of `@if` instead of `ngIf`.

HTML code:

```
@if (isLoggedIn) {
  <p>Welcome back!</p>
} @else {
  <p>Please log in.</p>
}
```

There is no need for `<ng-container>`, making templates cleaner.

Question 18: How does Angular 19+ optimize template reactivity and re-rendering?

Answer: It uses fine-grained reactivity (similar to signals in Angular 16) and reduces unnecessary component updates with zone-less change detection.

Consider an example of optimized re-rendering.

HTML code:

```
@let count = signal(0);
<button (click)="count.set(count() + 1)">Increase</button>
<p>Count: {{ count() }}</p>
```

Only the count updates, preventing unnecessary renders.

Question 19: What is the key template-related change in Angular 20?

Answer: The following are the expected major improvements:

- More SSR-friendly hydration.
- Enhanced deferred loading with better support for dynamic content.

Consider an example of Angular 20 smart hydration.

HTML code:

```
@defer (on idle)
  <app-user-profile></app-user-profile>
@end
```

Renders only when the browser is idle, improving performance.

Question 20: How do Angular 20 templates improve compatibility with standalone components?

Answer: Angular 20 is expected to further streamline the integration of templates with standalone components, enhancing their flexibility and usability in modern application development. This improvement could manifest as follows:

- **Native support for standalone contexts in templates:** Templates in Angular 20 might natively recognize standalone components as self-contained units, allowing direct use of their inputs, outputs, and directives without additional configuration.

  For example:

  ```
  <ng-container *ngTemplateOutlet="someTemplate"></ng-container>
  <ng-template #someTemplate>
    <app-standalone-comp></app-standalone-comp>
  </ng-template>
  ```

  In this example:

  - The **<ng-template>** defines reusable content (**`someTemplate`**).
  - **<ng-container>** serves as a placeholder that Angular can dynamically render using **`*ngTemplateOutlet`**.

- **Enhanced control flow integration:** The modern control flow syntax (**`@if`**, **`@for`**, **`@switch`**) could be optimized for standalone components, reducing boilerplate and improving readability. Templates might allow standalone components to leverage these constructs more efficiently, with better tree-shaking and lazy loading support.

  For example:

  ```
  @if (condition) {
    <app-standalone-comp />
  }
  ```

- **Simplified context passing with ng-template:** Templates in Angular 20 might improve how **`ng-template`** and **`*ngTemplateOutlet`** interact with standalone components, making data passing more intuitive. A standalone component could directly consume a template with a context object.

  For example:

  ```
  <ng-template #standaloneContent let-data="data">
    <p>{{ data }}</p>
  </ng-template>
  <app-standalone-comp *ngTemplateOutlet="standaloneContent; context: { data: 'Standalone Data' }" />
  ```

- **Better lazy loading support**: Angular 20 templates could enhance compatibility with lazy loaded standalone components, reducing runtime overhead. Using dynamic imports in templates might become more straightforward.

  For example:

```
@defer (when isReady) {
  <app-standalone-comp />
}
```

- **Type-safe template bindings**: Templates might offer tighter TypeScript integration for standalone components' inputs and outputs. Angular 20 could extend its type-checking capabilities to ensure that template bindings align with a standalone component's API, catching errors at compile time.

  For example:

```
@Component({
  standalone: true,
  selector: 'app-standalone-comp',
  template: '<p>{{ inputValue }}</p>',
})
export class StandaloneCompComponent {
  @Input() inputValue: string = '';
}
```

  In the parent template, **`<app-standalone-comp [inputValue]="someString" />`**.

  The template compiler could flag mismatches (e.g., passing a number instead of a string) more effectively.

- **Selectorless components**: One key improvement is the introduction of selectorless components, an experimental feature that allows developers to import and use components directly in templates without specifying a selector. This means you could use a component by its class name or another identifier, reducing boilerplate and making it easier to refactor component names without changing the template.

  For example, instead of **`<app-my-component></app-my-component>`**, you might import **`MyComponent`** and use it directly, which simplifies working with standalone components in templates.

Question 21: What template-related deprecations were removed in Angular 19 and 20?

Answer: In Angular 19 and upcoming Angular 20, the framework introduces and promotes new block syntax (e.g., **`@if`**, **`@for`**, **`@switch`**) as part of its effort to modernize and simplify template control flow. However, it is important to note that the traditional structural directives like **`*ngIf`**, **`*ngFor`**, and **`<ng-container>`** have not been deprecated or removed; they remain fully supported.

Instead of removal, Angular is encouraging a gradual migration to the newer, more declarative syntax to promote cleaner, more maintainable templates. Key updates (not deprecations) are as follows:

- **New @if syntax**: Introduced as a cleaner, more intuitive alternative to **`*ngIf`**, shown as follows:

```
@if (isLoggedIn) {
  <p>Welcome back!</p>
}
@else {
  <p>Please log in.</p>
}
```

- **New @for syntax**: An alternative to `*ngFor` that enhances readability and supports local variables more clearly.

```
@for (item of items; track item.id) {
  <li>{{ item.name }}</li>
}
```

- **Use of @defer for performance optimization**: Enables lazy rendering of blocks, especially useful for large or non-critical template sections. Replaces some scenarios where `<ng-container>` was previously used for deferred logic.

Some additional things to consider are as follows:

- `*ngIf`, `*ngFor`, and `<ng-container>` are still valid and officially supported.
- The new syntax is opt-in and meant to improve template clarity, not to break backward compatibility.
- Developers are encouraged to adopt the new syntax gradually as part of modern Angular best practices.

Template syntax and performance optimization

Question 22: How does Angular optimize DOM updates in templates for better performance?

Answer: Angular optimizes DOM updates using the following:

- **Change detection**: Tracks component changes and updates only affected parts of the DOM.
- **OnPush strategy**: Updates only when input properties change.
- **TrackBy in ngFor**: Prevents unnecessary re-renders in lists.

Consider the following example of using OnPush strategy to optimize updates:

```
import { Component, ChangeDetectionStrategy, Input } from '@angular/core';
@Component({
  selector: 'app-user',
  template: `<p>{{ user.name }}</p>`,
  changeDetection: ChangeDetectionStrategy.OnPush
})
export class UserComponent {
  @Input() user!: { name: string };
}
```

This ensures Angular updates only when the user object reference changes, reducing unnecessary re-renders.

Question 23: How does Angular handle asynchronous data in templates using async pipes?

Answer: The async pipe automatically subscribes and unsubscribes to observables and promises in templates.

Consider an example of fetching data using async pipe:

```
import { Component } from '@angular/core';
import { Observable, of, delay } from 'rxjs';
@Component({
  selector: 'app-data',
  template: `<p>Data: {{ data$ | async }}</p>`,
})
export class DataComponent {
```

```
  data$: Observable<string> = of('Hello, Angular!').pipe(delay(2000));
}
```

async pipe automatically unsubscribes when the component is destroyed.

Question 24: What is ngClass, and how can it dynamically apply CSS classes in templates?

Answer: **ngClass** dynamically adds or removes CSS classes based on conditions.

Consider an example of dynamic class binding.

HTML code:

```
<p [ngClass]="{ 'active': isActive, 'disabled': !isActive }">Status</p>
<button (click)="toggle()">Toggle</button>
```

TypeScript code:

```
export class AppComponent {
  isActive = false;
  toggle() { this.isActive = !this.isActive; }
}
```

If **isActive = true**, the active class is applied.

If **isActive = false**, the disabled class is applied.

Question 25: What is ngStyle, and how can it be used to dynamically style elements?

Answer: **ngStyle** dynamically sets inline styles. Consider an example of dynamic styling using **ngStyle**.

HTML code:

```
<p [ngStyle]="{ 'color': isActive ? 'green' : 'red' }">Dynamic Text</p>
```

If **isActive = true**, the text is green; otherwise, it is red.

Question 26: How do local template variables improve component communication?

Answer: Local template variables (**#variable**) allow direct access to DOM elements and child components. Consider an example of using local template variables.

HTML code:

```
<input #nameInput type="text">
<button (click)="showValue(nameInput.value)">Show Name</button>
```

TypeScript code:

```
export class AppComponent {
  showValue(value: string) { console.log(value); }
}
```

Clicking the button logs the input value.

Question 27: What are @ViewChild and @ViewChildren, and how do they interact with templates?

Answer: **@ViewChild** gets a single child component or DOM element, while **@ViewChildren** gets multiple child components or DOM elements. Consider an example of using **@ViewChild**.

HTML code:

```
<input #myInput type="text">
<button (click)="focusInput()">Focus</button>
```

TypeScript code:

```
import { Component, ViewChild, ElementRef } from '@angular/core';
@Component({
```

```
  selector: 'app-root',
  templateUrl: './app.component.html',
})
export class AppComponent {
  @ViewChild('myInput') inputRef!: ElementRef;
  focusInput() {
    this.inputRef.nativeElement.focus();
  }
}
```

Clicking the button focuses the input field.

Question 28. How does template-driven form binding work in Angular?

Answer: Template-driven forms use **`ngModel`** for two-way data binding.

Let us consider an example of a basic template-driven form. To use **`[(ngModel)]`**, you must import **`FormsModule`** in the module where the component is declared:

```
import { FormsModule } from '@angular/forms';
```

Without this, Angular will throw an error at runtime because **`ngModel`** is part of the template-driven forms API, which is provided by **`FormsModule`**.

HTML code:

```
<form #userForm="ngForm">
  <input type="text" name="username" [(ngModel)]="username">
  <button (click)="submit()">Submit</button>
</form>
```

TypeScript code:

```
export class AppComponent {
  username = '';
  submit() { console.log(this.username); }
}
```

Angular automatically manages form state and validation.

Question 29: What are lifecycle hooks, and how do they interact with templates?

Answer: Lifecycle hooks control a component's behavior at different stages of its existence, allowing developers to respond to changes in state, inputs, and rendering. Lifecycle hooks interact with templates in the following manner:

- **ngOnInit()**: Runs once after the component is created, commonly used for initialization logic.
- **ngOnChanges()**: Executes when input properties change, enabling responses to new values.
- **ngDoCheck()**: Used for custom change detection when Angular's default detection is insufficient.
- **ngAfterViewInit()**: Runs after the view is fully initialized, often used for DOM-related logic.

Other hooks, such as **`ngDoCheck`**, **`ngAfterContentInit`**, and **`ngAfterContentChecked`**, provide further control over the interaction between the component's lifecycle and its template.

Each hook allows precise control over component rendering and updates, ensuring optimal behavior within Angular templates.

For example: Using `ngOnInit`:

```
export class AppComponent implements OnInit {
  ngOnInit() {
```

```
    console.log('Component Initialized');
  }
}
```

The logs component is initialized when the component loads.

Question 30: How can you debug Angular templates effectively?

Answer: To debug Angular templates effectively, you can use the following methods:

- **Use console.log()**: Debug template expressions.
- **Angular DevTools**: Inspect change detection.
- **Augury Chrome extension**: Augury Chrome extension is no longer actively maintained. Use Angular DevTools as a modern alternative.
- **Debugger in Chrome**: Pause execution in DevTools.

Refer to an example of debugging with **`console.log()`**.

HTML code:

```
<p>{{ user?.name }}</p>
<button (click)="debug()">Debug</button>
```

TypeScript code:

```
export class AppComponent {
  user = { name: 'Anil' };
  debug() { console.log(this.user); }
}
```

Clicking the button logs the user to the console for debugging.

Template features in standalone components

Question 31: How do templates work in standalone components without NgModules?

Answer: In Angular's standalone components, templates work the same way as in traditional components, but they do not require an NgModule to function. Instead, each component is self-contained and declares its own dependencies.

For example: Standalone component with a template:

```
import { Component } from '@angular/core';
@Component({
  selector: 'app-hello',
  standalone: true, // Declares this as a standalone component
  template: `<h1>Hello, {{ name }}!</h1>`,
})
export class HelloComponent {
  name = 'Angular';
}
```

It works as follows:

- The **`standalone: true`** property eliminates the need for NgModule.
- The template is directly embedded using **`template`** property.
- The component can be used directly in another standalone component or application bootstrap.

Question 32: How do imports work in templates of standalone components?

Answer: Since standalone components do not belong to an NgModule, they declare their own dependencies explicitly using the imports property.

For example: Importing other components and directives:

```
import { Component } from '@angular/core';
import { CommonModule } from '@angular/common'; // Importing Angular built-in directives
import { HelloComponent } from './hello.component'; // Importing another standalone component
@Component({
  selector: 'app-main',
  standalone: true,
  template: `
    <app-hello></app-hello> <!-- Using imported component -->
    <p *ngIf="isVisible">This is conditionally displayed.</p>
  `,
  imports: [CommonModule, HelloComponent], // Declare required dependencies
})
export class MainComponent {
  isVisible = true;
}
```

It works in the following manner:

- `imports: [CommonModule, HelloComponent]` explicitly declares dependencies.
- Angular directives like `*ngIf` are available because `CommonModule` is imported.
- The `HelloComponent` can be used in the template since it is explicitly imported.

Question 33: What are the key template-related advantages of standalone components?

Answer: Standalone components in Angular offer several key template-related advantages, making them a powerful feature for building modular and efficient applications. Refer to the following list for a detailed breakdown:

- **No need for NgModule**: Components work independently without being declared inside a module.
- **Better encapsulation**: Each component explicitly declares its dependencies, making it more modular.
- **Faster development**: Developers can create and use components without worrying about module-level configuration.
- **Simplified codebase**: Reduces unnecessary boilerplate by eliminating module-related declarations.

Question 34: How does Angular handle template dependencies in standalone components?

Answer: In standalone components, Angular resolves dependencies at the component level rather than relying on a module-wide configuration.

For example: Standalone component with dependency resolution:

```
import { Component } from '@angular/core';
import { FormsModule } from '@angular/forms'; // Importing a module for forms
@Component({
  selector: 'app-user-input',
  standalone: true,
```

```
  template: `
    <input [(ngModel)]="name" placeholder="Enter name" />
    <p>Hello, {{ name }}!</p>
  `,
  imports: [FormsModule], // Importing FormsModule explicitly
})
export class UserInputComponent {
  name = '';
}
```

Its working is as follows:

- The component imports only what it needs (**`FormsModule`** for **`ngModel`**).
- No need to register **`FormsModule`** inside an **`NgModule`**; it is declared locally.
- Dependencies are resolved per component, reducing unnecessary imports.

Question 35: How do Angular templates in standalone components improve build performance?

Answer: Standalone components speed up builds and optimize performance by doing the following:

- **Tree-shaking optimization**: Only the imported dependencies are bundled in the final build, reducing the application size.
- **Faster compilation**: Angular does not have to analyze an entire NgModule graph; it compiles components individually.
- **Better code splitting**: Since standalone components declare their own dependencies, the Angular compiler can lazy load smaller chunks, improving initial load times.
- **Reduced change detection complexity**: Standalone components have faster change detection cycles by limiting dependencies, thus improving runtime performance.

SSR and hydration in Angular templates

Question 36: How does Angular handle SSR with templates?

Answer: Angular handles SSR with templates primarily through Angular Universal, which allows Angular applications to be rendered on the server instead of directly in the browser. This process is beneficial for improving initial load performance and enhancing SEO since the content is available in the HTML response before the Angular application takes over on the client side.

The following is a detailed breakdown of how Angular handles SSR with templates:

- **Angular Universal**: Angular Universal is a set of tools and libraries that enable Angular applications to run in a Node.js environment, which can render the application's components and templates on the server side. This results in static HTML pages being generated and sent to the client on the first load, shown as follows:
    - **SSR**: When a user requests a page, Angular Universal renders the application on the server, generating static HTML for the entire page (or at least for the parts of the page that do not require client-side interaction).
    - **Template rendering**: Angular templates are processed server-side using the Angular **ahead-of-time** (**AOT**) compiler, converting them into JavaScript code that can be executed on the server to generate the HTML output.

- **Template compilation and rendering**: This is done in the following manner:
    - **AOT compilation**: Angular uses the AOT compiler to compile templates and components ahead-of-time . During SSR, Angular uses precompiled templates to generate static HTML on the server before sending it to the browser.
    - **Server-side change detection**: When rendering the application on the server, Angular performs change detection to ensure that the view reflects the latest state of the data before generating the HTML.

  The HTML output from the server will include the resolved templates, such as the content generated by `*ngIf`, `*ngFor`, and other structural directives.
- **Hydration**: After the server has rendered and sent the HTML to the browser, the Angular client-side application takes over. This process is called **hydration**, where Angular attaches event listeners, initializes client-side behaviors, and replaces any static content with dynamic content as needed.

  Hydration ensures the app becomes interactive without needing to reload the page. The static HTML provided by SSR is enhanced with the dynamic capabilities of Angular, such as user interactions and data updates.
- **SEO benefits**: SEO optimization can be done as follows:
    - **Pre-rendered content**: SSR improves SEO by sending fully rendered HTML to the browser, which search engines can easily crawl. This is especially useful for SPAs, where content is typically dynamically loaded by JavaScript.
    - **Meta tags**: Angular Universal can also generate dynamic meta tags and titles based on the content rendered on the server, improving SEO for different pages.
- **Handling directives and bindings in templates**: Angular templates often contain structural directives like `*ngIf`, `*ngFor`, and `ngSwitch`. These are processed by Angular during SSR as follows:
    - **ngIf**: If the condition is false, the element and its children are excluded from the generated HTML on the server.
    - **ngFor**: The server performs the iteration and generates the HTML for each item in the collection, ensuring that the correct number of elements are included in the HTML response.
    - **ngSwitch**: Similar to `*ngIf`, `ngSwitch` evaluates the expression server-side, and the correct template content is rendered based on the condition.

  All directives and bindings are correctly handled server-side before the HTML is sent to the client, ensuring that the content is consistent when it reaches the browser.
- **Dynamic imports and lazy loading**: Angular supports **dynamic imports** in templates, allowing for the lazy loading of certain components or modules. This improves performance by loading only the necessary resources in the following manner:
    - **SSR support**: During SSR, Angular ensures that only the components and modules that are needed to render the initial page are loaded. The remaining parts are lazily loaded after the initial HTML is sent to the client.
    - **Client-side hydration**: On the client-side, dynamic imports allow Angular to load and render the remaining components once the client application takes over.
- **Partial hydration**: Angular 19+ introduced **partial hydration**, which improves performance by selectively hydrating parts of the page that require interactivity. Not all components need to be interactive immediately, so Angular only hydrates the components that are necessary for the user experience. This is done through the following methods:
    - **Selective hydration**: This minimizes the JavaScript payload by ensuring that only interactive components are hydrated and the rest remain static until needed.

- **Stateful hydration**: The state on the client-side is synchronized with the state rendered on the server, ensuring the view remains consistent when the client app takes over.

- **Handling template states**: SSR is often used with **stateful templates**, where data is fetched on the server (such as from APIs or databases) before rendering the page. This ensures that the server sends a fully populated page with dynamic content, like user-specific data or dynamic lists, so that the user sees the complete page on the first load without needing additional API calls.
- **Server-side template cache**: In some cases, Angular Universal can use **template caching** to improve SSR performance. By caching rendered HTML on the server, Angular can serve subsequent requests faster, reducing the time required to generate the page for each user.

Question 37: What is template hydration, and how does Angular 19 improve it?

Answer: Template hydration is the process of making a pre-rendered (SSR) template interactive in the browser by attaching event listeners, bindings, and Angular directives. The following are the improvements in hydration in Angular 19:

- **Partial hydration**: Components hydrate only when needed, reducing JavaScript execution time.
- **Streaming hydration**: Large templates hydrate progressively, improving user experience.
- **Better DOM matching**: Angular reuses existing server-rendered HTML instead of rebuilding it, reducing flickering.

An example of hydration in Angular 19 is as follows:

```
import { enableHydration } from '@angular/core';
bootstrapApplication(AppComponent, {
  providers: [enableHydration()],
});
```

It results in faster hydration, reduced JavaScript processing, and improved interaction speed.

Question 38: How does Angular optimize template rendering in SSR environments?

Answer: The following are the optimizations in SSR template rendering:

- **Static content pre-rendering**: Angular renders static parts of the template once on the server, reducing re-rendering.
- **Efficient hydration with incremental activation**: Instead of hydrating the entire page at once, Angular activates only the visible parts first.
- **Lazy loading in SSR mode**: Angular does not load unnecessary components until required, making SSR templates lightweight.
- **Minimal DOM manipulation**: Uses server-rendered DOM instead of rebuilding elements from scratch in the browser.

For example: Using SSR with lazy loading:

```
import { Routes } from '@angular/router';
export const routes: Routes = [
  {
    path: 'dashboard',
    loadComponent: () => import('./dashboard.component').then(m => m.DashboardComponent),
  },
];
```

This results in faster rendering, lower JavaScript execution time, and better performance for complex apps.

Question 39: What are incremental hydration techniques in Angular templates?

Answer: Incremental hydration is a technique where different parts of the SSR-rendered page become interactive progressively, rather than all at once. The following are the key techniques that Angular uses for incremental hydration:

- **Component-level hydration**: Components hydrate only when needed, avoiding unnecessary JavaScript execution.
- **Event-driven activation**: Angular hydrates a section only if a user scrolls to it, instead of on page load.
- **Optimized change detection**: Angular reuses server-generated content and avoids unnecessary change detection.

For example: Using deferred views for incremental hydration:

```
@defer {
  <app-dashboard></app-dashboard>
} when viewport
```

The benefits include faster initial loads, reduced CPU usage, and better performance on slow networks.

Question 40: How does Angular 19 improve template performance in prerendered applications?

Answer: Angular 19 introduces many improvements to template performance in prerendered applications, which can significantly enhance the loading speed and responsiveness of Angular applications. These optimizations help ensure that an application's content is quickly available to users and also improve efficiency for prerendered or SSR applications. Here is how Angular 19 improves template performance in prerendered applications:

- **Partial hydration**: Angular 19 introduces partial hydration, a key performance improvement for SSR and prerendered applications. With partial hydration, the following benefits are seen:
    - **Selective hydration**: Only the components that need to be interactive are hydrated, rather than hydrating the entire application. This means that non-interactive content remains static while only the necessary interactive components are initialized on the client side.
    - **Reduced JavaScript payload**: By hydrating fewer components, the initial JavaScript payload is significantly reduced, leading to faster load times and better performance, especially on slower networks or devices.
    - **Improved time to interactive**: Partial hydration allows the application to become interactive faster by focusing only on the critical parts of the page, which improves the perceived performance of the application.
- **Stateful hydration**: Another important performance feature in Angular 19 is stateful hydration, which ensures that the client-side application syncs correctly with the server-rendered content in the following manner:
    - **Client-server state alignment**: Angular ensures that the application's state remains consistent between the server-rendered HTML and the client-side app. This minimizes discrepancies and prevents unnecessary re-renders after the client app is bootstrapped.
    - **Faster interactivity**: With stateful hydration, the client-side app does not have to re-fetch or re-render the entire view, as the state is already preloaded from the server. This results in a smoother transition from SSR to **client-side rendering** (**CSR**) and provides a faster and more seamless user experience.
- **Optimized template rendering with lazy loading**: Angular 19 optimizes how templates are rendered in prerendered applications by improving support for lazy loading, shown as follows:
    - **Lazy load only what is needed**: Angular 19 ensures that only the required components and modules are lazily loaded when they are needed, rather than loading the entire application

upfront. This improves both the initial loading time and the subsequent user interactions, as only the necessary parts of the application are fetched.

  - **Efficient preloading**: Preloaded modules or resources can be loaded while the user is interacting with other parts of the app, ensuring a smoother experience. This reduces delays during navigation by ensuring that required resources are fetched in the background.

- **Optimized template change detection**: Angular 19 enhances the performance of template change detection by improving how Angular tracks changes and updates views in SSR and prerendered applications, providing the following benefits:
  - **Faster change detection**: Angular 19 optimizes the change detection process to ensure that only the components that need updating are checked and rendered rather than rechecking the entire component tree.
  - **Server-side change detection**: During SSR, Angular can now efficiently detect and render changes on the server, ensuring that only necessary updates are made when the content is first generated. This results in less computational overhead during the prerendering process.
- **Efficient rendering of dynamic content**: In prerendered applications, dynamic content (such as lists or data fetched from APIs) is often part of the initial page render. Angular 19 improves how this dynamic content is handled as follows:
  - **Smarter rendering of dynamic lists**: Angular 19 ensures that lists and dynamic elements are rendered efficiently without unnecessary re-renders or DOM manipulation. It uses intelligent caching and optimization strategies to ensure that only the parts of the list that need to be updated are modified.
  - **Handling of ngFor and ngIf**: Structural directives like `*ngFor` and `*ngIf` are optimized to reduce the number of times they need to be processed, ensuring faster template rendering.
- **Improved template parsing and compilation**: Angular 19 introduces enhancements to the template parsing and compilation processes, which improve the performance of prerendered applications in the following manner:
  - **Faster AOT compilation**: AOT compilation has been further optimized in Angular 19. This means that Angular compiles templates more efficiently at build time, reducing the time required to render templates on the server.
  - **Reduced template size**: Angular 19 optimizes the size of the templates generated during AOT compilation, ensuring that the templates sent to the server are as small and efficient as possible. This reduces the overhead of rendering templates on both the server and the client.
- **Optimized static rendering**: Angular 19 also improves the handling of static content in SSR and prerendered applications, shown as follows:
  - **Optimized static assets**: Angular ensures that static content (like images, styles, and scripts) is optimized and efficiently served alongside the prerendered HTML. This reduces the time it takes to load the application, as the necessary assets are already available when the HTML is served.
  - **Prerendered pages with minimal overhead**: When prerendering the application, Angular 19 ensures that there is minimal overhead in generating and serving the static HTML, resulting in faster response times.

Template best practices and common mistakes

Question 41: What are common performance pitfalls in Angular templates, and how can they be avoided?

Answer: The following are the common performance pitfalls and solutions:

- **Using functions inside templates**
  - **Common pitfall**: `<p>{{ calculateValue() }}</p>`

    This triggers recalculation on every change detection cycle.
  - **Solution**: Compute the value in the component and store it in a variable.
- **Not using trackBy in *ngFor**
  - **Common pitfall**: `*ngFor="let item of items"`

    It re-renders the entire list.
  - **Solution**: Use `trackBy` to track elements by unique ID, shown in the following TypeScript code:

    ```
    trackByFn(index: number, item: any) {
    return item.id;
    }
    ```
- **Overusing *ngIf and *ngSwitch**
  - **Common pitfall**: Frequent use of `*ngIf` or `*ngSwitch` leads to DOM removal and recreation, which can cause performance issues and loss of component state (e.g., form values). It also results in cluttered and complex templates.
  - **Solution**: Use `[hidden]` or `ngClass` to toggle visibility without DOM removal. Centralize logic in the component using variables, and break complex sections into child components. In Angular 17+, prefer `@if` and `@switch` for cleaner and more efficient control flow.
- **Using too many event bindings ((click), (input))**
  - **Common pitfall**: `<button (click)="heavyFunction()">Click</button>`
  - **Solution**: Use `@HostListener()` for optimized event handling.
- **Heavy computation in change detection**
  - **Solution**: Use `ChangeDetectionStrategy.OnPush` to optimize.

Final tip: **Profile performance with Angular DevTools to detect expensive operations.**

Question 42: **How does Angular prevent XSS in templates?**

Answer: Angular automatically escapes malicious content to prevent XSS attacks by doing the following:

- **Auto-escaping in interpolation ({{}})**: Angular escapes any untrusted content inside `{{}}`, preventing script execution.
- **Security in property binding ([property])**: Angular sanitizes untrusted HTML.

  For example: `<div [innerHTML]="userInput"></div>`
- **Explicitly trusted content (DomSanitizer)**: If you need to display dynamic content safely, use the following TypeScript code:

  ```
  this.safeHtml = this.sanitizer.bypassSecurityTrustHtml(userInput);
  ```

Final tip: **Never use `innerHTML` with direct user inputs.**

Question 43: **What are the benefits of using structural directives efficiently in templates?**

Answer: The following are the key benefits of using structural directives efficiently:

- **Efficient DOM manipulation**: Directives like `*ngIf`, `*ngFor`, and `*ngSwitch` optimize how elements are created or destroyed.
- **Conditional rendering**: Controls visibility efficiently (`*ngIf` avoids unnecessary elements in the DOM).

- **Dynamic lists with trackBy**: Improves performance by reducing unnecessary DOM re-renders.
- **Better readability**: Keeps templates clean and easy to manage.

Final tip: **Avoid nesting multiple structural directives; instead, use `<ng-container>`.**

Question 44: Why is it important to avoid complex expressions inside Angular templates?

Answer: Complex expressions in templates run on every change detection cycle, leading to performance issues. For example:

HTML code:

```
<p>{{ expensiveCalculation() }}</p>
```

This runs on every UI update, even if the data has not changed.

The best practice here is to compute values beforehand in the component using the following TypeScript code:

```
computedValue = this.expensiveCalculation();
```

```
Then bind: <p>{{ computedValue }}</p>.
```

Final tip: **Keep templates lightweight and delegate logic to the component.**

Question 45: How can lazy loading improve template performance in large applications?

Answer: The following are the benefits of lazy loading:

- **Faster initial load time**: It loads only required components, reducing bundle size.
- **Better memory management**: Keeps unnecessary modules out of memory until needed.
- **Improves navigation speed**: Large apps feel more responsive.

For example: Lazy loading a component in a standalone app:

```
const routes: Routes = [
  {
    path: 'dashboard',
    loadComponent: () => import('./dashboard.component').then(m => m.DashboardComponent)
  }
];
```

Final tip: **Always lazy load large modules and rarely used features.**

Question 46: Why should you avoid using functions inside Angular templates?

Answer: You should avoid using functions inside Angular templates, as every function inside a template is re-executed on every change detection cycle.

For example: The following HTML code is an example of a bad practice:

```
<p>{{ calculateTotal() }}</p>
```

The preceding code leads Angular to call `calculateTotal()` every time a change happens, even if the result is the same. To avoid this issue, use precomputed variables.

TypeScript code:

```
total = this.calculateTotal();
```

HTML code:

```
<p>{{ total }}</p>
```

Final tip: **Never use computational functions directly in the template.**

Question 47: What are some best practices for optimizing template rendering performance?

Answer: The following key best practices optimize template rendering performance:

- **Use ChangeDetectionStrategy.OnPush**: Reduces unnecessary re-renders.
- **Minimize use of *ngIf and *ngFor**: Prefer hidden for visibility toggling.
- **Use trackBy in *ngFor**: Prevents full list re-rendering.
- **Lazy load components**: Loads only the needed templates.
- **Avoid inline functions in templates**: Move logic to components.

Final tip: **Optimize bindings, directives, and change detection for better performance.**

Question 48: How does Angular handle template security vulnerabilities?

Answer: Angular handles template security vulnerabilities through the following security features:

- **Auto-sanitization of user input**: Prevents XSS attacks.
- **Content security policy (CSP) support**: Restricts unsafe scripts.
- **DomSanitizer for trusted content**: Ensures safe dynamic content rendering.

Final tip: **Never trust user input; always sanitize untrusted content.**

Question 49: What are the latest Angular 20 optimizations for template compilation?

Answer: The following are the key optimizations in Angular 20:

- **Faster compilation with AOT improvements**: Reduces build time.
- **Incremental compilation for standalone components**: It speeds up re-compilation.
- **Optimized hydration techniques**: Improves SSR template interaction.
- **Better change detection batching**: Reduces unnecessary UI updates.

Final tip: **Keep Angular updated to leverage the latest optimizations.**

Question 50: How can Angular templates be structured for better maintainability?

Answer: The following best practices are recommended in terms of structure for better maintainability of Angular templates:

- **Keep templates small**: Split complex UIs into reusable components.
- **Use template reference variables (#ref)**: Improves readability and event handling.
- **Avoid inline styles and logic**: Move logic to components and styles to separate files.
- **Follow a consistent naming convention**: Ensures code clarity and maintainability.

Final tip: **A well-structured template ensures scalability, readability, and performance..**

Conclusion

In this chapter, we explored the fundamental concepts of Angular templates, which are key to defining the user interface and binding data between the model and the view. We discussed the basic syntax, enhancements, and features of Angular templates, as well as techniques for optimizing their performance. Additionally, we examined how templates in standalone components work, the impact of SSR and hydration, and provided practical guidance on best practices and common mistakes to avoid in Angular templates.

In the next chapter, we will shift our focus to directives, where we will learn how to extend HTML's capabilities, create reusable behaviors, and manipulate DOM elements dynamically in Angular.

CHAPTER 4
Concepts of Directives

Introduction

Directives are one of the core building blocks of Angular applications. They allow developers to extend HTML capabilities by creating custom behaviors and reusable components. Angular provides three types of directives: component directives, structural directives, and attribute directives. Understanding these directive types and their applications is essential for building dynamic and interactive web applications.

In this chapter, we will explore the concepts behind Angular directives, their structure, and how to use them effectively. We will also discuss best practices to optimize directive usage within an Angular project.

Structure

This chapter covers the following topics:

- Basic concepts of directives
- Advanced directive usage and custom directives
- Directives in Angular 18, 19, and 20
- Optimizing structural directives
- Directive debugging, testing, and best practices

Objectives

By the end of this chapter, you will understand the purpose and significance of directives in Angular, differentiate between structural, attribute, and component directives, learn how to create and use custom directives effectively, gain insights into the latest directive features in Angular 20, and implement best practices for directive usage in real-world applications. This chapter will provide hands-on examples and code snippets to help solidify your understanding of Angular directives and their powerful capabilities.

Basic concepts of directives

Question 1: What are directives in Angular, and how are they categorized?

Answer: Directives in Angular are special instructions used to modify the behavior, appearance, or structure of DOM elements. The types of directives in Angular are as follows:

- **Structural directives:** These modify the DOM structure.

  For example: `*ngIf`, `*ngFor`, `*ngSwitch`

- **Attribute directives:** These change the appearance or behavior of elements.

  For example: `ngClass`, `ngStyle`, `ngModel`

- **Custom directives:** Custom directives refer to user-defined Angular directives that extend HTML behavior. These are not a separate type of directive but can be either:
  - **Custom attribute directives:** These are used to change the appearance or behavior of DOM elements (e.g., changing styles, listening to events).
  - **Custom structural directives:** These are used to add or remove elements from the DOM using `<ng-template>` and `ViewContainerRef`.

  For example: `appHighlight` (custom directive for highlighting text)

Question 2: What is the difference between structural, attribute, and custom directives?

Answer: Angular directives can be classified into the following three main types based on their purpose and functionality:

- **Structural directives (@if, @for, @switch, @defer):** Used to add, remove, or manipulate elements dynamically in the DOM.

  For example:

  ```
  @if (isLoggedIn) {
    <p>Welcome, User!</p>
  } @else {
    <p>Please log in.</p>
  }
  ```

  Other examples:
  - `*ngIf`, `*ngFor`, `*ngSwitch` (pre-Angular 17)
  - `@if`, `@for`, `@switch`, `@defer` (Angular 17+)

- **Attribute directives (ngClass, ngStyle, ngModel):** Used to modify the appearance or behavior of an existing element.

  For example:

  ```
  <p [ngClass]="{'highlight': isActive}">Styled Text</p>
  ```

  Other examples are `ngStyle`, `ngModel`.

- **Custom directives (appHighlight, appTooltip):** Used to create reusable logic for custom behaviors.

  For example:

  ```
  @Directive({
    selector: '[appHighlight]'
  })
  export class HighlightDirective {
    @HostBinding('style.backgroundColor') bgColor = 'yellow';
  ```

```
}
```

Other examples are **appTooltip**, **appAutoFocus**.

These three directives have the following key difference:

- Structural directives (**@if**, **@for**, **@switch**, **@defer**) modify the DOM structure by adding or removing elements.
- Attribute directives (**ngClass**, **ngStyle**) only change appearance or behavior without affecting the DOM structure.
- Custom directives are user-defined to extend Angular functionality.

Question 3: What are built-in Angular directives?

Answer: Angular provides several built-in directives, categorized into the following:

- **Structural directives**: Modify the DOM structure. These include the following:
  - ***ngIf or @if**: Conditionally adds or removes elements.
  - ***ngFor or @for**: Iterates over a list of items efficiently (supports **trackBy** for performance).
  - ***ngSwitch or @switch**: Conditionally renders one of multiple elements.
  - **@defer**: Lazily loads parts of a template for better performance.
- **Attribute directives**: These modify element appearance or behavior.
  - **ngClass**: Dynamically applies CSS classes.
  - **ngStyle**: Dynamically sets inline styles.
  - **ngModel**: Enables two-way data binding (Only available in forms module).
  - **ngOptimizedImage (new)**: Optimizes images automatically for better performance.

Question 4: What is ngIf, and how does it work in Angular templates?

Answer: The directives (***ngIf** or **@if**) conditionally render elements based on a Boolean expression.

For example: Using ***ngIf**/**@if** for conditional rendering:

HTML code: Using *ngIf

```
<p *ngIf="isLoggedIn">Welcome, User!</p>
<button (click)="toggleLogin()">Toggle Login</button>
```

HTML code: Using @if

```
<div> @if (isLoggedIn) { <p>Welcome, User!</p> } </div>
```

TypeScript code:

```
export class AppComponent {
  isLoggedIn = false;
  toggleLogin() { this.isLoggedIn = !this.isLoggedIn; }
}
```

If **isLoggedIn = true**, the paragraph is shown; otherwise, it is removed.

Question 5: What is ngFor, and how does it improve list rendering in Angular?

Answer: The directives (***ngFor** or **@for**) dynamically render a list based on an array.

For example: To display a list of items, run the following code:

HTML code: Using ***ngFor**:

```
<ul>
  <li *ngFor="let item of items; let i = index">
```

```
    {{ i + 1 }}. {{ item }}
  </li>
</ul>
```

HTML code: Using **`@for`**:

```
<ul>
  @for (item, i of items; track item) {
    <li>{{ i + 1 }}. {{ item }}</li>
  }
</ul>
```

TypeScript code:

```
export class AppComponent {
  items = ['Apple', 'Banana', 'Orange'];
}
```

The preceding codes allow efficient rendering of lists with automatic reactivity.

Question 6: How do *ngSwitch or @switch directives work, and when should they be used?

Answer: The directives (**`*ngSwitch`** or **`@switch`**) are used for conditional rendering based on a variable's value. For example:

HTML code: Using **`*ngSwitch`**:

```
<div [ngSwitch]="role">
  <p *ngSwitchCase="'admin'">Admin Panel</p>
  <p *ngSwitchCase="'user'">User Dashboard</p>
  <p *ngSwitchDefault>Select a Role</p>
</div>
```

HTML code: Using **`@switch`**:

```
<div>
  @switch (role) {
    @case ('admin') {
      <p>Admin Panel</p>
    }
    @case ('user') {
      <p>User Dashboard</p>
    }
    @default {
      <p>Select a Role</p>
    }
  }
</div>
```

TypeScript code:

```
export class AppComponent {
  role = 'admin';
}
```

It is useful for handling multiple conditional views.

Question 7: What is ngClass, and how can it be used to dynamically assign Cascading Style Sheets (CSS) classes?

Answer: **`ngClass`** dynamically applies CSS classes based on conditions.

For example: Dynamic class binding:

HTML code:

```
<p [ngClass]="{ 'active': isActive, 'disabled': !isActive }">Status</p>
<button (click)="toggle()">Toggle</button>
```

TypeScript code:

```
export class AppComponent {
  isActive = false;
  toggle() { this.isActive = !this.isActive; }
}
```

It adds **`'active'`** if **`isActive = true`**, else adds **`'disabled'`**.

Question 8: What is ngStyle, and how can it be used to apply dynamic styles?

Answer: **`ngStyle`** applies inline styles dynamically.

For example: Using `ngStyle`:

```
<p [ngStyle]="{ 'color': isActive ? 'green' : 'red' }">Dynamic Text</p>
```

It changes text color based on a Boolean value.

Question 9: How does ng-template differ from a regular template in Angular?

Answer: **`ng-template`** is an invisible container that does not render unless explicitly called. It is used for dynamic rendering and template reuse.

For example: Using **`ng-template`**:

HTML code:

```
<ng-template #message>
  <p>This is a hidden message</p>
</ng-template>
<button (click)="showMessage = true">Show</button>
<div *ngIf="showMessage">
  <ng-container *ngTemplateOutlet="message"></ng-container>
</div>
```

TypeScript code:

```
export class AppComponent {
  showMessage = false;
}
```

It allows delayed or conditional rendering.

Question 10: How do ng-container and ng-template differ in Angular?

Answer: Both **`ng-container`** and **`ng-template`** are structural elements in Angular, but they serve different purposes. The following are the key differences between **`ng-container`** and **`ng-template`**:

- **ng-container**:
    - Used to group multiple elements without introducing additional wrapper elements in the DOM.

    - It does not render any actual HTML element in the DOM. It acts purely as a logical container for structural directives like **`*ngIf`**, **`*ngFor`**, or **`@if`**.
    - It helps structure templates cleanly without affecting layout or CSS.
    - It is ideal when you need to apply multiple structural directives but want to avoid extra **`<div>`** or **`<span>`** tags.
    - Useful for conditional rendering of multiple elements without extra **`<div>`** wrappers.
    - **For example**:

```
<ng-container *ngIf="isLoggedIn">
  <p>Welcome, User!</p>
  <button (click)="logout()">Logout</button>
</ng-container>
```

- **ng-template**:
    - Used to define hidden content that will be rendered only when explicitly used.
    - It does not render in the DOM until referenced using **`*ngIf`**, **`ngTemplateOutlet`**, or **`@defer`**.
    - Useful for lazy rendering, dynamic content loading, and reusing template blocks.
    - **For example**:

```
<ng-template #loading>
  <p>Loading, please wait...</p>
</ng-template>
<div *ngIf="isLoading; else loading">
  <p>Content Loaded!</p>
</div>
```

Advanced directive usage and custom directives

Question 11: **What are custom directives in Angular, and how do you create them?**

Answer: Custom directives in Angular extend the behavior of elements in the DOM. Unlike components, directives do not have their own templates, but they can modify elements, listen to events, or apply styles dynamically. Refer to the following example:

1. **Create a custom directive (appHighlight)**: The following directive changes the background color of an element when hovered over:

```
import { Directive, ElementRef, HostListener, Renderer2 } from '@angular/core';
@Directive({
  selector: '[appHighlight]'
})
export class HighlightDirective {
  constructor(private el: ElementRef, private renderer: Renderer2) {}
  @HostListener('mouseenter') onMouseEnter() {
    this.renderer.setStyle(this.el.nativeElement, 'backgroundColor', 'yellow');
  }
  @HostListener('mouseleave') onMouseLeave() {
    this.renderer.removeStyle(this.el.nativeElement, 'backgroundColor');
  }
}
```

2. **Use the custom directive appHighlight in the component template**: Add the following code:

```
<p appHighlight>Hover over me to see the highlight effect!</p>
```

Output: Here is a simple visual showing how the **`appHighlight`** directive changes the background color when hovering over an element:

Hover over me to see
the highlight effect!

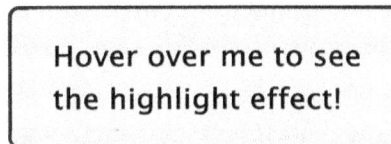

Figure 4.1: *Highlight custom directives*

Question 12: How does the @Directive decorator work in Angular?

Answer: The **`@Directive`** decorator marks a class as a directive in Angular. It tells Angular how to apply logic to an element. For example:

1. **Create a custom directive**: The following code will create a custom directive:

```
@Directive({
  selector: '[appCustomDirective]'
})
export class CustomDirective {
  constructor() {
    console.log('Custom directive initialized');
  }
}
```

2. **Use the directive `appCustomDirective` in a component**: Execute the following code:

```
<p appCustomDirective>Text with a custom directive</p>
```

This directive can be attached to an element to execute specific logic when Angular processes the component.

Question 13: What is ElementRef, and how is it used inside directives?

Answer: **`ElementRef`** provides direct access to the DOM element associated with the directive. However, direct manipulation of the DOM is not recommended due to security concerns.

`ElementRef` is a wrapper provided by Angular that gives direct access to the DOM element to which a directive or component is attached. It is commonly used in attribute directives to read or modify the element's properties, styles, or classes.

Unlike **`document.getElementById()`**, **`ElementRef`** does not perform a query; it is automatically injected by Angular and bound to the host element. Consider the following example:

- **Create a custom directive using ElementRef**: The following code will allow you to change the text color:

```
import { Directive, ElementRef } from '@angular/core';
@Directive({
  selector: '[appTextColor]'
})
export class TextColorDirective {
  constructor(private el: ElementRef) {
    el.nativeElement.style.color = 'blue';
```

```
    }
}
```

- **Use the directive appTextColor in a component**: This directive will help you to change the text color:

```
<p appTextColor>This text will appear in blue.</p>
```

The best practice when working with **ElementRef** is to avoid the direct use of **ElementRef.nativeElement** in general, especially in web workers or server-side rendering. Prefer using Angular's Renderer2 for safe, platform-agnostic DOM manipulation.

Question 14: What is Renderer2, and how does it help in directive development?

Answer: **Renderer2** is a safer alternative to **ElementRef**, as it allows modifying elements without directly interacting with the DOM. Consider the following example:

1. **Create a directive**: To change font size, create a directive using **Renderer2** as follows:

```
import { Directive, ElementRef, Renderer2 } from '@angular/core';
@Directive({
  selector: '[appFontSize]'
})
export class FontSizeDirective {
  constructor(private el: ElementRef, private renderer: Renderer2) {
    this.renderer.setStyle(this.el.nativeElement, 'font-size', '20px');
  }
}
```

2. **Using appFontSize directive in component**: This will change the font size, shown as follows:

```
<p appFontSize>This text has increased font size.</p>
```

Output: Here is an illustration showing how the **appFontSize** directive increases the font size of a paragraph element:

This text has increased font size.

Figure 4.2: Renderer2 custom FontSize directives

Question 15: How can you listen to DOM events inside a custom directive?

Answer: Angular provides **@HostListener** to listen to events like click, mouse enter, etc. For example:

1. **Creating a directive for listening to click events**: To do so, run the following code:

```
import {Directive, ElementRef, HostListener} from '@angular/core';
@Directive({
  selector: '[appClick]'
})
export class ClickDirective {
  constructor(private el: ElementRef) {}
  @HostListener('click') onClick() {
    alert('Element clicked!');
  }
}
```

2. **Use appClick directive**: Use the directive in a component for click events, shown as follows:

   ```
   <button appClick>Click Me</button>
   ```

Question 16: What is HostListener, and how does it work in Angular directives?

Answer: `@HostListener` allows binding to DOM events inside a directive.

Refer to the following example to change the background on hover:

```
import { Directive, ElementRef, HostListener, Renderer2 } from '@angular/core';
@Directive({
  selector: '[appHoverHighlight]'
})
export class HoverHighlightDirective {
  constructor(private el: ElementRef, private renderer: Renderer2) {}
  @HostListener('mouseenter') onMouseEnter() {
    this.renderer.setStyle(this.el.nativeElement, 'backgroundColor', 'lightgray');
  }
  @HostListener('mouseleave') onMouseLeave() {
    this.renderer.removeStyle(this.el.nativeElement, 'backgroundColor');
  }
}
```

Question 17: What is HostBinding, and how can it be used inside a directive?

Answer: `@HostBinding` binds a directive property to an element's property or style dynamically. Consider the following example:

1. **Create a directive for toggling a CSS class**: The code is as follows:

   ```
   import { Directive, HostBinding, HostListener } from '@angular/core';
   @Directive({
     selector: '[appBorderToggle]'
   })
   export class BorderToggleDirective {
     @HostBinding('class.border-highlight') isHighlighted = false;
     @HostListener('mouseover') onMouseOver() {
       this.isHighlighted = true;
     }
     @HostListener('mouseleave') onMouseLeave() {
       this.isHighlighted = false;
     }
   }
   ```

2. **Create CSS class for toggling**: The following code will create a CSS class for toggling:

   ```
   .border-highlight {
     border: 2px solid red;
   }
   ```

3. **Use appBorderToggle directive**: Use the directive in the component:

   ```
   <p appBorderToggle>Hover over me to see the border effect.</p>
   ```

Question 18: How can you pass input properties to a directive?

Answer: Directives can receive values using the **`@Input()`** decorator. For example:

1. **Create a directive**: To customize the highlight color, create a directive as follows:

```
import { Directive, ElementRef, Input, Renderer2 } from '@angular/core';
@Directive({
  selector: '[appCustomHighlight]'
})
export class CustomHighlightDirective {
  @Input('appCustomHighlight') highlightColor = 'yellow';
  constructor(private el: ElementRef, private renderer: Renderer2) {}
  ngOnInit() {
    this.renderer.setStyle(this.el.nativeElement, 'backgroundColor', this.
highlightColor);
  }
}
```

2. **Use the directive**: Use **`appCustomHighlight`** in the component as follows:

```
<p appCustomHighlight="lightblue">This text has a light blue background.</p>
```

Question 19: How do directives interact with parent components?

Answer: Directives can communicate with parent components via **`@Output()`** events. For example:

1. **Create a directive**: Create a custom directive to emit an event to the parent component as follows:

```
import { Directive, EventEmitter, HostListener, Output } from '@angular/core';
@Directive({
  selector: '[appClickTracker]'
})
export class ClickTrackerDirective {
  @Output() clicked = new EventEmitter<void>();
  @HostListener('click') onClick() {
    this.clicked.emit();
  }
}
```

2. **Define parent component**: Add the event handler as follows:

```
export class AppComponent {
  onElementClicked() {
    alert('Child element clicked!');
  }
}
```

3. **Use directive and parent component event**: The usage is shown as follows:

```
<button appClickTracker (clicked)="onElementClicked()">Click Me</button>
```

Question 20. What are the key best practices for writing custom directives?

Answer: When developing custom directives in Angular, the following best practices ensure they are efficient, reusable, and maintainable:

- Use **`Renderer2`** instead of **`ElementRef`** to manipulate the DOM securely.
- Use **`@HostBinding`** and **`@HostListener`** for better integration with host elements.
- Minimize direct DOM manipulation to keep the directive reusable.
- Use **`@Input()`** properties to allow dynamic behavior customization.
- Ensure proper memory management by unsubscribing from events when needed.

Directives in Angular 18, 19, and 20

Question 21: What are the latest enhancements to directives in Angular 18?

Answer: Angular 18 introduced improvements to directives, making them more efficient and reusable. Key enhancements include the following:

- **Improved dependency injection**: Directives now support better provider scoping.
- **More efficient change detection**: Directives update only when required.
- **Optimized Renderer2 performance**: Reduced overhead when applying styles dynamically.
- **Support for standalone components**: Directives integrate more seamlessly with standalone APIs.

For example:

1. **Improved custom directive in Angular 18**: The improvements can be seen in the following code:

```
import { Directive, ElementRef, Renderer2 } from '@angular/core';
@Directive({
  selector: '[appAutoFocus]',
  standalone: true // Now works without being declared in a module
})
export class AutoFocusDirective {
  constructor(private el: ElementRef, private renderer: Renderer2) {}
  ngOnInit() {
    this.renderer.setAttribute(this.el.nativeElement, 'autofocus', 'true');
  }
}
```

2. **Use the custom directive**: The usage is shown as follows:

```
<input appAutoFocus />
```

The preceding directive automatically focuses an input field when loaded, without needing to be declared in an NgModule.

Question 22: How does Angular 19 optimize structural directive performance?

Answer: Angular 19 introduced template block directives (**`@if`**, **`@for`**, **`@switch`**), which are faster and more readable than traditional structural directives (**`*ngIf`**, **`*ngFor`**, **`*ngSwitch`**). The following are the key optimizations in structural directives:

- **Better change detection**: Only updates relevant parts of the DOM.
- **Faster iteration with @for**: Reduces re-rendering overhead.
- **Efficient conditional rendering with @if**: Improves readability and performance.

Question 23: What is the @if directive in Angular 19, and how does it compare to ngIf?

Answer: The **`@if`** directive (introduced in Angular 19) replaces **`*ngIf`**, offering better readability and performance. The following are the key differences between **`@if`** and **`*ngIf`**:

- **Syntax**: `@if` uses a cleaner, block-based structure (`@if(condition) { ... }`), while `*ngIf` relies on attribute-based syntax.
- **Performance**: `@if` optimizes rendering by avoiding unnecessary DOM updates, whereas `*ngIf` can trigger a full re-render.
- **Readability**: `@if` provides better code organization, especially for complex conditions, while `*ngIf` can become harder to manage in larger templates.

For example: Using `@if`:

```
@if (isLoggedIn) {
  <p>Welcome back, user!</p>
} @else {
  <p>Please log in.</p>
}
```

Question 24: **What is the @for directive in Angular 19, and how does it improve iteration?**

Answer: The `@for` directive is a new, optimized alternative to `*ngFor` introduced in Angular 19 as part of the block template syntax. It improves list rendering performance by using incremental DOM updates, which means Angular updates only the parts of the list that actually change, rather than re-rendering the entire list. The following are key benefits:

- **Incremental updates**: Unlike `*ngFor`, which may re-render the entire list, `@for` updates only the changed items, improving performance for large or dynamic lists.
- **Encouraged identity tracking**: While `@for` can track items by reference by default, it is strongly recommended to define a track expression (e.g., track item.id) to uniquely identify list items.
- **More readable syntax**:

  ```
  @for (item of items; track item.id) {
    <li>{{ item.name }}</li>
  }
  ```

Clarification on identity tracking:

- The claim that `@for` removes the need for `trackBy` is incorrect.
- Without an explicit track expression, Angular tracks by object reference, which can cause inefficient updates if object instances change without identity changes.
- Always use a track expression (similar to `trackBy` in `*ngFor`) when possible, especially when working with mutable lists or API responses.

Question 25: **What is the @switch directive in Angular 19, and how does it compare to ngSwitch?**

Answer: `@switch` replaces `*ngSwitch` for better readability and performance.

For example: Using @switch:

```
@switch (userRole) {
  @case ('admin') {
    <p>Admin Dashboard</p>
  }
  @case ('user') {
    <p>User Dashboard</p>
  }
  @default {
    <p>Guest View</p>
```

```
  }
}
```

@switch is more readable and efficient than ***ngSwitch**.

Question 26: How do template block directives introduced in Angular 19 improve reusability?

Answer: Template block directives (**@if**, **@for**, **@switch**) reduce boilerplate and improve maintainability.

For example: Reusable @if in a component:

```
@for (product of products) {
  @if (product.inStock) {
    <p>{{ product.name }} is available</p>
  } @else {
    <p>{{ product.name }} is out of stock</p>
  }
}
```

Using **@if** simplifies templates, improving readability.

Question 27: What performance improvements were made to directives in Angular 20?

Answer: Angular 20 optimized directives with the following improvements:

- **Improved change detection**: Only updates relevant elements.
- **Optimized hydration**: Faster SSR.
- **Better standalone support**: Directives work seamlessly without modules.

Question 28: How does Angular 20 improve directive hydration for SSR?

Answer: Hydration in Angular 20 allows pre-rendered directives to hydrate efficiently, reducing re-renders.

For example: Use hydration with directives, shown as follows:

```
import { Directive, ElementRef } from '@angular/core';
@Directive({
  selector: '[appHydrate]',
  standalone: true
})
export class HydrateDirective {
  constructor(private el: ElementRef) {}
  ngOnInit() {
    console.log('Hydrated:', this.el.nativeElement);
  }
}
```

Pre-rendered elements hydrate faster, improving SSR performance.

Question 29: What are the best practices for using directives in Angular 20+?

Answer: Angular 20+ introduces enhanced performance, standalone components, and optimized directives. The following best practices ensure efficient and maintainable Angular applications:

- **Use template block directives (@if, @for, and @switch)**: These offer better performance than ***ngIf**, ***ngFor**, and ***ngSwitch** by reducing unnecessary re-renders.
- **Prefer Renderer2 over ElementRef**: Ensures safer DOM manipulations and enhances security.

- **Optimize hydration for SSR**: Use hydration-friendly directives to improve server-side rendering performance.
- **Use standalone directives**: Reduces module dependencies and simplifies the application structure.
- **Use directive inputs efficiently**: Avoid unnecessary bindings to improve performance.
- **Use structural directives efficiently (@defer)**: Optimize loading by deferring non-critical content.
- **Use attribute directives for DOM manipulation instead of JavaScript**: Keeps logic declarative and improves maintainability.
- **Avoid complex logic inside templates**: Move logic to component classes to enhance readability and maintainability.
- **Use custom directives for reusable logic**: Encapsulate behavior to improve code reusability and organization.
- **Ensure proper cleanup in directives**: Unsubscribe from observables and remove event listeners to prevent memory leaks.
- **Use directive composition API for advanced scenarios (Angular 16+)**: Composes multiple behaviors efficiently in a directive.
- **Secure directives against XSS attacks**: Sanitize user inputs and avoid direct innerHTML bindings.

Following these best practices ensures better performance, maintainability, and security in Angular applications.

Question 30: How does Angular 20 improve the rendering of directives in large-scale applications?

Answer: Angular 20 introduces several optimizations to enhance directive rendering in large-scale applications, improving performance and efficiency in the following manner:

- **Incremental rendering**: Instead of re-rendering entire components, Angular 20 updates only the elements that have changed, reducing processing overhead.
- **Improved memory management**: Unused directives are automatically freed, reducing memory consumption and improving application stability.
- **SSR and hydration enhancements**: SSR now supports faster template loading with improved hydration, leading to better performance and smoother client-side interactions.

These improvements make Angular 20 more efficient, especially for large-scale applications with complex directive usage.

For example: Efficient rendering with @for:

```
@for (product of products; track product.id) {
  <app-product-card [product]="product"></app-product-card>
}
```

It renders only modified items, improving scalability.

Optimizing structural directives

Question 31: How does Angular optimize ngFor for better performance?

Answer: Angular optimizes `*ngFor` by using change detection strategies and efficient DOM updates. The following are some of the key optimizations in `ngFor` for better performance:

- **trackBy function**: Prevents unnecessary re-renders.
- **Minimal DOM manipulations**: Updates only changed items.
- **OnPush change detection**: Reduces performance overhead.

For example: Using trackBy in `*ngFor`:

HTML code:

```
<div *ngFor="let item of items; trackBy: trackById">
  {{ item.name }}
</div>
```

TypeScript code:

```
trackById(index: number, item: any) {
  return item.id; // Only re-renders when ID changes
}
```

The **`trackById`** function helps avoid unnecessary re-rendering when data updates.

Question 32: What is the trackBy function in ngFor, and why is it important?

Answer: Earlier, Angular 17 used **`trackBy`** function in **`*ngFor`**. The **`trackBy`** function in **`*ngFor`** helps Angular efficiently identify items in a list when rendering changes. By default, Angular tracks items by reference. When using **`trackBy`**, Angular uses a unique identifier (like an ID) to determine which items changed, were added, or removed, thereby improving performance and avoiding unnecessary DOM updates. Consider the following example (**`*ngFor`** with **`trackBy`**):

HTML:

```
<div *ngFor="let user of users; trackBy: trackByUserId">
  {{ user.name }}
</div>
```

TypeScript:

```
trackByUserId(index: number, user: any): number {
  return user.id;
}
```

However, after Angular 17, a new syntax is used, where a track expression is required in **`@for`**. The **`@for`** directive (introduced in Angular 17) requires or strongly encourages a track expression to uniquely identify list items for incremental DOM updates. Unlike **`*ngFor`**, which optionally uses **`trackBy`**, **`@for`** can track items by a unique property, such as item.id, enabling Angular to efficiently update only changed elements in the DOM.

Consider the following example (**`@for`** syntax):

```
@for (user of users; track user.id) {
  <p>{{ user.name }}</p>
}
```

This allows Angular to avoid re-rendering unchanged items and significantly improves performance for large or dynamic lists.

Question 33: How does lazy loading work with directives?

Answer: Angular lazy loads directives to improve performance and reduce initial bundle size. To lazy load a directive in Angular, you must:

- Mark the directive with **`standalone: true`**.
- Load it using **`import()`** syntax.
- Use it with structural directives like **`*ngIf`** or via **`@defer`** or **`NgComponentOutlet`** with dynamic injection.

Consider an example of lazy loading a standalone structural directive.

highlight.directive.ts:

```
import { Directive, ElementRef, OnInit } from '@angular/core';
@Directive({
  selector: '[appHighlight]',
  standalone: true
})
export class HighlightDirective implements OnInit {
  constructor(private el: ElementRef) {}
  ngOnInit() {
    this.el.nativeElement.style.backgroundColor = 'yellow';
  }
}
```

app.component.ts:

```
import { Component } from '@angular/core';
@Component({
  selector: 'app-root',
  standalone: true,
  template: `
    @defer (when true; loading) {
      <div *ngComponentOutlet="highlighted"></div>
    }
  `
})
export class AppComponent {
  highlighted = () =>
    import('./highlight.directive').then(m => m.HighlightDirective);
}
```

Lazy loading ensures that directives are loaded only when needed, reducing initial load time.

Question 34: How do structural directives affect change detection in Angular?

Answer: Structural directives (`@if`, `@for`) influence change detection by conditionally adding or removing elements.

For example: Optimized change detection with `@if`:

```
@if (isVisible) {
  <p>This element appears dynamically</p>
}
```

Using `@if` avoids unnecessary DOM updates, improving performance.

Question 35: What are the common performance pitfalls when using directives?

Answer: The following are the common pitfalls to avoid when using directives:

- **Not using trackBy**: Causes unnecessary re-renders.
- **Overusing HostListener**: Too many event listeners slow down performance.

- **Manipulating DOM directly**: Use Renderer2 instead.
- **Heavy computations in directives**: Keep logic lightweight.

Question 36: **How do directives improve DOM manipulation in Angular applications?**

Answer: Directives encapsulate DOM logic, making it easier to manage without breaking Angular's change detection.

For example: Changing background color using a directive:

```
@Directive({
  selector: '[appHighlight]'
})
export class HighlightDirective {
  constructor(private el: ElementRef, private renderer: Renderer2) {}
  @HostListener('mouseenter') onMouseEnter() {
    this.renderer.setStyle(this.el.nativeElement, 'backgroundColor', 'yellow');
  }
  @HostListener('mouseleave') onMouseLeave() {
    this.renderer.setStyle(this.el.nativeElement, 'backgroundColor', 'white');
  }
}
```

Using directives is safer than directly modifying the DOM.

Question 37: **How can you create a reusable structural directive in Angular?**

Answer: A custom structural directive lets you dynamically add or remove elements.

For example:

1. **Create a *appUnless directive**: Create the directive as follows:

   ```
   import { Directive, Input, TemplateRef, ViewContainerRef } from '@angular/core';
   @Directive({
     selector: '[appUnless]'
   })
   export class UnlessDirective {
     @Input() set appUnless(condition: boolean) {
       if (!condition) {
         this.viewContainer.createEmbeddedView(this.templateRef);
       } else {
         this.viewContainer.clear();
       }
     }
     constructor(private templateRef: TemplateRef<any>, private viewContainer:
   ViewContainerRef) {}
   }
   ```

2. **Use *appUnless directive in the component**: An example is shown as follows:

   ```
   <p *appUnless="isLoggedIn">You are not logged in</p>
   ```

The **`*appUnless`** directive replaces **`*ngIf`**, but with opposite logic.

Question 38: How does directive-based lazy loading differ from module-based lazy loading?

Answer: Directive-based and module-based lazy loading are two different strategies to optimize Angular applications by loading resources only when required. The differences are as follows:

- **Directive-based lazy loading**: This loads only the directive when needed, reducing the application's initial load time and keeping it lightweight. Let us look at a few examples.

  Standalone directive:

```
// my-directive.directive.ts
import { Directive, ElementRef, OnInit } from '@angular/core';
@Directive({
  selector: '[appMyDirective]',
  standalone: true
})
export class MyDirective implements OnInit {
  constructor(private el: ElementRef) {}
  ngOnInit() {
    this.el.nativeElement.style.border = '2px solid green';
  }
}
```

  Lazy load with @defer (Angular 17+):

```
@Component({
  selector: 'app-root',
  standalone: true,
  imports: [],
  template: `
    @defer (when true; loading) {
      <div @loadDirective>Lazy Loaded Directive</div>
    }
  `
})
export class AppComponent {
  async loadDirective() {
    const { MyDirective } = await import('./my-directive.directive');
    // Use this with dynamic injection if needed via ViewContainerRef
  }
}
```

  To truly apply a directive lazily:

  - Use `ViewContainerRef` with `inject()` and `createComponent()`.
  - Wrap the directive logic in a component and lazy load that component.
  - Always mark the directive as `standalone: true`.

- **Module-based lazy loading**: This loads an entire feature module on demand, which is useful for larger sections of an application but may introduce additional overhead.

For example:

```
const routes: Routes = [
  { path: 'dashboard', loadChildren: () => import('./dashboard/dashboard.module').
then(m => m.DashboardModule) }
];
```

In this lazy loading example, the **DashboardModule** is loaded only when the user navigates to the **/dashboard** route.

Question 39: **What is a directive lifecycle hook, and how does it differ from a component lifecycle?**

Answer: Lifecycle hooks in Angular allow directives and components to respond to changes in their state and perform necessary actions at specific points during their existence. While directives and components share some lifecycle hooks, components have additional hooks for view and content initialization. The differences are as follows:

- **Directive lifecycle hooks**: Directives primarily use hooks like **ngOnInit**, **ngOnChanges**, **ngDoCheck**, and **ngOnDestroy** to manage their behavior and interactions with the DOM.
- **Component lifecycle hooks**: Components include the same hooks as directives but also have **ngAfterViewInit** and **ngAfterContentInit**, which handle view and content initialization for projected content and child components.

For example: Using **ngOnInit** in a directive:

```
@Directive({ selector: '[appLog]' })
export class LogDirective implements OnInit {
  ngOnInit() {
    console.log('Directive Initialized');
  }
}
```

Directives focus on elements, while components manage UI logic.

Question 40: **What are the key memory management considerations when using directives?**

Answer: Proper memory management is essential when using directives to prevent performance issues and memory leaks in Angular applications. The following best practices help ensure efficient resource usage:

- **Avoid memory leaks**: Unsubscribe from event listeners and observables to prevent unnecessary memory consumption.
- **Use ngOnDestroy**: Implement this lifecycle hook to clean up resources, such as subscriptions and event handlers, when the directive is destroyed.
- **Minimize direct DOM manipulation**: Instead of directly modifying the DOM, use Renderer2 to ensure safe and optimized updates.

For example: Cleaning up in **ngOnDestroy**:

```
@Directive({
  selector: '[appEventCleanup]'
})
export class EventCleanupDirective implements OnDestroy {
  private subscription: Subscription;
  constructor(private el: ElementRef) {
    this.subscription = fromEvent(this.el.nativeElement, 'click').subscribe(() => {
      console.log('Clicked');
```

```
    });
  }
  ngOnDestroy() {
    this.subscription.unsubscribe();
  }
}
```

This **appEventCleanup** directive prevents memory leaks by unsubscribing from the event listener in the **ngOnDestroy** lifecycle hook.

Directive debugging, testing, and best practices

Question 41: What are the common mistakes when using Angular directives?

Answer: The following are a few common mistakes that users make when using Angular directives:

- **Not using trackBy in *ngFor**: Causes unnecessary re-renders.
- **Direct DOM manipulation**: Use **Renderer2** instead of **ElementRef.nativeElement**.
- **Memory leaks**: Forgetting to unsubscribe from event listeners.
- **Overusing HostListener**: Too many listeners slow performance.
- **Using attribute directives incorrectly**: Modify behavior, not structure.

For example: Avoid direct DOM manipulation:

Correct (Using Renderer2):

```
this.renderer.setStyle(this.el.nativeElement, 'color', 'red');
```

Incorrect (Using ElementRef.nativeElement directly):

```
this.el.nativeElement.style.color = 'red'; // Avoid this
```

Question 42: How can you debug issues related to Angular directives?

Answer: Debugging Angular directives effectively helps identify issues in their behavior and interactions within the application. The following techniques can assist in troubleshooting:

- **Use Angular DevTools**: Inspect and analyze directives in real-time to track their properties and lifecycle.
- **Console logging**: Add logs inside lifecycle hooks like **ngOnInit** and **ngOnChanges** to monitor directive execution.
- **Breakpoints in Chrome DevTools**: Set breakpoints in the directive's TypeScript file to pause execution and examine its state.
- **Check directive selector**: Ensure that the directive is applied correctly by verifying its selector in templates.

Using these debugging techniques can help quickly identify and resolve directive-related issues in Angular applications.

For example: Debugging with ngOnInit logging:

```
@Directive({ selector: '[appDebug]' })
export class DebugDirective implements OnInit {
  ngOnInit() {
    console.log('Directive initialized:', this);
  }
}
```

Expected console output:

```
Directive initialized: DebugDirective {…}
```

Explanation of the preceding example is as follows:

- When the Angular component containing this directive is rendered, **`ngOnInit()`** is called.
- The **`console.log`** statement logs **`Directive initialized:`** along with the directive instance (**`this`**), which includes its properties and metadata.
- If multiple elements have the **`appDebug`** directive, this message will appear once for each instance.

Question 43: How do you write unit tests for a custom directive?

Answer: Writing unit tests for a custom directive ensures that it behaves as expected in different scenarios. The following steps help in setting up effective tests:

- **Use TestBed to create a testing environment**: Configure **`TestBed`** to initialize the directive in an isolated testing module.
- **Mock dependencies like Renderer2 and ElementRef**: Replace real dependencies with mock objects to test directive behavior without direct DOM manipulation.

These practices help verify directive functionality and prevent regressions in Angular applications.

For example: Unit test for a custom directive:

```
import { ComponentFixture, TestBed } from '@angular/core/testing';
import { HighlightDirective } from './highlight.directive';
import { Component, ElementRef, Renderer2 } from '@angular/core';
@Component({
  template: `<p appHighlight>Test</p>`
})
class TestComponent {}
describe('HighlightDirective', () => {
  let fixture: ComponentFixture<TestComponent>;
  beforeEach(() => {
    TestBed.configureTestingModule({
      declarations: [TestComponent, HighlightDirective]
    });
    fixture = TestBed.createComponent(TestComponent);
  });
  it('should apply highlight', () => {
    const paragraph: HTMLElement = fixture.nativeElement.querySelector('p');
    expect(paragraph.style.backgroundColor).toBe('yellow');
  });
});
```

This unit test verifies that the **`HighlightDirective`** correctly applies a background color to the **`<p>`** element when initialized.

Question 44: How does Angular handle directive scoping in standalone components?

Answer: In standalone components, Angular does not rely on modules to provide directives. Instead, directives must be explicitly imported to be available within the component's template. The following key points explain how directive scoping works:

- **Standalone components require explicit import of directives**: Unlike module-based components, standalone components must manually import any directive they use.
- **Directives must be declared in the imports array of the component**: To apply a directive in a standalone component, it must be included in the imports array within the component's metadata.

For example: Using a directive in a standalone component:

```
@Component({
  selector: 'app-example',
  standalone: true,
  imports: [HighlightDirective],
  template: `<p appHighlight>Standalone Component</p>`
})
export class ExampleComponent {}
```

Directives are no longer globally available, they must be explicitly imported.

Question 45: How do directives interact with dependency injection in Angular?

Answer: Angular directives support DI just like components, allowing them to use services and other dependencies efficiently. The following key points explain how directives interact with DI:

- **Directives can inject services like any other Angular component**: Services can be injected into a directive's constructor to provide shared functionality.
- **Use @Injectable({ providedIn: 'root' }) for global services**: This ensures the service is available application-wide without needing to be explicitly provided in a module or component.

For example: Injecting a service in a directive:

```
@Directive({ selector: '[appLogger]' })
export class LoggerDirective {
  constructor(private loggerService: LoggerService) {
    this.loggerService.log('Directive initialized');
  }
}
```

Directives can leverage Angular's DI system for efficiency.

Question 46: What is the impact of directives on page load performance?

Answer: Directives can influence page load performance based on their complexity and usage. Optimizing their implementation ensures a smoother user experience. Key performance considerations include:

- **Too many structural directives (@if, @for) can slow rendering**: Excessive use of these directives can increase DOM manipulations, leading to performance bottlenecks.
- **Heavy computation inside directives affects initial load time**: Performing complex logic within directives can delay rendering and degrade responsiveness.
- **Lazy loading directives reduce page load time**: Loading directives only when needed improves efficiency and optimizes resource usage.

Consider the following example of lazy loading a directive:

```
// highlight.directive.ts
import { Directive, ElementRef, OnInit } from '@angular/core';
@Directive({
  selector: '[appHighlight]',
  standalone: true
```

```
})
export class HighlightDirective implements OnInit {
  constructor(private el: ElementRef) {}
  ngOnInit() {
    this.el.nativeElement.style.backgroundColor = 'lightyellow';
  }
}
// app.component.ts or loader file
export const lazyDirective = () =>
  import('./highlight.directive').then(m => m.HighlightDirective);
```

Lazy loading delays loading until required, improving performance.

A few points to consider are given as follows:

- This **lazyDirective** function correctly imports a standalone directive using dynamic **import()**.
- However, this directive cannot be applied via **[directive]="..."**, as that syntax is invalid in Angular.
- Instead, you can use it via **@defer** (Angular 17+ block syntax), or dynamically inject it using **ViewContainerRef.createComponent()**, if wrapped in a component.

Question 47: How do directives work with reactive forms in Angular?

Answer: Directives can enhance reactive forms by adding custom validation, dynamic behavior, and reusable form controls. The following key points highlight their role in reactive forms:

- **Directives can be used to validate form inputs dynamically**: Custom directives can apply validation rules to form controls, ensuring user input meets specific requirements.
- **Use ControlValueAccessor for custom form controls**: Implementing **ControlValueAccessor** allows directives to integrate seamlessly with Angular's form API, enabling custom form elements to work like native inputs.

For example: Custom validator directive for reactive forms:

```
@Directive({
  selector: '[appEmailValidator]',
  providers: [{ provide: NG_VALIDATORS, useExisting: EmailValidatorDirective, multi: true
}]
})
export class EmailValidatorDirective implements Validator {
  validate(control: AbstractControl): ValidationErrors | null {
    return control.value.includes('@') ? null : { invalidEmail: true };
  }
}
```

This directive validates email input fields by ensuring they contain an **@** symbol, integrating seamlessly with Angular's reactive forms validation system.

Question 48: What security concerns should be considered when using directives?

Answer: The following security risks must be kept in mind when using directives:

- **Direct DOM manipulation**: Can lead to XSS vulnerabilities.
- **Unsafe event handling**: Avoid direct innerHTML assignments.
- **Third-party dependencies**: Validate external libraries.

For example: Preventing XSS with sanitizer:

```
constructor(private sanitizer: DomSanitizer) {}
safeHtml(value: string) {
  return this.sanitizer.bypassSecurityTrustHtml(value);
}
```

This **`safeHtml`** method prevents the execution of malicious scripts by sanitizing HTML content, allowing only safe, trusted content to be rendered in the application.

Question 49: How do directives improve reusability in large-scale applications?

Answer: Directives enhance maintainability and scalability by enabling reusable functionality across different parts of an application. The key benefits include:

- **Encapsulate reusable UI logic**: Directives allow common UI behaviors to be defined once and applied across multiple components.
- **Reduce duplicate code in multiple components**: By centralizing logic in directives, developers can avoid repetition and keep components clean.
- **Provide cross-application consistency**: Using directives ensures a uniform behavior and styling across the application, improving maintainability.

Let us look at a reusable tooltip directive example that supports:

- Custom text via **`@Input()`**
- DOM-safe creation and removal using **`Renderer2`**
- Style and positioning
- Cleanup on mouse leave

Refer to the following code:

```
@Directive({ selector: '[appTooltip]' })
export class TooltipDirective implements OnDestroy {
  @Input('appTooltip') tooltipText = '';
  private tooltipEl: HTMLElement | null = null;
  constructor(private el: ElementRef, private r: Renderer2) {}
  @HostListener('mouseenter') show() {
    if (!this.tooltipText) return;
    this.tooltipEl = this.r.createElement('span');
    this.r.setProperty(this.tooltipEl, 'innerText', this.tooltipText);
    ['absolute', '#333', '#fff'].forEach((v, i) =>
    this.r.setStyle(this.tooltipEl!, ['position', 'background', 'color'][i], v));
    [['top', '100%'], ['padding', '4px 8px'], ['zIndex', '1000']]
    .forEach(([k, v]) => this.r.setStyle(this.tooltipEl!, k, v));
    this.r.setStyle(this.el.nativeElement, 'position', 'relative');
    this.r.appendChild(this.el.nativeElement, this.tooltipEl);
  }
  @HostListener('mouseleave') hide() { this.destroy(); }
  ngOnDestroy() { this.destroy(); }
  private destroy() {
    if (this.tooltipEl) {
```

```
      this.r.removeChild(this.el.nativeElement, this.tooltipEl);
      this.tooltipEl = null;
    }
  }
}
```

A single tooltip directive can be used across multiple components.

Question 50: What are the expected future enhancements for directives in upcoming Angular versions?

Answer: Angular is advancing toward better performance, reactivity, and developer experience for directives. Key future enhancements include:

- Improved SSR hydration for faster server-side rendering
- Enhanced structural directives like **`@if`**, **`@for`**, and **`@switch`**
- Smarter lazy loading to reduce initial load time
- Better debugging tools for easier development and troubleshooting

These updates aim to make directives more efficient, flexible, and developer-friendly.

Conclusion

Directives are a powerful feature in Angular that enhance reusability, maintainability, and performance. By using structural and attribute directives effectively, developers can create dynamic and efficient applications. Key best practices, such as leveraging Renderer2, optimizing hydration for SSR, and ensuring proper memory management, help maintain scalable Angular applications. Additionally, future Angular versions are expected to bring further enhancements to directives, making them even more efficient.

In the next chapter, we will explore signals in Angular, a modern state management approach that improves reactivity and optimizes change detection. Signals provide a more efficient and predictable way to manage data flow in Angular applications.

Join our Discord space

Join our Discord workspace for latest updates, offers, tech happenings around the world, new releases, and sessions with the authors:

https://discord.bpbonline.com

Chapter 5
Concepts of Signals

Introduction

Signals play a crucial role in Angular applications by enabling reactive programming patterns that improve state management, change detection, and performance optimizations. Unlike traditional event-driven paradigms, signals provide a more structured and declarative way to handle data changes, making applications more predictable and efficient. This chapter explores the fundamental concepts of signals, their implementation, and their advantages in Angular development.

Structure

This chapter covers the following topics:

- Basics of signals
- Signal function
- Signal-based state management
- Latest features in signals
- Signals in real-world applications

Objectives

By the end of this chapter, you will have a clear understanding of the core concepts and benefits of signals in Angular. You will learn how to implement and use different types of signals effectively, integrating them into Angular components to enhance reactivity and maintainability. Additionally, you will gain insights into best practices and performance optimizations, avoiding common pitfalls while working with signals. Finally, you will explore real-world applications of signals, particularly in state management, reactive forms, and server-side rendering, enabling you to build more efficient and scalable Angular applications.

Basics of signals

Question 1: What are signals in Angular, and why were they introduced?

Answer: Signals were introduced in Angular 16+ as a reactive state management mechanism. Unlike traditional RxJS observables, which require manual subscriptions and complex change detection, signals provide a more intuitive and efficient way to manage state changes in Angular applications.

Angular signals form a system that granularly tracks how and where your state is used throughout an application, allowing the framework to optimize rendering updates. The following are the key features of signals:

- **Automatic dependency tracking**: No need for manual subscriptions.
- **Optimized change detection**: Signals update only the affected part of the UI.
- **Push-based rendering**: Unlike **Zone.js**, which runs change detection globally, signals only update relevant components.
- **Composable and readable API**: Simple syntax without needing observables.

Before signals, Angular primarily relied on the following:

- **RxJS observables**: Powerful but complex and required manual subscriptions.
- **Change detection mechanism**: The default change detection strategy led to unnecessary re-renders.
- **@Input() and @Output() for component communication**: Could become cumbersome in deeply nested components.

The problems with traditional state management are as follows:

- Manual subscriptions (**.subscribe()**) needed to be cleaned up using **ngOnDestroy()**.
- Change detection triggered too often, leading to performance overhead.
- Deeply nested components required complex event-driven communication.

Angular signals were introduced to solve these issues by providing the following:

- Automatic tracking of dependencies.
- Optimized reactivity without requiring manual subscriptions.
- Efficient rendering, reducing unnecessary change detection.

Understanding how signals work is essential for efficient communication and event handling in software systems. signals track dependencies automatically and notify Angular when a value changes. Unlike RxJS, they do not require **.subscribe()** to update the UI.

For example: Basic signal implementation:

```
import { signal } from '@angular/core';
export class CounterComponent {
  count = signal(0); // Declaring a Signal
  increment() {
    this.count.set(this.count() + 1); // Updating the Signal
  }
}
```

When **count.set()** is called, Angular automatically updates the UI.

For example: Using **set()** and **update()** with Angular signals:

The following are the key differences between **set()**, **update()** and **mutate()**:

- **set(value)**: Directly replaces the current signal value with a new one.

- **update(callback)**: Modifies the value based on its previous state.
- **mutate(callback)**: The **`mutate()`** method allows modifying the state of objects or arrays inside a signal without replacing the entire value. This is useful when working with complex data structures like arrays or objects.

Knowing when to use **`mutate()`** is key to efficiently updating state and managing data changes in applications in the following cases:

- When working with objects or arrays inside signals.
- When modifying data instead of replacing it.
- When performance optimization is needed, as it avoids unnecessary re-renders.

For example: Using **`set()`** to directly change a value:

```
import { Component, signal } from '@angular/core';
@Component({
  selector: 'app-name-changer',
  standalone: true,
  template: `
    <p>Current Name: {{ name() }}</p>
    <button (click)="changeName()">Change Name</button> `
})
export class NameChangerComponent {
  name = signal('Anil');
  changeName() {
    this.name.set('Reena'); // Directly sets a new value
  }
}
```

In the preceding example, the signal is initially set to **`Anil`** and is updated to **`Reena`** when the button is clicked using the **`set()`** method.

For example: Using **`update()`** to modify a value based on the previous state:

```
import { Component, signal } from '@angular/core';
@Component({
  selector: 'app-counter',
  standalone: true,
  template: `
    <p>Counter: {{ counter() }}</p>
    <button (click)="increment()">Increment</button> `
})
export class CounterComponent {
  counter = signal(0);
  increment() {
    this.counter.update(value => value + 1); // Updates based on previous value
  }
}
```

In the preceding example, the counter signal is initialized at 0, and each button click dynamically increments its value using the **update()** method.

For example: Using **mutate()** to mutate an object inside a signal:

```
import { Component, signal } from '@angular/core';
@Component({
  selector: 'app-user',
  standalone: true,
  template: `
    <p>Name: {{ user().name }}</p>
    <p>Age: {{ user().age }}</p>
    <button (click)="increaseAge()">Increase Age</button>
  `
})
export class UserComponent {
  user = signal({ name: 'Anil', age: 35 });
  increaseAge() {
    this.user.mutate(u => u.age += 1); // Mutates the object without replacing it
  }
}
```

The user signal stores an object with **name** and **age**. Clicking the button directly modifies the age without replacing the entire object.

For example: Using **mutate()** to mutate an array inside a signal:

```
import { Component, signal } from '@angular/core';
@Component({
  selector: 'app-items',
  standalone: true,
  template: `
   <ul>
      @for (item of items()) {
        <li>{{ item }}</li>
      }
    </ul>
    <button (click)="addItem()">Add Item</button> `
})
export class ItemsComponent {
  items = signal(['Apple', 'Banana']);
  addItem() {
    this.items.mutate(list => list.push('Orange')); // Mutates the array directly
  }
}
```

The items signal starts with two values: **Apple** and **Banana**. Clicking the button adds **Orange** without replacing the entire array.

For example: You can use signals with computed and effects as follows:

- **Computed signal (derived state)**: Computed signals derive their value from other signals automatically.

  For example:

  ```
  import { signal, computed } from '@angular/core';
  export class CounterComponent {
  count = signal(0);
  doubleCount = computed(() => this.count() * 2); // Derived State
  increment() {
  this.count.set(this.count() + 1);
  }
  }
  ```

  Whenever `count` updates, `doubleCount` is recalculated automatically.

- **Effect signal (side effects)**: Effects allow you to perform side effects when signals change.

  For example:

  ```
  import { signal, effect } from '@angular/core';
  export class CounterComponent {
  count = signal(0);
  constructor() {
  effect(() => {
  console.log(`Count changed to: ${this.count()}`);
  });
  }
  increment() {
  this.count.set(this.count() + 1);
  }
  }
  ```

  Whenever `count` changes, the effect runs automatically (e.g., logging or API calls).

Signals are ideal for scenarios where you need a lightweight and efficient state management solution. They provide fine-grained updates without full change detection and serve as a simpler alternative to RxJS for managing UI state.

RxJS is the go-to choice when working with complex asynchronous data streams, such as WebSockets or multi-step API calls. It also excels in scenarios requiring debouncing, throttling, or advanced reactive operators.

Signals offer several key benefits, shown as follows, over RxJS, making them a powerful choice for state management:

- **Setup complexity**: RxJS requires `.subscribe()`, `.pipe()`, and `.unsubscribe()`, whereas signals offer simple, direct access with `.set()` and `.update()`.
- **Performance**: RxJS triggers global change detection, while signals optimize local updates, reducing unnecessary re-renders.
- **Memory management**: RxJS requires manual unsubscribing to avoid memory leaks, but signals manage memory automatically.
- **State tracking**: RxJS needs `BehaviorSubject` or `ReplaySubject` for state tracking, whereas signals track dependencies automatically.

- **Ease of use**: RxJS can be complex with chaining operators, while signals provide a simpler, more intuitive API for managing state.

Question 2: How do signals differ from RxJS observables?

Answer: The following are the key differences between RxJS observables and signals:

- **Push vs. pull model**:
  - RxJS observables use a push-based model, where values are emitted asynchronously and require subscriptions.
  - Signals use a pull-based model, where values are read synchronously and update automatically when dependencies change.
- **Change detection**:
  - Observables trigger global change detection, leading to performance overhead.
  - Signals optimize local change detection, reducing unnecessary re-renders.
- **Memory management**:
  - Observables require manual subscription management (**`unsubscribe()`** to avoid memory leaks).
  - Signals handle memory automatically with built-in dependency tracking.

For example: Signals vs. observables:

```
import { Component, Signal, signal, computed, effect } from '@angular/core';
import { Observable, of } from 'rxjs';
@Component({
  selector: 'app-signal-example',
  standalone: true,
  template: `
    <p>RxJS Observable: {{ data$ | async }}</p>
    <p>Signal Value: {{ count() }}</p>  `,
})
export class SignalExampleComponent {
  // RxJS Observable
  data$: Observable<number> = of(10);
  // Angular Signal
  count = signal(10);
}
```

Signals provide a more streamlined approach to state management by eliminating the need for the async pipe while ensuring automatic and efficient update tracking.

Question 3: How do you create a simple signal in Angular?

Answer: The following syntax is used to create a simple signal in Angular:

```
const count = signal(0);
```

For example: Creating and updating a signal:

```
import { Component, signal } from '@angular/core';
@Component({
  selector: 'app-counter',
  standalone: true,
```

```
  template: `
    <p>Counter: {{ count() }}</p>
    <button (click)="increment()">Increment</button>  `,
})
export class CounterComponent {
  count = signal(0); // Create a Signal with initial value 0
  increment() {
    this.count.set(this.count() + 1); // Update Signal
  }
}
```

Question 4: What are writable signals, and what is the syntax for defining a writable signal?

Answer: Writable signals can be updated using **`.set()`** or **`.update()`**. These are ideal for state management in Angular components.

For example:

```
import { Component, signal } from '@angular/core';
@Component({
  selector: 'app-writable-signal',
  standalone: true,
  template: `
    <p>Value: {{ value() }}</p>
    <button (click)="changeValue()">Change Value</button>  `,
})
export class WritableSignalComponent {
  value = signal('Hello');
  changeValue() {
    this.value.set('Angular Signals!');
  }
}
```

Question 5: How do you read the value of a signal?

Answer: To read the value of a signal, use the syntax as follows:

```
const mySignal = signal(100);
console.log(mySignal()); // Read value
```

For example:

```
import { Component, signal } from '@angular/core';
@Component({
  selector: 'app-read-signal',
  standalone: true,
  template: `<p>Current Value: {{ count() }}</p>`,
})
export class ReadSignalComponent {
  count = signal(5);
  logValue() {
```

```
    console.log(this.count()); // Reading the signal value
  }
}
```

Question 6: What are computed signals, and how do they work?

Answer: Computed signals automatically recompute when dependencies change. They cannot be updated manually.

For example:

```
import { Component, signal, computed } from '@angular/core';
@Component({
  selector: 'app-computed-signal',
  standalone: true,
  template: `<p>Double Count: {{ doubleCount() }}</p>`,
})
export class ComputedSignalComponent {
  count = signal(5);
  doubleCount = computed(() => this.count() * 2);
}
```

When **count** changes, **doubleCount** updates automatically.

Question 7: What are effect signals, and when should you use them?

Answer: Effect signals run side effects when the dependent signals change. They are used for logging, API calls, or updating the DOM.

For example:

```
import { Component, signal, effect } from '@angular/core';
@Component({
  selector: 'app-effect-signal',
  standalone: true,
  template: `<p>Value: {{ value() }}</p>`,
})
export class EffectSignalComponent {
  value = signal(10);
  constructor() {
    effect(() => {
      console.log('Value changed:', this.value());
    });
  }
}
```

The preceding code logs every time a value changes.

Question 8: How do signals improve reactivity in Angular?

Answer: The following are the key benefits of signals in Angular:

- Automatic dependency tracking.
- Optimized local updates, reducing unnecessary renders.
- No need for manual subscriptions (unlike RxJS).

For example: Auto-tracking UI updates:

```
import { Component, signal, computed } from '@angular/core';
@Component({
  selector: 'app-signal-reactivity',
  standalone: true,
  template: `<p>Price with Tax: {{ priceWithTax() }}</p>`,
})
export class SignalReactivityComponent {
  price = signal(100);
  taxRate = signal(0.1);
  priceWithTax = computed(() => this.price() * (1 + this.taxRate()));
}
```

In the preceding code, when **`price`** or **`taxRate`** changes, **`priceWithTax`** updates automatically.

Question 9: How does Angular detect changes in signals?

Answer: Angular tracks changes in signals through the following:

- Signals track dependencies internally.
- No need for manual **`detectChanges()`** like in **`ChangeDetectorRef`**.
- More efficient than **`@Input()`** for props.

For example:

```
import { Component, signal } from '@angular/core';
@Component({
  selector: 'app-detect-signal',
  standalone: true,
  template: `<p>Value: {{ value() }}</p>`,
})
export class DetectSignalComponent {
  value = signal(1);
  updateValue() {
    this.value.set(this.value() + 1);
  }
}
```

Updating **`value`** in the preceding code automatically triggers UI updates.

Question 10: What are the key advantages of using signals over traditional state management?

Answer: The key advantages of using signals over traditional state management are as follows:

- **Simplified state management**: No need for complex RxJS operators (**`mergeMap`**, **`switchMap`**).
- **Optimized change detection**: Local updates instead of triggering the entire app.
- **Better memory management**: No manual **`unsubscribe()`** calls.
- **Automatic dependency tracking**: Unlike BehaviorSubject, signals track dependencies without extra boilerplate.
- **Less complexity**: Fewer concepts than RxJS and NgRx.

For example: Traditional state management vs. signals:

- Create a component with RxJS (complex) for state management as follows:

```
import { Component } from '@angular/core';
import { BehaviorSubject } from 'rxjs';
@Component({
  selector: 'app-rxjs-example',
  template: `<p>Value: {{ value$ | async }}</p>`,
})
export class RxjsExampleComponent {
  value$ = new BehaviorSubject<number>(0);
  updateValue() {
    this.value$.next(this.value$.value + 1);
  }
}
```

- Create a component with signals (simpler) for state management, shown as follows:

```
import { Component, signal } from '@angular/core';
@Component({
  selector: 'app-signals-example',
  template: `<p>Value: {{ value() }}</p>`,
})
export class SignalsExampleComponent {
  value = signal(0);
  updateValue() {
    this.value.set(this.value() + 1);
  }
}
```

Thus, signals require less code, are easier to manage, and are more performant.

Question 11: What are the limitations of signals in Angular, and how can they be mitigated?

Answer: Although signals improve reactivity and simplify state management in Angular, they have some limitations, which are as follows:

- **No built-in async handling**
  - **Issue**: Signals do not natively support async operations like HTTP calls.
  - **Solution**: Use RxJS for async data and update signals manually.
- **No built-in operators like RxJS**
  - **Issue**: Lacks RxJS features like **`map`**, **`filter`**, and **`combineLatest`**.
  - **Solution**: Use computed signals for derived state.
- **No automatic side effects**
  - **Issue**: Signals do not trigger side effects automatically.
  - **Solution**: Use **`effect()`** for logging, API calls, or analytics.
- **Limited debugging support**
  - **Issue**: No dedicated DevTools like NgRx or Redux.
  - **Solution**: Use manual logging with **`effect()`** or Angular Profiler.

- **Not a full replacement for RxJS**
  - **Issue**: RxJS is still better for WebSockets, multi-step APIs, and state synchronization.
  - **Solution**: Use both signals and RxJS together where needed.
- **Limited SSR hydration support**
  - **Issue**: Signals hydration is still improving in SSR.
  - **Solution**: Use Angular 20+ hydration optimizations

Thus, it is advised to ensure the following best practices:

- Use signals for component state and UI updates.
- Use RxJS for async data streams and complex state management.
- Combine both for optimal performance in large-scale applications.

Signal function

Question 12. What is the toSignal function, and how does it convert observables to signals?

Answer: **`toSignal`** is a utility function in Angular that converts an observable into a signal. It allows seamless integration of RxJS with Angular's reactivity model. It has the following key benefits:

- Enables signals-based reactivity while still using RxJS.
- Eliminates the need for async pipes in templates.
- Improves performance by reducing unnecessary re-renders.

Question 13: What are the key differences between @let, async, and toSignal?

Answer: Understanding the differences between **`@let`**, **`async`**, and **`toSignal`** helps in choosing the right approach for state management and reactivity in Angular. The comparison is as follows:

- **@let**: Used for template-based variable declaration, allowing efficient state management without extra change detection. It is optimized for signals and computed values.
- **async Pipe**: Subscribes and unsubscribes to observables inside templates but triggers change detection on every emission, which can cause unnecessary re-renders.
- **toSignal**: Converts an observable into a signal, reducing template re-renders and bridging the gap between RxJS and Angular's reactivity model.

Some of the best use cases are as follows:

- Use **`@let`** for lazy evaluation and computed values.
- Use async for handling HTTP streams or live updates.
- Use **`toSignal`** for better performance and state stability with observables.

Question 14: When should you use @let instead of async in templates?

Answer: Use **`@let`** in the following cases:

- You want lazy evaluation (values update only when used).
- You want better performance with fewer change detections.
- You work with computed values inside templates.

Use async in the following cases:

- You need direct observable support without signals.
- You are handling HTTP streams, WebSockets, or live updates.

Question 15. How does toSignal improve performance compared to async?

Answer: The `toSignal` function enhances performance by optimizing state management and reducing unnecessary re-renders. Compared to the async pipe, `toSignal` improves performance in the following manner:

- Reduces change detection cycles by eliminating direct template subscriptions.
- Keeps state stable, unlike async, which re-renders on every emission.
- Automatically unsubscribes, avoiding memory leaks.

Question 16: Can @let and async be used together in the same template?

Answer: Yes, `@let` and async can be used together in the same template. However, it is not recommended. A better alternative is to convert the observable using `toSignal()` and use `@let` inside the template.

Question 17: What are the advantages of using @let over async for managing observables?

Answer: Using `@let` instead of async for managing observables offers several advantages, particularly in performance and maintainability. `@let` is a better choice for the following reasons:

- It gives better performance as it re-renders only when needed.
- Scoped variables reduce template clutter.
- It allows for easier debugging as it avoids unnecessary async handling.

Question 18: How does toSignal work under the hood in Angular's reactivity model?

Answer: `toSignal()` performs the following functions:

- Subscribes to an observable (internally).
- Caches the latest emitted value.
- Updates only when needed, reducing change detection overhead.
- Automatically unsubscribes when the component is destroyed.

Question 19: How can toSignal help improve real-time applications like chat apps?

Answer: In real-time applications like chat apps, `toSignal` enhances performance and responsiveness by efficiently managing live data streams. It helps in the following manner:

- Converts live chat streams (WebSockets) into reactive state.
- Reduces unnecessary template updates, ensuring smooth UI performance.
- Works seamlessly with computed signals for message filtering, formatting, etc.

Question 20. What are some real-world scenarios where toSignal is preferred over async?

Answer: The `toSignal` function is preferred over async in scenarios where real-time data handling and performance optimization are crucial. Some common use cases include:

- Dashboard widgets (stock prices, weather updates).
- Live notifications (real-time alerts in SaaS apps).
- Streaming data (IoT dashboards, trading apps).
- Performance-critical UIs (gaming leaderboards, analytics panels).

Question 21: How does toSignal help optimize Angular apps using signals and observables?

Answer: The `toSignal` function optimizes Angular applications by seamlessly integrating signals with observables while minimizing performance overhead. It enhances efficiency in the following manner:

- Bridges RxJS and signals without extra change detection overhead.
- Provides a single, reactive value, thus avoiding unnecessary template updates.
- Eliminates async boilerplate, making code cleaner and more maintainable.

Question 22: How can you integrate toSignal with state management libraries like NgRx?

Answer: Integrating **`toSignal`** with state management libraries like NgRx allows for a more reactive and efficient approach to handling application state. It can be integrated as follows:

1. Use **`toSignal(store.select(selectData))`** to convert NgRx selectors into signals.
2. Combine it with computed signals for derived state.
3. Use **`effect()`** to trigger state updates based on signals.

Question 23: How does toSignal function help reduce unnecessary re-renders in components?

Answer: The **`toSignal`** function helps optimize component performance by minimizing unnecessary re-renders. It achieves this in the following manner:

- Signals update only when accessed (unlike async, which updates on every emission).
- Avoids change detection triggers in OnPush components.
- Efficient memory management (automatically unsubscribes).

The best practice is to use **`toSignal()`** for stateful observables and async for streaming data.

Signal-based state management

Question 24: How do you use signals inside Angular components?

Answer: Signals are used inside Angular components to manage state reactively. They can be created using the **`signal()`** function and used directly in templates without triggering unnecessary re-renders.

Here is an example of using signals in a standalone Angular component for efficient state management:

```
import { Component, signal } from '@angular/core';
@Component({
  selector: 'app-counter',
  standalone: true,
  template: `
    <p>Counter: {{ counter() }}</p>
    <button (click)="increment()">Increment</button>
  `
})
export class CounterComponent {
  counter = signal(0); // Creating a signal
  increment() {
    this.counter.update(value => value + 1); // Updating the signal reactively
  }
}
```

Explanation of the example is as follows:

- **Signal initialization**: The counter signal starts with a value of 0.
- **Reactive updates**: The **`increment()`** method updates the signal's value without triggering unnecessary change detection.
- **Direct template usage**: The **`counter()`** function is called inside the template without subscriptions or async pipes.

This approach makes state management simpler and more efficient in Angular components.

Question 25: How do you update a signal's value?

Answer: You can update a signal using the following:

- **.set(newValue)**: Directly assigns a new value to the signal.
- **.update(prevValue => modifiedValue)**: Updates the current value based on the previous state.

For example:

```
import { Component, signal } from '@angular/core';
@Component({
  selector: 'app-counter',
  standalone: true,
  template: `<p>Count: {{ count() }}</p>
    <button (click)="reset()">Reset</button>
    <button (click)="increment()">Increment</button>`
})
export class CounterComponent {
  count = signal(0);
  reset() {
    this.count.set(0); // Directly setting a new value
  }
  increment() {
    this.count.update(value => value + 1); // Updating based on previous value
  }
}
```

In the preceding example, this approach ensures efficient state updates while maintaining a highly responsive and optimized UI.

Question 26: How do you pass signals as input properties to child components?

Answer: Use the `@Input` decorator to pass signals to child components. The child component can access them as read-only values.

Question 27. How do you bind a signal to an Angular template?

Answer: To bind a signal to an Angular template, use interpolation, shown as follows:

```
<p>{{ mySignal() }}</p>
```

Since signals are functions, calling them retrieves the current value.

Question 28: How do you use signals with event handlers in Angular?

Answer: You can update signals inside event handlers as follows:

```
<button (click)="counter.update(c => c + 1)">Increment</button>
```

Question 29: Can you use signals in Angular services? If yes, how?

Answer: Yes, signals can be used inside services to manage global state. Services provide a shared signal that components can read and update.

Question 30: How do you create a computed signal that depends on multiple signals?

Answer: Use the `computed()` function to create a signal that reacts to other signals, shown as follows:

```
const fullName = computed(() => firstName() + ' ' + lastName());
```

Question 31: How do you prevent unnecessary computations in computed signals?

Answer: Computed signals only recalculate when dependencies change, avoiding unnecessary computations automatically.

Question 32: How do you debug signals in an Angular application?

Answer: Use `console.log(mySignal())` or Angular DevTools to inspect signal values.

Question 33: What are the limitations of using signals in Angular?

Answer: While signals offer a powerful state management approach in Angular, they come with certain limitations. Some key considerations are as follows:

- No built-in support for asynchronous streams like RxJS.
- Not compatible with every RxJS operator.
- May require migration effort for existing apps using observables.

Question 34: How do you replace RxJS with signals in an existing Angular application?

Answer: Migrating from RxJS to signals in an existing Angular application involves adapting state management and reactivity. You can make the transition as follows:

- Convert `BehaviorSubject` to `signal()`.
- Replace observable with `toSignal()`.
- Use `effect()` instead of `subscribe()`.

Question 35: How do signals integrate with Angular's change detection mechanism?

Answer: Signals trigger updates only where they are used, reducing unnecessary re-renders compared to RxJS.

Question 36: How do you use signals in forms and reactive state management?

Answer: Signals can store form values and update the UI reactively when inputs change.

Question 37: What is the difference between signals and BehaviorSubject in state management?

Answer: In state management, both signals and BehaviorSubject help manage reactive data, but they function differently in terms of tracking dependencies and updating values. The comparison is as follows:

- **Signals**: Automatically track dependencies and avoid unnecessary updates.
- **BehaviorSubject**: Requires manual subscription and `.next()` calls.

Question 38: How do you use signals in Angular services for global state management?

Answer: Define a shared signal in a service and expose methods to update it, similar to a store.

Question 39: How do you perform side effects in signals using effect()?

Answer: Use `effect()` to run logic when a signal changes, shown as follows:

```
effect(() => console.log(count()));
```

Question 40: Can signals work with Angular Directives? If yes, how?

Answer: Yes, signals can be used in directives to dynamically update properties without extra change detection.

Question 41: How do you dispose of a signal when a component is destroyed?

Answer: Signals are automatically garbage-collected, but `effect()` should be cleaned up using `onDestroy()`.

Question 42: How do signals impact performance compared to observables?

Answer: Signals optimize reactivity by reducing change detection cycles, making them faster than observables for UI updates.

Question 43: How do you handle asynchronous operations with signals?

Answer: Use **`toSignal()`** to convert an observable into a signal, allowing async data handling while leveraging Angular's reactivity model.

Latest features in signals

Question 44: What new features were introduced in Angular 18 for signals?

Answer: Angular 18 introduced signals as a built-in reactivity system. Key features include the following:

- Automatic dependency tracking for better performance.
- **`computed()`** and **`effect()`** for derived values and side effects.
- **`toSignal()`** function for converting observables to signals.
- Improved change detection, reducing unnecessary updates.

Question 45: How does Angular 19 optimize signals for better reactivity?

Answer: Angular 19 introduced optimizations for signals as follows:

- Enhancing dependency tracking to minimize re-computations.
- Improving garbage collection for unused signals.
- Faster template updates by prioritizing signal-based rendering.

Angular 19+ introduces three new ways to load data using signals:

- **resource**: A promise-based loader for fetching and updating data asynchronously.

  Example usage:

  ```
  import { resource } from '@angular/core';
  const userResource = resource(async () => {
    const response = await fetch('https://api.example.com/user');
    return response.json();
  });
  ```

  Here, **`userResource()`** triggers the function, fetches data from the API, and resolves it using a promise.

- **rxResource**: An observable-based loader, ideal for reactive programming.

  Example usage:

  ```
  import { rxResource } from '@angular/core';
  import { of, delay } from 'rxjs';
  const timeResource = rxResource(() => {
    return of(new Date()).pipe(delay(1000)); // Emits the current date after 1 second
  });
  ```

  Here, **`timeResource`** emits a new value whenever it is invoked, utilizing RxJS observables to provide more control over data streams.

- **httpResource**: Extends resource, using **`HttpClient`** for API requests.

  Example usage:

  ```
  import { httpResource } from '@angular/core';
  import { HttpClient } from '@angular/common/http';
  export class UserService {
    constructor(private http: HttpClient) {}
  ```

```
  userResource = httpResource(() => this.http.get('https://api.example.com/user'));
}
```

This approach makes it easier to integrate with Angular's **HttpClient** while ensuring optimal performance.

All three serve the same purpose: fetching data, updating locally, and loading resources asynchronously, but differ in their implementation approach.

Question 46: What are signal-based lifecycle hooks, and how do they work in Angular 19?

Answer: Angular 19 introduced signal-based lifecycle hooks like **onSignalDestroy()**, which allow cleanup logic when a signal is no longer needed. This improves memory management.

Question 47: How does Angular 20 integrate signals with HTTP client?

Answer: Angular 20 simplifies HTTP requests with signals as follows:

- Allowing **toSignal(http.get(…))** to fetch and update UI reactively.
- Reducing the need for async pipes and manual subscriptions.
- Enhancing caching mechanisms using signals.

Question 48: What are signal-based inputs in Angular 20, and how do they improve performance?

Answer: Angular 20 introduced signal-based **@Input()** properties, which perform the following actions:

- Reactively update child components without triggering unnecessary change detection.
- Allow direct bindings without **ChangeDetectorRef.markForCheck()**.
- Improve component rendering efficiency.

Question 49: How does Angular 20 handle form reactivity using signals?

Answer: Forms in Angular 20 leverage signals as follows:

- Using **signal()** for real-time form state tracking.
- Removing the need for **BehaviorSubject** in form updates.
- Providing better integration with Angular's reactive forms.

Question 50: What are signal-based view models, and how do they enhance component state management?

Answer: Signal-based view models are introduced in Angular 20 for managing UI state efficiently. They perform the following actions:

- Store component state using **signal()**.
- Use **computed()** for derived values.
- Minimize unnecessary component re-renders.

Question 51: How does Angular 20 simplify state management using signals?

Answer: Angular 20 replaces complex state management patterns as follows:

- Standalone signals instead of global stores like NgRx.
- Direct template bindings with **signal()** instead of observables.
- Better debugging tools for tracking state changes.

Question 52: How do signals improve SSR in Angular 20?

Answer: Signals in Angular 20 improve SSR as follows:

- Hydration speed is improved by tracking dependencies more efficiently.
- JavaScript overhead is reduced, as they do not require manual subscriptions.
- Seamless state synchronization between server and client.

Question 53: What are the best practices for migrating to signals in Angular 20 applications?

Answer: When migrating to signals in Angular 20, it is important to follow best practices to ensure efficient and maintainable state management. The following are key recommendations for a smooth transition:

- Convert `BehaviorSubject` to `signal()` for local state.
- Use `toSignal()` for observables instead of async pipe.
- Replace `ChangeDetectorRef` calls with signal-based updates.
- Use `computed()` and `effect()` for reactive UI changes.
- Avoid overusing signals where simple properties suffice.

Signals in real-world applications

Question 54: How do you use signals for real-time updates in an Angular application?

Answer: Signals enable real-time updates by reacting to changes in data sources like WebSockets or APIs. Using `effect()`, you can automatically update the UI when data changes without manual subscriptions.

Question 55: How do you combine signals with dependency injection in Angular?

Answer: Signals can be injected into services to create a centralized state. This allows components to react to state changes without using RxJS or global stores.

Question 56: How do you use signals to optimize performance in large Angular applications?

Answer: Signals reduce unnecessary re-renders by updating only dependent components. Using `computed()` ensures that derived values are recalculated only when needed.

Question 57: What are the best practices for using signals in enterprise applications?

Answer: When implementing signals in enterprise applications, following best practices ensures scalability, maintainability, and performance optimization. Consider these key guidelines:

- Use `signal()` for local component state to manage isolated state effectively.
- Use `computed()` for derived state to ensure efficient recalculations based on dependencies.
- Centralize shared state in Angular services for better state management and reusability across components.
- Optimize performance by avoiding deeply nested computed properties to prevent unnecessary re-evaluations and improve responsiveness.

Question 58: How do signals improve reactivity in Angular applications compared to Zone.js?

Answer: Signals eliminate the need for `Zone.js` by tracking dependencies directly, leading to more efficient change detection and faster UI updates.

Question 59: How do you integrate signals with GraphQL in Angular applications?

Answer: By converting GraphQL queries into signals using `toSignal()`, you can ensure reactive data updates without manually subscribing to observables.

Question 60: How do signals improve state synchronization between components?

Answer: Signals allow components to react instantly to state changes without requiring input/output properties or event emitters.

Question 61: What are some real-world use cases where signals outperform RxJS?

Answer: Signals offer a more intuitive and efficient approach to state management in Angular applications, reducing boilerplate code and improving performance. The following are some real-world scenarios where signals provide a clear advantage over RxJS:

- **Form state management without BehaviorSubject**: Signals simplify local state handling without requiring explicit subscriptions.
- **Real-time dashboards without manual subscriptions**: Signals automatically track dependencies and update UI efficiently without `.subscribe()` calls.
- **Component-based caching without ReplaySubject**: Signals enable lightweight caching at the component level without the overhead of RxJS Subjects.

Question 62: What are the key challenges when adopting signals in an existing Angular application?

Answer: While signals offer significant benefits in state management, transitioning from **Reactive Extensions for JavaScript** (**RxJS**) can present certain challenges. Developers must carefully address these obstacles to ensure a smooth migration. Here are some key challenges to consider:

- **Migrating from RxJS to signals requires refactoring**: Existing RxJS-based logic, such as `BehaviorSubject` and observable chains, needs to be rewritten using signals.
- **Lack of direct support for all RxJS operators**: Some advanced RxJS patterns, like complex transformations using `switchMap` or `combineLatest`, may require alternative approaches.
- **Learning curve for developers used to RxJS**: Teams familiar with RxJS must adapt to the new reactive model and rethink state management strategies.

Question 63: What future improvements are expected for signals in upcoming Angular versions?

Answer: As signals continue to evolve in Angular, future updates are expected to enhance their capabilities and integration within the framework. Some anticipated improvements are as follows:

- **Deeper integration with state management libraries**: Better support for centralized state management solutions like NgRx or Akita.
- **Improved debugging tools for tracking signal dependencies**: Enhanced developer tools to visualize and debug signal-based state changes more efficiently.
- **Optimized performance for large-scale applications**: Further refinements to ensure minimal overhead and better scalability in enterprise-grade applications.

Question 64: How do signals affect Angular's Zone.js and change detection mechanism?

Answer: Signals reduce the reliance on Zone.js by triggering updates only where needed, leading to more efficient change detection.

Question 65: How can you optimize performance by using signals in complex UI updates?

Answer: When handling complex UI updates, signals can enhance performance by reducing unnecessary computations and improving reactivity. To achieve optimal efficiency, follow these best practices:

- **Use computed() to prevent unnecessary recalculations**: This ensures that derived values are only updated when dependencies change.
- **Avoid deep nesting of signals**: It minimizes excessive recalculations and keeps state management simple and efficient.
- **Implement lazy loading patterns with effect()**: This defers expensive computations or API calls until they are truly needed.

Question 66: How do signals help reduce unnecessary component re-renders in Angular?

Answer: Signals update only the components that depend on them, unlike traditional change detection, which affects the entire component tree.

Question 67: What is the best way to migrate from RxJS-based state management to Signals?

Answer: Migrating from RxJS to signals in Angular requires a structured approach to ensure a smooth transition and maintainability. The key steps are as follows:

- **Replace BehaviorSubject with signal()**: Use signals for managing local component state instead of manually emitting values.
- **Convert observable streams using toSignal()**: Transform existing RxJS observables into signals to seamlessly integrate reactive data.
- **Use computed() for derived state instead of map()**: Replace RxJS transformation operators like `map()` with `computed()` to automatically track dependencies.

Question 68: How do you handle large-scale application state using signals efficiently?

Answer: You can manage global state while keeping performance high using dependency tracking by creating a signal-based store.

Question 69: How does Angular 20 improve signal-based dependency injection?

Answer: Angular 20 enhances DI by allowing signals to be injected directly into services and components, improving state management.

Question 70: How do you use signals with NgRx or other state management libraries?

Answer: Integrating signals with **Angular Reactive Extensions** (**NgRx**) or other state management libraries enhances reactivity while maintaining structured state handling. Users can effectively use signals in combination with the following libraries:

- **Convert selectors into computed() for efficient updates**: Use `computed()` to derive state values dynamically, ensuring updates only occur when necessary.
- **Replace BehaviorSubject with signal()**: Manage local component state with `signal()` instead of manually handling `BehaviorSubject`.

  Use toSignal() to bridge observables with signals: Seamlessly integrate existing NgRx selectors or store observables into signals for better performance.

Question 71: Can you create custom signal-based hooks in Angular? If yes, how?

Answer: Yes, custom hooks can be created using `signal()`, `computed()`, and `effect()` to encapsulate reusable logic.

Question 72: How do you combine signals with async operations like Fetch API or WebSockets?

Answer: Integrating signals with asynchronous operations ensures efficient reactivity in Angular applications. Users can handle async data using signals as follows:

- **Use toSignal() to convert async observables into signals**: Convert HTTP requests, WebSocket streams, or other async data sources into signals for seamless reactivity.
- **Trigger updates using effect() when data changes**: Utilize `effect()` to respond to new data updates, ensuring real-time UI updates without manual subscriptions.

Question 73: What are signal-based lifecycle hooks in Angular 19 and 20, and how do they work?

Answer: Signal-based lifecycle hooks allow cleanup (`onSignalDestroy()`) and optimize component state handling.

Question 74: How does Angular handle memory management and garbage collection for signals?

Answer: Angular automatically cleans up unused signals, unlike RxJS, where manual unsubscription is required.

Question 75: How can you create a shared store using signals across multiple modules?

Answer: Define a signal-based service and inject it where needed, ensuring global state management.

Question 76: What is the difference between signals and React's signals API (if available)?

Answer: React's signals (if introduced) would focus on fine-grained reactivity, but Angular signals are natively optimized for change detection.

Question 77: How do signals improve SSR in Angular 20?

Answer: Signals enhance SSR performance in Angular 20 by optimizing reactivity and reducing unnecessary computations. They contribute to better SSR in the following manner:

- **Faster hydration due to dependency tracking**: Signals automatically track dependencies, enabling quicker client-side hydration without excessive re-computation.
- **Reduced server-side computation for rendering templates**: Signals minimize redundant calculations, improving server-side performance and response times.
- **Optimized data fetching with toSignal()**: `toSignal()` helps efficiently convert observables to signals, ensuring streamlined data handling during SSR.

Conclusion

In this chapter, we explored signals, a powerful new reactivity model introduced in Angular 20. Unlike traditional RxJS-based state management, signals provide automatic dependency tracking, eliminate unnecessary re-computations, and simplify state handling. By leveraging signal(), computed(), and effect(), developers can build highly efficient, reactive applications with minimal boilerplate.

We also covered best practices for migrating from RxJS to signals, optimizing performance in complex UI updates, and integrating signals with NgRx, Fetch API, WebSockets, and SSR. As signals continue to evolve, they promise to streamline state management in Angular applications, offering a more intuitive and performant alternative to existing solutions.

With a strong understanding of signals, in the next chapter, we will look at dependency injection and explore how it enables modular, scalable, and testable applications by efficiently managing service dependencies.

Join our Discord space

Join our Discord workspace for latest updates, offers, tech happenings around the world, new releases, and sessions with the authors:

https://discord.bpbonline.com

Chapter 6
Concepts of Dependency Injection

Introduction

In modern software development, **dependency injection** (**DI**) is a fundamental design pattern that enhances code maintainability, testability, and scalability. It is widely used in frameworks like Angular and React to manage dependencies efficiently. DI allows developers to decouple components by providing dependencies externally rather than having them created within the component itself. This approach follows the IoC principle, enabling better modularization and code reusability.

This chapter explores the core concepts of DI, its advantages, various types, and its practical applications in real-world software development. By the end of this chapter, you will have a strong understanding of DI and how to implement it effectively in your projects.

Structure

This chapter covers the following topics:

- Basics of dependency injection in Angular
- Advanced dependency injection concepts

Objectives

By the end of this chapter, you should be able to understand the importance and principles of DI, identify and differentiate various types of DI, implement DI in different programming languages and frameworks, recognize the advantages and challenges associated with DI, and apply best practices to ensure efficient usage of DI in software development.

This chapter lays the foundation for writing clean, scalable, and maintainable code using DI principles.

Basics of dependency injection in Angular

Question 1: What is DI in Angular, and why is it important?

Answer: DI is a design pattern used in Angular to manage dependencies efficiently. It allows classes (like services, components, and directives) to receive dependencies from an external source rather than creating them manually. The importance of DI in Angular is as follows:

- **Reduces tight coupling**: Promotes modular and maintainable code.
- **Improves testability**: Dependencies can be easily mocked or replaced in unit tests.
- **Enhances code reusability**: Services can be injected wherever needed without recreating instances.
- **Manages object lifecycle**: Angular automatically handles the creation and destruction of dependencies.

Angular's DI system is a powerful feature that improves modularity, testability, and performance. It allows efficient management of services and dependencies at different levels, reducing code complexity and ensuring reusability.

Angular has a built-in DI framework that provides dependencies where needed, improving code reusability, maintainability, and testability.

Using loose coupling in DI has the following benefits:

- **Without DI**: Components create their dependencies, making them tightly coupled.
- **With DI**: Dependencies are injected, making components independent of specific implementations.
- **Improved testability**: Mock services can be injected easily during unit testing.
- **Code reusability**: Services can be reused across multiple components and modules.
- **Better maintainability**: Changes in dependencies do not require modifications in multiple places.
- **Performance optimization**: Angular's DI framework ensures efficient lazy loading and tree-shakable providers, reducing app size.

Angular's DI system follows these three main steps:

1. Declare the dependency (service).
2. Register the dependency (provider).
3. Inject the dependency (consumer).

For example: Using DI in Angular:

Let us create a simple service and inject it into a component as follows:

1. **Create a service**: Generate a service using the Angular CLI as follows:

   ```
   ng generate service services/logger
   ```

   This creates a **`logger.service.ts`** file.

   ```
   import { Injectable } from '@angular/core';
   @Injectable({
     providedIn: 'root',  // Registers service at the root level (Singleton)
   })
   export class LoggerService {
     log(message: string) {
       console.log(`[Logger]: ${message}`);
     }
   }
   ```

In Angular, services play a crucial role in managing shared data and business logic across different components. When defining a service, the **`@Injectable()`** decorator and the **`providedIn`** property help control how the service is provided and accessed within the application:

- **`@Injectable()`** tells Angular that this service can be injected.
- **`providedIn: 'root'`** makes this a singleton service available throughout the app.

2. **Inject the service into a component**: Now, let us use **`LoggerService`** in a component as follows:

```
import { Component } from '@angular/core';
import { LoggerService } from '../services/logger.service';
@Component({
  selector: 'app-home',
  template: `<button (click)="logMessage()">Log Message</button>`,
})
export class HomeComponent {
  constructor(private loggerService: LoggerService) {}  // Dependency Injection
  logMessage() {
    this.loggerService.log('Button clicked!');
  }
}
```

In Angular, services are commonly injected into components or other services to promote reusability and maintainability. The **`LoggerService`** is an example of such a service that helps in logging messages efficiently:

- The **`LoggerService`** is injected in the constructor.
- The **`logMessage()`** method uses the service to log a message.

Angular provides different types of DI to handle dependencies at various levels, which are as follows:

- **Constructor injection (most common)**: Injects the dependency via the constructor.

  For example:

```
constructor(private myService: MyService) { }
```

- **Setter injection**: Uses a setter method to inject the dependency.

  For example:

```
private _myService: MyService;
set service(service: MyService) {
    this._myService = service;
}
```

- **Injector injection (manual injection)**: Uses the **`inject()`** function (introduced in Angular 14) to inject dependencies without a constructor.

  For example:

```
import { inject } from '@angular/core';
export class MyComponent {
  private myService = inject(MyService);
}
```

- **DI in Angular standalone components (Angular 16+)**: Angular standalone components do not rely on NgModules, but DI still works similarly. Uses **`inject(LoggerService)`** instead of constructor injection, and defines local providers inside the component.

For example:

```
import { Component, inject } from '@angular/core';
import { LoggerService } from './services/logger.service';
@Component({
  selector: 'app-standalone',
  standalone: true,
  template: `<button (click)="logMessage()">Log</button>`,
  providers: [LoggerService]  // Providing service locally
})
export class StandaloneComponent {
  private loggerService = inject(LoggerService);  // Inject without constructor
  logMessage() {
    this.loggerService.log('Standalone Component Log');
  }
}
```

The best practices for DI are as follows:

- **Use (providedIn: 'root') for singleton services**: Ensures a single instance and improves performance with tree-shaking.
- **Provide services in feature modules only when necessary**: Helps prevent unwanted instances across lazy loaded modules.
- **Avoid injecting dependencies in multiple levels**: Injecting at both module and component levels can create multiple instances.
- **Use the inject() function for standalone components**: Recommended for Angular 16+ to avoid constructor-based injection.
- **Use InjectionToken for configuration values**: Helps provide non-class-based dependencies in DI.

By following best practices and understanding DI at different levels (global, module, and component), developers can create scalable and efficient Angular applications.

Question 2: How does the Angular DI system work?

Answer: Angular's DI system consists of the following components:

- **Providers**: Define how dependencies should be created.
- **Injectors**: Maintain dependency instances and provide them when needed.
- **Dependencies**: The actual services, components, or objects being injected.

In Angular's DI system, dependencies are provided and managed by the injector to ensure efficient resource utilization. The process works as follows:

- A component, directive, or service requests a dependency in its constructor.
- The injector checks if the requested dependency is already created.
    - o If available, it returns the existing instance.
    - o If not available, it creates a new instance using the Provider and stores it.
- The dependency is injected into the requesting class.

Question 3: What is the @Injectable decorator, and why is it used?

Answer: The `@Injectable()` decorator marks a class as available for DI. It tells Angular that this class can be instantiated and injected as a service.

Angular's DI system provides a structured way to manage services and their availability within an application. It is used for the following reasons:

- Ensures that Angular's DI system can manage the service.
- Allows the service to be provided at different levels (root, module, or component).
- Enables hierarchical injection.

For example:

```
import { Injectable } from '@angular/core';
@Injectable({
  providedIn: 'root' // Makes it a singleton across the app
})
export class DataService {
  getData() {
    return 'Hello from DataService!';
  }
}
```

Question 4: What is the difference between providedIn: 'root' and providedIn: 'any'?

Answer: When using the **`providedIn`** property in Angular services, the choice between **`'root'`** and **`'any'`** affects how the service is provided and shared across modules. The key differences include:

- **Scope**:
    - **`providedIn: 'root'`** creates a singleton instance that is shared across the entire application.
    - **`providedIn: 'any'`** creates a new instance of the service for each module that injects it.
- **Sharing**:
    - With **`providedIn: 'root'`**, the service is shared across all lazy loaded modules.
    - With **`providedIn: 'any'`**, different lazy loaded modules receive their own instances of the service.
- **Use case**:
    - **`providedIn: 'root'`** is best for services that should be globally accessible and shared across the app.
    - **`providedIn: 'any'`** is useful when separate instances are needed for different modules to maintain an isolated state.

For example:

```
@Injectable({
  providedIn: 'any'
})
export class AuthService {
  // This service will have different instances in different modules
}
```

Question 5: What is the role of the injector in Angular?

Answer: The injector is responsible for managing and providing dependencies. It maintains a container of registered providers and resolves dependencies when requested.

Roles of the injector are as follows:

- Creates instances of services and provides them to classes.

- Manages instances to avoid duplicate service objects.
- Follows hierarchical injection to allow scoped dependency management.

For example:

```
constructor(private injector: Injector) {
  const dataService = this.injector.get(DataService);
  console.log(dataService.getData());
}
```

Question 6: **What is hierarchical DI in Angular, and how does it work?**

Answer: Hierarchical DI means that Angular maintains multiple injectors in a tree-like structure, allowing different parts of an application to have separate instances of a service.

Hierarchical DI has the following benefits:

- **Root injector**: Available globally across the application (`providedIn: 'root'`).
- **Module injector**: Services registered in a module are available only within that module.
- **Component injector**: Services provided in a component are available only in that component and its children.

For example:

```
@Component({
  selector: 'app-child',
  templateUrl: './child.component.html',
  providers: [DataService] // New instance of DataService for this component
})
export class ChildComponent {
  constructor(private dataService: DataService) {}
}
```

Question 7: **What are the different provider scopes available in Angular?**

Answer: Angular provides different ways to scope services, illustrated as follows:

- **Application-wide (providedIn: 'root')**: The service is a singleton and shared across the app.
- **Module-level (providedIn: MyModule)**: The service is available only in the specified module.
- **Component-level (providers array in @Component)**: A new instance is created for the component and its children.
- **Dynamic Injector (injector.get())**: Service is manually retrieved at runtime.

Question 8: **How do services get registered in Angular's DI system?**

Answer: Services in Angular are registered using providers. The following are the methods to register a service:

For example: Using **`providedIn`** in **`@Injectable()`** (recommended):

```
@Injectable({ providedIn: 'root' })
export class DataService {}
```

For example: Using providers array in **`@NgModule`**:

```
@NgModule({
  providers: [DataService]
})
export class AppModule {}
```

For example: Using providers in **`@Component`**:

```
@Component({
  providers: [DataService]
})
```

Question 9: How can we provide dependencies at the module, component, and service levels?

Answer: In Angular, dependencies can be provided at different levels to control their scope and availability within the application. The provisioning can be done as follows:

- **At the module level**: Use the providers array in **`@NgModule`** or **`providedIn: 'root'`**.
- **At the component level**: Define providers in **`@Component`**.
- **At the service level**: Use **`@Injectable({ providedIn: 'root' })`**.

For example:

```
@NgModule({
  providers: [GlobalService] // Available to the entire module
})
export class AppModule {}
@Component({
  selector: 'app-test',
  providers: [LocalService] // Only available in this component and its children
})
export class TestComponent {}
```

Question 10: How do you use the @Inject decorator, and when is it needed?

Answer: The **`@Inject()`** decorator is used when:

- A service depends on an interface or a non-class token.
- A service uses an opaque token.
- DI tokens are needed explicitly.

For example: Using a token for injection:

```
import { Inject, InjectionToken } from '@angular/core';
export const API_URL = new InjectionToken<string>('API_URL');
@Injectable({
  providedIn: 'root'
})
export class ApiService {
  constructor(@Inject(API_URL) private apiUrl: string) {
    console.log('API URL:', this.apiUrl);
  }
}
```

Advanced dependency injection concepts

Question 11: What are multi-providers in Angular, and how are they used?

Answer: Multi-providers allow multiple instances of a provider token to exist within the DI system instead of overriding previous instances. This is useful for collecting and aggregating services dynamically.

For example:

```
import { Injectable, InjectionToken } from '@angular/core';
export const MULTI_SERVICE = new InjectionToken<string[]>('MULTI_SERVICE');
@Injectable({ providedIn: 'root' })
export class ServiceA {
  getData() { return 'ServiceA Data'; }
}
@Injectable({ providedIn: 'root' })
export class ServiceB {
  getData() { return 'ServiceB Data'; }
}
// Register multiple providers for the same token
@NgModule({
  providers: [
    { provide: MULTI_SERVICE, useClass: ServiceA, multi: true },
    { provide: MULTI_SERVICE, useClass: ServiceB, multi: true }
  ]
})
export class AppModule { }
```

This allows all registered services to be injected as an array.

Question 12: **How do you create and use an abstract class with DI in Angular?**

Answer: An abstract class in Angular DI is used to define a common service contract without implementing it. This helps enforce a structure while allowing multiple implementations.

For example:

```
export abstract class LoggerService {
  abstract log(message: string): void;
}
@Injectable({ providedIn: 'root' })
export class ConsoleLoggerService extends LoggerService {
  log(message: string) { console.log('Console Logger:', message); }
}
// Provide the abstract class with a concrete implementation
@NgModule({
  providers: [{ provide: LoggerService, useClass: ConsoleLoggerService }]
})
export class AppModule { }
```

This enables DI to inject the `LoggerService`, which is actually an instance of `ConsoleLoggerService`.

Question 13: **What are token-based providers, and how do they work?**

Answer: Token-based providers use `InjectionTokens` to define dependencies that are not tied to a specific class. This is useful for injecting non-class values like configurations.

For example:

```
import { InjectionToken } from '@angular/core';
```

```
export const API_URL = new InjectionToken<string>('API_URL');
@NgModule({
  providers: [{ provide: API_URL, useValue: 'https://api.example.com' }]
})
export class AppModule { }
// Injecting the token in a service
@Injectable({ providedIn: 'root' })
export class ApiService {
  constructor(@Inject(API_URL) private apiUrl: string) {}
}
```

Here, API_URL is an **`InjectionToken`** that provides a string value.

Question 14: What is InjectionToken, and when should it be used?

Answer: **`InjectionToken <T>`** is a generic token used when you need to inject values that are not tied to a class, such as configuration objects or environment variables.

It should be used in the following cases:

- When injecting primitive values (strings, numbers, etc.).
- When dealing with multiple instances of a service.
- When injecting interfaces that do not have a concrete class.

For example:

```
export const CONFIG = new InjectionToken<{ apiUrl: string }>('config');
@NgModule({
  providers: [{ provide: CONFIG, useValue: { apiUrl: 'https://example.com' } }]
})
export class AppModule { }
```

Question 15: How does Angular resolve dependencies in nested modules?

Answer: Angular uses a hierarchical DI system, meaning services provided at the root level (**`providedIn: 'root'`**) are available throughout the application. However, services provided in a feature module are scoped to that module unless explicitly shared.

If a module provides a service, that service is available only to components declared within the module unless re-exported.

Question 16: What is the difference between useClass, useExisting, useValue, and useFactory?

Answer: In Angular's DI system, different provider configurations determine the manner in which a service or value is supplied. The key differences between these configurations are as follows:

- **useClass**: Provides an instance of a specific class.
- **useExisting**: Reuses an already provided service.
- **useValue**: Provides a fixed value.
- **useFactory**: Uses a factory function to create an instance.

Example of useFactory:

```
export function loggingFactory(): LoggerService {
  return new ConsoleLoggerService();
}
```

```
@NgModule({
  providers: [{ provide: LoggerService, useFactory: loggingFactory }]
})
export class AppModule { }
```

Question 17: How can you create a factory provider in Angular?

Answer: A factory provider dynamically creates service instances at runtime.

For example:

```
export function apiServiceFactory(logger: LoggerService) {
  return new ApiService(logger, 'https://api.example.com');
}
@NgModule({
  providers: [{ provide: ApiService, useFactory: apiServiceFactory, deps: [LoggerService]
}]
})
export class AppModule { }
```

Here, **`apiServiceFactory`** provides an instance of **`ApiService`** with dependencies.

Question 18: What are optional dependencies in Angular, and how do you handle them?

Answer: Optional dependencies allow services to be injected only if they exist, avoiding runtime errors when a service is unavailable.

Example using @Optional decorator:

```
constructor(@Optional() private logger?: LoggerService) { }
```

If **`LoggerService`** is not provided, the component will still work.

Question 19: How do you mock services and inject them in Angular unit tests?

Answer: Mocking services is essential for testing components without actual dependencies.

Example using TestBed:

```
const mockApiService = { getData: () => of(['mockData']) };
beforeEach(() => {
  TestBed.configureTestingModule({
    providers: [{ provide: ApiService, useValue: mockApiService }]
  });
});
```

Here, **`useValue`** provides a mock implementation of **`ApiService`**.

Question 20: What is tree-shakable DI, and how does Angular optimize DI?

Answer: Tree-shakable DI ensures that services are only included in the final bundle if they are used. If a service is marked with **`providedIn: 'root'`**, but never injected, Angular removes it during the build process. It is beneficial as it significantly reduces bundle size and improves performance.

Question 21: What improvements were made to DI in Angular 18?

Answer: Angular 18 introduced several enhancements to its DI system, improving performance, efficiency, and debugging capabilities. The key improvements are as follows:

- **Optimized dependency resolution**: Faster provider lookup and module bootstrapping.
- **Tree-shakable multi-providers**: Unused multi-providers are removed from the final bundle.

- **Improved debugging**: Enhanced DevTools support for analyzing DI trees.
- **Standalone component DI**: Services can be provided directly within standalone components.

Question 22: How does Angular 19 optimize provider tree management?

Answer: Angular 19 introduced optimizations to provider tree management, enhancing performance, isolation, and debugging. The key improvements include:

- **Better lazy loaded module isolation**: Prevents accidental service sharing between modules.
- **Faster provider lookup**: Optimized resolution in nested modules.
- **Improved debugging tools**: Visualized provider scopes in `DevTools`.
- **Efficient service overriding**: Improved handling of `useExisting` and `useFactory`.

Question 23: What are the DI-related optimizations in Angular 20?

Answer: Angular 20 introduced DI-related optimizations to enhance efficiency and performance. The key improvements are as follows:

- **Signal-based dependency resolution**: More efficient provider updates without change detection overhead.
- **Faster service instantiation**: Reduced object creation overhead.
- **Memory-optimized DI trees**: Better garbage collection for unused services.
- **Enhanced SSR support**: Improved async DI handling for server-side rendering.
- **Advanced tree-shaking**: More aggressive removal of unused providers.

Question 24: How does Angular 20 improve DI performance for SSR?

Answer: Angular 20 brings significant performance enhancements to DI for SSR, improving efficiency and resource management. The key improvements include:

- **Pre-resolved dependencies**: Reduces server processing time.
- **Lower memory usage**: Improved DI instance disposal after SSR execution.
- **Async service injection**: Non-blocking execution for dependencies like API calls.
- **Provider caching**: Reuses instances instead of recreating them for each request.

Question 25: What are the best practices for optimizing DI in Angular 20+?

Answer: To optimize DI in Angular 20 and beyond, following best practices ensures better performance, scalability, and maintainability. Key recommendations include:

- Use `providedIn: 'root'` for global singletons.
- Scope services to feature modules (`providedIn: 'any'`) when needed.
- Leverage signal-based DI for better reactivity.
- Optimize lazy loaded modules to prevent unnecessary service sharing.
- Use factory providers (`useFactory`) for dynamic DI.
- Avoid circular dependencies by refactoring or using `useExisting`.
- Ensure proper service disposal in SSR to prevent memory leaks.
- Use multi-providers (`multi: true`) for extensible services.
- Utilize `DevTools` to analyze DI trees and optimize performance.

Question 26: What is the difference between singleton and non-singleton services in Angular DI?

Answer: In Angular's DI system, services can be configured as either singleton or non-singleton, depending on how they are provided and used within the application.

The key differences between singleton and non-singleton services include:

- **Singleton services**:
  - Defined using **`providedIn: 'root'`**.
  - A single instance is shared across the entire application.
  - **Example**: Authentication, API services.
- **Non-singleton services**:
  - Defined using **`providedIn: 'any'`** or in specific modules or components.
  - A new instance is created for each module or component that injects it.
  - **Example**: Feature-specific services that need an independent state.

Question 27: **How does Angular handle DI in standalone components?**

Answer: Angular allows standalone components to manage their own dependencies without relying on **`NgModules`**. The key aspects of DI in standalone components are as follows:

- Standalone components can provide their own dependencies using the providers array.
- Dependencies can be injected just like in traditional module-based components.
- Services provided inside a standalone component are scoped to that component and its children.

For example:

```
@Component({
  standalone: true,
  selector: 'app-example',
  template: `<p>Standalone Component</p>`,
  providers: [ExampleService] // Scoped to this component
})
export class ExampleComponent {
  constructor(private exampleService: ExampleService) {}
}
```

Question 28: **How can you inject dependencies dynamically in Angular?**

Answer: In Angular, dependencies can be injected dynamically to allow greater flexibility and runtime configuration. This can be achieved through the following approaches:

- **Using injector service**: Inject dependencies at runtime using **`Injector.create()`** or **`inject()`**.

  For example:

  ```
  constructor(private injector: Injector) {}
  const dynamicService = this.injector.get(DynamicService);
  ```

- **Factory providers (useFactory)**: Generate dependencies dynamically based on conditions.

  For example:

  ```
  { provide: SomeService, useFactory: () => new SomeService(config) }
  ```

- **Using inject tokens (InjectionToken)**: Create dynamic, configurable dependencies.

  For example:

  ```
  export const API_URL = new InjectionToken<string>('apiUrl');
  ```

Question 29: **What is the impact of lazy loaded modules on DI in Angular?**

Answer: Lazy loaded modules create their own DI context, meaning:

- Services provided in a lazy loaded module are **not shared** with other modules by default.

- If a service is defined with **`providedIn: 'root'`**, it remains a singleton across lazy loaded modules.
- If a service is registered inside a lazy module, each lazy module gets its own instance.

However, there are potential issues, which are outlined as follows:

- Unintended multiple instances of a service.
- Unexpected behavior when sharing services between eagerly and lazily loaded modules.

Question 30: How can we override a service provider at the component level?

Answer: Use the providers array inside the component decorator to override a service for that component and its children.

For example:

```
@Component({
  selector: 'app-child',
  template: `<p>Child Component</p>`,
  providers: [{ provide: DataService, useClass: MockDataService }] // Overrides global
DataService
})
export class ChildComponent {
  constructor(private dataService: DataService) {}
}
```

This ensures the component uses a different instance of **`DataService`**, without affecting the rest of the application.

Question 31: What are the best practices for managing global vs. local providers in Angular DI?

Answer: Effectively managing global and local providers in Angular's DI system helps optimize performance and resource usage. The best practices include:

- Use **`providedIn: 'root'`** for global services to ensure a single instance across the app.
- Provide services at the module level when they are needed only in specific feature modules to avoid unnecessary memory usage.
- Use component-level providers when a service should have a unique instance per component instance.
- Avoid unnecessary service instantiations by not providing the same service at multiple levels unless required.

Question 32: How does Angular handle circular dependencies in DI?

Answer: Circular dependencies occur when two or more services depend on each other directly or indirectly.

Angular resolves this using forward declarations (**`@Inject`** with **`InjectionToken`**), shown as follows:

```
constructor(@Inject(forwardRef(() => SomeService)) private someService: SomeService) {}
```

Refactor dependencies by breaking them into separate services or introducing event-driven patterns (e.g., observables).

Lazy loading services can also help avoid circular dependencies.

Question 33: How does Angular DI improve performance compared to manual service instantiation?

Answer: Angular's DI system enhances performance by efficiently managing service instantiation and resource allocation. Key benefits over manual service instantiation include:

- **Optimized object creation**: Services are instantiated only when needed, reducing memory overhead.
- **Tree-shakable providers**: Unused services are removed during the build process, reducing bundle size.

- **Singleton pattern**: Ensures only one instance is created globally, preventing redundant object creation.
- **Efficient change detection**: Angular injects dependencies efficiently, reducing the number of checks needed in the application lifecycle.

Question 34: How can you inject platform-specific services in Angular?

Answer: In Angular, platform-specific services can be injected to tailor functionality based on the runtime environment. This can be achieved through the following methods:

- **Use factory providers**: Use (`useFactory`) to inject different services based on the platform.

  For example:

  ```
  export function platformServiceFactory() {
    return isMobilePlatform() ? new MobileService() : new WebService();
  }
  { provide: PlatformService, useFactory: platformServiceFactory }
  ```
- **Conditional imports**: Use **`import()`** dynamically inside services to load platform-specific implementations.
- **Environment-based injection**: Use **`InjectionToken`** to provide platform-specific values based on environment settings.

Question 35: What are the key security considerations when using DI in Angular applications?

Answer: When using DI in Angular applications, security best practices help protect against vulnerabilities and unauthorized access. Key considerations are as follows:

- **Avoid injecting unsanitized data**: Never inject untrusted user input into services.
- **Use DI for configuration data**: Prevent hardcoded secrets by injecting environment variables securely.
- **Restrict service exposure**: Use encapsulation (component-level providers) to limit access to sensitive services.
- **Prevent dependency manipulation**: Ensure dependencies are properly registered and cannot be overridden maliciously.
- **Use Angular's built-in security mechanisms**: Leverage Angular's **`DomSanitizer`** and **`HttpClient`** to prevent XSS and injection attacks.

Question 36: What is injection context in Angular?

Answer: Injection context in Angular refers to the runtime environment where dependencies are being injected. It provides additional metadata and contextual information when resolving dependencies within Angular's DI system.

With the introduction of the **`inject()`** function in Angular 14+, injection context plays a critical role in determining how and where dependencies are resolved.

Question 37: Why is injection context important?

Answer: Injection context helps in the following:

- Determining where a dependency is being injected (component, service, directive, etc.).
- Providing additional context-aware functionalities for better state management.
- Enhancing Angular's DI flexibility by improving lazy loading, dynamic injections, and scoped providers.

Question 38: How does injection context work?

Answer: Whenever **`inject()`** is used, it automatically gets access to the current injection context, which includes the following:

- The current injector (where the dependency is being resolved from).
- The scope (e.g., root, module, component, directive).
- The runtime environment (inside a constructor, service, or a standalone component).

For example: Using injection context with `inject()`:

Let us see how **`inject()`** utilizes injection context:

- **Traditional DI using constructor injection**:

  ```
  import { Injectable } from '@angular/core';
  @Injectable({
    providedIn: 'root'
  })
  export class LoggerService {
    log(message: string) {
      console.log(`[Logger]: ${message}`);
    }
  }
  ```

- **Injecting it in a component**:

  ```
  import { Component } from '@angular/core';
  import { LoggerService } from './services/logger.service';
  @Component({
    selector: 'app-home',
    template: `<button (click)="logMessage()">Log Message</button>`,
  })
  export class HomeComponent {
    constructor(private loggerService: LoggerService) {}  // Constructor Injection
    logMessage() {
      this.loggerService.log('Button clicked!');
    }
  }
  ```

- **Using inject() with injection context (Angular 14+)**: Instead of injecting via the constructor, we can use **`inject()`**, which automatically retrieves the injection context:

  ```
  import { Component, inject } from '@angular/core';
  import { LoggerService } from './services/logger.service';
  @Component({
    selector: 'app-standalone',
    standalone: true,
    template: `<button (click)="logMessage()">Log</button>`,
    providers: [LoggerService]
  })
  export class StandaloneComponent {
    private loggerService = inject(LoggerService);  // Uses Injection Context
    logMessage() {
      this.loggerService.log('Standalone Component Log');
  ```

```
  }
}
```

In Angular, the **inject()** function provides a more flexible and context-aware way to retrieve dependencies. Key advantages include:

- **inject(LoggerService)** gets context-aware dependency resolution.
- It automatically determines where the dependency should be provided.

The following are use cases of injection context:

- **Dynamic DI**: With **inject()**, dependencies can be resolved dynamically without requiring constructor injection.

  For example:

```
import { inject } from '@angular/core';
import { ActivatedRoute } from '@angular/router';
export class MyComponent {
  private route = inject(ActivatedRoute);  // Injection Context provides
ActivatedRoute
}
```

  Angular's injection context simplifies dependency retrieval, enhancing flexibility and reducing boilerplate. Key benefits are as follows:

  - No need to manually pass **ActivatedRoute** via the constructor.
  - The injection context ensures the correct instance is used.

- **Scoped dependency resolution**: Injection context ensures dependencies are resolved within the correct scope.

  For example: Using **inject()** in a service factory provider:

```
import { Injectable, inject } from '@angular/core';
import { HttpClient } from '@angular/common/http';
@Injectable({
  providedIn: 'root',
  useFactory: () => {
    const http = inject(HttpClient); // Inject HttpClient dynamically
    return new DataService(http);
  }
})
export class DataService {
  constructor(private http: HttpClient) {}
  fetchData() {
    return this.http.get('/api/data');
  }
}
```

  Using **inject(HttpClient)** in Angular optimizes dependency management by ensuring efficient resource utilization. The following are the key benefits:

  - **inject(HttpClient)** ensures **HttpClient** is provided only when needed.
  - This reduces unnecessary constructor-based injections.

- **Signal-based DI (Angular 16+)**: Angular 16 introduced signals, which can also leverage **`inject()`**.

  For example:

```
import { Component, Signal, computed, effect, inject } from '@angular/core';
import { AuthService } from './services/auth.service';
@Component({
  selector: 'app-dashboard',
  standalone: true,
  template: `User: {{ username() }}`
})
export class DashboardComponent {
  private authService = inject(AuthService);
  username: Signal<string> = computed(() => this.authService.getUsername());
  constructor() {
    effect(() => console.log(this.username()));
  }
}
```

  Angular's injection context enhances dependency management and reactivity in authentication services. Key benefits include:

  - The injection context ensures **`AuthService`** is correctly injected.
  - Signals reactively update when the authentication state changes.

Question 39: **What are the key benefits of injection context?**

Answer: The injection context in Angular modernizes and simplifies DI, offering benefits, such as the following:

- **Eliminating boilerplate code**: No need to inject dependencies in the constructor.
- **Supporting standalone components**: Works without modules, simplifying dependency management.
- **Optimizing lazy loading and scoped providers**: Creates module-specific service instances instead of sharing globally.
- **Improves performance with tree-shaking providers**: Removes unused services from the final build, reducing bundle size.
- **Enhances SSR**: Resolves dependencies efficiently for SSR applications.
- **Better debugging and error handling**: Provides clear DI error messages and improves debugging.
- **Enhancing reactivity**: It enhances reactivity with signals.

By leveraging **`inject()`**, developers can build more scalable, efficient, and maintainable Angular applications.

Question 40: **What are the best practices for using injection context in Angular applications?**

Answer: Injection context in Angular simplifies DI by allowing services to be injected directly within functions, eliminating the need for constructor-based DI in some cases.

The following are the best practices for effectively using injection context in Angular applications:

- **Prefer inject() over constructor-based DI**: Use **`inject()`** inside services, factory functions, and lifecycle hooks instead of constructors where applicable.
- **Use in standalone components**: **`inject()`** simplifies dependency management in standalone components.
- **Utilize in signals and effects**: Works well with Angular signals for reactive state management.

- **Ensure lazy loading support**: `inject()` respects hierarchical DI, making it useful in lazy loaded modules.
- **Use InjectionToken for configurable dependencies**: Helps manage dynamic values and configuration-based injections.
- **Avoid overusing inject()**: Use it selectively where it provides real benefits without overcomplicating DI.
- **Maintain testability**: Ensure injected dependencies are easily mockable for unit testing.

By following these best practices, injection context improves code clarity, performance, and maintainability in Angular applications.

Conclusion

DI in Angular is a powerful design pattern that enhances modularity, reusability, and maintainability by efficiently managing dependencies. By leveraging DI, Angular optimizes service instantiation, improves performance, and provides a scalable way to share functionality across components, directives, and services. Best practices such as using providedIn, factory providers, and injection tokens help ensure efficient and secure dependency management. With advancements in Angular, including signal-based DI and standalone component support, DI continues to evolve, making Angular applications more efficient and flexible.

In the next chapter, we will explore the concepts of routing in Angular. We will cover how Angular's router enables navigation between views, lazy loading, route guards, and advanced routing strategies to build dynamic, single-page applications efficiently.

Chapter 7
Concepts of Routing

Introduction

Routing is a fundamental concept in Angular that enables navigation between different views in a **single page application** (**SPA**). Unlike traditional multi-page applications, where each navigation request loads a new page, Angular uses client-side routing to dynamically update the view without a full-page reload. This approach improves performance and provides a seamless user experience.

Angular's router module manages application navigation, allowing developers to define routes, pass parameters, protect routes using guards, and implement lazy loading for better performance. Understanding routing concepts is essential for building scalable and efficient Angular applications.

Structure

This chapter covers the following topics:

- Basics of Angular routing
- Advanced routing concepts
- Route navigation and state management
- Angular latest version routing enhancements
- Error handling and performance optimization

Objectives

By the end of this chapter, you will have a comprehensive understanding of Angular's routing system and its significance in building dynamic web applications. You will learn to configure and define routes using the RouterModule, implement various navigation techniques for seamless user interaction, and pass parameters and query strings between different views. Additionally, you will explore route guards to manage access control and authentication, optimize application performance using lazy loading, and implement child routes for better application structure. Furthermore, you will understand how to handle invalid URLs with wildcard and redirect routes, as well as track navigation events using the Angular router lifecycle.

Basics of Angular routing

Question 1: What is routing in Angular, and why is it important?

Answer: Routing in Angular allows navigation between different views (**components**) within a SPA without requiring a full page reload. It enhances user experience, performance, and maintainability by enabling dynamic content updates. It uses the **Angular router**, a built-in module (`RouterModule`), to map URLs to specific components, enabling the app to dynamically update the displayed content based on the browser's URL. The router interprets URL paths, matches them to predefined routes, and renders the associated components in a designated `<router-outlet>` placeholder in the app's template.

For instance, a URL like `/home` might display a `HomeComponent`, while `/products` loads a `ProductListComponent`. Angular routing also supports advanced features like route parameters (e.g., `/product/123`), query parameters, nested routes, and lazy loaded modules. The breakdown of Angular routing benefits is as follows:

- **Improves performance**: Prevents full-page reloads, speeding up navigation by updating only necessary components.
- **Enhances user experience**: Provides smooth, seamless transitions without page refresh, mimicking a native app feel.
- **Manages application state**: Ties state to dynamic URLs and uses route guards for access control and data pre-fetching.
- **Lazy loading support**: Loads feature modules on demand, reducing initial load time and optimizing resources.
- **Modular design**: It supports organizing the app into feature modules, enhancing scalability and maintainability.
- **Control and security**: Route guards allow developers to restrict access or pre-fetch data, ensuring the app behaves logically and securely.

In essence, Angular routing is the backbone of navigation and structure in an SPA, making it essential for creating interactive, efficient, and user-friendly web applications.

Question 2: How do you set up routing in an Angular application?

Answer: Set up routing in an Angular project as follows:

1. Create a new Angular project with routing: `ng new my-app --routing`
2. Define routes in `app-routing.module.ts`, shown as follows:

```
import { NgModule } from '@angular/core';
import { RouterModule, Routes } from '@angular/router';
import { HomeComponent } from './home/home.component';
import { AboutComponent } from './about/about.component';
const routes: Routes = [
  { path: 'home', component: HomeComponent },
  { path: 'about', component: AboutComponent },
  { path: '', redirectTo: '/home', pathMatch: 'full' }
];
@NgModule({
  imports: [RouterModule.forRoot(routes)],
  exports: [RouterModule]
})
export class AppRoutingModule {}
```

3. Use `<router-outlet>` in `app.component.html`:

```
<router-outlet></router-outlet>
```

4. Add navigation links:

```
<a routerLink="/home">Home</a>
<a routerLink="/about">About</a>
```

Question 3: What is the purpose of the RouterModule in Angular?

Answer: The `RouterModule` is an essential Angular module that facilitates routing within an application. It serves the following purposes:

- **Defines application routes** using `RouterModule.forRoot()` for the main application and `RouterModule.forChild()` for feature modules.
- **Registers route configurations** and provides core routing services such as router and ActivatedRoute.
- **Manages navigation and route handling**, including route parameters, guards, and lazy loading for optimized performance.

Question 4: What is the difference between forRoot() and forChild() in Angular routing?

Answer: In Angular, routing configuration depends on whether it is set up in the root module or a feature module. The difference lies in how routing services and configuration are initialized:

- **RouterModule.forRoot(routes)**:
  - Used **once in the root module** (`AppModule`) to configure global application routes.
  - Provides **singleton services** such as the router, location, and route guards.
  - Should **not be used in feature modules**, as doing so may cause duplicated router instances.
- **RouterModule.forChild(routes)**:
  - Used in **feature modules** to define **module-specific routes**.
  - Does **not re-register router providers**, which avoids unintended side effects.

Consider the following examples:

In AppRoutingModule (Root):

```
@NgModule({
  imports: [RouterModule.forRoot(appRoutes)],
  exports: [RouterModule]
})
export class AppRoutingModule {}
```

In FeatureModule:

```
@NgModule({
  imports: [RouterModule.forChild(featureRoutes)],
  exports: [RouterModule]
})
export class FeatureModule {}
```

The best practices are as follows:

- Always use `forRoot()` only once in the root module.
- Use `forChild()` in any lazy loaded or shared feature modules to avoid conflicts.
- Using `forRoot()` more than once can lead to unexpected routing behavior or duplicated service instances.

Question 5: How do you define a basic route in an Angular application?

Answer: Define a route by mapping a path to a component in the routes array inside **app-routing.module.ts** as follows:

```
const routes: Routes = [
  { path: 'dashboard', component: DashboardComponent },
  { path: '', redirectTo: '/dashboard', pathMatch: 'full' }
];
```

Question 6: What is the RouterOutlet, and how does it work?

Answer: The **<router-outlet>** directive acts as a placeholder where the matching route's component is rendered.

For example:

```
<h1>My Angular App</h1>
<router-outlet></router-outlet>
```

In Angular, route navigation determines which component is displayed based on the URL. The following examples illustrate this behavior:

- If the user navigates to **/home**, Angular renders **HomeComponent**.
- If the user navigates to **/about**, Angular renders **AboutComponent**.

Question 7: How can you navigate between routes in Angular?

Answer: There are two ways to navigate between routes, which are as follows:

- Using **routerLink** in templates:

```
<a routerLink="/home">Go to Home</a>
<a routerLink="/about">Go to About</a>
```

- Using router service in TypeScript:

```
import { Router } from '@angular/router';
constructor(private router: Router) {}
goToAbout() {
  this.router.navigate(['/about']);
}
```

Question 8: What are route parameters, and how do you pass them in Angular?

Answer: Route parameters allow passing dynamic values (e.g., user IDs, product IDs) in the URL.

For example:

- Defining a route with parameters:

```
const routes: Routes = [
  { path: 'product/:id', component: ProductComponent }
];
```

- Passing parameters in navigation:

```
<a [routerLink]="['/product', productId]">View Product</a>
```

Question 9: How can you access route parameters inside a component?

Answer: Use the **ActivatedRoute** service to access parameters.

For example:

```
import { ActivatedRoute } from '@angular/router';
```

```
constructor(private route: ActivatedRoute) {}
ngOnInit() {
  this.route.paramMap.subscribe(params => {
    let id = params.get('id');
    console.log('Product ID:', id);
  });
}
```

Question 10: What is a wildcard route, and when should it be used?

Answer: A wildcard route (**) is a catch-all route for undefined URLs. It is used for 404 pages or handling incorrect routes.

For example:

```
const routes: Routes = [
  { path: '**', component: NotFoundComponent }
];
```

This ensures that if the user enters an invalid URL, they are redirected to the `Not Found` page instead of seeing a blank page.

Advanced routing concepts

Question 11: What are child routes in Angular, and how do you configure them?

Answer: Child routes allow nesting routes inside a parent route, which is useful for structuring modules like dashboard, user profiles, or settings.

This is useful when you want a consistent layout (like a dashboard or tabs) and change only a portion of the view based on navigation. Let us look at some examples of child routes.

Routing configuration (app-routing.module.ts):

```
const routes: Routes = [
  {
    path: 'dashboard',
    component: DashboardComponent,
    children: [
      { path: 'stats', component: StatsComponent },
      { path: 'reports', component: ReportsComponent }
    ]
  },
  { path: '', redirectTo: 'dashboard', pathMatch: 'full' }
];
```

Dashboard component template (dashboard.component.html):

```
<h2>Dashboard</h2>
<nav>
  <a routerLink="stats">Stats</a> |
  <a routerLink="reports">Reports</a>
</nav>
```

```
<!-- Child views appear here -->
<router-outlet></router-outlet>
```

App component template (app.component.html):

```
<!-- Root level router outlet -->
<router-outlet></router-outlet>
```

The following is the resulting behavior:

- Visiting **/dashboard/stats** displays the **StatsComponent** inside the dashboard layout.
- Visiting **/dashboard/reports** displays the **ReportsComponent** in the same layout.

Thus, child routes do the following:

- Child routes allow you to nest views and build structured UIs.
- They use a second **<router-outlet>** inside the parent component.
- Useful for modular pages like dashboards, tabs, or multi-step forms.

Question 12: **What is lazy loading in Angular routing, and how does it improve performance?**

Answer: Lazy loading loads modules only when needed, reducing the initial bundle size and improving performance. Consider an example of lazy loading a feature module:

```
const routes: Routes = [
  { path: 'users', loadChildren: () => import('./users/users.module').then(m => m.UsersModule)
}
];
```

It improves application speed by loading only necessary parts of the app.

Question 13: **What is the difference between eager loading and lazy loading in Angular?**

Answer: Eager loading and lazy loading are two strategies for managing module loading in Angular:

- **Eager loading** loads all modules at application startup, which can lead to longer initial load times but ensures that all features are immediately available. It is ideal for small applications, where performance impact is minimal.
- **Lazy loading**, on the other hand, loads modules only when needed, reducing the initial load time and improving performance. It is beneficial for large applications where different sections are accessed at different times.

Angular supports different module loading strategies to optimize application performance and resource management:

- **Eager loading**: Modules are imported directly in **AppModule**, making them available immediately.
- **Lazy loading**: Uses **loadChildren** to dynamically load feature modules only when they are accessed, reducing initial load time. Also, lazy loading is recommended for optimizing performance in larger applications.

Question 14: **How does Angular handle redirects in routing?**

Answer: Angular uses the **redirectTo** property to redirect users to a specific route.

For example: Redirecting from **/** to **/home**:

```
const routes: Routes = [
  { path: '', redirectTo: 'home', pathMatch: 'full' },
  { path: 'home', component: HomeComponent }
];
```

It prevents users from landing on a blank page by setting a default route.

Question 15: What are route guards in Angular, and why are they needed?

Answer: Route guards control access to routes based on conditions like authentication, user roles, or permissions. They help prevent unauthorized access and improve security.

Question 16: What are the different types of route guards in Angular?

Answer: Angular provides five types of route guards, which are as follows:

- **CanActivate**: Prevents access if a condition is not met.
- **CanActivateChild**: Controls access to child routes.
- **CanDeactivate**: Prevents leaving a route if conditions fail (e.g., unsaved changes).
- **Resolve**: Fetches data before route activation.
- **CanLoad**: Prevents a lazy loaded module from loading if a condition is not met.

Guards improve security and user flow control in apps.

Question 17: How do you implement CanActivate and CanDeactivate route guards?

Answer: In Angular, route guards are used to control navigation:

- `CanActivate` determines if a route can be accessed.
- `CanDeactivate` checks whether a user can leave the current route or component.

The implementation can be done as follows:

- **Functional guards (recommended for Angular 15+)**

  Example of CanActivateFn:

```
// auth.guard.ts
import { CanActivateFn } from '@angular/router';
export const authGuard: CanActivateFn = (route, state) => {
  const isLoggedIn = localStorage.getItem('token') !== null;
  return isLoggedIn;
};
```

  Example of CanDeactivateFn:

```
// exit.guard.ts
import { CanDeactivateFn } from '@angular/router';
export const exitGuard: CanDeactivateFn<MyComponent> = (component, route, state) => {
  return component.hasUnsavedChanges
    ? confirm('You have unsaved changes. Leave anyway?')
    : true;
};
```

  Using functional guards in routes:

```
const routes: Routes = [
  {
    path: 'dashboard',
    component: DashboardComponent,
    canActivate: [authGuard],
    canDeactivate: [exitGuard]
  }
];
```

- **Class-based guards (legacy approach):**

```
@Injectable({ providedIn: 'root' })
export class AuthGuard implements CanActivate {
  canActivate(): boolean {
    return !!localStorage.getItem('token');
  }
}
const routes: Routes = [
  { path: 'dashboard', component: DashboardComponent, canActivate: [AuthGuard] }
];
```

Recommendation: Use functional guards (**`CanActivateFn`**, **`CanDeactivateFn`**) for simplified syntax, better tree-shaking, and fewer boilerplate classes.

Guards provide security and prevent unintended actions.

Question 18: What is resolve guard in Angular, and how does it work?

Answer: The resolve guard fetches data before the route is activated, ensuring the component loads with data.

For example:

```
@Injectable({ providedIn: 'root' })
export class UserResolver implements Resolve<User> {
  constructor(private userService: UserService) {}
  resolve(route: ActivatedRouteSnapshot): Observable<User> {
    return this.userService.getUser(route.paramMap.get('id'));
  }
}
```

Usage in routing:

```
const routes: Routes = [
  { path: 'profile/:id', component: ProfileComponent, resolve: { user: UserResolver } }
];
```

It ensures components load only when data is available.

Question 19: How does Angular handle route-based authentication?

Answer: Angular provides several mechanisms to secure routes and control user access, which are as follows:

- Using **`CanActivate`** guard to restrict unauthorized access.
- JWT tokens and Interceptors for secure API calls.
- Role-based access control for admin or user dashboards.
- Prevents unauthenticated users from accessing protected routes.

Question 20: How do you handle protected routes in Angular?

Answer: Protecting routes in Angular ensures that only authorized users can access certain parts of the application. This can be achieved through the following steps:

1. **Use CanActivate:** Implement route guards to restrict access based on authentication status.
2. **Redirect unauthorized users:** Navigate unauthorized users to the login page if access is denied.
3. **Use JWT tokens:** Authenticate users securely by validating **JSON Web Tokens (JWT)** in API requests.

Example of a protected route:

```
const routes: Routes = [
  { path: 'dashboard', component: DashboardComponent, canActivate: [AuthGuard] },
  { path: 'login', component: LoginComponent }
];
```

It ensures only authenticated users can access sensitive areas.

Route navigation and state management

Question 21: How do you navigate programmatically using the router service?

Answer: You can navigate programmatically in Angular using the router service's **`navigate()`** or **`navigateByUrl()`** methods.

For example:

```
constructor(private router: Router) {}
// Navigate to '/dashboard'
this.router.navigate(['/dashboard']);
// Navigate with parameters
this.router.navigate(['/profile', userId]);
```

Question 22: What is the difference between navigateByUrl() and navigate()?

Answer: Angular provides the following two methods for programmatic navigation, each serving different use cases:

- **navigateByUrl(url: string):** Takes a URL as a string and navigates directly.
- **navigate(commands: any[], extras?: NavigationExtras):** More flexible, allowing array-based commands and additional options (query params, fragments, etc.).

For example:

```
this.router.navigateByUrl('/dashboard');
this.router.navigate(['/dashboard'], { queryParams: { id: 1 } });
```

Question 23: How do you pass query parameters in Angular routing?

Answer: Use the **`queryParams`** option in **`navigate()`**, shown as follows:

```
this.router.navigate(['/products'], { queryParams: { category: 'electronics' } });
```

You can also pass query parameters by using the following template:

```
<a [routerLink]="['/products']" [queryParams]="{ category: 'electronics' }">View Electronics</
a>
```

Question 24: How can you retrieve query parameters from the URL in Angular?

Answer: Use **`ActivatedRoute`** to read query parameters.

For example:

```
constructor(private route: ActivatedRoute) {}
ngOnInit() {
  this.route.queryParams.subscribe(params => {
    console.log(params['category']); // 'electronics'
  });
}
```

Question 25: How does Angular support navigation extras like skipLocationChange and replaceUrl?

Answer: Angular provides the following navigation extras to control the manner in which route changes are handled in the browser history:

- **skipLocationChange: true**: Navigates without adding the URL to browser history.
- **replaceUrl: true**: Replaces the current URL in history instead of pushing a new entry.

For example:

```
this.router.navigate(['/dashboard'], { skipLocationChange: true });
this.router.navigate(['/dashboard'], { replaceUrl: true });
```

Question 26: What is ActivatedRoute, and how does it help in retrieving route information?

Answer: `ActivatedRoute` provides access to the current route's parameters, query parameters, and data.

For example:

```
constructor(private route: ActivatedRoute) {}
ngOnInit() {
  console.log(this.route.snapshot.paramMap.get('id')); // Get route param
}
```

Question 27: How does Angular handle back and forward navigation in routes?

Answer: Angular provides location service for handling navigation history.

For example:

```
constructor(private location: Location) {}
// Navigate back
this.location.back();
// Navigate forward
this.location.forward();
```

Question 28: What is the location service in Angular, and how does it work with routing?

Answer: The location service interacts with the browser's history API to control navigation.

For example:

```
import { Location } from '@angular/common';
constructor(private location: Location) {}
goBack() {
  this.location.back();
}
```

Question 29: What is routerLinkActive, and how can it be used to style active links?

Answer: `routerLinkActive` applies a class when the link is active.

For example:

```
<a routerLink="/home" routerLinkActive="active">Home</a>
```

You can also apply multiple classes as follows:

```
<a routerLink="/dashboard" routerLinkActive="active highlighted">Dashboard</a>
```

Question 30: How does the route reuse strategy work in Angular?

Answer: `RouteReuseStrategy` is a powerful Angular interface that allows developers to customize the behavior of route navigation, particularly by caching and reusing route components instead of destroying and recreating them every time a route is revisited. This is especially useful for:

- Preserving component state
- Improving navigation performance
- Avoiding unnecessary API calls or reinitialization

Let us look at an example of caching components using **RouteReuseStrategy** with standalone components. To demonstrate how to cache a component (e.g., **ProductListComponent**) so that when the user navigates away and comes back, the component retains its state without being destroyed and recreated.

This is useful for large lists, dashboards, or tabbed interfaces where performance and user experience matter. Follow the given steps:

1. **Define the custom route reuse strategy**:

```
//app/route-reuse-strategy.ts
import {
  RouteReuseStrategy,
  ActivatedRouteSnapshot,
  DetachedRouteHandle
} from '@angular/router';
export class CustomReuseStrategy implements RouteReuseStrategy {
  private cache = new Map<string, DetachedRouteHandle>();
  shouldDetach(route: ActivatedRouteSnapshot): boolean {
    return route.routeConfig?.path === 'products';
  }
  store(route: ActivatedRouteSnapshot, handle: DetachedRouteHandle): void {
    if (route.routeConfig?.path && handle) {
      this.cache.set(route.routeConfig.path, handle);
    }
  }
  shouldAttach(route: ActivatedRouteSnapshot): boolean {
    return route.routeConfig?.path === 'products' && this.cache.has(route.routeConfig.
path);
  }
  retrieve(route: ActivatedRouteSnapshot): DetachedRouteHandle | null {
    return route.routeConfig?.path
      ? this.cache.get(route.routeConfig.path) || null
      : null;
  }
  shouldReuseRoute(future: ActivatedRouteSnapshot, curr: ActivatedRouteSnapshot):
boolean {
    return future.routeConfig === curr.routeConfig;
  }
}
```

2. **Create the routing file**:

```
//app/app.routes.ts
import { Routes } from '@angular/router';
import { HomeComponent } from './home.component';
```

```
import { ProductListComponent } from './product-list.component';
export const routes: Routes = [
  { path: '', component: HomeComponent },
  { path: 'products', component: ProductListComponent }
];
```

3. **Configure the application**:

```
// app/app.config.ts
import { ApplicationConfig } from '@angular/core';
import { provideRouter } from '@angular/router';
import { routes } from './app.routes';
import { RouteReuseStrategy } from '@angular/router';
import { CustomReuseStrategy } from './route-reuse-strategy';
export const appConfig: ApplicationConfig = {
  providers: [
    provideRouter(routes),
    { provide: RouteReuseStrategy, useClass: CustomReuseStrategy }
  ]
};
```

4. **Bootstrap the application**:

```
//main.ts
import { bootstrapApplication } from '@angular/platform-browser';
import { AppComponent } from './app.component';
import { appConfig } from './app.config';
bootstrapApplication(AppComponent, appConfig)
  .catch(err => console.error(err));
```

5. **Create the root component**:

```
//app/app.component.ts
import { Component } from '@angular/core';
import { RouterOutlet } from '@angular/router';
@Component({
  selector: 'app-root',
  standalone: true,
  imports: [RouterOutlet],
  template: `
    <h1>Angular 19: Caching Component Example</h1>
    <router-outlet></router-outlet>
  `

})
export class AppComponent {}
```

6. **Create the home component**:

```
// app/home.component.ts
import { Component } from '@angular/core';
```

```
import { RouterLink } from '@angular/router';
@Component({
  standalone: true,
  selector: 'app-home',
  imports: [RouterLink],
  template: `
    <h2>Home</h2>
    <a routerLink="/products">Go to Product List</a>
  `
})
export class HomeComponent {}
```

7. **Create the product list component (cached)**:

```
// app/product-list.component.ts
import { Component, OnInit } from '@angular/core';
import { RouterLink } from '@angular/router';
@Component({
  standalone: true,
  selector: 'app-product-list',
  imports: [RouterLink],
  template: `
    <h2>Product List</h2>
    <ul>
      <li *ngFor="let product of products">{{ product }}</li>
    </ul>
    <a routerLink="/">Back to Home</a>
  `
})
export class ProductListComponent implements OnInit {
  products = Array.from({ length: 20 }, (_, i) => `Product #${i + 1}`);
  ngOnInit(): void {
    console.log('ProductListComponent initialized');
  }
}
```

The result is as follows:

- Navigate to **`/products`**
- Scroll or interact with the component
- Go back to **/** (home page)
- **Navigate again to /products**: The component is restored with state retained; **`ngOnInit()`** is not called again

This can optimize performance by caching route components instead of destroying and recreating them.

Angular latest version routing enhancements

Question 31: What are the latest improvements in Angular 18 for routing?

Answer: Angular 18 introduced several routing improvements, focusing on performance and developer experience:

- **Improved route matching**: Faster and more efficient route recognition.
- **Enhanced guards and resolvers**: Async handling improved to prevent unnecessary re-execution.
- **Better lazy loading**: Optimized route-based code splitting.
- **Debugging enhancements**: More detailed error messages for incorrect routes.

Example of improved route matching:

```
const routes: Routes = [
  { path: 'home', component: HomeComponent, pathMatch: 'full' },
  { path: '**', redirectTo: 'home' } // Optimized wildcard matching
];
```

Question 32: How does Angular 19 optimize lazy loading performance?

Answer: Angular 19 introduced optimizations such as the following:

- **Faster module federation**: Dynamic imports for micro-frontends.
- **Deferred loading with signals**: Improves initial load time.
- **Pre-built route hints**: Reduces parsing overhead.

Example of lazy loading optimization:

```
const routes: Routes = [
  { path: 'dashboard', loadComponent: () => import('./dashboard.component').then(m =>
m.DashboardComponent) }
];
```

Question 33: What improvements were made to @RouteConfig in Angular 19?

Answer: Angular 19 introduced several enhancements to the router system, particularly in the context of standalone components:

- **Fully standalone routing setup**: You can now define routes using **`provideRouter()`** without any NgModules.
- **Improved type safety**: Route definitions now offer better TypeScript inference for parameters and route configuration.
- **Signal-based reactivity (preview)**: Angular's signal system integrates better with route state management and reactive guards.

For example:

```
import { provideRouter } from '@angular/router';
import { ProfileComponent } from './profile.component';
const routes = [
  { path: 'profile', component: ProfileComponent }
];
export const appConfig = {
  providers: [provideRouter(routes)]
};
```

In summary:

- **@RouteConfig** is not part of Angular and should not be referenced in modern Angular books or tutorials.
- Angular 19 continues to improve standalone routing, but not through any **@RouteConfig** mechanism.

Question 34: How does Angular 20 handle router preloading strategies?

Answer: Angular 20 introduced the following:

- **Signal-based preloading**: Routes are preloaded dynamically based on state.
- **Smarter link predictions**: Prefetches routes before user clicks.
- **Improved network-aware loading**: Loads assets based on connection speed.

Example of custom preloading strategy:

```
export class CustomPreload implements PreloadingStrategy {
  preload(route: Route, load: () => Observable<any>): Observable<any> {
    return route.data?.['preload'] ? load() : of(null);
  }
}
const routes: Routes = [
  { path: 'reports', loadChildren: () => import('./reports.module'), data: { preload: true
} }
];
```

Question 35: What changes were introduced in Angular 20 for standalone route configurations?

Answer: Angular 20 introduces several improvements to standalone route configurations, making routing more streamlined and efficient. The key enhancements include:

- **Fully standalone router modules**: Standalone components can now configure their own routing without requiring the **RouterModule**. This reduces module dependencies and simplifies the overall routing structure.
- **Automatic route composition**: Angular 20 makes it easier to nest standalone components within routes. Route definitions are more intuitive, allowing better organization and maintainability without additional configuration complexity.
- **Enhanced lazy loading support**: The lazy loading mechanism is further optimized to minimize bundle size, ensuring that only the required routes and components are loaded when needed. This leads to improved performance and reduced initial load time.

These updates make Angular's routing system more modular, efficient, and developer-friendly, especially for large-scale applications.

Example of standalone route definition in Angular 20:

```
const routes = [
  { path: '', component: HomeComponent },
  { path: 'dashboard', loadComponent: () => import('./dashboard.component').then(m =>
m.DashboardComponent) }
];
bootstrapApplication(AppComponent, {
  providers: [provideRouter(routes)]
});
```

Question 36: How does Angular 20 improve the handling of route animations?

Answer: Angular 20 introduces enhancements to route animations, making transitions smoother and more performance-efficient. The key improvements are as follows:

- **Route-specific animations**: Animations are now applied only when a route change occurs, reducing unnecessary re-rendering. Developers can define animations that trigger during navigation, improving the user experience.
- **Better performance with signals**: With the introduction of signal-based rendering, Angular 20 optimizes animations by reducing the re-render overhead. This ensures that animations are processed efficiently without affecting the application's performance.
- **Improved query parameter handling**: Query parameters are now better managed during route transitions, preventing abrupt visual changes and ensuring smooth animations when navigating between routes with different query parameters.

These improvements enhance the overall responsiveness of Angular applications by making route transitions more fluid and resource-efficient.

Example of route animation in Angular 20:

```
const slideAnimation = trigger('routeAnimations', [
  transition('* <=> *', [
    style({ opacity: 0 }),
    animate('300ms ease-in', style({ opacity: 1 }))
  ])
]);
@Component({
  animations: [slideAnimation],
  template: `<div @routeAnimations>Content Here</div>`
})
export class AnimatedComponent {}
```

Question 37: How do new signals in Angular 19+ enhance routing performance?

Answer: Angular 19+ introduces signal-based reactivity, significantly improving routing performance by optimizing how route-related data is managed. The key enhancements include:

- **Reactive route listeners**: Traditional route listeners often trigger unnecessary change detection cycles, leading to performance overhead. With signals, route listeners update reactively, ensuring that only relevant changes trigger updates. This eliminates unnecessary processing and improves efficiency.
- **Signal-based route parameters**: Instead of manually subscribing to **`ActivatedRoute`** parameters, Angular now allows developers to use signals for route params. This makes reactive programming more seamless, as components can automatically respond to parameter changes without the need for explicit subscriptions and unsubscriptions.
- **Efficient component re-renders**: With signals, Angular ensures that only the affected components re-render when route changes occur. This targeted update mechanism prevents unnecessary re-renders of unrelated components, reducing processing time and improving the overall responsiveness of applications.

By leveraging these signal-based enhancements, Angular 19+ optimizes routing performance, reducing memory usage and making applications more efficient and scalable.

For example: Using signals for route params in Angular 19+:

```
import { Component } from '@angular/core';
import { ActivatedRoute } from '@angular/router';
```

```
import { map } from 'rxjs/operators';
import { toSignal } from '@angular/core/rxjs-interop';
@Component({
  selector: 'app-profile',
  template: `<p>User ID: {{ userId() }}</p>`,
  standalone: true
})
export class ProfileComponent {
  userId = toSignal(
    this.route.paramMap.pipe(
      map(params => params.get('id'))
    )
  );
  constructor(private route: ActivatedRoute) {}
}
```

The explanation is as follows:

- **`toSignal()`** bridges RxJS and Angular signals, keeping your app reactive.
- This approach works well with:
    - ActivatedRoute.paramMap
    - queryParamMap
    - HTTP calls
    - Any other observable-based APIs

Error handling and performance optimization

Question 38: How do you handle route errors in Angular applications?

Answer: Handling route errors in Angular ensures a smooth user experience and prevents application crashes. Common strategies include:

- **Using a fallback route (404 Page)**: Redirects users to a custom error page when they navigate to an unknown route.

  For example:

  ```
  const routes: Routes = [
    { path: 'home', component: HomeComponent },
    { path: '**', component: NotFoundComponent } // Catch-all route
  ];
  ```

- **Using route guards (CanActivate)**: Prevents navigation to unauthorized or unavailable routes.

  For example:

  ```
  @Injectable({ providedIn: 'root' })
  export class AuthGuard implements CanActivate {
    constructor(private authService: AuthService, private router: Router) {}
    canActivate(): boolean {
      if (!this.authService.isLoggedIn()) {
  ```

```
        this.router.navigate(['/login']);
        return false;
      }
      return true;
    }
  }
```

- **Handling errors in route resolvers**: If a resolver fails (e.g., API call error), redirect or display an error message.

  For example:

```
  @Injectable({ providedIn: 'root' })
  export class DataResolver implements Resolve<any> {
    constructor(private dataService: DataService, private router: Router) {}
    resolve(): Observable<any> {
      return this.dataService.getData().pipe(
        catchError(() => {
          this.router.navigate(['/error']);
          return EMPTY;
        })
      );
    }
  }
```

- **Using ErrorHandler for global route errors**: Catches unexpected errors across all routes.

  For example:

```
  @Injectable()
  export class GlobalErrorHandler implements ErrorHandler {
    handleError(error: any): void {
      console.error('Route Error:', error);
      alert('Something went wrong!');
    }
  }
```

Question 39: **What is catchError in Angular routing, and how does it work?**

Answer: The **`catchError`** is an RxJS operator used to handle errors in observables. In Angular routing, it is commonly used in route resolvers and HTTP requests to ensure smooth application behavior, even when errors occur. The key points of **`catchError`** are as follows:

- **Prevents application crashes**: When an error occurs in an observable (such as a failed API call in a resolver), **`catchError`** intercepts it and prevents the error from propagating further. This ensures that the application does not crash due to unhandled exceptions.
- **Returns a fallback value**: Instead of allowing the error to break the app, **`catchError`** can return a default value. This helps maintain user experience by providing alternative content when the expected data is unavailable.
- **Navigates to an error page**: If necessary, **`catchError`** can trigger a redirection to an error-handling route, ensuring that users receive a clear message when something goes wrong instead of facing a blank or broken page.

For example: Handling errors in a route resolver:

```
@Injectable({ providedIn: 'root' })
export class UserResolver implements Resolve<any> {
  constructor(private userService: UserService, private router: Router) {}
  resolve(): Observable<any> {
    return this.userService.getUserData().pipe(
      catchError(error => {
        console.error('User data fetch failed:', error);
        this.router.navigate(['/error']);
        return of(null); // Return a fallback value
      })
    );
  }
}
```

The RxJS **catchError** is a powerful tool in Angular routing that enhances application stability by managing errors in observables. By returning fallback values or redirecting users to error pages, it ensures a smoother user experience even when unexpected issues arise.

Question 40: **What is route preloading, and how can it improve performance?**

Answer: Route preloading is a technique in Angular where lazy loaded modules are loaded in the background after the initial page load, reducing delays when users navigate to those routes.

The following are the performance benefits:

- **Faster navigation**: Preloads modules before they are needed.
- **Reduces perceived load time**: Users do not wait for route-dependent assets.
- **Optimized user experience**: Prevents visible lag when switching pages.

For example: Enabling preloading in Angular:

```
import { PreloadAllModules, provideRouter } from '@angular/router';
const routes: Routes = [
  { path: 'dashboard', loadChildren: () => import('./dashboard.module').then(m =>
m.DashboardModule) }
];
bootstrapApplication(AppComponent, {
  providers: [provideRouter(routes, { preloadingStrategy: PreloadAllModules })]
});
```

Question 41: **What are the different route preloading strategies available in Angular?**

Answer: Angular provides various preloading strategies to optimize module loading and improve application performance. These strategies determine how lazy loaded modules are fetched in the background. The strategies are as follows:

- **No preloading (default)**: Modules are only loaded when accessed. Also, there is no background fetching.
- **PreloadAllModules (eager preloading)**: Preloads all lazy loaded modules immediately after app boot.

  For example:

```
provideRouter(routes, { preloadingStrategy: PreloadAllModules })
```

- **Custom preloading strategy**: Preloads only selected modules based on conditions.

  For example:

```
export class CustomPreloadingStrategy implements PreloadingStrategy {
  preload(route: Route, load: () => Observable<any>): Observable<any> {
    return route.data?.['preload'] ? load() : of(null);
  }
}
const routes: Routes = [
  { path: 'reports', loadChildren: () => import('./reports.module'), data: { preload: true } }
];
```

Question 42: How does Angular handle 404 pages with routing?

Answer: Angular uses wildcard ('**') routes to handle unknown paths.

For example: Creating a 404 page:

```
const routes: Routes = [
  { path: 'home', component: HomeComponent },
  { path: '**', component: NotFoundComponent } // 404 page
];
```

Example of redirecting to a 404 page dynamically: Use **`ngOnInit()`** for navigation logic to avoid early side effects:

```
import {Component, OnInit} from '@angular/core';
import {Router} from '@angular/router';
@Component({
  selector: 'app-some-component',
  standalone: true,
  template: `Redirecting...`
})
export class SomeComponent implements OnInit {
  constructor(private router: Router) {}
  ngOnInit(): void {
    this.router.navigateByUrl('/not-found');
  }
}
```

Alternative (preferred for route protection): If redirection is based on access rules (e.g., auth check, invalid data), it is even better to handle it in a route guard:

```
import { CanActivateFn } from '@angular/router';
import { inject } from '@angular/core';
export const redirectIfInvalid: CanActivateFn = (route, state) => {
  const isValid = false; // replace with your logic
  const router = inject(Router);
  if (!isValid) {
```

```
    router.navigateByUrl('/not-found');
    return false;
  }
  return true;
};
```

Then use this guard in your route config:

```
{
  path: 'dashboard',
  canActivate: [redirectIfInvalid],
  component: DashboardComponent
}
```

Question 43: How can you optimize route transitions and animations in Angular?

Answer: To enhance user experience and improve performance, Angular provides several techniques to optimize route transitions and animations. The following strategies help to create smooth navigation while reducing unnecessary processing:

- **Use route-based animations**: Animates page transitions between routes for a better visual experience.

  For example:

  ```
  const slideAnimation = trigger('routeAnimations', [
    transition('* <=> *', [
      style({ opacity: 0 }),
      animate('300ms ease-in', style({ opacity: 1 }))
    ])
  ]);
  ```

- **Optimize lazy loading**: Load components only when needed and avoid loading unnecessary dependencies.
- **Minimize change detection**: Uses **`ChangeDetectionStrategy.OnPush`** to improve performance by reducing the number of change detection cycles.

  For example:

  ```
  @Component({
    changeDetection: ChangeDetectionStrategy.OnPush
  })
  ```

Question 44: What are the best practices for structuring routes in large Angular applications?

Answer: Properly structuring routes in large Angular applications improves maintainability, scalability, and performance. The following best practices ensure a well-organized and efficient routing system:

- **Use feature modules for scalability**: Keeps route definitions modular.

  For example:

  ```
  const routes: Routes = [
    { path: 'dashboard', loadChildren: () => import('./dashboard.module').then(m =>
  m.DashboardModule) }
  ];
  ```

- **Implement route guards for security**: Use **`CanActivate`** for access control.
- **Use a clear folder structure**: Shown as follows:

For example:

```
/app
  /core
  /features
    /dashboard
      - dashboard.module.ts
      - dashboard.routing.ts
```

- **Optimize for SEO**: Add **meta** tags dynamically.

  For example:

  ```
  constructor(private meta: Meta) {
    this.meta.updateTag({ name: 'description', content: 'Page description' });
  }
  ```

Question 45: How can you debug common routing issues in Angular?

Answer: Debugging routing issues in Angular requires a systematic approach to identify misconfigurations and errors. The following techniques help diagnose and resolve common problems effectively:

- **Enable Angular router debugging**: Logs routing events in the console for better visibility into navigation issues.

  For example:

  ```
  import { Router } from '@angular/router';
  constructor(private router: Router) {
    this.router.events.subscribe(event => console.log(event));
  }
  ```

- **Check pathMatch and redirectTo conflicts**: Ensures routes are defined in the correct order to avoid unexpected redirections.
- **Verify lazy loading module imports**: Ensures modules are correctly loaded in **loadChildren** to prevent navigation failures.
- **Use Chrome DevTools and Augury extension**: Helps visualize Angular's router state and detect configuration errors.
- **Check for duplicate router outlet usage**: Avoids multiple **<router-outlet>** elements in the same view, which can cause unexpected behavior.

Conclusion

In this chapter, we explored the fundamental and advanced concepts of Angular routing, covering everything from basic route configuration to lazy loading, route guards, and performance optimizations. We discussed best practices for structuring routes in large applications, debugging common routing issues, and leveraging Angular's latest features for improved navigation and animations. A well-structured routing strategy enhances user experience and application maintainability.

In the next chapter, we will explore Angular forms, exploring template-driven forms and reactive forms, form validation, handling user inputs, and best practices for managing form data efficiently.

Chapter 8
Concepts of Forms

Introduction

Forms are a fundamental part of web applications, allowing users to input and submit data. Angular provides a robust framework for handling forms efficiently with two primary approaches: Template-driven forms and reactive forms. Each approach has its advantages and is suited to different use cases.

This chapter explores the key concepts, structure, and best practices for working with forms in Angular. It provides insights into form validation, data binding, handling user input, and integrating forms with services.

Structure

This chapter covers the following topics:

- Basics of Angular forms
- Form validation and error handling
- Advanced form handling
- Forms enhancements with the latest versions
- Form submissions and API integration

Objectives

By the end of this chapter, readers will have a comprehensive understanding of the importance and implementation of forms in Angular applications. Readers will learn to distinguish between template-driven and reactive forms, implementing validation techniques to improve user experience. Additionally, the readers will gain the ability to handle user input dynamically using Angular form controls, integrate forms with backend services for seamless data submission, and apply best practices for efficient form management and error handling.

Basics of Angular forms

Question 1: What are forms in Angular, and why are they important?

Answer: Forms in Angular are used to handle user input, validation, and data submission. They allow users to interact with the application, enter data, and trigger events. The importance of forms is as follows:

- Enable structured data input from users.
- Support real-time validation to improve user experience.
- Bind user input directly to the component's model.
- Facilitate form submission and handling efficiently.

There are two main types of forms: template-driven forms and reactive forms.

Question 2: What is the difference between template-driven forms and reactive forms in Angular?

Answer: Template-driven forms use a declarative approach where form logic is written in HTML templates. They rely on directives like **ngModel** for data binding and are best suited for simple, static forms. Validation is handled using Angular directives as required.

Reactive forms take a programmatic approach using TypeScript code. They utilize **FormControl** and **FormGroup** to define form structures and manage state. The validators API provides robust validation, making it ideal for complex, dynamic forms requiring advanced logic and reactive behavior.

Question 3: How do you create a template-driven form in Angular?

Answer: Complete the following steps to create a template-driven form:

1. Import **FormsModule** in **app.module.ts**:
   ```
   import { NgModule } from '@angular/core';
   import { FormsModule } from '@angular/forms';
   @NgModule({
     imports: [FormsModule]
   })
   export class AppModule { }
   ```
2. Create an HTML form using **ngModel**:
   ```
   <form #userForm="ngForm">
     <input type="text" [(ngModel)]="user.name" name="name" required />
     <button type="submit" [disabled]="userForm.invalid">Submit</button>
   </form>
   ```
3. Define the model in the component:
   ```
   export class AppComponent {
     user = { name: '' };
   }
   ```

Question 4: How do you create a reactive form in Angular?

Answer: To create a reactive form, proceed with the steps as follows:

1. Import **ReactiveFormsModule**:
   ```
   import { ReactiveFormsModule } from '@angular/forms';
   @NgModule({
     imports: [ReactiveFormsModule]
   })
   export class AppModule { }
   ```

2. Create a form using **FormGroup**:

```
import { Component } from '@angular/core';
import { FormGroup, FormControl } from '@angular/forms';
@Component({
  selector: 'app-user-form',
  templateUrl: './user-form.component.html'
})
export class UserFormComponent {
  userForm = new FormGroup({
    name: new FormControl(''),
    email: new FormControl('')
  });
  submitForm() {
    console.log(this.userForm.value);
  }
}
```

3. Bind the form in HTML:

```
<form [formGroup]="userForm" (ngSubmit)="submitForm()">
  <input type="text" formControlName="name" />
  <input type="email" formControlName="email" />
  <button type="submit">Submit</button>
</form>
```

Question 5: What is FormGroup, and how is it used in reactive forms?

Answer: A **FormGroup** is a fundamental building block of Angular's reactive forms module. It is used to group multiple form controls (**FormControl**) together, allowing you to manage the form as a whole, track the state of multiple fields, and perform validation on groups of controls.

For example: To create a reactive form using **FormGroup**, complete the following steps:

1. **Use Angular FormGroup to create a reactive form**: In the component, create a **FormGroup** instance that contains multiple **FormControl** elements like name and email, shown as follows:

```
// Creating a FormGroup with multiple FormControls
userForm = new FormGroup({
  name: new FormControl('', [Validators.required, Validators.minLength(3)]),
  email: new FormControl('', [Validators.required, Validators.email])
});
```

2. **Access Angular form and retrieve form values**:

   this.userForm.value: Returns an object with the form's values.

   For example, **`console.log(this.userForm.value); //{ name: '', email: '' }`**

3. **Validate Angular form using FormGroup to track form state**:
   - **this.userForm.valid**: Returns true if all controls are valid.
   - **this.userForm.invalid**: Returns true if any control is invalid.
   - **this.userForm.touched**: Returns true if any control has been interacted with.

4. **Dynamically update reactive form values:**

```
this.userForm.patchValue({name:'Anil Singh'});
```

A **FormGroup** allows you to manage multiple form fields, track their state, and apply validation easily. It is an essential part of Angular's reactive forms for handling complex forms in a structured and scalable way.

Question 6: What is FormControl, and how does it work in Angular forms?

Answer: **FormControl** is an individual input control inside a **FormGroup**. It manages the state (value, validation, status) of a single form field.

Please refer to the example in *Answer 5*.

Question 7: What is FormArray, and when should it be used?

Answer: The **FormArray** is used when dealing with a dynamic list of form controls, such as multiple addresses or phone numbers. Consider the following example:

1. **Dynamically add form fields:**

```
// Creating a FormArray with multiple FormControls
addresses = new FormArray([
  new FormControl('Address 1'),
  new FormControl('Address 2')
]);
//Add Address method to add a new address
addAddress() {
  this.addresses.push(new FormControl('New Address here.'));
}
```

2. **Use and bind to the reactive form using addresses array object in the HTML from:**

```
<div *ngFor="let address of addresses.controls; let i = index">
  <input [formControl]="address" />
</div>
<button (click)="addAddress()">Add Address</button>
```

Question 8: How do you bind form inputs using ngModel in template-driven forms?

Answer: In template-driven forms, Angular provides the **[(ngModel)]** directive to enable two-way data binding between form inputs and component properties. This ensures that when a user updates the input field, the component's data model is automatically updated, and vice versa.

For example: Use the **[(ngModel)]** directive for two-way data binding, shown as follows:

1. **Use [(ngModel)] directive in the HTML control:**

```
<input type="text" [(ngModel)]="user.name" name="name" required />
```

2. **Create a component and define the model that will store form input values:**

```
export class AppComponent {
  //Data model bound to form inputs
  user ={name:'Anil Singh'};
}
```

The key features of **ngModel** in template-driven forms are as follows:

- **Two-way data binding:** Angular **[(ngModel)]** ensures synchronization between the UI and the component model. For example, if the user enters a name, **user.name** is updated automatically.
- **Binding with name attribute:** The name attribute is required for **ngModel** to work within a **<form>**.

- **Form validation**: Use required for mandatory fields and disable the submit button if fields are empty.
- **Reactive updates**: Any changes in the input field update the component model dynamically.

Question 9: What is the role of FormBuilder in Angular forms?

Answer: **`FormBuilder`** simplifies form creation in reactive forms by reducing boilerplate code.

For example: The code will look like the following without **`FormBuilder`**:

```
constructor(private fb: FormBuilder) {}
this.userForm = this.fb.group({
  name: [''],
  email: ['']
});
```

FormBuilder has the following benefits:

- Less code.
- Better readability.
- Easy dynamic form handling.

Question 10: How do you initialize form values dynamically in Angular Forms?

Answer: In Angular Forms, you can initialize form values dynamically in both reactive forms and template-driven forms.

In reactive forms, you can set initial values using the following:

- The **`FormControl`** constructor
- The **`setValue()`** method updating the entire form.
- The **`patchValue()`** method updating specific fields.

Consider the following example:

1. **Define the FormBuilder with initial values**:
   ```
   this.userForm = this.fb.group({
     name: ['Anil'],
     email: ['anil.singh@code-sample.com']
   });
   ```
2. **Use setValue() method to update form dynamically**:
   ```
   this.userForm.setValue({ name: 'Anil', email: 'anil.singh@code-sample.com' });
   ```
3. **Use patchValue() method to partially update**:
   ```
   this.userForm.patchValue({ name: 'Anil Singh' });
   ```
4. **Bind dynamic data in HTML inputs with the following code**:
   ```
   <input type="text" formControlName="name" />
   <input type="email" formControlName="email" />
   ```

Form validation and error handling

Question 11: What are the different types of form validation in Angular?

Answer: Angular supports the following three types of validation:

- Built-in validation (e.g., **`required`**, **`minLength`**, **`maxLength`**, **`pattern`**).
- Custom validation (user-defined functions to enforce specific rules).
- Asynchronous validation (validation using external services, like checking username availability).

Question 12: How do you implement built-in validators like required, minLength, and maxLength?

Answer: Built-in validators are provided by Angular's **`Validators`** class.

Example in reactive forms:

```
this.form = new FormGroup({
  username: new FormControl('', [Validators.required, Validators.minLength(3), Validators.
maxLength(10)])
});
```

Example in template-driven forms:

```
<input type="text" name="username" ngModel required minlength="3" maxlength="10">
```

Question 13: How do you create custom validators in Angular forms?

Answer: Custom validators are functions that return an error object or null.

For example:

```
function noSpecialChars(control: FormControl) {
  const forbidden = /[^a-zA-Z0-9]/.test(control.value);
  return forbidden ? { specialCharsNotAllowed: true } : null;
}
```

The following is an example of usage in reactive forms:

```
this.form = new FormGroup({
  username: new FormControl('', [noSpecialChars])
});
```

Question 14: What is ValidatorFn, and how is it used in Angular?

Answer: **`ValidatorFn`** is a function type for custom validators.

For example:

```
const noWhitespace: ValidatorFn = (control: AbstractControl) => {
  return control.value.includes(' ') ? { noWhitespace: true } : null;
};
this.form = new FormGroup({
  username: new FormControl('', [noWhitespace])
});
```

Question 15: How do you implement asynchronous validation in Angular forms?

Answer: Use **`AsyncValidatorFn`** for asynchronous validation.

For example:

```
function checkUsername(control: AbstractControl): Observable<ValidationErrors | null> {
  return timer(1000).pipe(
    map(() => control.value === 'admin' ? { usernameTaken: true } : null)
  );
}
this.form = new FormGroup({
  username: new FormControl('', [], checkUsername)
});
```

Question 16: How do you display validation messages dynamically?

Answer: To display validation messages dynamically, use Angular's **`*ngIf`** in the template, shown as follows:

```
<input formControlName="username">
<div *ngIf="form.controls.username.errors?.required">Username is required.</div>
<div *ngIf="form.controls.username.errors?.minlength">Too short.</div>
```

Here is a visual example showing how a validation message is displayed dynamically when the username field is left empty:

Username is required.

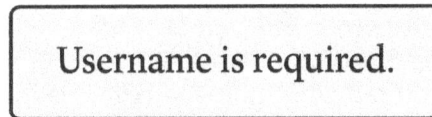

Figure 8.1: Dynamically display validation message

Question 17: What is updateOn in Angular forms, and how does it improve validation performance?

Answer: **`updateOn`** defines when validation is triggered (change, blur, submit).

For example:

```
this.form = new FormGroup({
  username: new FormControl('', { validators: [Validators.required], updateOn: 'blur' })
});
```

This improves performance by reducing validation checks on every keystroke.

Question 18: How do you disable form controls dynamically?

Answer: You can disable form controls as follows:

```
this.form.controls['username'].disable();
```

You can enable form controls as follows:

```
this.form.controls['username'].enable();
```

Question 19: How do you mark a form control as touched or dirty programmatically?

Answer: In Angular reactive forms, you can programmatically mark a form control as touched or dirty to trigger validation messages or UI updates.

The **`markAsTouched()`** method marks the control as touched, indicating that the user has interacted with it. This is useful for triggering validation messages. The **`markAsDirty()`** method marks the control as dirty, meaning the value has changed. This is useful for tracking modifications.

For example: Marking a form control as touched or dirty:

```
export class UserFormComponent {
  userForm = new FormGroup({
    username: new FormControl('', [Validators.required]),
    email: new FormControl('', [Validators.required, Validators.email])
  });
  markAsTouched() {
    this.userForm.controls['username'].markAsTouched();
    this.userForm.controls['email'].markAsTouched();
  }
  markAsDirty() {
```

```
        this.userForm.controls['username'].markAsDirty();
        this.userForm.controls['email'].markAsDirty();
    }
}
```

The **markAsTouched()** method is useful for triggering validation messages when a form is submitted without user interaction. The **markAsDirty()** method helps track modified fields for saving or confirming unsaved changes. By using these methods, you can improve user experience and validation workflows in Angular forms.

Question 20: How do you reset a form and clear validation errors in Angular?

Answer: In Angular reactive forms, you can reset a form and clear validation errors using the reset() method. This method restores all form controls to their initial state, clearing both values and validation statuses, shown as follows:

- **Resetting the form completely:** The **reset()** method resets all form fields to null or their default values while also clearing validation errors.

  For example, **this.form.reset();**

- **Resetting the form without clearing specific values:** If you want to reset the form but retain some default values, you can pass an object to **reset()**.

  For example, **this.form.reset({ username: 'default' });**

The **reset()** method ensures that all fields return to their original state and removes validation errors. If you need to keep certain values, pass an object with default values while calling **reset()**.

Advanced form handling

Question 21: What is the difference between patchValue() and setValue() in Angular forms?

Answer: In Angular reactive forms, both **setValue()** and **patchValue()** are used to update form values dynamically, but they behave differently, shown as follows:

- **setValue():** The **setValue()** method is strict, meaning it requires all form controls to be updated. If any control is missing from the object, Angular will throw an error.
- **patchValue():** The **patchValue()** method is flexible and allows updating only specific form controls. It does not require all controls to be included in the object.

Refer to the example in *Answer 10*, which uses both **setValue()** and **patchValue()** methods.

Question 22: How do you dynamically add and remove form controls in a reactive form?

Answer: To dynamically add and remove form controls in a reactive form, use **addControl()** and **removeControl()**, shown as follows:

```
this.form.addControl('email', new FormControl(''));
this.form.removeControl('email');
```

For dynamic forms, refer to the following code:

```
const control = new FormControl('');
(this.form.get('dynamicControls') as FormGroup).addControl('newField', control);
```

Question 23: How do you handle form arrays with dynamic input fields?

Answer: In Angular reactive forms, a **FormArray** is used to manage dynamic form controls, allowing users to add or remove input fields dynamically.

The steps to handle dynamic form arrays are as follows:

1. Use **FormArray** to store multiple **FormGroup** instances.
2. Add or remove controls dynamically using methods like **push()** and **removeAt()**.
3. Bind the form array in the template using ***ngFor**.

Consider the following example:

1. **Initializing FormArray, add item, and remove item:**

```
this.form = new FormGroup({
  items: new FormArray([])
});
//this method dynamically adds a new input field
addItem() {
  (this.form.get('items') as FormArray).push(new FormControl(''));
}
//this method removes an input field at the specified index
removeItem(index: number) {
  (this.form.get('items') as FormArray).removeAt(index);
}
```

2. **Bind the form array in the HTML template using *ngFor:**

```
<div formArrayName="items">
  <div *ngFor="let item of form.get('items').controls; let i = index">
    <input [formControlName]="i">
    <button (click)="removeItem(i)">Remove</button>
  </div>
</div>
<button (click)="addItem()">Add Item</button>
```

Using **FormArray**, you can efficiently manage dynamic form fields in Angular applications.

Question 24: How can you listen to form control value changes in Angular?

Answer: In Angular reactive forms, you can listen to value changes using the **valueChanges** observable. This allows you to track real-time updates when users interact with form fields. It can be done in the following manner:

- **Listening to a single form control's value changes**: To listen to changes for a specific form control, use **valueChanges** on that control:

```
this.form.get('name')?.valueChanges.subscribe(value => {
  console.log('New value:', value);
});
```

- **Listening to the entire form's value changes**: To track changes across the entire form, subscribe to **valueChanges** on the **FormGroup**:

```
this.form.valueChanges.subscribe(values => {
  console.log('Form values changed:', values);
});
```

The following are the key features of **valueChanges**:

- The **valueChanges** observable is triggered whenever a form control's value changes.

- Subscribing to **valueChanges** on a single control helps monitor specific fields.
- Subscribing at the form level helps track updates across all fields.

Using **valueChanges**, you can implement real-time validation, data tracking, and dynamic UI updates in Angular forms

Question 25: How do you handle nested form groups in Angular?

Answer: In Angular reactive forms, a **FormGroup** can contain other **FormGroup** instances, allowing you to structure complex forms with nested controls. This is useful for handling grouped data such as user profiles, addresses, or payment details.

The steps to handle nested form groups are as follows:

1. Create a parent **FormGroup** that contains a child **FormGroup**.
2. Define nested controls inside the child **FormGroup**.
3. Access nested controls using the **get()** method in the component or template.

Consider the following example:

1. **Create nested form groups for user and address:**

```
userForm = new FormGroup({
    name: new FormControl('', Validators.required),
    email: new FormControl('', [Validators.required, Validators.email]),
    address: new FormGroup({
      street: new FormControl('', Validators.required),
      city: new FormControl('', Validators.required),
      zip: new FormControl('', Validators.required)
    })
  });
```

2. **Accessing nested form controls in the component:**

```
this.userForm.get('address.street')?.value; // Gets street value
```

Question 26: What is statusChanges, and how does it help in form state tracking?

Answer: The **statusChanges** is an observable in Angular reactive forms that emits whenever the validation status of a form control, form group, or form array changes. It helps developers track the state of a form in real-time, making it easier to implement validation messages, enable and disable buttons, and take actions based on form validity.

The working of **statusChanges** is as follows:

- When a form control's validity status changes (e.g., from **VALID** to **INVALID** or vice versa), **statusChanges** emits a new status.
- It can be used at different levels:
    - **FormControl:** Tracks the status of an individual input field.
    - **FormGroup:** Tracks the overall status of multiple controls within the group.
    - **FormArray:** Tracks the status of a collection of form controls.

The observable emits one of the following values:

- **VALID:** The form/control has passed all validations.
- **INVALID:** The form/control has failed validation.
- **PENDING:** Async validation is in progress.
- **DISABLED:** The form/control is disabled and not validated.

Consider the following example:

- **Tracking statusChanges for a single FormControl:**

```
export class ExampleComponent {
  nameControl = new FormControl('');
  constructor() {
    this.nameControl.statusChanges.subscribe(status => {
      console.log('Name Control Status:', status);
    });
  }
}
```

- **Tracking statusChanges for a FormGroup:**

```
export class FormExampleComponent {
  userForm = new FormGroup({
    name: new FormControl('', Validators.required),
    email: new FormControl('', Validators.email)
  });
  constructor() {
    this.userForm.statusChanges.subscribe(status => {
      console.log('Form Status:', status);
    });
  }
}
```

The following are use cases of statusChanges:

- **Displaying validation messages in real-time:** Helps in dynamically updating UI elements based on validation status.
- **Disabling the submit button based on form status:**

```
<button [disabled]="userForm.invalid">Submit</button>
```

- **Logging validation status for debugging:** Useful for tracking validation issues in complex forms.
- **Triggering actions on status change:** Can be used to send a notification, enable or disable elements, or show alerts when the form becomes valid or invalid.

Question 27: How do you implement conditional validation in Angular forms?

Answer: Conditional validation in Angular forms allows developers to apply or remove validation rules dynamically based on specific conditions. This is useful when certain fields should only be required based on user input, selection, or other logic.

The following is the method for conditional validation:

- **Using setValidators() and updateValueAndValidity():** The `setValidators()` method is used to apply new validators dynamically, and `updateValueAndValidity()` ensures the form control updates accordingly.

  Consider the following example:

```
toggleValidation() {
  const ageControl = this.form.get('age');
```

```
    if (this.form.get('isAdult')?.value) {
      ageControl?.setValidators([Validators.required, Validators.min(18)]);
    } else {
      ageControl?.clearValidators();
    }
    ageControl?.updateValueAndValidity();
  }
```

The following are the use cases of conditional validation:

- **Dynamic required fields**: Based on a dropdown or checkbox selection.
- **Conditional email or phone validation**: If the user selects **Contact via Email**, require an email address.
- **Address fields based on shipping Option**: Require an address if **Home Delivery** is chosen.
- **Multi-step forms**: Apply validation rules based on step progression.

Question 28: **How can you submit a form programmatically in Angular?**

Answer: In Angular, you can submit a form programmatically by marking all fields as touched, validating the form, and handling the submission logic.

An example of programmatic form submission is as follows:

```
submitForm() {
  this.form.markAllAsTouched();
  if (this.form.valid) {
    console.log('Form Submitted:', this.form.value);
  }
}
```

The following are the steps for programmatic submission:

1. **markAllAsTouched()**: Marks all controls as touched to trigger validation messages.
2. **Check form.valid**: Ensures submission happens only if the form is valid.
3. **Submit the form data**: Handle form data (e.g., send it to an API).

Question 29: **How do you access form controls inside a component using @ViewChild?**

Answer: In template-driven forms, you can use **`@ViewChild`** to get a reference to the form inside a component. An example of accessing form controls with **`@ViewChild`** is as follows:

```
export class MyFormComponent implements AfterViewInit {
  @ViewChild('myForm') myForm!: NgForm;
  ngAfterViewInit() {
    console.log('Form Controls:', this.myForm.controls);
  }
}
```

The following is an explanation of the preceding **`@ViewChild`** example:

- **@ViewChild('myForm') myForm!: NgForm**: Captures the form reference using **`#myForm`** from the template.
- **ngAfterViewInit()**: Runs after the view is initialized, ensuring the form is accessible and logs the form controls (**`myForm.controls`**) to inspect values and validation.

Question 30: What are the best practices for handling large and complex forms in Angular?

Answer: When dealing with large and complex forms in Angular, performance and maintainability are crucial. Here are some best practices to ensure smooth form handling:

- **Use reactive forms for better control**: Reactive forms provide better scalability, testability, and flexibility compared to template-driven forms. They allow dynamic form control creation and validation.
- **Break down forms into multiple FormGroup components**: Instead of managing a massive form in a single component, divide it into smaller, manageable FormGroup sections and use nested forms.
- **Lazy load form modules when possible**: If the form is part of a feature module, consider lazy loading it to improve initial application load time.
- **Use async validation wisely to avoid unnecessary API calls**: Avoid excessive API calls by implementing debounce time in async validators and triggering them only when necessary.
- **Use debounceTime when listening to valueChanges**: When subscribing to `valueChanges`, use `debounceTime()` to reduce the number of updates and improve performance.
- **Optimize form rendering using trackBy in loops**: When rendering form controls dynamically in an `*ngFor` loop, use `trackBy` to minimize DOM updates and improve performance.

Forms enhancements with the latest versions

Question 31: What are the key improvements in Angular 18 related to Forms?

Answer: Angular 18 has introduced several enhancements to forms, including the following:

- **Improved form control performance**: Optimized internal handling of form updates for better efficiency.
- **Stronger type safety**: More accurate type inference for `FormGroup`, `FormControl`, and `FormArray`.
- **Enhanced form reset behavior**: Allows better control over resetting form states and values.
- **Built-in async validation enhancements**: Improved support for handling async validators without unnecessary re-evaluations.

Question 32: How does Angular 19 improve form validation and performance?

Answer: Angular 19 introduces several enhancements to form validation, improving both efficiency and usability, which include the following:

- **New updateOn enhancements**: Allows better control over when validation runs ('change', 'blur', 'submit').
- **Improved error handling**: More efficient error tracking in `FormGroup`.
- **Faster change detection**: Optimized internal structures to reduce the number of unnecessary validations.
- **Built-in validation summary API**: Provides an easier way to display all validation errors.

Consider an example. Developers have more control over when validation runs ('change', 'blur', 'submit'), reducing unnecessary validations and improving performance:

```
this.form = new FormGroup({
  email: new FormControl('', {
    validators: [Validators.required, Validators.email],
    updateOn: 'blur'
  })
});
```

Question 33: What new form APIs were introduced in Angular 19?

Answer: Angular 19 introduces several improvements to the forms API, enhancing flexibility, performance, and type safety. These updates help developers handle complex form scenarios more efficiently, shown as follows:

- **markAsPending()**: This method allows marking a form control as pending without immediately triggering validation, useful for handling async operations like server-side validation. This is also known as delayed validation triggering.
- **Enhanced hasError() for better error handling**: The `hasError()` method now offers more precise error checks with improved type inference, making validation logic cleaner and more reliable.
- **Improved FormBuilder API for flexible initialization**: The `FormBuilder` API now supports better default values and initialization options, simplifying form creation and reducing boilerplate code.
- **Stronger typed forms for safer development**: With improved TypeScript support, `FormGroup` and `FormArray` now ensure stricter type checking, reducing runtime errors and improving developer experience.

An example is given as follows:

```
export class AppComponent {
  userForm: FormGroup<{ email: FormControl<string> }>;
  constructor(private fb: FormBuilder) {
    this.userForm = this.fb.group({
      email: new FormControl('', {nonNullable: true, validators:   [Validators.required,
Validators.email] })
    });
  }
  submitForm() {
    this.userForm.get('email')?.markAsPending(); // Simulating async validation
    console.log('Form Submitted:', this.userForm.value);
  }
}
```

Question 34: How does Angular 20 improve reactive forms with better state management?

Answer: Angular 20 introduces the following enhancements to reactive forms, making state management more efficient and intuitive:

- **Signals integration for reactive state updates**: Forms can now leverage Angular signals, allowing more efficient and reactive state management without unnecessary change detection cycles.
- **Improved immutable form handling**: Angular 20 enhances support for immutable form states, making it easier to work with state management libraries like NgRx while preventing unintended mutations.
- **Optimized nested form updates**: When updating deeply nested form values, Angular now minimizes unnecessary re-renders, improving performance in complex forms.
- **FormStatusSignal for reactive status tracking**: A new API, `FormStatusSignal`, provides a reactive way to track form status (`VALID`, `INVALID`, `PENDING`), eliminating the need for manual subscriptions.
- **Better error management with typed forms**: Stronger TypeScript support ensures better error handling when working with `FormGroup`, reducing runtime issues and improving debugging.
- **Performance improvements for large forms**: Angular 20 introduces internal optimizations that make form validations and updates more efficient, especially in large-scale applications.

Consider the following example of Angular 20 reactive forms with improved state management:

```
import {Component, Signal, computed, signal} from '@angular/core';
import {FormBuilder, FormControl, FormGroup, Validators} from '@angular/forms';
export class AppComponent {
  userForm: FormGroup<{email: FormControl<string>; address: FormControl<string> }>;
  //Reactive Signals for Status Management
  formStatus: Signal<string>;
  constructor(private fb: FormBuilder) {
    this.userForm = this.fb.group({
      email: new FormControl('', { nonNullable: true, validators: [Validators.required, 
Validators.email] }),
      address: new FormControl('', { nonNullable: true })
    });
    //Using Signals to track form status reactively
    this.formStatus = toSignal(this.userForm.statusChanges,{initialValue: 'VALID' });
  }
  get emailControl() {
    return this.userForm.get('email') as FormControl;
  }
  submitForm() {
    this.userForm.markAsPending(); //Simulate async validation
    console.log('Form Submitted:', this.userForm.value);
  }
}
```

If you are using Angular signals, ensure your project is updated to Angular 20. This example demonstrates the following:

- Signals integration for reactive form updates
- Optimized nested form updates to reduce unnecessary re-renders
- Using **FormStatusSignal** for tracking form status
- Immutable form handling for better state management

Question 35: How does the new signals API in Angular 20 impact form handling?

Answer: The new signals API in Angular 20 impacts form handling in the following manner:

- **Reactive form status**: Forms can now use signals to update UI based on state changes efficiently.
- **Efficient change detection**: Signals prevent unnecessary re-renders in complex forms.
- **Better performance**: Reduces form re-evaluation cycles, improving large form performance.

For example: Using signals with forms:

```
import { signal, effect } from '@angular/core';
const email = signal('');
effect(() => console.log(email()));
this.form.get('email')?.valueChanges.subscribe(value => email.set(value));
```

Question 36: What are the recommended form handling strategies in Angular 20?

Answer: Angular 20 introduces powerful enhancements to form handling, making it more efficient, scalable, and easier to maintain. To effectively manage forms in modern Angular applications, developers should follow these best practices:

- **Use signals for state tracking**: Improves UI performance by reducing unnecessary re-renders.
- **Leverage updateOn**: Use `updateOn: 'blur'` or `updateOn: 'submit'` for better validation efficiency.
- **Avoid direct template access**: Use reactive forms instead of manually referencing DOM elements.
- **Lazy load form modules**: Reduces initial load time for complex forms.
- **Use trackBy for dynamic form fields**: Prevents unnecessary re-rendering of input fields.

Question 37: How does Angular 20 improve form change detection for large forms?

Answer: Managing large forms efficiently has always been a challenge, especially when handling frequent updates. Angular 20 introduces several optimizations to improve form change detection, ensuring better performance and responsiveness in complex applications, shown as follows:

- **Optimized dirty checking**: Angular 20 reduces unnecessary dirty or touched checks for better performance.
- **Form-level signals**: Allows selective UI updates when specific form controls change.
- **Improved event batching**: Groups multiple form updates together to prevent excessive re-renders.
- **Efficient async validators**: Reduces redundant API calls by tracking previous async validation requests.
- **Smarter markAsTouched() and markAsDirty() Behavior**: These methods now work more efficiently, ensuring only the necessary controls are marked without triggering unnecessary updates.

For example: Using signals for efficient form updates:

```
import {toSignal} from '@angular/core/rxjs-interop';
formState = toSignal(this.form.valueChanges, {
  initialValue: this.form.value
});
```

Form submissions and API integration

Question 38: How do you submit an Angular form and handle HTTP requests?

Answer: To submit an Angular form and handle an HTTP request, use Angular's `HttpClient` inside a service. Reactive forms make handling submissions more structured.

For example:

```
onSubmit() {
  if (this.form.valid) {
    this.http.post('https://api.example.com/submit', this.form.value).subscribe({
      next: (response) => console.log('Form submitted successfully', response),
      error: (error) => console.error('Error submitting form', error),
    });
  }
}
```

The best practice is to disable the submit button when the form is invalid to prevent unnecessary submissions. This can be done as follows:

```
<button [disabled]="form.invalid">Submit</button>
```

Question 39: How do you bind a reactive form to an API response?

Answer: Use **`patchValue()`** or **`setValue()`** to bind API data to form fields.

For example:

```
this.http.get('https://api.example.com/user/1').subscribe((data) => {
  this.form.patchValue({
    name: data.name,
    email: data.email,
  });
});
```

The best practice is to use **`patchValue()`** when updating a subset of form fields and **`setValue()`** when updating all fields.

Question 40: How do you prepopulate a form with data from an API?

Answer: Prepopulate the form by calling an API on component initialization and using **`patchValue()`**, shown as follows:

```
ngOnInit() {
  this.http.get<User>('https://api.example.com/user/1').subscribe(user => {
    this.form.patchValue(user);
  });
}
```

The best practice is to use a loading state (**`isLoading = true`**) to prevent user interaction until data is loaded.

Question 41: How do you handle errors returned from an API in Angular forms?

Answer: Use **`catchError`** to handle API errors and display validation messages dynamically.

For example:

```
this.http.post('https://api.example.com/submit', this.form.value).pipe(
  catchError((error: HttpErrorResponse) => {
    this.form.setErrors({ apiError: error.message });
    return throwError(() => error);
  })
).subscribe();
```

The best practice is to show error messages in the UI for a better user experience, shown as follows:

```
<div *ngIf="form.errors?.apiError">{{ form.errors.apiError }}</div>
```

Question 42: What is the role of asyncValidators in API-based validation?

Answer: Async validators allow form validation using API calls, such as checking if an email is already registered.

For example:

```
emailExistsValidator(control: AbstractControl) {
  return this.http.get(`https://api.example.com/check-email/${control.value}`).pipe(
    map(response => response.exists ? { emailTaken: true } : null),
    catchError(() => of(null))
  );
}
```

```
this.form = new FormGroup({
  email: new FormControl('', [Validators.required], [this.emailExistsValidator.bind(this)])
});
```

The best practice is to debounce API requests to avoid excessive calls.

Question 43: How do you optimize form submissions to prevent duplicate requests?

Answer: Preventing duplicate form submissions is crucial to ensure a smooth user experience and avoid unnecessary API calls. Angular provides several strategies to handle this effectively, which are outlined as follows:

- **Disable the submit button while submitting**: Prevents users from clicking the submit button multiple times while a request is in progress.
- **Use switchMap() to cancel previous requests**: The `switchMap()` operator in RxJS cancels any ongoing API request if a new one is triggered, ensuring only the latest submission is processed.
- **Throttle user input using debounceTime()**: Helps prevent rapid consecutive submissions by adding a delay before sending the request.

Consider the following example:

1. **Create a submit button method for disable**:

```
onSubmit() {
  if (this.form.valid) {
    this.isSubmitting = true;
    this.http.post('https://api.example.com/submit', this.form.value).subscribe({
      next: () => this.isSubmitting = false,
      error: () => this.isSubmitting = false
    });
  }
}
```

2. **Use the disabling button to prevent the user from clicking multiple times**:

```
<button [disabled]="isSubmitting">Submit</button>
```

Question 44: What are the security considerations when handling form submissions?

Answer: Ensuring security in form submissions is critical to protect user data and prevent common attacks. The key security best practices are as follows:

- **Use cross-site request forgery (CSRF) protection**: Implement CSRF tokens to prevent unauthorized form submissions from third-party sites.
- **Sanitize and escape user input**: Prevent XSS attacks by properly escaping or sanitizing user input before rendering it in the UI.
- **Implement rate limiting and bot protection**: Use CAPTCHAs or rate limiting to prevent automated bots from submitting forms repeatedly.
- **Secure API endpoints with authentication and authorization**: Ensure that API requests are authenticated and restrict access based on user roles.
- **Use HTTPS for secure data transmission**: Always transmit form data over HTTPS to prevent data interception (man-in-the-middle attacks).

Question 45: What are the best performance optimization techniques for Angular forms?

Answer: Optimizing Angular forms ensures better responsiveness, reduced lag, and a smooth user experience. The key techniques are outlined as follows:

- **Use updateOn: 'blur' or 'submit'**: This will reduce unnecessary validations, shown as follows:
```
new FormControl('', { validators: [Validators.required], updateOn: 'blur' });
```
- **Use trackBy in ngFor**: This optimizes rendering of dynamic forms, shown in the following code:
```
<div *ngFor="let field of formArray.controls; trackBy: trackByFn"></div>
```
- **Use signals for efficient state management**: Signals can be used in Angular 20+ as follows:
```
import { toSignal } from '@angular/core/rxjs-interop';
formStatus = toSignal(this.form.statusChanges, {
  initialValue: this.form.status
});
```
- **Lazy load forms**: Lazy loading reduces the initial bundle size.

Conclusion

This chapter provided a comprehensive understanding of Angular forms, covering essential topics such as reactive and template-driven forms, validation techniques, performance optimizations, security best practices, and the latest enhancements in Angular 20. By implementing these strategies, developers can create efficient, scalable, and secure form-based applications. Mastering Angular forms ensures better user experience, reduced performance overhead, and improved maintainability in modern web applications.

The next chapter will explore Angular's HTTP Client, a powerful module for making API calls and handling server interactions. We will cover key topics such as performing HTTP requests (GET, POST, PUT, DELETE), handling responses and errors, optimizing network performance with caching and interceptors, and using RxJS operators for better API management. Understanding these concepts will help in building robust, efficient, and secure data-driven applications.

CHAPTER 9
Concepts of HTTP Client

Introduction

In modern web applications, communication between the client and server plays a crucial role in data exchange. The HTTP Client is a fundamental component that facilitates this interaction by making HTTP requests and handling responses. Understanding the concepts of the HTTP Client is essential for building dynamic applications that rely on RESTful APIs, third-party services, and remote data sources.

This chapter covers the core principles of HTTP Client usage, focusing on how Angular provides a built-in HTTP Client module for seamless integration with APIs. Readers will learn how to make GET, POST, PUT, DELETE, and other HTTP requests efficiently while handling responses, errors, and performance optimizations.

Structure

This chapter covers the following topics:

- Basics of Angular HTTP Client
- Advanced Angular HTTP Client features
- Working with APIs and data handling
- HTTP Client enhancements in the latest version
- Performance optimization and security
- Advanced authentication and authorization

Objectives

By the end of this chapter, readers will have a comprehensive understanding of HTTP Client concepts in web applications. They will be able to efficiently utilize Angular's **`HttpClientModule`** for API interactions and perform various HTTP operations such as GET, POST, PUT, and DELETE. Additionally, they will learn to handle API responses and errors using observables while implementing request headers, authentication mechanisms, and interceptors. Readers will also gain practical knowledge on securing requests and working with HTTP interceptors in complex apps. Finally, they will be equipped with the best practices to apply in real-world Angular applications.

Basics of Angular HTTP Client

Question 1: What is the Angular HTTP Client, and why is it used?

Answer: The Angular **`HttpClient`** module is a built-in service for making HTTP requests to a backend server. It is used to communicate with the **Representational State Transfer Application Programming Interface** (**REST API**) for data retrieval, submission, and manipulation. The following are the key benefits of using the Angular HTTP Client:

- Provides built-in support for observables using RxJS.
- Handles JSON data automatically.
- Supports interceptors for request or response modification.
- Allows setting headers, query parameters, and error handling.

The following figure shows how Angular uses the HTTP client to make API calls and handle responses in a service-component setup:

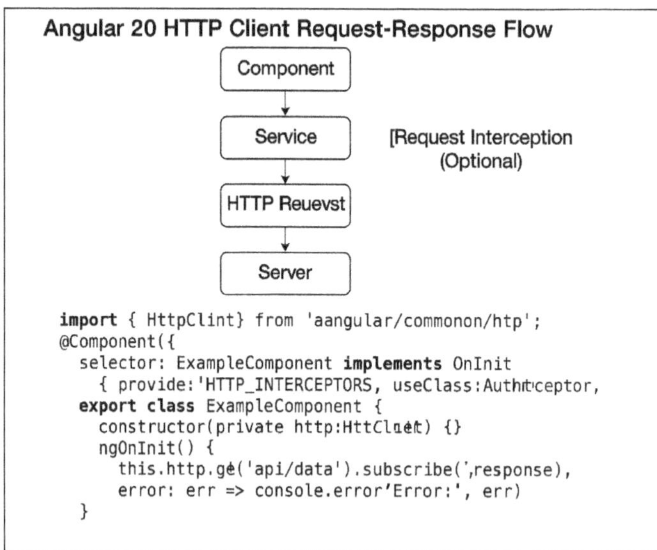

Figure 9.1: Angular HTTP client request-response flow

Question 2: How do you set up HTTP Client in an Angular application?

Answer: To use **`HttpClient`**, import **`HttpClientModule`** in **`app.module.ts`** or in a feature module. Consider the following example:

```
import { HttpClientModule } from '@angular/common/http';
@NgModule({
  imports: [HttpClientModule]
})
export class AppModule { }
```

Then, inject HttpClient in a service or component as follows:

```
import { HttpClient } from '@angular/common/http';
constructor(private http: HttpClient) {}
```

Question 3: How do you make a simple HTTP GET request using Angular HTTP Client?

Answer: Use **`http.get()`** to fetch data from an API. Consider the following example:

```
this.http.get<User[]>('https://api.example.com/users').subscribe(users => {
  console.log(users);
});
```

The best practice is to always unsubscribe when making requests inside a component to avoid memory leaks, shown as follows:

```
export class MyComponent implements OnInit, OnDestroy {
  subscription!: Subscription;
  constructor(private http: HttpClient) {}
  ngOnInit() {
    this.subscription = this.http.get('/api/data').subscribe(data => {
      // handle response
    });
  }
  ngOnDestroy() {
    this.subscription.unsubscribe();
  }
}
```

This ensures that the subscription is properly cleaned up when the component is destroyed, preventing potential memory leaks.

Question 4: How do you make a POST request using Angular HTTP Client?

Answer: Use `http.post()` to send data to an API. Consider the following example:

```
const user = { name: 'anil', email: 'anil.singh@code-sample.com' };
this.http.post('https://api.example.com/users', user).subscribe(response => {
  console.log('User created:', response);
});
```

The best practice is to use headers to send content-type information when required, as follows:

```
const headers = new HttpHeaders({ 'Content-Type': 'application/json' });
this.http.post(url, body, { headers }).subscribe();
```

Question 5: What is the difference between GET, POST, PUT, and DELETE requests in Angular HTTP Client?

Answer: In Angular, the `HttpClient` module is used to make HTTP requests. The difference between GET, POST, PUT, and DELETE requests in Angular's `HttpClient` is as follows:

- **GET request:**
    - Used to retrieve data from the server.
    - Does not modify any resources.
    - Typically used for fetching data like lists, details, etc.

  An example of GET is as follows:

  ```
  this.http.get('https://api.example.com/items').subscribe(response => {
    console.log(response);
  });
  ```

- **POST request:**
    - Used to send data to the server to create a new resource.

- Sends data in the request body.
- The response usually contains the newly created resource.

An example of POST is as follows:

```
const newItem = { name: 'New Item', price: 100 };
this.http.post('https://api.example.com/items', newItem).subscribe(response => {
  console.log(response);
});
```

- **PUT request**:
  - Used to update an existing resource on the server.
  - Sends the entire updated object in the request body.
  - If the resource does not exist, it may create a new one (depends on the API implementation).

An example of PUT is as follows:

```
const updatedItem = { id: 1, name: 'Updated Item', price: 150 };
this.http.put('https://api.example.com/items/1', updatedItem).subscribe(response => {
  console.log(response);
});
```

- **DELETE request**
  - Used to remove a resource from the server.
  - Generally, it does not send a body, only the resource identifier in the URL.

An example of DELETE is as follows:

```
this.http.delete('https://api.example.com/items/1').subscribe(response => {
  console.log(response);
});
```

Question 6: How do you send request headers in Angular HTTP Client?

Answer: Use `HttpHeaders` to send custom headers.

For example:

```
const headers = new HttpHeaders({
  'Authorization': 'Bearer my-token',
  'Custom-Header': 'value'
});
this.http.get('https://api.example.com/data', { headers }).subscribe();
```

The best practice is to use HTTP interceptors for setting headers globally.

Question 7: How do you send query parameters in an HTTP request?

Answer: Use `HttpParams` to add query parameters dynamically. Consider an example:

```
const params = new HttpParams().set('page', '1').set('limit', '10');
this.http.get('https://api.example.com/users', { params }).subscribe();
```

The alternative is to append multiple parameters dynamically as follows:

```
const params = new HttpParams({ fromObject: { page: '1', limit: '10' } });
```

Question 8: What is the HttpHeaders class, and how is it used?

Answer: `HttpHeaders` is used to define custom headers in HTTP requests. Consider the following example:

```
const headers = new HttpHeaders({
```

```
  'Authorization': 'Bearer my-token',
  'Content-Type': 'application/json'
});
this.http.get('https://api.example.com/users', { headers }).subscribe();
```

It offers the following key benefits:

- Allows immutable headers (modifications create a new instance).
- Helps enforce security and authentication.

Question 9: How do you handle response types in Angular HTTP Client?

Answer: Use the **`responseType`** option to specify the expected response format. Consider the following example:

```
this.http.get('https://api.example.com/file', { responseType: 'blob' }).subscribe(file => {
  console.log(file);
});
```

The common response types are as follows:

- **'json' (default)**: Parses response as JSON.
- **'text'**: Treats response as a plain string.
- **'blob'**: Used for binary data like images.

Question 10: What is the purpose of the observe option in HTTP requests?

Answer: The observe option allows accessing the full HTTP response, including headers and status codes. Consider the following example:

```
this.http.get('https://api.example.com/users', { observe: 'response' }).subscribe(response
=> {
  console.log(response.headers.get('Content-Length'));  // Access headers
  console.log(response.body);  // Access data
});
```

It has the following use cases:

- Fetching headers or status codes.
- Handling paginated responses with headers like X-total-count.

Advanced HTTP Client features

Question 11: What is the difference between HttpClientModule and HttpClient?

Answer: **`HttpClientModule`** and **`HttpClient`** are both part of Angular's HTTP communication mechanism, but they serve different purposes, shown as follows:

- **HttpClientModule**: This is an Angular module that needs to be imported in the root module (or any feature module) to enable HTTP functionalities. It provides the necessary configuration for making HTTP requests in Angular applications.

  For example:

  ```
  import { HttpClientModule } from '@angular/common/http';
  @NgModule({
    imports: [HttpClientModule],
  })
  export class AppModule {}
  ```

- **HttpClient**: This is a service provided by Angular that allows making HTTP requests (GET, POST, PUT, DELETE, etc.). It is used in components or services to interact with REST APIs.

  For example:

  ```
  import { HttpClient } from '@angular/common/http';
  constructor(private http: HttpClient) {}
  this.http.get('https://api.example.com/data').subscribe(data => console.log(data));
  ```

Thus, **`HttpClientModule`** enables HTTP functionality in an Angular app, while **`HttpClient`** is the service used to perform actual HTTP requests.

Question 12: How do you handle HTTP errors in Angular?

Answer: You can handle HTTP errors using the **`catchError`** operator from RxJS in an Angular service. Consider the following example:

```
import { HttpClient, HttpErrorResponse } from '@angular/common/http';
import { catchError } from 'rxjs/operators';
import { throwError } from 'rxjs';
constructor(private http: HttpClient) {}
getData() {
  return this.http.get('https://api.example.com/data').pipe(
    catchError(this.handleError)
  );
}
private handleError(error: HttpErrorResponse) {
  let errorMessage = 'Unknown error!';
  if (error.error instanceof ErrorEvent) {
    errorMessage = `Client-side error: ${error.error.message}`;
  } else {
    errorMessage = `Server-side error: ${error.status} - ${error.message}`;
  }
  return throwError(() => new Error(errorMessage));
}
```

Question 13: What is the catchError operator in RxJS, and how is it used in HTTP requests?

Answer: The **`catchError`** operator in RxJS is used to handle errors in an observable stream. It allows catching HTTP errors and returning a fallback value or throwing a custom error. In Angular, **`catchError`** is commonly used with **`HttpClient`** to manage HTTP request failures gracefully. Consider the following example of handling HTTP errors in an API call:

```
import {HttpClient} from '@angular/common/http';
import {catchError} from 'rxjs/operators';
import {throwError, Observable} from 'rxjs';
constructor(private http: HttpClient) { }
getData(): Observable<any> {
  return this.http.get('https://api.example.com/data').pipe(
    catchError(error => {
      console.error('Error occurred:', error);
      return throwError(() => new Error('Something went wrong, please try again.'));
    })
```

```
  );
}
```

This ensures that any error encountered during the API call is handled properly instead of breaking the application.

Question 14: How do you retry failed HTTP requests in Angular?

Answer: Use the **retry** operator from RxJS to automatically retry failed HTTP requests.

For example:

```
import { retry } from 'rxjs/operators';
this.http.get('https://api.example.com/data').pipe(
  retry(3) // Retries the request up to 3 times before failing
).subscribe();
```

Question 15: What is an interceptor, and how does it work with HTTP requests?

Answer: An interceptor is a service that intercepts HTTP requests or responses globally. It is used for logging, authentication, request modification, etc.

For example:

1. **Create an HTTP interceptor:**

   ```
   import { HttpInterceptor, HttpRequest, HttpHandler, HttpEvent } from '@angular/
   common/http';
   import { Observable } from 'rxjs';
   export class AuthInterceptor implements HttpInterceptor {
     intercept(req: HttpRequest<any>, next: HttpHandler): Observable<HttpEvent<any>> {
       console.log('Request intercepted:', req);
       return next.handle(req);
     }
   }
   ```

2. **Register the interceptor in the provider's array:**

   ```
   import { HTTP_INTERCEPTORS } from '@angular/common/http';
   providers: [
     { provide: HTTP_INTERCEPTORS, useClass: AuthInterceptor, multi: true }
   ]
   ```

Question 16: How do you add an authentication token to all outgoing HTTP requests?

Answer: Use an interceptor to automatically append the token to each request.

For example:

```
export class AuthInterceptor implements HttpInterceptor {
  intercept(req: HttpRequest<any>, next: HttpHandler): Observable<HttpEvent<any>> {
    const token = 'your-auth-token';
    const clonedReq = req.clone({
      setHeaders: { Authorization: `Bearer ${token}` }
    });
    return next.handle(clonedReq);
  }
}
```

Question 17: What is HttpParams, and how do you use it for sending multiple parameters?

Answer: `HttpParams` is used to send query parameters in an HTTP request.

For example:

```
import { HttpParams } from '@angular/common/http';
const params = new HttpParams()
  .set('page', '1')
  .set('size', '10');
this.http.get('https://api.example.com/data', { params }).subscribe();
```

Question 18: How do you cancel an HTTP request in Angular?

Answer: Use the `AbortController` in the latest versions of Angular.

For example:

```
const controller = new AbortController();
this.http.get('https://api.example.com/data', { signal: controller.signal })
  .subscribe();
setTimeout(() => {
  controller.abort(); // Cancels the request
  console.log('Request canceled');
}, 2000);
```

Question 19: How do you handle request timeouts in Angular HTTP Client?

Answer: Use the `timeout` operator from RxJS.

For example:

```
import { timeout, catchError } from 'rxjs/operators';
import { throwError } from 'rxjs';
this.http.get('https://api.example.com/data').pipe(
  timeout(5000), // Request fails if it takes more than 5 seconds
  catchError(error => throwError(() => new Error('Request timed out')))
).subscribe();
```

Question 20: What is the difference between map() and tap() in Angular HTTP requests?

Answer: In Angular, the `map()` and `tap()` operators are used with observables to process data from HTTP requests. While both can interact with the response, they serve different purposes, shown as follows:

- **map():** Transforms the response data before passing it to the next operator or subscriber. It is used when you need to modify the API response.
- **tap():** Performs a side effect (such as logging or debugging) without modifying the response data. It is mainly used for debugging purposes.

For example:

```
import { map, tap } from 'rxjs/operators';
this.http.get('https://api.example.com/data').pipe(
  tap(data => console.log('Original data:', data)), // Logs data without modifying it
  map(data => (data as any[]).filter(item => item.active)) // Transforms data
).subscribe(filteredData => console.log('Filtered data:', filteredData));
```

Working with APIs and data handling

Question 21: How do you consume a REST API in Angular?

Answer: Use the **HttpClient** service to make API calls.

For example:

```
import { HttpClient } from '@angular/common/http';
import { Component, OnInit } from '@angular/core';
@Component({
  selector: 'app-example',
  templateUrl: './example.component.html',
})
export class ExampleComponent implements OnInit {
  constructor(private http: HttpClient) {}
  ngOnInit() {
    this.http.get('https://api.example.com/data').subscribe(data => {
      console.log(data);
    });
  }
}
```

Question 22: How do you send form data using HTTP Client?

Answer: Use **FormData** to send multipart or form-data content.

For example:

```
const formData = new FormData();
formData.append('name', 'John Doe');
formData.append('file', selectedFile);
this.http.post('https://api.example.com/upload', formData).subscribe();
```

Question 23: How do you send JSON data in an HTTP POST request?

Answer: Use **HttpClient.post** with a JSON object and appropriate headers.

For example:

```
const data = { name: 'Anil Singh', age: 35 };
this.http.post('https://api.example.com/users', data, {
  headers: { 'Content-Type': 'application/json' }
}).subscribe();
```

Question 24: How do you fetch and display data from an API in an Angular component?

Answer: Use a service to fetch data and bind it in the component template.

An example of service is as follows:

```
import { HttpClient } from '@angular/common/http';
import { Injectable } from '@angular/core';
@Injectable({ providedIn: 'root' })
export class DataService {
  constructor(private http: HttpClient) {}
  getData() {
```

```
    return this.http.get<any[]>('https://api.example.com/data');
  }
}
```

An example of component is as follows:

```
import { Component, OnInit } from '@angular/core';
import { DataService } from '../services/data.service';
@Component({
  selector: 'app-data-list',
  template: `<ul><li *ngFor="let item of data">{{ item.name }}</li></ul>`,
})
export class DataListComponent implements OnInit {
  data: any[] = [];
  constructor(private dataService: DataService) {}
  ngOnInit() {
    this.dataService.getData().subscribe(res => this.data = res);
  }
}
```

Question 25: How do you implement pagination using HTTP requests?

Answer: Use query parameters to request data for specific pages.

For example:

```
const page = 1;
const size = 10;
this.http.get(`https://api.example.com/data?page=${page}&size=${size}`).subscribe();
```

Question 26: How do you implement infinite scrolling using HTTP Client?

Answer: Use a scroll event to load additional data as the user scrolls.

For example:

```
import { Component, HostListener } from '@angular/core';
import { HttpClient } from '@angular/common/http';
@Component({
  selector: 'app-infinite-scroll',
  template: `<div *ngFor="let item of data">{{ item.name }}</div>`,
})
export class InfiniteScrollComponent {
  data: any[] = [];
  page = 1;
  constructor(private http: HttpClient) {
    this.loadMore();
  }
  @HostListener('window:scroll', [])
  onScroll() {
    if (window.innerHeight + window.scrollY >= document.body.offsetHeight) {
      this.loadMore();
    }
```

```
  }
  loadMore() {
    this.http.get<any[]>(`https://api.example.com/data?page=${this.page++}`)
      .subscribe(res => this.data.push(...res));
  }
}
```

Question 27: How do you handle file uploads using Angular HTTP Client?

Answer: Use **`FormData`** to append the file and send it via POST.

For example:

```
const formData = new FormData();
formData.append('file', selectedFile);
this.http.post('https://api.example.com/upload', formData).subscribe();
```

Question 28: How do you download a file from a server using HTTP Client?

Answer: Use **`responseType: 'blob'`** to receive binary data or download a file.

For example:

```
this.http.get('https://api.example.com/file', { responseType: 'blob' })
  .subscribe(blob => {
    const url = window.URL.createObjectURL(blob);
    const a = document.createElement('a');
    a.href = url;
    a.download = 'filename.pdf';
    a.click();
    window.URL.revokeObjectURL(url);
  });
```

Question 29: How do you work with Blob and ArrayBuffer response types in Angular?

Answer: Use **`responseType: 'blob'`** for binary files and **`responseType: 'arraybuffer'`** for raw data.

An example of blob is as follows:

```
this.http.get('https://api.example.com/image', { responseType: 'blob' })
  .subscribe(blob => {
    const url = URL.createObjectURL(blob);
    window.open(url);
  });
```

An **`ArrayBuffer`** example is as follows:

```
this.http.get('https://api.example.com/data', { responseType: 'arraybuffer' })
  .subscribe(buffer => {
    console.log(new Uint8Array(buffer));
  });
```

Question 30: How do you handle multiple API calls efficiently in Angular?

Answer: In Angular, handling multiple API calls efficiently ensures better performance and a seamless user experience. This can be achieved using RxJS operators like **`forkJoin`**, **`mergeMap`**, and **`combineLatest`**, depending on the requirement.

The following examples show the use of **`forkJoin`**, **`mergeMap`**, and **`combineLatest`** from RxJS:

- **Example of using forkJoin (waits for all calls to complete):**

```
import { forkJoin } from 'rxjs';
forkJoin([
  this.http.get('https://api.example.com/users'),
  this.http.get('https://api.example.com/orders')
]).subscribe(([users, orders]) => {
  console.log(users, orders);
});
```

- **Example of using mergeMap (executes sequentially, dependent calls):**

```
import { mergeMap } from 'rxjs';
this.http.get('https://api.example.com/users/1').pipe(
  mergeMap(user => this.http.get(`https://api.example.com/orders/${user.id}`))
).subscribe(orderDetails => {
  console.log(orderDetails);
});
```

- **Example of using combineLatest (handles real-time changes together):**

```
import { combineLatest } from 'rxjs';
combineLatest([
  this.http.get('https://api.example.com/stocks'),
  this.http.get('https://api.example.com/currency-rates')
]).subscribe(([stocks, rates]) => {
  console.log(stocks, rates);
});
```

HTTP Client enhancements in the latest version

Question 31: What improvements were made to the Angular HTTP Client in Angular 18?

Answer: In Angular 18, a significant change was the deprecation of **`HttpClientModule`**. Developers are now encouraged to use the **`provideHttpClient()`** function for configuring HTTP services. This shift aims to streamline HTTP client configuration and promote a more modular approach.

Question 32: How does Angular 19 optimize HTTP requests?

Answer: Angular 19 introduced several features to enhance performance, indirectly benefiting HTTP requests as follows:

- **Incremental hydration:** This feature improves SSR by allowing faster initial page loads and smoother interactions. While not directly related to HTTP requests, it enhances the overall performance of applications that rely on HTTP data fetching.
- **Route-level render modes:** Developers can specify rendering strategies (server-side, client-side, or pre-rendered) for each route, optimizing how and when HTTP requests are made during the rendering process.

Question 33: What new HTTP Client features were introduced in Angular 19?

Answer: While Angular 19 focused on performance and rendering enhancements, there were no specific new features added directly to the HTTP Client. However, the introduction of the resource function allows developers to define data dependencies with automatic state management, which can be used alongside native **`fetch()`** for data retrieval.

Question 34: How does Angular 20 improve request cancellation and error handling?

Answer: As of now, Angular 20 has not been officially released, and specific details about improvements in request cancellation and error handling are not available. Developers are encouraged to follow Angular's official channels for updates on upcoming features.

Question 35: How does the new signals API in Angular 20 impact HTTP Client usage?

Answer: The signals API is an experimental feature introduced in Angular 19, providing reactive primitives for state management. While it offers a new way to handle reactivity, its direct impact on HTTP Client usage is still under exploration. Developers should monitor official Angular communications for guidance on integrating signals with HTTP operations.

Question 36: What are the best practices for HTTP request performance optimization in Angular 20?

Answer: In the context of Angular 19, best practices for optimizing HTTP request performance include the following:

- **Using incremental hydration**: Enhances SSR applications by improving load times and interactivity.
- **Implementing route-level render modes**: Allows fine-grained control over rendering strategies, optimizing when and how HTTP requests are made.
- **Leveraging the resource function**: Manages data dependencies efficiently, ensuring that HTTP requests are made only when necessary.

These practices aim to reduce unnecessary HTTP requests and improve application responsiveness.

Question 37: How does Angular 20 handle automatic request retries?

Answer: Specific details about automatic request retries in Angular 20 are not available, as the version has not been officially released. In Angular 19 and earlier versions, developers can implement automatic retries using RxJS operators like `retry` and `retryWhen` in combination with the HTTP Client.

Performance optimization and security

Question 38: How do you improve the performance of HTTP requests in Angular?

Answer: To optimize HTTP requests in Angular, follow these best practices:

- **Use caching**: Avoid making unnecessary requests by caching data.
- **Minimize API calls**: Use RxJS operators like `debounceTime()` and `distinctUntilChanged()`.
- **Lazy load modules**: Load modules and data only when needed.
- **Use pagination and infinite scrolling**: Reduce payload size.
- **Enable compression**: Gzip responses from the server.
- **Batch requests**: Use `forkJoin()`, `mergeMap()` or `combineLatest()` to make parallel calls (from RxJS).
- **Use signals (Angular 16+)**: Improve reactivity and performance.

Question 39: What are the best practices for caching HTTP requests?

Answer: Caching HTTP requests improves performance by reducing redundant network calls. Here are some best practices for implementing caching effectively in Angular:

- **Validate input on both client and server**: Never rely solely on client-side validation; always validate and sanitize input on the server to prevent malicious data injection.
- **Use HTTP interceptors**: Implement an interceptor to cache GET requests and serve cached responses when available.
- **Leverage RxJS shareReplay**: Use the `shareReplay` operator to cache and share API responses across multiple subscribers.
- **Set cache expiry**: Define an expiration time for cached data to ensure freshness.

- **Use local storage or session storage**: Store frequently accessed data in **localStorage** or **sessionStorage** for persistence.
- **Invalidate cache on data change**: Clear or update the cache when the data is modified to prevent stale responses.
- **Use service-level caching**: Store API responses in a service variable for short-term caching within a session.

The following are some examples:

- Use RxJS **shareReplay()** as follows:

  ```
  this.http.get('https://api.example.com/data')
    .pipe(shareReplay(1)) // Caches the latest value
    .subscribe();
  ```

- Use Angular's service for caching by running the following code:

  ```
  private cache = new Map<string, any>();
  getData(): Observable<any> {
    if (this.cache.has('data')) {
      return of(this.cache.get('data'));
    }
    return this.http.get('https://api.example.com/data').pipe(
      tap(data => this.cache.set('data', data))
    );
  }
  ```

- Use HTTP Interceptors to cache requests.
- Use browser storage (**LocalStorage**, **IndexedDB**).

Question 40: How do you implement request debouncing in Angular?

Answer: Use **debounceTime()** to limit API calls when users type in search fields.

For example:

```
searchControl.valueChanges.pipe(
  debounceTime(500),
  distinctUntilChanged(),
  switchMap(value => this.http.get(`https://api.example.com/search?q=${value}`))
).subscribe();
```

Question 41: How do you prevent duplicate API calls in Angular applications?

Answer: To optimize performance and avoid unnecessary network requests, Angular provides RxJS operators that help prevent duplicate API calls, shown as follows:

- Use **switchMap()** to cancel previous requests.
- Use **take(1)** to ensure only one request is made.

The following examples help to prevent duplicate API calls in Angular:

- **Example of using switchMap() (cancels previous requests)**:

  ```
  searchSubject.pipe(
    debounceTime(300),
    switchMap(query => this.http.get(`https://api.example.com/users?search=${query}`))
  ).subscribe(response => console.log(response));
  ```

- **Example of using take(1) (ensures only one request):**
```
this.http.get('https://api.example.com/user/1')
  .pipe(take(1))
  .subscribe(response => console.log(response));
```

Question 42: How do you secure API requests in an Angular application?

Answer: To protect API requests and prevent unauthorized access, follow these best practices:

- **Use HTTPS**: Secure communication using **Secure Sockets Layer** (**SSL**).
- **Add authentication tokens**: Use **JSON Web Token** (**JWT**) or OAuth to authenticate API requests..
- **Use cross-origin resource sharing (CORS) properly**: Restrict allowed origins.
- **Sanitize user inputs**: Prevent SQL and XSS attacks.
- **Avoid storing secrets in frontend**: Never store API keys, authentication tokens, or sensitive data in client-side code or local storage.
- **Use security headers**: Implement **Content Security Policy** (**CSP**), **HTTP Strict Transport Security** (**HSTS**), and X-Frame-Options.

Question 43: How do you refresh an authentication token using an HTTP interceptor?

Answer: In Angular applications, authentication tokens (e.g., JWT) expire after a certain period. To ensure continuous user access without requiring re-login, we implement token refreshing using an HTTP Interceptor. This allows us to intercept 401 Unauthorized errors, request a new token, and retry failed requests automatically.

The process works as follows:

1. The user makes an API request.
2. If the token is valid, the request proceeds normally.
3. If the token has expired (401 error):
    a. The interceptor pauses all requests.
    b. It requests a new token from the refresh endpoint.
    c. Once received, it retries the original request.
4. If the refresh token also fails, the user is logged out.

For example:
```
@Injectable()
export class AuthInterceptor implements HttpInterceptor {
  constructor(private authService: AuthService) {}
  intercept(req: HttpRequest<any>, next: HttpHandler) {
    const token = this.authService.getToken();
    let authReq = req;
    if (token) {
      authReq = req.clone({
        setHeaders: { Authorization: `Bearer ${token}` }
      });
    }
    return next.handle(authReq).pipe(
      catchError(error => {
        if (error.status === 401) {
          return this.authService.refreshToken().pipe(
```

```
          switchMap(newToken => {
            const newReq = req.clone({
              setHeaders: { Authorization: `Bearer ${newToken}` }
            });
            return next.handle(newReq);
          })
        );
      }
      return throwError(() => error);
    })
  );
 }
}
```

The benefits of using an interceptor for token refresh are as follows:

- **Automatic token management**: Users do not need to log in repeatedly.
- **Prevents duplicate requests**: Ensures only one refresh request is sent.
- **Cleaner code**: Avoids adding token logic in every API request.

Question 44: What are the security risks of HTTP requests in Angular, and how can you mitigate them?

Answer: When making HTTP requests in Angular applications, several of the following security risks must be addressed to prevent attacks and data breaches.

- **Cross-site scripting (XSS)**: Attackers can inject malicious scripts into web pages. Use Angular's built-in `DomSanitizer` to prevent this.
- **CSRF**: Unauthorized requests can be sent from an authenticated user. Mitigate this by using CSRF tokens from the backend.
- **Man-in-the-middle (MITM) attacks**: Attackers can intercept HTTP requests. Always use HTTPS and apply secure headers to prevent this.
- **Insecure JWT storage**: Storing tokens in `LocalStorage` makes them vulnerable to XSS attacks. Instead, store JWT tokens in `HttpOnly` cookies for better security.
- **CORS exploits**: Improperly configured CORS can expose your API to unauthorized origins. Always restrict API access to trusted origins.

Implementing the preceding security measures allows you to significantly reduce the risks associated with HTTP requests in Angular applications.

Question 45: How do you test HTTP Client requests in Angular?

Answer: Use `HttpTestingController` from Angular's testing module.

Conduct unit testing with `HttpClient` as follows:

```
import { HttpClientTestingModule, HttpTestingController } from '@angular/common/http/
testing';
describe('MyService', () => {
  let service: MyService;
  let httpMock: HttpTestingController;
  beforeEach(() => {
    TestBed.configureTestingModule({
      imports: [HttpClientTestingModule],
      providers: [MyService]
```

```
    });
    service = TestBed.inject(MyService);
    httpMock = TestBed.inject(HttpTestingController);
  });
  it('should fetch data', () => {
    const mockData = { name: 'John' };
    service.getData().subscribe(data => {
      expect(data).toEqual(mockData);
    });
    const req = httpMock.expectOne('https://api.example.com/data');
    expect(req.request.method).toBe('GET');
    req.flush(mockData);
  });
  afterEach(() => {
    httpMock.verify();
  });
});
```

Advanced authentication and authorization

Question 46: How do you implement JWT authentication in Angular?

Answer: To implement JWT authentication in Angular, follow these steps:

- **Login form**: Collect user credentials.
- **Send login request**: Send credentials to the backend and receive a JWT token.
- **Store JWT securely**: Store the token in `HttpOnly` cookies or session storage.
- **Attach token to HTTP requests**: Use an HTTP interceptor to add the token to every request.
- **Protect routes**: Use Auth Guards to restrict access to authenticated users.

For example: Create a login API call as follows:

```
login(username: string, password: string) {
  return this.http.post<{ token: string }>('/api/auth/login', { username, password }).pipe(
    tap(response => localStorage.setItem('token', response.token))
  );
}
```

Question 47: How do you store and manage authentication tokens securely in Angular?

Answer: To protect authentication tokens and prevent unauthorized access, follow these best practices:

- **Use HttpOnly cookies**: More secure than local storage since they are not accessible by JavaScript.
- **Session storage (limited security)**: Use this only for non-sensitive apps.
- **Angular services**: Manage authentication state using a service.
- **Auto logout on expiration**: Use RxJS timer to log out users when the token expires.

Question 48: How do you automatically attach authentication tokens to every HTTP request?

Answer: Use an HTTP interceptor to append the token to all outgoing requests.

For example:

```
@Injectable()
```

```
export class AuthInterceptor implements HttpInterceptor {
  intercept(req: HttpRequest<any>, next: HttpHandler) {
    const token = localStorage.getItem('token');
    if (token) {
      req = req.clone({ setHeaders: { Authorization: `Bearer ${token}` } });
    }
    return next.handle(req);
  }
}
```

Question 49: What is role-based authentication, and how do you implement it in Angular?

Answer: Role-based authentication ensures that only users with specific roles can access certain parts of an application. It is implemented as follows:

- **Assign roles in JWT**: Backend issues a token containing user roles.
- **Decode JWT in Angular**: Extract roles from the token after authentication.
- **Use guards to restrict access**: Implement **Route Guards (CanActivate)** to prevent unauthorized users from accessing protected routes.

For example: Create a role-based route guard as follows:

```
import {Injectable} from '@angular/core';
import {CanActivate, Router} from '@angular/router';
import {AuthService} from './auth.service';
@Injectable({ providedIn: 'root' })
export class RoleGuard implements CanActivate {
  constructor(private authService: AuthService, private router: Router) {}
  canActivate(): boolean {
    const role = this.authService.getRole();
    if (role === 'admin') {
      return true;
    }
    this.router.navigate(['/unauthorized']);
    return false;
  }
}
```

Question 50: How do you create an authentication guard (AuthGuard) in Angular to protect routes?

Answer: Use **`AuthGuard`** to prevent unauthorized access.

For example:

```
@Injectable({ providedIn: 'root' })
export class AuthGuard implements CanActivate {
  constructor(private authService: AuthService, private router: Router) {}
  canActivate(): boolean {
    if (!this.authService.isAuthenticated()) {
      this.router.navigate(['/login']);
      return false;
    }
```

```
    return true;
  }
}
```

Register guard in routing module as follows:

```
{ path: 'dashboard', component: DashboardComponent, canActivate: [AuthGuard] }
```

Question 51: How do you implement refresh tokens in Angular for session management?

Answer: Use a refresh token stored securely in an **`HttpOnly`** cookie to get a new access token when it expires.

For example:

```
refreshToken() {
  return this.http.post<{ accessToken: string }>('/api/auth/refresh', {}).pipe(
    tap(response => localStorage.setItem('token', response.accessToken))
  );
}
```

The best practice is to use an HTTP Interceptor to automatically refresh tokens before they expire.

Question 52: What is OAuth2, and how do you integrate it with Angular applications?

Answer: OAuth2 is an authorization framework that allows users to log in using third-party providers like *Google*, *Facebook*, or *GitHub*. To integrate OAuth2 in Angular, complete the following steps:

1. Register the application with an OAuth provider (e.g., Google).
2. Use OAuth login API to redirect users to the provider's authentication page.
3. Receive authorization code and exchange it for an access token.
4. Use token in API requests.

For example: Integrate Google OAuth login as follows:

```
window.location.href = 'https://accounts.google.com/o/oauth2/auth?...';
```

For Angular OAuth2 implementation, you can use angular-oauth2-oidc library.

Question 53: How do you handle token expiration and force user logout in Angular?

Answer: To ensure security, expired tokens should be detected, and users should be logged out or prompted to refresh their session. Here is how to implement it:

- **Decode JWT and check expiry:** Use **`jwt-decode`** to extract the expiration time.
- **Set auto logout timer:** Use **`setTimeout()`** to log out users when the token expires.
- **Refresh token automatically:** Use an HTTP interceptor.

For example: Set an automatic logout timer as follows:

```
if (Date.now() > tokenExpiry) {
  this.authService.logout();
}
```

Question 54: How do you protect API endpoints using CORS and security headers in Angular?

Answer: To prevent unauthorized access and enhance security, API endpoints should be protected using CORS and security headers, using the following steps:

- Enable CORS on the backend.
- Restrict allowed origins and only allow trusted domains.
- Set secure HTTP headers in the backend.

For example:

- CORS configuration in Express.js:
  ```
  app.use(cors({ origin: 'https://yourdomain.com', credentials: true }));
  ```
- Security headers:
  ```
  app.use(helmet()); // Adds security headers
  ```

Question 55: How do you implement Single Sign-On (SSO) authentication in Angular?

Answer: SSO allows users to log in once and access multiple applications without re-authenticating. Complete the following steps to implement SSO in Angular:

1. **Use OAuth2 or OpenID Connect (OIDC)**: Integrate with identity providers like Okta, Auth0, or **`Keycloak`**.
2. **Redirect to identity provider**: Authenticate users using a shared login system.
3. **Use access token**: Once authenticated, store the token and use it for API requests.

For example: Use **`Keycloak`** in Angular as follows:

```
import { KeycloakService } from 'keycloak-angular';
constructor(private keycloakService: KeycloakService) {}
login() {
  this.keycloakService.login();
}
logout() {
  this.keycloakService.logout();
}
```

The libraries for SSO in Angular are as follows:

- **`angular-oauth2-oidc`** (for OAuth2)
- **`keycloak-angular`** (for **`Keycloak`**)
- **`auth0-angular`** (for Auth0)

Conclusion

In this chapter, we covered the Angular HTTP Client, exploring how to handle API requests efficiently and securely. We discussed various HTTP methods, such as GET, POST, PUT, DELETE, error handling with RxJS operators, authentication techniques, token management, caching strategies, and security best practices. By leveraging interceptors, role-based authentication, and secure API communication, developers can build robust and scalable Angular applications.

In the next chapter, we will explore SSR and hybrid rendering in Angular. This includes how SSR improves performance and SEO, the role of Angular Universal, and the benefits of hybrid approaches that combine client-side and server-side rendering for optimal user experience.

CHAPTER 10
Concepts of SSR and Hybrid Rendering

Introduction

In modern web development, rendering strategies play a crucial role in determining application performance, **search engine optimization** (**SEO**), and user experience. Traditional **client-side rendering** (**CSR**) often faces challenges related to slower initial page loads and SEO limitations. To overcome these challenges, **server-side rendering** (**SSR**) and hybrid rendering have emerged as efficient approaches.

SSR involves rendering pages on the server before sending them to the client, reducing the time-to-first-paint and enhancing SEO capabilities. On the other hand, hybrid rendering combines both SSR and CSR to optimize performance and user interactivity. This chapter explores the fundamental concepts, benefits, and implementation strategies of SSR and hybrid rendering in modern web applications, especially in the context of Angular.

Structure

This chapter covers the following topics:

- SSR and hybrid rendering basics
- Performance optimization and enhancements
- Implementation and configuration
- Hybrid and dynamic rendering
- Hydration and state management in SSR
- Security and authentication
- Performance and optimization

Objectives

This chapter aims to provide a clear understanding of SSR and its role in modern web development. You will learn how Angular Universal enables SSR in Angular applications, understand the concept of hybrid rendering, and learn how SSR improves performance and SEO. You will be able to compare SSR, CSR, and hybrid rendering to determine the best approach for different use cases and learn best practices to optimize SSR and hybrid rendering implementations in Angular projects. This chapter will equip you with the necessary knowledge to make informed decisions when choosing the right rendering strategy for your Angular applications.

SSR and hybrid rendering basics

Question 1: What is SSR in Angular, and how does it improve performance?

Answer: SSR in Angular refers to rendering Angular applications on the server before sending the HTML to the browser. This is different from CSR, where the browser downloads and compiles JavaScript to generate the UI.

The following figure illustrates the workflows of CSR, SSR, and hybrid rendering:

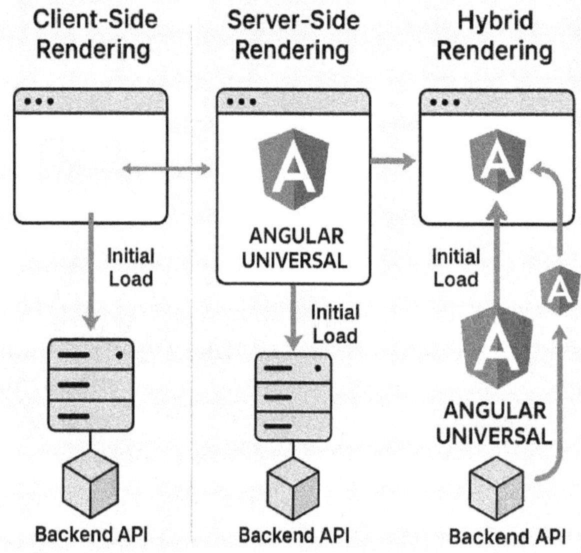

Figure 10.1: CSR, SSR, and hybrid rendering

The performance benefits of SSR are as follows:

- **Faster initial load**: The user sees content immediately because HTML is pre-rendered.
- **Better SEO**: Search engine crawlers can easily index pre-rendered HTML.
- **Improved social sharing**: Meta tags are rendered correctly.
- **Improved perceived performance**: Users see content before JavaScript fully loads.
- **Works well on slow networks**: Users see content before JavaScript loads.

SSR enhances web performance by rendering content on the server before delivering it to the browser. When a user requests a page, the server pre-renders the HTML and sends it, allowing the browser to display content instantly. Angular then hydrates the page, enabling full interactivity.

SSR is particularly useful for SEO-focused applications such as blogs, e-commerce sites, and news platforms. It is also beneficial for apps that rely on meta tags for social sharing and content-heavy pages that require fast loading times.

For example: Implementing SSR in Angular:

1. Install Angular Universal (SSR):
```
ng add @angular/platform-server
```
2. Serve the Application with SSR:
```
npm run dev:ssr
```

Question 2: What is hybrid rendering in Angular, and how does it differ from pure SSR or CSR?

Answer: Hybrid rendering in Angular combines both SSR and CSR to optimize performance. It provides a balance between the benefits of SSR (like faster initial load and better SEO) and CSR (like interactivity and dynamic content).

The differences between SSR, CSR, and hybrid rendering are as follows:

- **CSR**:
  - **Where rendering happens**: The browser renders content using JavaScript.
  - **Performance impact**: Slower initial load but interactive after the application has fully loaded (hydration).
- **SSR**:
  - **Where rendering happens**: The server generates HTML and sends it to the browser.
  - **Performance impact**: Faster initial load because the page is pre-rendered on the server, but may increase server load.
- **Hybrid rendering**:
  - **Where rendering happens**: Some content is rendered on the server, and some on the client.
  - **Performance impact**: Offers the best of both worlds by balancing the benefits of SSR (fast initial load and SEO-friendly) and CSR (dynamic content and interactivity).

Question 3: How does Angular Universal enable SSR in an Angular application?

Answer: Angular Universal is the official SSR solution for Angular. It enables server-side rendering by allowing an Angular app to be executed on the server before sending it to the client.

The steps to enable Angular Universal in an Angular app are as follows:

1. **Add Angular Universal**: `ng add @angular/platform-server`
2. **Modify Angular config**: Update `angular.json` and create a server module.
3. **Serve the application with SSR**: `npm run dev:ssr`

Question 4: What are the key benefits and drawbacks of using Angular Universal for SSR?

Answer: The benefits of Angular Universal (SSR) are as follows:

- **Improves SEO**: Pre-rendered HTML helps search engines crawl the content.
- **Faster First Contentful Paint (FCP)**: Users see content immediately.
- **Supports social media sharing**: Generates metadata previews correctly.

The drawbacks of Angular Universal are as follows:

- **Increased server load**: Every request requires server processing.
- **Complex setup**: Requires additional configuration.
- **State management challenges**: Server-rendered state must sync with the client after hydration.

Question 5: How does SSR improve SEO and initial load performance in Angular applications?

Answer: SSR enhances SEO and initial load performance in Angular applications by optimizing content delivery and improving search engine visibility.

- Key aspects of SEO improvement include:
  - **Pre-rendered HTML**: With SSR, the server sends a fully rendered HTML page, which search engines can easily crawl and index without needing to execute JavaScript.
  - **Better search engine visibility**: Content is accessible right away, improving indexing and making your site more discoverable.

- Key aspects of initial load performance include:
  - **Faster First Contentful Paint (FCP)**: Users see content immediately because the HTML is pre-rendered on the server, reducing the waiting time for the browser to load JavaScript.
  - **No waiting for JavaScript**: The browser does not have to wait for JavaScript to compile before showing content, improving perceived speed.

SSR improves SEO by making the HTML content crawlable and indexed by search engines, and it boosts initial load performance by delivering pre-rendered content, reducing load times, and improving user experience.

Performance optimization and enhancements

Question 6: How has Angular 18 optimized SSR performance compared to previous versions?

Answer: In Angular 18, SSR performance has been enhanced through the introduction of partial hydration. This technique allows the server to render static content while deferring non-essential components, reducing the initial load time. The client then hydrates these deferred components as needed, leading to faster interactive times.

For example: Consider a dashboard with several widgets. With partial hydration, the server renders the main structure and critical widgets, while less critical widgets are rendered on the client side when required.

Question 7: What are streaming SSR capabilities introduced in Angular 18, and how do they work?

Answer: Angular 18 introduced streaming SSR, enabling the server to send HTML content to the client in chunks as it is rendered. This allows the browser to begin displaying content before the entire page is rendered, improving perceived performance.

For example, when rendering a blog post with multiple sections, streaming SSR sends each section to the client as soon as it is ready, allowing users to start reading the first sections while the rest are still being processed.

Question 8: How does Angular 19's hybrid rendering strategy improve dynamic content loading?

Answer: Angular 19 introduced a hybrid rendering strategy that combines SSR, CSR, and build-time prerendering **Static Site Generation** (**SSG**). This approach allows developers to specify the rendering mode for each route, optimizing performance and user experience.

For example: In an e-commerce application, the following happens:

- Static pages like the homepage and product listings can be prerendered at build time (SSG).
- Dynamic pages requiring user-specific data, such as the user profile, can be rendered on the server (SSR).
- Interactive features like a live chat can be rendered on the client side (CSR).

This selective rendering ensures that each part of the application loads efficiently based on its content.

Question 9: What is partial prerendering in Angular 20, and how does it help with SEO?

Answer: Partial prerendering in Angular 20 allows developers to prerender specific parts of a page at build time, serving static HTML for these sections. This ensures that critical content is immediately available to users and search engine crawlers, enhancing SEO.

For example: For a news website, the latest headlines can be prerendered, ensuring they are instantly visible and crawlable, while the rest of the content loads dynamically.

Question 10: How does Angular 20 optimize hydration for faster rendering on the client-side?

Answer: Angular 20 introduced optimized hydration techniques that enhance the process of attaching event listeners and restoring the application state on the client side without re-rendering the entire **Document Object Model** (**DOM**). This leads to faster interactive times and a smoother user experience.

For example: In a server-rendered form, Angular 20's optimized hydration ensures that input fields and buttons are immediately interactive upon page load without waiting for the full JavaScript bundle to initialize.

These advancements in Angular versions 18 through 20 collectively enhance performance, SEO, and user experience by leveraging improved rendering and hydration strategies.

Implementation and configuration

Question 11: How do you set up an Angular Universal project from scratch?

Answer: To set up an Angular Universal project from scratch, follow these steps:

1. **Create a new Angular project**: Run the following code:
   ```
   ng new my-angular-universal-app
   cd my-angular-universal-app
   ```
2. **Add Angular Universal**: Use the Angular CLI to add Angular Universal to the project as follows:
   ```
   ng add @nguniversal/express-engine
   ```
   This command automatically updates the project and adds files necessary for SSR.
3. **Build and run the Universal App**: Run the following commands:
   ```
   npm run build:ssr
   npm run serve:ssr
   ```
   Your Angular Universal app will now run on **http://localhost:4000/**.

Example output: When you visit the site, the HTML source will contain pre-rendered content, improving SEO and initial load performance.

Question 12: What changes are required in the angular.json and server.ts files for SSR?

Answer: For implementing SSR in an Angular application, modifications are required in both the **`angular.json`** and **`server.ts`** files:

- **Changes in angular.json are as follows**:
  ```
  Modify the server builder to ensure SSR builds properly.
  "server": {
    "builder": "@angular-devkit/build-angular:server",
    "options": {
      "outputPath": "dist/my-angular-universal-app-server",
      "main": "server.ts",
      "tsConfig": "tsconfig.server.json"
    }
  }
  ```
- **Changes in server.ts are as follows**:
  ```
  Modify server.ts to include Express middleware and handle SSR requests:
  import 'zone.js/node';
  import express from 'express';
  import { existsSync } from 'fs';
  import { join } from 'path';
  import { ngExpressEngine } from '@nguniversal/express-engine';
  import { AppServerModule } from './src/main.server';
  const app = express();
  const distFolder = join(process.cwd(), 'dist/my-angular-universal-app/browser');
  ```

```
const indexHtml = existsSync(join(distFolder, 'index.original.html')) ? 'index.original.html' : 'index.html';
app.engine('html', ngExpressEngine({ bootstrap: AppServerModule }));
app.set('view engine', 'html');
app.set('views', distFolder);
app.use(express.static(distFolder, { maxAge: '1y' }));
app.get('*', (req, res) => {
  res.render(indexHtml, { req });
});
app.listen(4000, () => {
  console.log(`Node Express server running on http://localhost:4000`);
});
```

Example scenario: After making these changes, running **`npm run serve:ssr`** will serve your app using Express with SSR enabled.

Question 13: How do you configure lazy loaded modules to work correctly with SSR?

Answer: Lazy loaded modules need to work both on the client and server.

The key changes include the following:

1. Use **`import()`** instead of **`loadChildren`** in **`app-routing.module.ts`**:

```
const routes: Routes = [
  {
    path: 'lazy',
    loadChildren: () => import('./lazy/lazy.module').then(m => m.LazyModule)
  }
];
```

2. Ensure modules are imported in **`app.server.module.ts`**:

```
Modify app.server.module.ts to include lazy loaded modules:
import { NgModule } from '@angular/core';
import { ServerModule } from '@angular/platform-server';
import { AppModule } from './app.module';
import { AppComponent } from './app.component';
@NgModule({
  imports: [
    AppModule,
    ServerModule
  ],
  bootstrap: [AppComponent],
})
export class AppServerModule {}
```

Example problem: Without these configurations, SSR may fail to pre-render lazy loaded modules, resulting in blank pages on the server.

Question 14: What are TransferState and state rehydration, and how do they optimize SSR?

Answer: **`TransferState`** is a mechanism that allows passing data from the server to the client to prevent duplicate API calls. State rehydration refers to restoring this state in the client.

For example: To implement **`TransferState`** in a service, execute the following steps:

1. **First, import TransferState and create a service to utilize TransferState**:

```
//Create a service that utilizes TransferState to store and retrieve data.
import { Injectable } from '@angular/core';
import { HttpClient } from '@angular/common/http';
import { TransferState, makeStateKey } from '@angular/platform-browser';
import { Observable } from 'rxjs';
import { tap } from 'rxjs/operators';
const DATA_KEY = makeStateKey<any>('serverData');
@Injectable({
  providedIn: 'root'
})
export class DataService {
  constructor(private http: HttpClient, private transferState: TransferState) {}
  getData(): Observable<any> {
    const storedData = this.transferState.get(DATA_KEY, null);
    if (storedData) {
      return new Observable(observer => {
        observer.next(storedData);
        observer.complete();
      });
    } else {
      return this.http.get('https://api.example.com/data').pipe(
        tap(data => this.transferState.set(DATA_KEY, data)) // Store data in
TransferState
      );
    }
  }
}
```

2. **Now, using TransferState to fetch data in a component**:

```
//Use the DataService to retrieve data without making duplicate API calls.
import { Component, OnInit } from '@angular/core';
import { DataService } from './data.service';
@Component({
  selector: 'app-data',
  template: `<div *ngIf="data">Data: {{ data | json }}</div>`
})
export class DataComponent implements OnInit {
  data: any;
```

```
    constructor(private dataService: DataService) {}
    ngOnInit() {
      this.dataService.getData().subscribe(response => {
        this.data = response;
      });
    }
  }
```

By implementing **TransferState** and state rehydration, SSR applications eliminate redundant API calls, enhance performance, and provide a seamless user experience.

Question 15: How do you handle JSON Web Token (JWT), cookies authentication in an SSR-enabled Angular app?

Answer: Authentication in an SSR-enabled Angular app requires securely managing session-based (cookies) or token-based (JWT) authentication while ensuring that authentication data persists across server and client transitions.

The following example demonstrates how to implement JWT and cookie-based authentication in an SSR-enabled Angular application.

- **Example 1: Using cookies for authentication**:

  Cookies work well with SSR because they are sent with each HTTP request. To set a cookie on login, run the following command:

  ```
  res.cookie('auth', token, { httpOnly: true, secure: true });
  ```

  In Angular, read the cookie using **HttpClient** with **withCredentials: true**:

  ```
  this.http.get('https://api.example.com/user', { withCredentials: true });
  ```

- **Example 2: Using JWT authentication**:

  Store the JWT in a cookie or send it via HTTP headers. To send JWT in an HTTP request, run the following:

  ```
  const headers = new HttpHeaders().set('Authorization', `Bearer ${token}`);
  this.http.get('https://api.example.com/protected', { headers });
  ```

Handling authentication in SSR: Modify **server.ts** to extract authentication headers, shown as follows:

```
app.use((req, res, next) => {
  const token = req.cookies['auth'];
  req.headers.authorization = token ? `Bearer ${token}` : '';
  next();
});
```

Without proper authentication handling in an SSR-enabled Angular application, users may experience session inconsistencies, leading to unexpected logouts when switching between client-side and server-rendered pages. However, by implementing authentication correctly, such as storing JWTs in HTTP-only cookies, authentication remains persistent across both client and server requests, ensuring a seamless and secure user experience.

Hybrid and dynamic rendering

Question 16: How does Angular handle dynamic API content rendering in SSR?

Answer: Angular Universal fetches API data on the server before rendering and sends the pre-rendered HTML to the client. To avoid duplicate API calls, **TransferState** is used to pass data from the server to the client.

For example: Fetching **application programming interface** (**API**) data in SSR:

```
Service: data.service.ts
import { Injectable, Inject, PLATFORM_ID } from '@angular/core';
import { HttpClient } from '@angular/common/http';
import { TransferState, makeStateKey } from '@angular/platform-browser';
import { isPlatformServer } from '@angular/common';
import { Observable } from 'rxjs';
import { tap } from 'rxjs/operators';
const API_DATA_KEY = makeStateKey<any>('apiData');
@Injectable({ providedIn: 'root' })
export class DataService {
  constructor(
    private http: HttpClient,
    private transferState: TransferState,
    @Inject(PLATFORM_ID) private platformId: Object
  ) {}
  getData(): Observable<any> {
    if (this.transferState.hasKey(API_DATA_KEY)) {
      return new Observable(observer => {
        observer.next(this.transferState.get(API_DATA_KEY, null));
        observer.complete();
      });
    } else {
      return this.http.get('https://api.example.com/data').pipe(
        tap(data => {
          if (isPlatformServer(this.platformId)) {
            this.transferState.set(API_DATA_KEY, data);
          }
        })
      );
    }
  }
}
```

The key aspects of how it functions on both the server and client are as follows:

- **On the server**, API data is fetched and stored in **`TransferState`**.
- **On the client**, the data is retrieved from **`TransferState`**, preventing duplicate API calls.

Example scenario: Without **`TransferState`**, API requests will be made twice (once on the server, again on the client). With **`TransferState`**, the client receives pre-fetched data from the server, improving performance.

Question 17: **What are the best practices for caching SSR responses in an Angular Universal app?**

Answer: Caching improves performance by reducing redundant server processing. The best practices for caching in Angular Universal are as follows:

- **Use HTTP cache-control headers**:

  ```
  app.use((req, res, next) => {
    res.setHeader('Cache-Control', 'public, max-age=600, s-maxage=1200');
    next();
  });
  ```

  Caching settings help optimize performance by controlling how responses are stored and retrieved, shown as follows:

  - **max-age=600**: Browser caches the response for 10 minutes.
  - **s-maxage=1200**: CDN caches for 20 minutes.

- **Implement redis or in-memory caching for SSR responses**:

  ```
  import redis from 'redis';
  const cache = redis.createClient();
  app.get('*', (req, res, next) => {
    cache.get(req.url, (err, cachedResponse) => {
      if (cachedResponse) {
        return res.send(cachedResponse);
      }
      next();
    });
  });
  app.use((req, res, next) => {
    res.sendResponse = res.send;
    res.send = (body) => {
      cache.setex(req.url, 600, body); // Cache for 10 minutes
      res.sendResponse(body);
    };
    next();
  });
  ```

- **Use static pre-rendering for non-dynamic pages**: For static pages, pre-render them using the following command:

  ```
  ng run my-app:prerender
  ```

  This generates static HTML files for specific routes, reducing server load.

Example scenario: A news website pre-renders popular articles, caches responses using Redis, and sets HTTP caching headers to minimize redundant rendering.

Question 18: **How do you implement hybrid rendering where some pages are SSR while others use CSR?**

Answer: Hybrid rendering allows some pages to be SSR-rendered for SEO while others remain CSR-rendered for interactivity.

The solution is to use guards to enable CSR on specific routes.

For example: Define a NoSSRGuard for CSR-only pages:

```
import { Injectable, PLATFORM_ID, Inject } from '@angular/core';
import { CanActivate } from '@angular/router';
import { isPlatformBrowser } from '@angular/common';
```

```
@Injectable({ providedIn: 'root' })
export class NoSSRGuard implements CanActivate {
  constructor(@Inject(PLATFORM_ID) private platformId: Object) {}
  canActivate(): boolean {
    return isPlatformBrowser(this.platformId);
  }
}
```

For example: Apply the guard to a route:

```
const routes: Routes = [
  { path: 'dashboard', component: DashboardComponent, canActivate: [NoSSRGuard] },
  { path: 'blog', component: BlogComponent } // Rendered via SSR
];
```

This approach optimizes performance by using the appropriate rendering strategy for different parts of the application as follows:

- Dashboard is CSR-only and only loads in the browser.
- Blog is SSR-rendered for SEO benefits.

Example scenario: An e-commerce site uses SSR for product pages (for SEO) but CSR for the shopping cart (for faster updates).

Question 19: **How does Angular handle server-side rendering of third-party libraries that depend on the DOM?**

Answer: When using SSR in Angular, handling third-party libraries that depend on the DOM requires special consideration, as certain browser-specific objects are unavailable on the server.

Some third-party libraries rely on window, document, or **`localStorage`**, which are not available on the server.

The following solutions demonstrate how to use **`isPlatformBrowser`** and conditional imports:

- **Solution 1**: Use **`isPlatformBrowser`** to check the environment:

  ```
  import { isPlatformBrowser } from '@angular/common';
  import { PLATFORM_ID, Inject } from '@angular/core';
  constructor(@Inject(PLATFORM_ID) private platformId: any) {}
  ngOnInit() {
    if (isPlatformBrowser(this.platformId)) {
      // Run code that accesses the DOM
      const el = document.getElementById('example');
      el?.classList.add('active');
    }
  }
  ```

- **Solution 2**: Use conditional imports:

  If a library does not support SSR, load it only on the client.

  ```
  if (typeof window !== 'undefined') {
    import('some-browser-library').then((lib) => lib.init());
  }
  ```

Example scenario: A website using **`ngx-carousel`** (which relies on the DOM) crashes in SSR. The fix is to wrap it with **`isPlatformBrowser`**, ensuring it only runs in the browser.

Question 20: How do you integrate SSR with headless content management system (CMS) platforms like Strapi, Contentful, or Sanity?

Answer: Integrating SSR with headless CMS platforms like **`Strapi`**, **`Contentful`**, or **`Sanity`** involves fetching content dynamically on the server and passing it to the client for rendering.

Headless CMS platforms provide API-based content, which can be fetched and pre-rendered in Angular Universal.

Consider the following example:

1. **Fetch CMS content on the server**:

   Modify **`server.ts`** to fetch data from the CMS before rendering as follows:

   ```
   app.get('*', async (req, res) => {
     const response = await fetch('https://cms.example.com/posts');
     const data = await response.json();
     res.render('index.html', { req, providers: [{ provide: 'CMS_DATA', useValue: data
   }] });
   });
   ```

2. **Use TransferState to pass CMS data to the client**:

   ```
   const CMS_DATA_KEY = makeStateKey<any>('cmsData');
   @Injectable({ providedIn: 'root' })
   export class CmsService {
     constructor(private transferState: TransferState) {}
     getData(): any {
       return this.transferState.get(CMS_DATA_KEY, []);
     }
   }
   ```

3. **Display CMS data in a component**:

   ```
   export class BlogComponent {
     posts: any;
     constructor(private cmsService: CmsService) {
       this.posts = this.cmsService.getData();
     }
   }
   ```

Example scenario: A news website using **`Contentful`** pre-renders articles via SSR and uses **`TransferState`** to avoid duplicate API calls.

Hydration and state management in SSR

Question 21: What is hydration in SSR, and how does Angular 20 improve it?

Answer: Hydration is the process where Angular takes the server-rendered HTML and attaches event listeners to make it interactive on the client side.

The issue with traditional hydration is that in previous Angular versions, the client would re-render components, leading to flickering and redundant computations. Angular 20 enhances the hydration process by optimizing how components become interactive after server-side rendering. It introduces partial hydration, ensuring that only necessary components are hydrated instead of the entire page, improving performance and reducing unnecessary processing.

Example of partial hydration in Angular 20:

```
@Component({
  selector: 'app-hero',
  standalone: true,
  template: `<h1>{{ title }}</h1>`,
  hydration: true  // Enables partial hydration
})
export class HeroComponent {
  title = 'Welcome to Angular SSR';
}
```

The benefits of hydration in Angular 20 are as follows:

- **No repainting or flickering**: Reuses the server-rendered HTML instead of re-creating it.
- **Improved performance**: Reduces the JavaScript execution needed for rehydration.
- **Supports lazy loading**: Components hydrate only when they are needed.

Question 22: How do you manage global application state across SSR and CSR transitions?

Answer: Managing state across SSR and CSR ensures a smooth user experience without redundant API calls or page flickering. Let us look at some solutions:

- **Solution 1**: Using **`TransferState`** for temporary state:

  Use **`TransferState`** to share data between SSR and CSR, shown as follows:

  ```
  import { TransferState, makeStateKey } from '@angular/platform-browser';
  const USER_DATA_KEY = makeStateKey<any>('userData');
  export class UserService {
    constructor(private transferState: TransferState) {}
    getUserData() {
      return this.transferState.get(USER_DATA_KEY, null);
    }
  }
  ```

  When to use: API responses that need to be available during hydration.

- **Solution 2**: Using NgRx for persistent state:

  For a global state that needs to persist across navigation, run the following code:

  ```
  import { createReducer, on, createAction, createSelector, createFeatureSelector }
  from '@ngrx/store';
  // Actions
  export const setUser = createAction('[User] Set', (user: any) => ({ user }));
  // Reducer
  export const userReducer = createReducer(
    null,
    on(setUser, (state, { user }) => user)
  );
  // Selector
  export const selectUser = createFeatureSelector<any>('user');
  ```

Effective state management plays a crucial role in ensuring a smooth transition between SSR and CSR as:

- **Without state management**: Users see a flicker when switching from SSR to CSR.
- **With TransferState**: The transition is seamless, as SSR data is reused in CSR.

Question 23: What are the best strategies to prevent flickering or reloading issues during SSR hydration?

Answer: When Angular rehydrates a page, it might re-render elements, causing flickering. The best practices to prevent flickering are as follows:

- **Use TransferState for API data**: Prevents re-fetching data in the client.
- **Enable partial hydration (Angular 20+)**: Ensures only dynamic parts of the page are hydrated.
- **Avoid direct DOM manipulation**: Libraries that modify the DOM (**`document.createElement`**) may cause mismatches.

For example: Using TransferState to avoid API re-fetching:

```
const DATA_KEY = makeStateKey<any>('serverData');
@Injectable({ providedIn: 'root' })
export class ApiService {
  constructor(private transferState: TransferState, private http: HttpClient) {}
  getData() {
    if (this.transferState.hasKey(DATA_KEY)) {
      return of(this.transferState.get(DATA_KEY, null));
    } else {
      return this.http.get('https://api.example.com/data').pipe(
        tap(data => this.transferState.set(DATA_KEY, data))
      );
    }
  }
}
```

Optimizing hydration helps prevent unnecessary data reloads and enhances the user experience:

- **Without this optimization**: API data is reloaded after hydration, causing flickering.
- **With this optimization**: Pre-rendered data is reused, making hydration smooth.

Question 24: How do signals improve SSR and hydration performance in Angular 20?

Answer: Signals are reactive state management tools that improve reactivity and reduce unnecessary re-renders.

For example: Using signals for hydration in Angular 20:

```
import { signal } from '@angular/core';
export class CounterComponent {
  count = signal(0);
  increment() {
    this.count.update((value) => value + 1);
  }
}
```

Angular 20 introduces the following improvements that enhance performance and optimize UI updates during hydration:

- **Efficient rehydration**: Only updates parts of the UI that need changes.
- **No Zone.js Overhead**: Unlike traditional change detection, signals update only affected components.

Without **signals**, hydration triggers a re-render of the entire page, leading to unnecessary processing and reduced performance. However, with **signals**, only the specific component that undergoes changes gets updated, optimizing rendering and significantly improving application efficiency.

Question 25: What debugging tools can you use to identify and fix SSR-related performance issues?

Answer: Debugging SSR-related performance issues requires specialized tools to analyze rendering behavior, detect bottlenecks, and optimize performance. The following tools can help identify and resolve such issues effectively:

- **Angular universal profiler (Chrome DevTools Performance tab)**:
    - **Usage steps of universal profiler (Chrome tool)**:
        1. Open DevTools.
        2. Go to the performance tab.
        3. Finally, click record page load.
    - **Key benefits of DevTools are as follows**:
        - Detects slow-rendering components.
        - Identifies hydration bottlenecks for optimization.
- **ng.profiler.timeChangeDetection() (Angular Profiler tool)**:
    - **Usage step of Angular profiler**:
        1. Run in browser console: `ng.profiler.timeChangeDetection()`.
    - **Key benefits of Profiler tool are as follows**:
        - Measures time taken for hydration
        - Shows unnecessary change detection cycles
- **Lighthouse (Google Chrome extension)**:
    - **Usage steps of Google Chrome extension**:
        1. Open DevTools
        2. Go to Lighthouse
        3. Go to Run Report
    - **Key benefits are as follows**:
        - SEO score for SSR pages.
        - **First Contentful Paint** (FCP) analysis.

When troubleshooting SSR hydration issues, it is essential to identify unnecessary re-renders and optimize performance effectively. Let us look at the issue and solution:

- **Issue**: After hydration, the page re-renders completely.
- **Solution**:
    - Run `ng.profiler.timeChangeDetection()` to analyze change detection cycles.
    - Identify and eliminate unnecessary change detections.
    - Optimize rendering using `TransferState` and signals to ensure efficient hydration.

Security and authentication

Question 26: How do you securely handle user authentication in an SSR application without exposing sensitive data?

Answer: Handling authentication in an SSR-enabled Angular app requires securing JWT tokens, cookies, and session data to prevent data leaks. The following best practices help enhance security:

- **Use HTTP-only cookies for JWT tokens**: Avoid storing tokens in `localStorage` or exposing them in the HTML source. Instead, use secure, HTTP-only cookies, which are not accessible by JavaScript.

  For example: Setting a secure HTTP-only cookie (in `server.ts`):

  ```
  app.post('/login', (req, res) => {
    const token = generateJWT(req.body.user);
    res.cookie('auth_token', token, {
      httpOnly: true,
      secure: true,
      sameSite: 'Strict'
    });
    res.status(200).send({ message: 'Login successful' });
  });
  ```

  For example: Sending authenticated requests (Angular Service):

  ```
  this.http.get('/api/user', { withCredentials: true }).subscribe(user => {
    console.log(user);
  });
  ```

- **Use sessions or server-side token storage**: For better security, store session tokens in Redis instead of the client-side.

  For example: Redis-based session storage in Express:

  ```
  const session = require('express-session');
  const RedisStore = require('connect-redis')(session);
  app.use(session({
    store: new RedisStore({ client: redisClient }),
    secret: 'your-secret-key',
    resave: false,
    saveUninitialized: false,
    cookie: { secure: true, httpOnly: true }
  }));
  ```

These security measures effectively protect user authentication data and prevent potential vulnerabilities:

- **Prevents token theft via XSS**: Since cookies are HTTP-only, they cannot be accessed by malicious scripts.
- **No token exposure**: Sensitive authentication tokens are not stored in `localStorage` or embedded in the HTML source.
- **Enhanced session control**: Session-based authentication provides better management of user login states and security.

Question 27: What are the potential security risks of SSR in Angular, and how do you mitigate them?

Answer: SSR introduces new attack vectors that developers must address, which are as follows:

- **Sensitive data leakage**: Never include sensitive user data in **`res.render()`**. Use **`TransferState`** to safely share necessary data between the server and client.
- **Cross-site scripting (XSS)**: Sanitize user-generated content using Angular's built-in **`DomSanitizer`** to prevent script injection attacks.
- **Cross-site request forgery (CSRF)**: Implement CSRF protection using same-site cookies or CSRF tokens to prevent unauthorized requests.
- **Server-side request forgery (SSRF)**: Validate all server-side requests to external APIs and avoid directly using user input in API calls.
- **Cross-origin resource sharing (CORS) misconfigurations**: Restrict API access to trusted origins and avoid wildcard (*) settings in CORS policies.

Following these best practices ensures that your SSR-enabled Angular app remains secure against common web vulnerabilities.

Question 28: How do you prevent XSS and request forgery attacks in SSR?

Answer: To safeguard an SSR-enabled Angular application from **cross-site scripting** (**XSS**) and Request Forgery Attacks, implementing robust security measures is essential. The following practices help mitigate these risks:

- **Preventing XSS**: To prevent XSS attacks in Angular, you can use Angular's built-in sanitization methods to ensure user inputs are safely processed before being rendered in the DOM.

  For instance, consider a scenario where you display user-generated content (such as comments) on your website. Without sanitization, an attacker could inject malicious scripts.

  XSS attacks occur when an attacker injects malicious scripts into your app. Here is how you can handle it:

  For example: To prevent XSS, use malicious script and **`DomSanitizer`** as follows:

```
import {DomSanitizer} from '@angular/platform-browser';
export class UserCommentComponent {
  comment = '<img src="x" onerror="alert(\'XSS Attack\')">'; // Example of a
malicious script
  sanitizedComment;
  constructor(private sanitizer: DomSanitizer) {
    // Sanitize the comment to remove harmful scripts
    this.sanitizedComment = this.sanitizer.sanitize(SecurityContext.HTML, this.
comment);
  }
}
```

  For example: To prevent XSS, use built-in sanitization (**`DomSanitizer`** and **`SafeHtml`**) for sanitizing HTML, shown as follows:

```
//Angular automatically sanitizes untrusted HTML, but always use DomSanitizer for
dynamic content.
import {DomSanitizer, SafeHtml} from '@angular/platform-browser';
constructor(private sanitizer: DomSanitizer) {}
sanitizeHtml(unsafeHtml: string): SafeHtml {
  return this.sanitizer.bypassSecurityTrustHtml(unsafeHtml);
}
```

- **Preventing CSRF**: CSRF attacks occur when a malicious website tricks a user into making unauthorized requests to a trusted site where they are authenticated. To prevent CSRF in an Angular app, you can use same-site cookies as a security measure.

  For instance, when setting authentication cookies, you can use the `SameSite` attribute to restrict how cookies are sent in cross-origin requests:

  For example: To prevent CSRF, use same-site cookies:

  ```
  res.cookie('auth_token', token, {
    httpOnly: true,
    secure: true,
    sameSite: 'Strict'
  });
  ```

- **Implement CSRF tokens for API requests**:

  For example: Generating a CSRF token (Node.js backend):

  ```
  const csrf = require('csurf');
  app.use(csrf({ cookie: true }));
  ```

  For example: Sending CSRF token in Angular HTTP requests:

  ```
  this.http.post('/api/data', { data: 'test' }, {
    headers: { 'X-CSRF-Token': csrfToken }
  });
  ```

These security measures are effective because they address multiple vulnerabilities and ensure the integrity of user data and actions in the following manner:

- Prevents script injections via untrusted HTML.
- Blocks unauthorized requests from other sites.
- Ensures only the authenticated user can perform actions.

Question 29: How do you securely manage sessions and cookies in an SSR-enabled Angular application?

Answer: To securely manage sessions and cookies in an SSR-enabled Angular application, it is essential to implement best practices that protect sensitive data and ensure secure communication. The following steps help mitigate risks and enhance security:

- **Use secure, HTTP-only, and SameSite cookies**:

  ```
  res.cookie('session_id', sessionId, {
    httpOnly: true,
    secure: true,
    sameSite: 'Strict'
  });
  ```

- **Implement session expiration and rotation**: Rotate JWT tokens periodically to prevent session hijacking, shown as follows:

  ```
  res.cookie('auth_token', newToken, { expires: new Date(Date.now() + 3600000) }); // Expires in 1 hour
  ```

- **Use short-lived access tokens with refresh tokens**: Store access tokens in HTTP-only cookies and use refresh tokens only in a secure backend.

These security practices effectively protect session data and reduce the risk of attacks by addressing key vulnerabilities:

- No exposure of session tokens to JavaScript (prevents XSS token theft).
- Session expiration forces re-authentication, reducing risk.
- Access tokens are short-lived to reduce the attack window.

Question 30: How do you ensure sensitive user data is not exposed in the HTML source during SSR?

Answer: Never pass sensitive data directly in **`res.render()`**:

Example to avoid: This unintentionally exposes user details in the HTML:

```
app.get('*', (req, res) => {
  res.render('index.html', { user: req.user });
});
```

Use secure API calls instead: Store user data in a secure session and fetch it via API, shown as follows:

```
app.get('/api/user', (req, res) => {
  res.json({ username: req.user.name });
});
```

Fetch user data only on the client-side:

```
this.http.get('/api/user', { withCredentials: true }).subscribe(user => {
  this.username = user.username;
});
```

Remove sensitive headers from SSR responses: Use Helmet.js to strip unnecessary headers as follows:

```
const helmet = require('helmet');
app.use(helmet.hidePoweredBy());
```

To ensure sensitive user data remains secure during SSR, it is important to follow proper precautions when rendering HTML:

- **Without these precautions**: The SSR-generated HTML may include sensitive user data in view-source.
- **With these best practices**: Sensitive data is never exposed in the rendered HTML.

Performance and optimization

Question 31: How does Angular 20 handle incremental hydration for improved page rendering?

Answer: Incremental hydration allows Angular to progressively hydrate parts of the page instead of rendering everything at once. This reduces the load time and improves performance by only rehydrating interactive parts of the page when needed.

In Angular 20, incremental hydration is achieved by hydrating only the critical sections of the page first and progressively hydrating other sections as needed. This helps in improving the perceived performance as the interactive elements are ready quickly.

For example:

```
@NgModule({
  imports: [
    BrowserModule.withServerTransition({ appId: 'my-app' }),
    // other imports
  ],
  declarations: [AppComponent],
  bootstrap: [AppComponent],
})
```

```
export class AppModule {}
```

In this setup, only specific components that need to be interactive get hydrated on the client-side as users scroll or interact with them.

Question 32: What are the best strategies for caching SSR responses at the Content Delivery Network (CDN) level?

Answer: Caching SSR responses at the CDN level helps to serve pre-rendered pages faster by reducing the load on the server and improving page load times. Best practices include the following:

- **Cache HTML responses**: Cache the entire HTML output of SSR responses at the CDN to avoid hitting the backend server frequently.
- **Cache by URL path and query parameters**: Ensure that the cache key is based on URL paths and query parameters to serve personalized content if needed.
- **Set cache-control headers**: Use appropriate headers to define cache duration, such as **`Cache-Control: public, max-age=3600`** for one-hour caching.
- **Use stale-while-revalidate**: This strategy serves stale content while revalidating the cache in the background, providing a balance between fresh content and speed.

For example: `Cache-Control: public, max-age=3600, stale-while-revalidate=30`

Question 33: How does Angular handle SSR with Web Workers for better performance?

Answer: Web Workers in Angular are used for running JavaScript in background threads, improving application performance, particularly in SSR scenarios. Angular can offload specific tasks such as rendering and data fetching to Web Workers, reducing the main thread's workload and improving page load speed.

Angular Universal (SSR) leverages Web Workers to handle computationally expensive tasks in the background, such as:

- Data processing
- Fetching or caching data
- Preloading resources

For example:

```
import { Injectable } from '@angular/core';
import { TransferState } from '@angular/platform-browser';
import { HttpClient } from '@angular/common/http';
@Injectable()
export class DataService {
  constructor(private http: HttpClient, private transferState: TransferState) {}
  fetchData() {
    return new Observable(observer => {
      if (this.transferState.hasKey(DATA_KEY)) {
        observer.next(this.transferState.get(DATA_KEY, null));
      } else {
        this.http.get('/api/data').subscribe((data) => {
          this.transferState.set(DATA_KEY, data);
          observer.next(data);
        });
      }
    });
```

```
  }
}
```

In the preceding example, data fetching is managed using Web Workers, which allows Angular to continue executing other tasks without blocking the main thread.

Question 34: How do you optimize the Time to First Byte (TTFB) in an SSR Angular application?

Answer: To optimize TTFB in an SSR Angular application, complete the following steps:

1. **Pre-render HTML on the server**: Ensure the HTML is fully generated before being sent to the client, reducing the time spent on the client-side.
2. **Use a CDN**: Serve SSR responses from a CDN to reduce latency and increase download speed.
3. **Caching**: Cache the SSR content at the CDN level to prevent generating the same page repeatedly on the server.
4. **Optimize backend performance**: Use faster server-side rendering engines (e.g., use Node.js with Angular Universal) and optimize server-side APIs for faster data retrieval.
5. **HTTP/2 or HTTP/3**: Use HTTP/2 or HTTP/3 to minimize latency for serving assets.

For example:

```
Cache-Control: public, max-age=300, must-revalidate
```

This ensures that the cached HTML is served quickly to the user with minimal delay.

Question 35: How can you use server-side GraphQL rendering with Angular Universal for better API performance?

Answer: With GraphQL in Angular Universal, you can render API data on the server-side and pass it to the client, reducing the need for multiple client-side API calls and improving performance. By using SSR with GraphQL, you can fetch the data during SSR and inject it into the HTML, ensuring that the client does not need to make separate requests to fetch data on page load. The steps are as follows:

1. Fetch data on the server-side using GraphQL during SSR.
2. Inject the data into the rendered HTML using Angular's **`TransferState`** API.
3. Send pre-fetched data to the client, reducing the need for additional API calls.

For example:

```
import { HttpClient } from '@angular/common/http';
import { Injectable } from '@angular/core';
import { Apollo } from 'apollo-angular';
import gql from 'graphql-tag';
@Injectable({
  providedIn: 'root',
})
export class GraphQLService {
  constructor(private apollo: Apollo) {}
  fetchData() {
    return this.apollo.query({
      query: gql`
        query GetData {
          items {
            id
```

```
                name
            }
        }
      `,
    });
  }
}
```

This example uses Apollo to fetch data from a GraphQL endpoint on the server-side during SSR, then passes the data to the client.

Conclusion

In this chapter, we explored the concepts of SSR and hybrid rendering in Angular. SSR enhances SEO, improves initial load performance, and provides a better user experience by rendering content on the server before sending it to the client. Hybrid rendering, on the other hand, combines the benefits of both SSR and CSR, offering flexibility and optimization based on the application's needs. By leveraging these techniques, developers can create fast, SEO-friendly applications that deliver dynamic and responsive content.

The next chapter is about pipes in Angular. Pipes allow developers to transform data before displaying it in the view. We will cover various built-in pipes, how to create custom pipes, and how they can be used to enhance the functionality of your Angular applications.

Join our Discord space

Join our Discord workspace for latest updates, offers, tech happenings around the world, new releases, and sessions with the authors:

https://discord.bpbonline.com

CHAPTER 11
Concepts of Pipes

Introduction

In Angular, pipes are a powerful feature that transform data before displaying it in a template. They help format values such as dates, currency, percentages, and more, making the UI more readable and user-friendly. Pipes in Angular can be built-in or custom-defined to suit specific application needs.

Structure

This chapter covers the following topics:

- Basic pipes
- Custom pipes
- Advanced pipes
- Debugging and performance optimization

Objectives

By the end of this chapter, you will understand the purpose and functionality of Angular pipes, enabling you to utilize built-in pipes effectively, implement parameterized pipes for dynamic transformations, and develop custom pipes to meet specific formatting needs. You will also be able to differentiate between pure and impure pipes and their impact on performance, work with async pipes to manage asynchronous data streams efficiently, and follow best practices to optimize pipe usage in Angular applications.

Basic pipes

Question 1: What are pipes in Angular, and why are they used?

Answer: In Angular, pipes are used to transform data in templates. They allow you to format or modify data before displaying it, without changing the underlying data. Pipes are useful for formatting strings, dates, numbers, and other data types. Angular provides several built-in pipes, and you can also create custom pipes to meet your specific needs.

Pipes are a powerful feature in Angular that enhance code readability and maintainability. They help create cleaner and more readable templates, keep transformation logic separate from the component, and enable reusability across different parts of the application.

For example:

```
<p>{{ 'angular pipe example' | uppercase }}</p>
```

Here, the uppercase pipe transforms the string into uppercase: `ANGULAR PIPE EXAMPLE`.

Question 2: What is the syntax for using a pipe in an Angular template?

Answer: The basic syntax for using a pipe is shown as follows:

```
{{ value | pipeName:argument }}
```

Where:

- `value` is the data to be transformed.
- `pipeName` is the name of the pipe.
- `argument` is an optional parameter passed to the pipe (if needed).

For example:

```
<p>{{ 1234.5 | currency:'USD' }}</p> <!-- Output: $1,234.50 -->
```

Here, the currency pipe formats the number as currency in USD.

Question 3: What are some built-in pipes provided by Angular?

Answer: Angular provides several built-in pipes, including the following:

- **DatePipe**: Formats dates.
- **CurrencyPipe**: Formats numbers as currency.
- **DecimalPipe**: Formats numbers with decimal points.
- **JsonPipe**: Converts an object to a JSON string.
- **LowerCasePipe**: Converts a string to lowercase.
- **UpperCasePipe**: Converts a string to uppercase.
- **PercentPipe**: Formats numbers as percentages.
- **SlicePipe**: Extracts a subset of an array or string.
- **AsyncPipe**: Subscribes to observables and promises.

Question 4: How does the uppercase and lowercase pipe work in Angular?

Answer: The uppercase and lowercase pipes transform the case of a string as follows:

- **uppercase**: Converts the string to uppercase.
- **lowercase**: Converts the string to lowercase.

For example:

```
<p>{{ 'Hello World' | uppercase }}</p> <!-- Output: HELLO WORLD -->
<p>{{ 'HELLO WORLD' | lowercase }}</p> <!-- Output: hello world -->
```

In the preceding example:

- `'Hello World'` is converted to `HELLO WORLD` using the uppercase pipe.
- `'HELLO WORLD'` is converted to `hello world` using the lowercase pipe.

Question 5: What is the date pipe, and how do you format dates with it?

Answer: The date pipe is used to format date values. You can pass optional format strings to the date pipe to control how the date is displayed. Its syntax is as follows:

```
{{ value | date:'format' }}
```

The syntax consists of the following values:

- `value` is the date object or timestamp.
- `'format'` is an optional format string ('short', 'fullDate', 'yyyy-MM-dd', etc.).

For example:

```
<p>{{ today | date:'yyyy-MM-dd' }}</p> <!-- Output: 2025-02-16 -->
<p>{{ today | date:'fullDate' }}</p> <!-- Output: Sunday, February 16, 2025 -->
<p>{{ today | date:'short' }}</p> <!-- Output: 2/16/25, 10:30 AM -->
```

In this case, the date pipe formats the today variable in different formats, such as short, full, or custom.

Question 6: How does the currency pipe work, and how can you customize its format?

Answer: The currency pipe formats numbers as currency values, and you can customize the currency symbol, code, and decimal formatting. Its syntax is as follows:

```
{{ value | currency:'currencyCode':'symbolDisplay':'digitInfo' }}
```

Where:

- **currencyCode**: A three-letter currency code like 'USD', 'EUR', etc.
- **symbolDisplay**: 'code' to show the currency code, or 'symbol' to show the currency symbol.
- **digitInfo**: A string specifying the number of decimals, e.g., '1.2-2' (min 1, max 2).

For example:

```
<p>{{ 1234.5 | currency:'USD':'symbol':'1.2-2' }}</p> <!-- Output: $1,234.50 -->
<p>{{ 1234.5 | currency:'EUR':'code':'1.0-0' }}</p> <!-- Output: EUR 1,235 -->
```

In the first example, the currency pipe formats the value as USD currency with two decimal places, and in the second, the EUR currency code is displayed with no decimals.

Question 7: What is the difference between slice and JSON pipes?

Answer: The difference between slice and JSON pipes is as follows:

- **SlicePipe**: Slices an array or string into a subset. It is useful for limiting the display of elements in arrays or strings, illustrated as follows:
  ```
  <p>{{ 'Angular Pipes' | slice:0:7 }}</p> <!-- Output: Angular -->
  <p>{{ [1, 2, 3, 4, 5] | slice:1:4 }}</p> <!-- Output: [2, 3, 4] -->
  ```
- **JsonPipe**: Converts an object or array to a JSON-formatted string for display, shown as follows:
  ```
  <pre>{{ {name: 'John', age: 25} | json }}</pre>
  <!-- Output: {"name":"John","age":25} -->
  ```

Question 8: Can we use multiple pipes together in an Angular template? If yes, how?

Answer: Yes, you can chain multiple pipes together by separating them with a pipe (|). The output of one pipe becomes the input for the next.

For example:

```
<p>{{ '2025-02-16' | date:'fullDate' | uppercase }}</p>
<!-- Output: SUNDAY, FEBRUARY 16, 2025 -->
```

Here, the date pipe formats the date, and the uppercase pipe then converts the result to uppercase.

Question 9: What is a pure pipe, and how does it differ from an impure pipe?

Answer: A pure pipe in Angular is a pipe that only executes when its input data changes. This means Angular will only re-evaluate the pipe if it detects a change in the input reference or value. A pure pipe is the default type of pipe in Angular, and it provides better performance compared to impure pipes because it avoids unnecessary re-execution unless the input changes. The key concepts of pure pipes are as follows:

- **Input data change detection**: Angular performs change detection on the component and checks if the input to the pipe has changed. If the input remains the same, Angular does not execute the pipe again.
- **Optimization**: Pure pipes only re-run when input data changes, so they are optimized for performance, especially when dealing with large datasets or expensive transformations.

Consider an example. Let us assume you have a pipe that formats dates and receives a date object as input. The pipe will only execute if the date object reference changes, shown as follows:

```
<p>{{ date | date: 'short' }}</p>
```

In this case, the date pipe only executes when the date reference changes. If the value of the date object itself is modified but its reference stays the same (e.g., **`date.setDate(10)`**), Angular will not run the pipe again because the reference has not changed.

Consider an example for creating a pure pipe. In Angular, a pipe is pure by default, meaning it behaves like a pure pipe unless explicitly defined otherwise. You do not need to do anything special to make a pipe pure. However, the pure property is set to true by default in the **`@Pipe`** decorator, shown as follows:

```
@Pipe({
  name: 'uppercase',
  pure: true  // this is actually the default, so you can omit it
})
export class UppercasePipe implements PipeTransform {
  transform(value: string): string {
    return value.toUpperCase();
  }
}
```

In this case, the uppercase pipe will only execute when the value changes. If the reference remains the same, Angular will not execute the pipe again.

An impure pipe in Angular runs on every change detection cycle, regardless of whether the input data has changed. This type of pipe is useful when the data is dynamically changing (e.g., time, random numbers) or when the input is an object that can be mutated, but its reference does not change. The key concepts of impure pipes are as follows:

- **Runs on every change detection cycle**: Impure pipes will re-run every time Angular performs change detection, even if the data has not changed. This can negatively impact performance if the pipe contains expensive transformations and the change detection cycle occurs frequently.
- **Use cases**: Impure pipes are useful when dealing with continuously updating data, such as live time updates or random numbers.

Consider an example where you want to display a random number using a custom pipe. The random number changes every time Angular runs change detection, shown as follows:

```
@Pipe({
  name: 'randomNumber',
  pure: false  // this makes the pipe impure
})
export class RandomNumberPipe implements PipeTransform {
  transform(value: any): number {
    return Math.random();
  }
```

```
}
```

In this case, the randomNumber pipe will re-run every time Angular performs change detection, even if the input value does not change, because the output of the pipe is dynamic (i.e., a random number).

Let us look at an example of the creation of an impure pipe. To make a pipe impure, you need to set the pure property to false in the **@Pipe** decorator as follows:

```
@Pipe({
  name: 'randomNumber',
  pure: false  // Explicitly marking the pipe as impure
})
export class RandomNumberPipe implements PipeTransform {
  transform(value: any): number {
    return Math.random();
  }
}
```

In the preceding example, the **randomNumber** pipe will generate a new random number every time the Angular change detection cycle is triggered, regardless of whether the input data has changed.

The following are performance considerations for pure pipes:

- More efficient as they execute only when their input data changes.
- Angular optimizes pure pipes by skipping unnecessary executions, improving performance.

The following are performance considerations for impure pipes:

- Can impact performance, especially in large applications, as they run on every change detection cycle.
- Even if the input remains unchanged, impure pipes execute repeatedly, leading to potential inefficiencies.

Pure pipes can be used in the following cases:

- Ideal for transforming data that rarely changes.
- Best suited for immutable data types (e.g., strings, numbers).
- Recommended when performance optimization is a priority to reduce unnecessary computations.

Impure pipes can be used in the following cases:

- Useful for frequently changing or mutable data (e.g., random numbers, timestamps, or observable streams).
- Needed when the data reference remains the same, but its contents update dynamically (e.g., modified arrays or objects).

Pure pipes execute only when their input reference changes, making them highly efficient for static or immutable data. They help optimize rendering performance by reducing unnecessary computations. In contrast, impure pipes execute on every change detection cycle, making them suitable for frequently changing data but potentially impacting performance.

By default, all pipes in Angular are pure. To create an impure pipe, you must explicitly set pure: false in the **@Pipe** decorator. Understanding when to use each type of pipe ensures optimal performance and effective data transformations in your Angular applications.

Real-world example: Let us say you have a component that shows the current time. You can use an impure pipe because the time is always changing, shown as follows:

```
@Pipe({
  name: 'currentTime',
```

```
  pure: false  // this pipe should be impure
})
export class CurrentTimePipe implements PipeTransform {
  transform(value: any): string {
    const currentTime = new Date().toLocaleTimeString();
    return currentTime;
  }
}
```

In your template add the following:

```
<p>{{ currentTime | currentTime }}</p>
```

Here, the time will update every time Angular runs change detection, even though the value does not change. This is a valid use case for an impure pipe because the time value is dynamic.

Question 10: What is the async pipe, and how does it work with observables and promises?

Answer: The async pipe subscribes to an observable or promise and updates the template with the latest value emitted by the observable or resolved by the promise. It automatically handles subscribing and unsubscribing from the observable or promise.

An example with observable is as follows:

```
<p>{{ dataObservable | async }}</p>
```

An example with promise is as follows:

```
<p>{{ dataPromise | async }}</p>
```

This will automatically update the template whenever the observable emits new data or the promise resolves.

Custom pipes

Question 11: How do you create a custom pipe in Angular?

Answer: To create a custom pipe in Angular, you need to define a class that implements the **`PipeTransform`** interface and annotate the class with a **`@Pipe`** decorator. The transform method in the class is where you define the transformation logic for the input data.

Complete the following steps to create a custom pipe in Angular:

1. Define a class that implements **`PipeTransform`**.
2. Decorate the class with the **`@Pipe`** decorator and provide a name for the pipe.
3. Implement the transform method, which will contain the transformation logic.

For example:

```
import { Pipe, PipeTransform } from '@angular/core';
@Pipe({
  name: 'exclamation'
})
export class ExclamationPipe implements PipeTransform {
  transform(value: string, count: number = 1): string {
    return value + '!'.repeat(count);
  }
}
```

In the preceding example, the **`ExclamationPipe`** adds *n* exclamation marks to the end of the input string.

Question 12: What are the steps to create and register a custom pipe?

Answer: The following are the steps for creating and registering a custom pipe in Angular:

1. **Generate the pipe**: Use Angular CLI to generate the pipe, or manually create a file for the pipe as follows:

   ```
   ng generate pipe exclamation
   ```

2. **Implement the pipe logic**: Create a class that implements the **PipeTransform** interface and define the transformation logic inside the transform method (as shown in *Answer 11*).
3. **Register the Pipe**: Register the pipe in an Angular module's declarations array (e.g., in **app.module.ts**).

For example:

```
import { ExclamationPipe } from './exclamation.pipe';
@NgModule({
  declarations: [
    AppComponent,
    ExclamationPipe // Register the custom pipe here
  ],
  imports: [BrowserModule],
  providers: [],
  bootstrap: [AppComponent]
})
export class AppModule {}
```

The following is a step-by-step guide to creating and registering a custom pipe in a standalone component:

- **Create the custom pipe**: Define the pipe class and implement the transformation logic. Use **standalone**: true in the **@Pipe** decorator.

  For example:

  ```
  import { Pipe, PipeTransform } from '@angular/core';
  @Pipe({
    name: 'exclamation',
    standalone: true // Declare the pipe as standalone
  })
  export class ExclamationPipe implements PipeTransform {
    transform(value: string, count: number = 1): string {
      if (!value) return '';
      return value + '!'.repeat(count); // Adds exclamation marks
    }
  }
  ```

- **Register the pipe**: Import and register the pipe in the imports array of the standalone component.

  For example:

  ```
  import { Component } from '@angular/core';
  import { ExclamationPipe } from './exclamation.pipe'; // Import the custom pipe
  @Component({
    selector: 'app-root',
  ```

```
  template: `<p>{{ 'Hello' | exclamation:3 }}</p>`,
  standalone: true, // This component is standalone
  imports: [ExclamationPipe] // Register the custom pipe here
})
export class AppComponent {}
```

- **Use the pipe in the template**: Apply the pipe in the component's HTML template.

  For example: `<p>{{ 'Angular' | exclamation:3 }}</p> <!-- Output: Angular!!! -->`

- **Run the application**: Use **`ng serve`** to start the Angular application and test the pipe.

By using standalone components, you eliminate the need for registering the pipe in a module, making it simpler to create and use custom pipes.

Question 13: How do you pass arguments to a custom pipe?

Answer: To pass arguments to a custom pipe, you can simply add them after the pipe name in the template. These arguments are passed as additional parameters to the transform method of the pipe.

Refer to the following steps:

1. **Create an exclamation custom pipe class**:

```
// Define a custom pipe that appends a specified number of exclamation marks to a string.
@Pipe({
  name: 'exclamation'
})
export class ExclamationPipe implements PipeTransform {
  transform(value: string, count: number = 1): string {
    return value + '!'.repeat(count); // Add 'count' exclamation marks
  }
}
```

2. **Use the exclamation pipe in a component**:

```
// Apply the pipe in a template to modify text dynamically.
<p>{{ 'Hello' | exclamation:3 }}</p> <!-- Output: Hello!!! -->
```

The output is as follows:

`Hello!!!`

In the preceding example, the number 3 is passed as an argument to the transform method, adding three exclamation marks to the string **Hello**.

Question 14: How do you use a custom pipe inside a component?

Answer: To use a custom pipe inside a component, simply reference the pipe in the component's HTML template. Ensure that the pipe is registered in the component's module.

For example:

```
<p>{{ 'Angular' | exclamation:2 }}</p> <!-- Output: Angular!! -->
```

Question 15: How can you transform an array using a custom pipe?

Answer: You can transform an array using a custom pipe by processing the array elements in the transform method of the pipe. You can map, filter, or manipulate array elements as needed.

To transform each element in the array to uppercase before displaying it, you need to create a custom pipe called **`uppercaseArray`**.

Consider the following example of implementation:

1. **Create a custom pipe for applying uppercase on an array item**:

```
@Pipe({
  name: 'uppercaseArray'
})
export class UppercaseArrayPipe implements PipeTransform {
  transform(value: string[]): string[] {
    return value.map(item => item.toUpperCase());
  }
}
```

2. **Use the uppercaseArray pipe in the template**:

```
<ul>
  <li *ngFor="let item of ['apple', 'banana', 'cherry'] | uppercaseArray">
    {{ item }}
  </li>
</ul>
```

The output is as follows:

APPLE

BANANA

CHERRY

In this example, the **uppercaseArray** pipe transforms each element of the array to uppercase before displaying it in the list.

Question 16: How can you filter an array using a custom pipe?

Answer: A custom pipe can filter an array by using the filter method on the array inside the transform method. You can pass a criterion (e.g., a search term) as an argument.

Consider the following example:

1. **Create a custom pipe**:

```
import { Pipe, PipeTransform } from '@angular/core';
@Pipe({
  name: 'filterArray'
})
export class FilterArrayPipe implements PipeTransform {
  transform(value: any[], searchTerm: string): any[] {
    if (!Array.isArray(value) || !searchTerm) {
      return value;
    }
    const lowerSearch = searchTerm.toLowerCase();
    return value.filter(item =>
      item?.toString().toLowerCase().includes(lowerSearch)
    );
  }
}
```

2. **Use the FilterArrayPipe pipe in the template:**

```
<ul>
  <li *ngFor="let item of ['apple', 'banana', 'cherry'] | filterArray:'ap'">
    {{ item }}
  </li>
</ul>
```

The output is as follows:

`apple`

In this example, the **`FilterArray`** pipe filters the array to only show items that contain the substring **`"ap"`**. Therefore, only **`apple`** is displayed in the list.

Question 17: What is the best practice for handling null or undefined values in a custom pipe?

Answer: In custom pipes, it is important to handle null or undefined values to avoid runtime errors. The best practice is to check if the value is valid before performing any transformation.

For example:

```
@Pipe({
  name: 'safeExclamation'
})
export class SafeExclamationPipe implements PipeTransform {
  transform(value: string, count: number = 1): string {
    if (!value) return ''; // Handle null or undefined input gracefully
    return value + '!'.repeat(count);
  }
}
```

This pipe will return an empty string if the value is null or undefined.

Question 18: What are the performance implications of using custom pipes?

Answer: Using custom pipes can have performance implications, especially if they are impure or complex, as they are re-evaluated on every change detection cycle (if impure).

Pure pipes are generally more efficient because they only execute when the input data reference changes.

Impure pipes can negatively impact performance because they execute on every change detection cycle, even if the input data has not changed.

The best practices for using pipes are as follows:

- Use pure pipes wherever possible to optimize performance.
- Avoid using custom pipes for complex transformations that need to run on every cycle unless necessary.

Question 19: Can a custom pipe be used inside a component's TypeScript file instead of the template?

Answer: Yes, you can use a custom pipe inside a component's TypeScript file by manually invoking the transform method. To do this, you need to inject the pipe into your component's constructor.

For example:

```
import { Component } from '@angular/core';
import { ExclamationPipe } from './exclamation.pipe';
@Component({
  selector: 'app-root',
```

```
  template: `<p>{{ transformedText }}</p>`
})
export class AppComponent {
  transformedText: string;
  constructor(private exclamationPipe: ExclamationPipe) {
    this.transformedText = this.exclamationPipe.transform('Hello', 3);
  }
}
```

In this case, the transform method of the **ExclamationPipe** is called directly in the TypeScript file to set **transformedText**.

Question 20: How do you test a custom pipe in Angular?

Answer: To test a custom pipe in Angular, you can write unit tests using the Angular testing framework. You can use **TestBed** to configure the testing module and instantiate the pipe for testing.

For example:

```
import { ExclamationPipe } from './exclamation.pipe';
describe('ExclamationPipe', () => {
  let pipe: ExclamationPipe;
  beforeEach(() => {
    pipe = new ExclamationPipe();
  });
  it('should add exclamation marks to the end of the string', () => {
    expect(pipe.transform('Hello', 3)).toBe('Hello!!!');
  });
  it('should add one exclamation mark by default', () => {
    expect(pipe.transform('Hello')).toBe('Hello!');
  });
});
```

In the preceding example, we test the **ExclamationPipe** to ensure it behaves as expected, adding the correct number of exclamation marks to the input string.

Advanced pipes

Question 21: What is the difference between pure and impure pipes, and when should each be used?

Answer: Pure pipes are executed only when input references change, making them highly efficient and suitable for most use cases.

Impure pipes are executed on every change detection cycle, which can be useful for dynamic data like timestamps or non-reference-changing arrays, but can impact performance.

Please refer to *Answer 9* for detailed information and examples.

Question 22: How does Angular determine when to re-run a pipe?

Answer: Angular determines when to re-run a pipe by checking if the input reference has changed. For pure pipes, Angular checks if the object reference changes (not deep comparison). For impure pipes, Angular runs the pipe on every change detection cycle, even if the data has not changed.

Question 23: How do you create an impure custom pipe?

Answer: To create an impure pipe, you simply set the **`pure: false`** property in the **`@Pipe`** decorator. This forces Angular to run the pipe on every change detection cycle.

For example:

```
@Pipe({
  name: 'random',
  pure: false  // Set the pipe to be impure
})
export class RandomPipe implements PipeTransform {
  transform(value: any): any {
    return Math.random(); // Return a random number, changing each cycle
  }
}
```

Question 24: What are the benefits of using pure pipes over impure pipes?

Answer: Using pure pipes offers several advantages over impure pipes, particularly in terms of performance and predictability. The key benefits are as follows:

- **Performance**: Pure pipes are more efficient because they are only invoked when the input reference changes. This reduces unnecessary computation.
- **Predictability**: Pure pipes are predictable, as they only run when the data changes.

Use pure pipes if your data is immutable or does not change frequently.

Question 25: How does the async pipe automatically subscribe and unsubscribe from an observable?

Answer: The async pipe in Angular automatically subscribes to an observable or promise and returns the emitted values. When the component is destroyed or the value changes, the async pipe automatically unsubscribes to avoid memory leaks.

For example:

```
@Component({
  selector: 'app-root',
  template: `<div>{{ observableData | async }}</div>`
})
export class AppComponent {
  observableData = new Observable((observer) => {
    setTimeout(() => observer.next('Hello World'), 1000);
  });
}
```

In the preceding example, the async pipe subscribes to **`observableData`**, and Angular handles the subscription and unsubscription automatically.

Question 26: Can we use a pipe inside a directive? If yes, how?

Answer: Yes, you can use a pipe inside a directive by injecting it into the directive class and manually calling the transform method.

For example:

```
import { Directive, ElementRef, Input, OnChanges } from '@angular/core';
import { ExclamationPipe } from './exclamation.pipe';
```

```
@Directive({
  selector: '[appExclamation]'
})
export class ExclamationDirective implements OnChanges {
  @Input() appExclamation: string;
  @Input() exclamationCount: number = 1;
  constructor(private el: ElementRef, private exclamationPipe: ExclamationPipe) {}
  ngOnChanges() {
    const transformedValue = this.exclamationPipe.transform(this.appExclamation, this.
exclamationCount);
    this.el.nativeElement.textContent = transformedValue;
  }
}
```

Here, the **ExclamationPipe** is used inside a directive to modify the text content dynamically.

Question 27: How do you optimize an expensive computation inside a pipe?

Answer: To optimize expensive computations, you can do the following:

- **Use memoization**: Cache previous results to avoid recomputing values for the same input.
- **Limit recalculations**: Use pure pipes whenever possible to ensure the pipe only runs when the input data changes.

For example:

```
@Pipe({
  name: 'expensiveComputation',
  pure: true // Ensures it's only re-calculated when input changes
})
export class ExpensiveComputationPipe implements PipeTransform {
  private cache = new Map();
  transform(value: any): any {
    if (this.cache.has(value)) {
      return this.cache.get(value); // Return cached value
    }
    const result = this.expensiveComputation(value); // Perform expensive computation
    this.cache.set(value, result); // Cache the result
    return result;
  }
  private expensiveComputation(value: any): any {
    // Simulate an expensive computation
    return value * Math.random();
  }
}
```

Question 28: What are the performance issues with using impure pipes?

Answer: Impure pipes can impact performance significantly because they are executed on every change detection cycle. This is especially costly when dealing with large data sets or complex computations.

The following are the key impacts of using impure pipes:

- Increased CPU usage due to frequent execution.
- Slower change detection cycles.

Question 29: How does the safe navigation operator (?.) work with pipes in Angular?

Answer: The **safe navigation operator (?.)** in Angular is used to prevent errors when accessing properties of null or undefined. When used with pipes, it ensures that the pipe does not throw errors if the data is null or undefined.

For example:

```
<p>{{ user?.name | uppercase }}</p>
```

If the user is null or undefined, the safe navigation operator ensures no error is thrown, and the pipe does not execute.

Question 30: How can you use pipes dynamically inside a component instead of templates?

Answer: You can use pipes dynamically by calling their transform method inside the component's TypeScript file. Inject the pipe using Angular's dependency injection system.

For example:

```
import { Component } from '@angular/core';
import { ExclamationPipe } from './exclamation.pipe';
@Component({
  selector: 'app-root',
  template: '<p>{{ transformedText }}</p>',
  standalone: true,
  imports: [ExclamationPipe]
})
export class AppComponent {
  transformedText: string;
  constructor(private exclamationPipe: ExclamationPipe) {
    this.transformedText = this.exclamationPipe.transform('Hello', 3); // Using pipe in
TypeScript
  }
}
```

Question 31: What improvements have been introduced in pipes in Angular 18+?

Answer: In Angular 18+, improvements in pipes include the following:

- Better performance with pure pipes, reducing unnecessary recalculations.
- Improved support for signals and reactive programming with pipes.
- Enhanced lifecycle management for pipes in standalone components.

Question 32: How does Angular 19 optimize pipe execution for signals-based components?

Answer: Angular 19 optimizes pipe execution by leveraging signals. Signals track state changes more efficiently, allowing Angular to trigger pipe transformations only when the underlying signals change, reducing unnecessary executions.

Question 33: How do pipes interact with the new zone-less rendering in Angular 19+?

Answer: With zone-less rendering in Angular 19+, change detection is no longer automatically triggered by Angular's Zone.js. Pipes now need to be more explicit in responding to changes, particularly for impure pipes. Developers may need to manually trigger change detection or handle it via signals.

Question 34: What changes were made to async pipe in Angular 20?

Answer: Angular 20 introduced performance improvements for the async pipe, reducing unnecessary change detection cycles and improving the handling of observables and promises in templates.

Question 35: How can you use pipes efficiently with Angular hydration and hybrid rendering?

Answer: In hybrid rendering and hydration, Angular 20 optimizes pipes by deferring their execution until necessary, minimizing initial rendering time and improving performance during rehydration.

Question 36: What are deferred pipes, and how do they improve performance in Angular 20?

Answer: Deferred pipes in Angular 20 are executed lazily, meaning they are only triggered once the view has fully loaded or when specific conditions are met. This reduces initial load time and improves the perceived performance of the app.

Question 37: How does Angular 20 improve support for lazy loaded pipes?

Answer: Angular 20 introduced lazy loading support for pipes, allowing pipes to be loaded and executed only when needed. This helps to reduce the initial bundle size and also improves the application's performance.

Question 38: How can you integrate pipes with server-side rendering (SSR) and hydration?

Answer: In SSR and hydration, pipes are executed both on the server and the client. Angular optimizes the execution of pipes during hydration, ensuring that pipes do not re-execute unnecessarily, improving both initial rendering and client-side updates.

Question 39: How does the internationalization (i18n) pipe work in Angular 20?

Answer: The i18n pipe in Angular 20 supports advanced internationalization features, including locale-based formatting, translations, and string replacements. It dynamically transforms content based on the user's locale.

Question 40: What are the recommended changes in using pipes with Angular's signal-based components?

Answer: With signal-based components, Angular's pipes should be used more efficiently. Signals provide a more granular approach to data changes, reducing unnecessary updates. When using pipes, it is important to ensure that pipes are only invoked when signal values change, avoiding unnecessary recomputations.

Debugging and performance optimization

Question 41: How do you debug issues with pipes in Angular?

Answer: You can debug issues with pipes in Angular as follows:

- **Use console.log**: Inside the transform method of the pipe, add console.log statements to check the values passed and the results returned.
- **Check for pure or impure behavior**: Ensure that the pipe is correctly marked as pure or impure depending on how often it should be run.
- **Inspect change detection**: Use Angular DevTools to monitor how frequently your pipes are being executed during change detection.

For example:

```
@Pipe({
  name: 'debugPipe',
  pure: true
})
export class DebugPipe implements PipeTransform {
  transform(value: any): any {
    console.log('Transforming value:', value);  // Debugging the input value
```

```
    return value * 2;  // Just an example transformation
  }
}
```

Question 42: What are some common mistakes developers make when using pipes?

Answer: Some common mistakes include the following:

- **Using impure pipes unnecessarily**: This can lead to performance issues as the pipe will be run on every change detection cycle.
- **Not handling null or undefined values**: Pipes should account for potential null or undefined inputs to avoid runtime errors.
- **Using pipes for heavy computations**: Pipes should be kept lightweight, and expensive computations should be done in methods or services.

Question 43: When should you use a pipe versus a method in a component?

Answer: Deciding whether to use a pipe or a method in a component depends on the nature of the transformation or logic you need to perform. The following are some guidelines to help determine when to use each:

- **Use pipes in the following cases:**
  - You need to perform simple transformations in the template, such as formatting dates, numbers, or strings.
  - The transformation is stateless and can be reused in multiple places.
- **Use methods in the following cases:**
  - You need to perform more complex logic or operations that may have side effects.
  - The logic involves mutable state or conditions that change based on user interactions.

For example:

```
// Pipe for simple transformations
@Pipe({
  name: 'uppercase'
})
export class UppercasePipe implements PipeTransform {
  transform(value: string): string {
    return value.toUpperCase();
  }
}
// Method in component for complex logic
@Component({
  selector: 'app-complex-method',
  template: `<div>{{ complexCalculation() }}</div>`
})
export class ComplexMethodComponent {
  complexCalculation(): number {
    // Perform complex operations here
    return 42;
  }
}
```

Question 44: How can you optimize an expensive calculation inside a pipe?

Answer: You can optimize expensive calculations inside a pipe as follows:

- **Use memoization**: Cache results for specific inputs.
- **Use pure pipes**: Pure pipes only re-run when the input reference changes.
- **Limit recalculations**: Do heavy computations outside the pipe, or use a service to perform calculations.

An example with memorization is as follows:

```
@Pipe({
  name: 'expensiveComputation',
  pure: true
})
export class ExpensiveComputationPipe implements PipeTransform {
  private cache = new Map();
  transform(value: any): any {
    if (this.cache.has(value)) {
      return this.cache.get(value);
    }
    const result = this.expensiveComputation(value);
    this.cache.set(value, result);
    return result;
  }
  private expensiveComputation(value: any): any {
    // Simulate an expensive computation
    return value * Math.random();
  }
}
```

Question 45: What tools can you use to measure the performance impact of pipes in Angular?

Answer: To measure the performance impact, you can use the following tools:

- **Angular DevTools**: Provides performance profiling, which helps monitor the change detection cycles and pipe executions.
- **Chrome DevTools**: Use the performance tab to check the execution time and frequency of pipe transformations.
- **Profiling with console.time()**: Measure the execution time of pipe logic with custom **`console.time()`** and **`console.timeEnd()`** methods.

Question 46: How do pipes impact change detection, and how can you avoid unnecessary recalculations?

Answer: Pipes impact change detection by being executed when Angular checks for changes. To avoid unnecessary recalculations, do the following:

- **Use pure pipes**: They are only re-executed when the input reference changes.
- **Use ChangeDetectionStrategy.OnPush**: This ensures change detection is only triggered when input properties change.

An example with **`OnPush`** is as follows:

```
@Component({
  selector: 'app-on-push',
```

```
  changeDetection: ChangeDetectionStrategy.OnPush,
  template: `<div>{{ data | exclamation:2 }}</div>`
})
export class OnPushComponent {
  @Input() data: string;
}
```

Question 47: **Can pipes be used inside Angular directives?**

Answer: Yes, you can use pipes inside directives by injecting the pipe into the directive and manually calling the transform method.

For example:

```
import { Directive, ElementRef, Input, OnChanges } from '@angular/core';
import { ExclamationPipe } from './exclamation.pipe';
@Directive({
  selector: '[appExclamation]'
})
export class ExclamationDirective implements OnChanges {
  @Input() appExclamation: string;
  @Input() exclamationCount: number = 1;
  constructor(private el: ElementRef, private exclamationPipe: ExclamationPipe) {}
  ngOnChanges() {
    const transformedValue = this.exclamationPipe.transform(this.appExclamation, this.
exclamationCount);
    this.el.nativeElement.textContent = transformedValue;
  }
}
```

Question 48: **What are some real-world use cases for using pipes in enterprise applications?**

Answer: Pipes can be incredibly useful in enterprise applications for handling common data transformations and ensuring consistency across the application. Some real-world use cases are outlined as follows:

- **Date formatting**: To display dates in different formats based on the user's locale.
- **Currency formatting**: For dynamically displaying values with different currencies.
- **Custom filters**: Filtering lists of data (like showing active items in a list).
- **Text transformations**: Uppercasing or truncating strings based on certain conditions.

For example:

```
<p>{{ user.lastLoginDate | date: 'short' }}</p>
<p>{{ amount | currency: 'USD' }}</p>
```

Question 49: **How do you handle deep object transformations inside a pipe?**

Answer: For deep object transformations, it is recommended to use a service or avoid handling complex data structures directly inside a pipe, as pipes are meant for lightweight, stateless transformations. You can use recursion if needed, but you should be mindful of performance.

For example:

```
@Pipe({
  name: 'deepTransform'
```

```
})
export class DeepTransformPipe implements PipeTransform {
  transform(value: any): any {
    if (Array.isArray(value)) {
      return value.map(this.deepTransform);
    } else if (typeof value === 'object') {
      return Object.keys(value).reduce((acc, key) => {
        acc[key] = this.deepTransform(value[key]);
        return acc;
      }, {});
    }
    return value;
  }
  private deepTransform(value: any) {
    // Perform transformation logic (e.g., string manipulation, etc.)
    return value.toUpperCase();
  }
}
```

Question 50: What is the best practice for using pipes inside large Angular applications?

Answer: To ensure optimal performance and maintainability in large Angular applications, it is important to follow best practices when using pipes. The key practices include:

- Use pure pipes to minimize unnecessary recalculations.
- Keep pipes simple and focus on one transformation logic.
- Avoid complex logic inside pipes; use services for data transformations or heavy computations.
- Limit the use of impure pipes, as they can negatively affect performance due to frequent execution during change detection.

For example:

```
@Pipe({
  name: 'simplifyText',
  pure: true
})
export class SimplifyTextPipe implements PipeTransform {
  transform(value: string): string {
    // Simple transformation logic
    return value.trim().toLowerCase();
  }
}
```

Conclusion

In this chapter, we explored the power of pipes in Angular for transforming data in templates. We discussed how to create custom pipes, use built-in pipes, and understand the differences between pure and impure pipes. We also covered performance considerations, best practices, and real-world use cases for pipes in enterprise applications. By effectively leveraging pipes, you can write cleaner, more maintainable, and performant code in your Angular applications.

In the next chapter, we will explore NgModules, a fundamental building block of Angular applications. We will explore their role in organizing and structuring your application, how to define and use modules, and the importance of lazy loading for performance optimization. Understanding NgModules is crucial for building scalable and maintainable Angular applications.

CHAPTER 12
Concepts of NgModules

Introduction

NgModules have been a fundamental part of Angular for organizing and structuring an Angular application. They provide a way to group related components, services, directives, and pipes, making an application easier to manage and scale. However, with the introduction of newer features in Angular, such as standalone components, the role of NgModules has been evolving.

Angular 19 marks a major shift by making standalone components the default for new Angular projects. This encourages a more streamlined and modular architecture without requiring NgModules. However, NgModules are still fully supported and widely used, especially in large or legacy codebases.

Understanding NgModules remains important for maintaining and working with existing Angular applications. There is no official deprecation timeline, and both models can coexist within the same project.

Structure

This chapter covers the following topics:

- Basic NgModules
- Advanced NgModules
- Recent Angular and standalone features
- Debugging and performance optimization
- Real-world use cases and migration

Objectives

By the end of this chapter, readers will have a clear understanding of the role and purpose of NgModules in Angular applications. They will learn how to structure an Angular application by organizing components, directives, pipes, and services into appropriate modules. Additionally, they will gain insights into optimizing performance through lazy loading with NgModules, and how to bootstrap and organize Angular apps using the **@NgModule** decorator and its properties. Finally, readers will understand the process of migrating from NgModules to standalone components for new Angular code, as recommended starting with Angular 19.

Basic NgModules

Before diving into the modern Angular architecture, it is important to understand the foundational concepts that shaped earlier versions of the framework. One of the core building blocks of Angular applications for many years was the NgModule, which provided a way to organize related components, directives, pipes, and services into cohesive units, making it easier to manage dependencies and structure large applications.

Understanding how NgModules work is essential for developers maintaining legacy codebases or transitioning older projects to newer standards. While Angular has evolved significantly, the principles behind NgModules still offer valuable insights into modular design and dependency management.

> Note: **As of Angular 19, the Angular team has officially deprecated and removed the use of NgModules for all new code. Instead, standalone components should be used for new development. However, this chapter serves to help you understand and work with existing code that uses NgModules, which is still relevant for maintaining or refactoring legacy applications. The shift to standalone components is part of Angular's effort to simplify the framework and encourage a more modular, flexible approach to application development. Standalone components remove the need for NgModules, making code easier to maintain and reducing the overhead of managing multiple modules.**

Question 1: What is an NgModule in Angular?

Answer: An NgModule is a fundamental building block in Angular applications. It is a class that encapsulates a set of related functionalities and provides a way to organize the application into cohesive blocks. An NgModule defines the components, directives, pipes, and services that are part of a specific feature or a set of features in an application.

For example:

```
@NgModule({
  declarations: [AppComponent],
  imports: [BrowserModule],
  providers: [],
  bootstrap: [AppComponent]
})
export class AppModule { }
```

Question 2: Why do we need NgModules in an Angular application?

Answer: NgModules help in doing the following:

- **Organizing code**: Grouping related code together for better structure and maintainability.
- **Encapsulation**: Keeping different parts of the app (like features) isolated from each other to avoid clutter.
- **Lazy loading**: Enabling feature modules to be loaded only when needed, improving performance.
- **Dependency management**: Managing services and components that are available to the entire application or to specific parts.

Question 3: What are the key properties of the @NgModule decorator?

Answer: The **@NgModule** decorator has the following key properties:

- **declarations**: Declares the components, directives, and pipes that belong to this module.
- **imports**: Imports other modules that are required for the functionality of this module.

- **providers**: Specifies the services that are available for dependency injection throughout the module.
- **bootstrap**: Defines the root component(s) that Angular should bootstrap when the application starts (usually for the root module).

Question 4: What is the purpose of the declarations array in an NgModule?

Answer: The declarations array is used to declare the components, directives, and pipes that belong to the module. These are the building blocks of the module, and they can be used within the module and its templates.

For example:

```
@NgModule({
  declarations: [
    AppComponent,
    MyComponent,
    MyDirective
  ]
})
export class AppModule { }
```

Question 5: What is the imports array in an NgModule, and why is it needed?

Answer: The imports array is used to import other modules that are required for the current module to function. This helps in sharing functionality, such as directives, pipes, and services, across multiple modules.

For example:

```
@NgModule({
  imports: [
    BrowserModule,
    FormsModule
  ]
})
export class AppModule { }
```

Question 6: What does the providers array in an NgModule do?

Answer: The providers array is used to register services or providers that will be available for dependency injection throughout the module. These services can be injected into components, directives, and other services.

For example:

```
@NgModule({
  providers: [UserService, AuthService]
})
export class AppModule { }
```

Question 7: What is the bootstrap array, and when is it required in an NgModule?

Answer: The bootstrap array is used in the root module (usually AppModule) to define the root component that Angular should load when the application starts. It is required only in the root module.

For example:

```
@NgModule({
  bootstrap: [AppComponent]
})
export class AppModule { }
```

Question 8: How do you create a feature module in Angular?

Answer: To create a feature module, you define a new module using the **`@NgModule`** decorator, similar to how you define the root module. The feature module can include components, directives, pipes, and services related to a specific feature of the application.

For example:

```
@NgModule({
  declarations: [FeatureComponent],
  imports: [CommonModule],
  providers: []
})
export class FeatureModule { }
```

You can then import this feature module into the root module or other feature modules as needed.

Question 9: What is a shared module, and how do you use it in an Angular app?

Answer: A **`SharedModule`** is a module that contains common functionality (such as commonly used components, directives, or pipes) that needs to be reused across multiple feature modules. The goal is to avoid repeating code and maintain consistency.

For example:

```
@NgModule({
  declarations: [SharedComponent, SharedPipe],
  imports: [CommonModule],
  exports: [SharedComponent, SharedPipe]
})
export class SharedModule { }
```

You can then import the **`SharedModule`** into any other module that requires the shared functionality.

Question 10: What is the difference between BrowserModule and CommonModule in Angular?

Answer: In Angular, both **`BrowserModule`** and **`CommonModule`** are essential modules that provide commonly used features for applications. However, they serve different purposes and are typically imported based on the context of the application. The following are the key differences between **`BrowserModule`** and **`CommonModule`**:

- **BrowserModule**: It is required only in the root module (**`AppModule`**). It provides essential services and directives (like **`ngIf`** and **`ngFor`**) necessary for Angular applications to run in the browser. It is a higher-level module that includes features necessary for bootstrapping and running the app.
- **CommonModule**: It is used in feature modules and provides common directives (like **`ngIf`**, **`ngFor`**) and pipes (like date, currency). It is a lower-level module compared to **`BrowserModule`** and should be imported in feature modules, not the root module.

For example:

```
@NgModule({
  imports: [CommonModule], // Used in feature modules
})
export class FeatureModule { }
@NgModule({
  imports: [BrowserModule], // Used only in the root module
})
export class AppModule { }
```

Advanced NgModules

Question 11: How do lazy loaded modules work with NgModules?

Answer: Lazy loading in Angular enables the loading of feature modules only when they are required, which helps optimize the initial loading time of an application. To set up lazy loading, you define a feature module with its own routes and configure the Angular router to load it lazily when a specific route is accessed.

The following is an example demonstrating how to implement lazy loading in Angular using the following NgModules:

- Feature module (lazy loaded)
- App routing module

For example: Using feature module (lazy loaded):

```
@NgModule({
  declarations: [LazyComponent],
  imports: [CommonModule],
})
export class LazyModule { }
```

For example: Using app routing module:

```
const routes: Routes = [
  { path: 'lazy', loadChildren: () => import('./lazy/lazy.module').then(m => m.LazyModule)
}
];
```

Here, the **`LazyModule`** will be loaded only when the user navigates to the 'lazy' route.

Question 12: What are entryComponents, and how were they used before Angular Ivy?

Answer: Before Angular Ivy, **`entryComponents`** were used to explicitly declare components that would be dynamically loaded, such as components used in a modal or dialog. These components had to be included in the **`entryComponents`** array of the **`@NgModule`** metadata for Angular to know about them during runtime.

For example:

```
@NgModule({
  declarations: [DialogComponent],
  entryComponents: [DialogComponent]
})
export class AppModule { }
```

With Angular Ivy (introduced in Angular 9), the need for **`entryComponents`** has been largely eliminated. Ivy's improved compilation and tree-shaking mechanisms allow Angular to detect and include dynamically loaded components without requiring explicit declaration in **`entryComponents`**.

However, the **`entryComponents`** property still exists for edge cases, such as compatibility scenarios with older libraries or non-standard dynamic component loading strategies, where manual declaration may still be required.

Question 13: How do you create a Core Module in an Angular application?

Answer: A Core Module is used to contain singleton services, components, and other functionality that should only be instantiated once in the application. It is usually imported only in the root module (**`AppModule`**), not in feature modules, to ensure that services are singleton across the app.

For example:

```
@NgModule({
  providers: [AuthService, LoggerService],
  imports: [CommonModule],
})
export class CoreModule { }
```

You then import the **CoreModule** into your root module as follows:

```
@NgModule({
  imports: [CoreModule]
})
export class AppModule { }
```

Question 14: How do you prevent re-importing a module in Angular?

Answer: To prevent re-importing a module in Angular, use the **ForRoot** pattern in the module's **@NgModule** metadata. You can define a method like **forRoot()** that configures the module for the root and ensures it is imported only once.

For example:

```
@NgModule({
  imports: [CommonModule],
  providers: [SomeService],
})
export class SomeModule {
  static forRoot() {
    return {
      ngModule: SomeModule,
      providers: [SomeService] // Singleton service
    };
  }
}
```

Then import it in the **AppModule** as follows:

```
@NgModule({
  imports: [SomeModule.forRoot()]
})
export class AppModule { }
```

This pattern ensures the module and its services are only imported once.

Question 15: What is the difference between a root module and a feature module?

Answer: The difference between a root module and a feature module is as follows:

- **Root module (AppModule)**: The entry point of an Angular application. It is the module where the root component is bootstrapped and where global configurations (like routing and providers) are defined.
- **Feature module**: These are modules that represent distinct features of the application, such as a product catalog or user profile. Feature modules are typically lazy loaded to improve performance.

The following demonstrates how lazy loading works with feature modules:

- `AppModule` is the root module.
- `ProductModule` can be a feature module, imported and lazy loaded only when the user navigates to the product page.

Question 16: How do you structure a large-scale Angular application using NgModules?

Answer: In large-scale Angular applications, it is important to break down the app into smaller, feature-based modules to improve maintainability, testability, and scalability. The following is a typical structure:

- **CoreModule**: Contains singleton services, guards, and global components.
- **SharedModule**: Contains shared components, pipes, and directives.
- **Feature modules**: Each feature (like a user profile, admin panel, etc.) is encapsulated in its own module.
- **Lazy loaded modules**: Feature modules that are loaded on demand.

Question 17: What are singleton services, and how do they work with NgModules?

Answer: A **singleton service** is a service that has only one instance throughout the lifetime of the application. Singleton services are typically provided at the root level, meaning Angular's dependency injection system creates only one instance of the service for the entire application.

In Angular, services can be provided in the **`@NgModule's`** providers array, and this ensures that the service remains a singleton.

For example:

```
@NgModule({
  providers: [LoggerService]
})
export class CoreModule { }
@Injectable({
  providedIn: 'root'
})
export class LoggerService {
  log(message: string) {
    console.log(message);
  }
}
```

Question 18: How do you share components, directives, and pipes across multiple modules?

Answer: These are sequence-wise steps that users need to follow when sharing components, directives, and pipes across multiple modules. The sequence is given as follows:

1. Declare them in a shared module.
2. Export them from the shared module.
3. Import the shared module into any feature module or root module where you need to use these components.

These steps ensure that the components, directives, and pipes are available to other modules.

For example:

```
@NgModule({
  declarations: [SharedComponent, SharedDirective],
  exports: [SharedComponent, SharedDirective]
```

```
})
export class SharedModule { }
@NgModule({
  imports: [SharedModule]
})
export class FeatureModule { }
```

Question 19: What are the advantages and disadvantages of using NgModules?

Answer: The following are the advantages of using NgModules:

- **Modularization**: Helps in organizing the code into logical, cohesive blocks.
- **Lazy loading**: Improves performance by loading modules on demand.
- **Scalability**: Makes it easier to scale and maintain large applications by keeping features isolated.

The following are the disadvantages of using NgModules:

- **Complexity**: Can add complexity to an application, especially in very large applications.
- **Overhead**: Sometimes NgModules might seem like overkill for small applications.

Question 20: How do NgModules interact with Angular DI?

Answer: NgModules are an essential part of Angular's DI system. Providers registered within an NgModule (either at the module level or at the root level) are available for injection into components, services, and other providers within that module or any other modules that import it.

Angular uses the module system to manage and scope the instances of services, ensuring that services are instantiated in the appropriate context (singleton, lazy loaded, etc.).

For example:

```
@NgModule({
  providers: [SomeService]
})
export class SomeModule { }
@Injectable({
  providedIn: 'root' // Singleton service provided at the root level
})
export class SomeService { }
```

In this example, `SomeService` is registered in `SomeModule`, and it will be injected wherever it is needed, based on its provided scope.

Recent Angular and standalone features

Question 21: What changes have been introduced in NgModules with Angular 18+?

Answer: Angular 18+ brings several optimizations and enhancements to the way NgModules are used, especially in the context of signal-based components and new rendering strategies as follows:

- **Enhanced tree-shaking**: NgModules are better optimized for tree-shaking, ensuring that only used components, directives, and services are included in the final bundle.
- **Support for signals**: Angular 18+ improved compatibility with signal-based components, allowing for reactive programming paradigms within NgModules.

- **Improved lazy loading**: Lazy loading has become more efficient, especially when combined with Angular's new rendering strategies, reducing initial load times.

These changes streamline the use of NgModules and make it easier to integrate with newer Angular features while maintaining compatibility with older code.

Question 22: How does the standalone API introduced in Angular 14 impact NgModules?

Answer: The standalone API introduced in Angular 14 significantly reduced the reliance on NgModules for many common use cases. It allows you to create standalone components, directives, and pipes without needing to wrap them inside an NgModule. This simplifies component-based development, removes boilerplate, and can make code more modular.

The following are the key impacts of using standalone components:

- **No NgModule required for standalone components**: Standalone components can be directly declared and used without NgModules.
- **Simplified dependencies**: Standalone components can declare their dependencies directly using imports, eliminating the need to import entire modules when only a few components are needed.

For example:

```
@Component({
  selector: 'app-standalone',
  standalone: true,
  imports: [CommonModule]
})
export class StandaloneComponent {}
```

Here, **`StandaloneComponent`** does not require an NgModule.

Question 23: Can we use both standalone components and NgModules together in Angular 19+?

Answer: Yes, Angular 19+ fully supports using both standalone components and NgModules together. This hybrid approach allows you to progressively migrate from NgModules to standalone components or use standalone components for smaller, isolated features without needing to restructure the entire application. Here is how standalone components can be utilized effectively:

- Standalone components can be used in routes or as part of other components.
- NgModules can still be used to organize larger parts of the application, providing flexibility for both new and existing codebases.

For example:

```
@NgModule({
  declarations: [ExistingComponent],
  imports: [CommonModule],
  exports: [ExistingComponent]
})
export class FeatureModule {}
@Component({
  selector: 'app-standalone',
  standalone: true,
  imports: [CommonModule]
})
export class StandaloneComponent {}
```

In this example, both a **FeatureModule** (using NgModule) and **StandaloneComponent** (without NgModule) are used in the same application.

Question 24: What is the recommended approach for structuring applications in Angular 20?

Answer: Angular 20 continues to embrace flexibility with a focus on modular architecture. The recommended approach for structuring applications includes the following:

- **Standalone components**: Using standalone components for most of the application's UI pieces. This reduces boilerplate and simplifies development.
- **Feature modules**: Grouping related features into lazy loaded modules for performance optimization.
- **Core and shared modules**: Use a **CoreModule** for singleton services and essential functionality, and a **SharedModule** for commonly used components, directives, and pipes.
- **Hybrid structure**: Angular 20 supports hybrid applications, where parts of the app can use NgModules and others can leverage standalone components.

Question 25: How does NgModules work with the latest hydration and SSR improvements?

Answer: Angular's hydration and SSR improvements in versions 19 and 20 work seamlessly with NgModules. Hydration involves sending a fully rendered page from the server to the client, and NgModules play an important role in structuring the application on the server side.

The following are some key benefits related to SSR and performance optimization in Angular:

- **Hydration**: NgModules can be configured to use both SSR and hydration, where components inside the NgModule are rendered on the server and then rehydrated on the client without a full reload.
- **Optimized performance**: Angular optimizes module loading and rendering on the client side, improving **time-to-interactive** (**TTI**) and the user experience.

For example: SSR with NgModule:

```
@NgModule({
  imports: [BrowserModule.withServerTransition({ appId: 'my-app' }), AppRoutingModule],
  bootstrap: [AppComponent]
})
export class AppModule {}
```

Question 26: What are the performance benefits of moving from NgModules to standalone components?

Answer: Moving from NgModules to standalone components offers several performance benefits as follows:

- **Reduced bundle size**: Standalone components can be imported directly, meaning only the necessary components are included in the final bundle. This reduces the overhead compared to loading entire modules.
- **Faster load times**: Standalone components can be lazy loaded more easily, improving the initial load time by only loading components as needed.
- **Simplified codebase**: With fewer dependencies between components and NgModules, the application becomes easier to maintain and scale.

Question 27: How does lazy loading work differently in standalone API vs. NgModules?

Answer: With standalone API, lazy loading becomes even more flexible, shown as follows:

- **In NgModules**: You have to use **loadChildren** to configure lazy loaded modules in the routing configuration.
- **In standalone components**: You can directly lazy load standalone components without the need for an entire module.

For example: Lazy loading standalone component:

```
const routes: Routes = [
  {
    path: 'lazy',
    loadComponent: () => import('./lazy/lazy.component').then(m => m.LazyComponent)
  }
];
```

In this case, the `LazyComponent` is loaded lazily, without needing a wrapper module.

Question 28: How does Angular handle providers differently in standalone components?

Answer: Standalone components in Angular allow for more granular control over service providers. You can define providers directly in the component's metadata, making it possible to scope services to just that component or a group of components. This reduces the need to provide services at the module level.

For example:

```
@Component({
  selector: 'app-standalone',
  standalone: true,
  imports: [CommonModule],
  providers: [MyService]
})
export class StandaloneComponent {}
```

In this case, `MyService` is provided only for `StandaloneComponent`.

Question 29: What are the best practices for migrating a large app from NgModules to standalone components?

Answer: Migrating a large application from NgModules to standalone components can be a complex process, requiring careful planning and execution. The following best practices can help ensure a smooth transition:

- **Gradual migration**: Start by converting smaller, self-contained components into standalone components, especially those that do not depend on many services.
- **Hybrid approach**: Use standalone components where feasible, but keep NgModules for complex feature areas, lazy loading, and legacy code.
- **Ensure dependency management**: Make sure services, pipes, and other components are correctly scoped when migrating.
- **Optimize routing**: With standalone components, refactor the routing to use `loadComponent` instead of `loadChildren` for lazy loaded components.

Question 30: How do Angular signals interact with NgModules in the latest versions?

Answer: Angular signals, a reactive programming feature introduced in Angular 19+, allows for a more efficient and declarative approach to handling state changes. NgModules continue to support signals, but signals offer an alternative to RxJS or `EventEmitters` in some scenarios.

Signals can be integrated effectively in the following manner:

- **Signals** can be used alongside NgModules to create more reactive components and services without the need for observables or NgRx.
- The **signals API** allows for more efficient state management and can be used directly inside components, services, or even in NgModules.

For example:

```
import { signal } from '@angular/core';
@Component({
  selector: 'app-signal',
  template: `Value: {{ value() }}`
})
export class SignalComponent {
  value = signal(0);
  increment() {
    this.value.update(v => v + 1);
  }
}
```

This integrates signals into a typical Angular component setup.

Debugging and performance optimization

Question 31: How do you debug issues related to NgModules?

Answer: Debugging issues with NgModules can be challenging, especially in larger applications. The following are a few strategies:

- **Check module imports:** Ensure all necessary modules are imported in the correct NgModules. Missing imports can lead to runtime errors or undefined behaviors.
- **Use Angular Command Line Interface (CLI):** The Angular CLI can be used to generate and serve the app with debugging enabled. `ng serve` or `ng build --prod` can help identify issues related to module resolution.
- **Browser DevTools:** Utilize the browser's developer tools to inspect the console for errors related to missing components or services.
- **Debugging tools like Augury:** Augury is an Angular-specific Chrome extension that can help visualize the structure of NgModules, components, and routing.
- **Console logs and breakpoints:** Sometimes, adding logs or setting breakpoints in the component or module files can reveal missing or incorrectly configured parts.

Question 32: What are common mistakes developers make when working with NgModules?

Answer: Some common mistakes when working with NgModules include the following:

- **Overloading a module:** Placing too many unrelated components, directives, or pipes into a single module can lead to an overly complex and unmanageable structure.
- **Not exporting components:** If components, directives, or pipes are not exported, they will not be available for use in other modules, leading to errors in templates.
- **Circular dependencies:** Importing modules in a circular way can cause Angular to fail during compilation.
- **Incorrect use of imports and declarations:** Developers sometimes mix imports (which bring in other modules) with declarations (which register components, directives, and pipes) incorrectly.

Question 33: How do NgModules impact performance in large Angular applications?

Answer: NgModules impact performance in several ways as follows:

- **Lazy loading:** Proper use of lazy loaded modules can significantly improve initial load times, as only the essential modules are loaded initially.

- **Tree shaking**: If modules are structured correctly (i.e., keeping them small and focused), Angular's tree-shaking process can remove unused code, optimizing the bundle size.
- **Module resolution**: Large, poorly organized NgModules can result in unnecessary module imports, increasing the size of the application bundle and slowing down load times.
- **Memory overhead**: Each module has some memory overhead, so splitting the application into smaller, focused modules can improve performance.

Question 34: How can you optimize an Angular app with multiple feature modules?

Answer: Optimize an Angular app with multiple feature modules as follows:

- **Lazy load feature modules**: Load only the necessary feature modules at the time of need rather than loading everything upfront.
- **Use shared modules**: Put commonly used components, directives, and pipes in shared modules and import them only where needed to avoid repetition.
- **Optimize imports**: Avoid importing unnecessary modules into feature modules. Only import modules that provide functionality needed by that module.
- **Tree-shaking**: Ensure that the app's build configuration supports tree-shaking, which removes unused code.

Question 35: What tools can you use to analyze module dependencies and optimize loading?

Answer: Several tools can help analyze module dependencies and optimize loading as follows:

- **Webpack Bundle Analyzer**: This tool helps visualize the size of bundles, including the modules included in them. This is useful for identifying large, unoptimized bundles.
- **Source Map Explorer**: A tool that analyzes source maps and generates a visual representation of your bundle to help you identify which files take up the most space.
- **Angular CLI ng build --stats-json**: This command generates stats in JSON format, which can then be analyzed with tools like webpack-bundle-analyzer.
- **Angular DevTools (Augury)**: A Chrome extension for inspecting Angular applications that provides an overview of module dependencies and component trees.

Question 36: What are circular dependencies in NgModules, and how do you avoid them?

Answer: Circular dependencies occur when two or more modules depend on each other, creating a cycle that Angular's compiler cannot resolve. This can cause runtime errors or slow down the application.

Example of a circular dependency: Module A imports Module B, and Module B imports Module A.

To avoid common issues related to module dependencies and improve the maintainability of your Angular application, consider implementing the following strategies:

- **Restructure modules**: Split the code into smaller, more focused modules and ensure that the dependencies flow in one direction.
- **Use services to break dependencies**: If two modules depend on each other, consider moving shared logic to a service that can be injected into both modules.
- **Avoid unnecessary imports**: Only import what is necessary for a module to function.

Question 37: How does NgModules affect tree shaking and bundle optimization?

Answer: NgModules play a crucial role in Angular's tree-shaking and bundle optimization processes. Tree shaking is a method of removing unused code from the final bundle, and bundle optimization focuses on ensuring that the final output is as efficient and small as possible. NgModules contribute to both in the following manner:

- **Small modules**: By breaking your application into smaller, focused modules, unused code can be excluded more effectively, allowing tree shaking to remove unnecessary parts from the final bundle.

- **Correct module exports**: If unused components, directives, or services are not exported from modules, they will be excluded from the final bundle by tree shaking, resulting in a more optimized application.
- **Lazy loading**: By lazy loading feature modules, Angular ensures that only the necessary parts of the application are loaded initially, reducing the size of the initial bundle and optimizing the application load time.
- **Minification**: Tools like Terser are used in Angular to minify the final bundle, removing unnecessary whitespace, comments, and shortening variable names, which contributes to reducing the bundle size.
- **Code splitting**: Angular supports code splitting, where the application is divided into smaller chunks, ensuring that only the required code is loaded for each user interaction, leading to a faster and more efficient loading experience.
- **Preloading strategies**: Angular allows you to preload certain lazy loaded modules after the initial load, balancing the need for quick access to critical modules while optimizing the overall application size and load time.

By leveraging these strategies, Angular ensures that both tree shaking and bundle optimization work together to reduce the size and improve the performance of your application.

Question 38: How does Angular handle component encapsulation within an NgModule?

Answer: Angular uses **`ViewEncapsulation`** to manage component encapsulation as follows:

- **Emulated (default)**: Angular creates a shadow **Document Object Model** (**DOM**) for the component and adds unique attributes to the component's **Cascading Style Sheets** (**CSS**), ensuring styles do not leak into other components.
- **None**: The styles are not encapsulated, and they apply globally across the application.
- **ShadowDOM**: Uses the native shadow DOM browser feature to encapsulate styles and the component's template.

Component encapsulation is independent of NgModules. You can use any encapsulation mode within an NgModule to control the visibility of styles and templates.

Question 39: How do you handle internationalization (i18n) within NgModules?

Answer: Angular provides built-in i18n support for handling internationalization in NgModules as follows:

- **Translate pipes and services**: Use Angular's i18n pipe or third-party libraries like **`ngx-translate`** to manage translations.
- **Define translations**: In each NgModule, you can define translations in different languages and use them in components, templates, and services.
- **LocaleData**: Angular allows you to configure the application's locale data and format dates, numbers, and currencies based on the selected language.

For example:

```
@NgModule({
  imports: [CommonModule, I18nModule],
  providers: [{ provide: LOCALE_ID, useValue: 'en' }]
})
export class AppModule {}
```

Question 40: How do you integrate AngularFire or Firebase with NgModules?

Answer: AngularFire is the official library for Firebase integration with Angular, and it integrates seamlessly with NgModules. The process flows in the following manner:

1. **Install AngularFire**: First, you need to install the **`@angular/fire`** library via **`npm`** to enable Firebase integration.

2. **Set up Firebase configuration**: Next, configure Firebase in the **AppModule** or another appropriate NgModule, including setting up the Firebase project credentials.
3. **Use Firebase services**: Finally, you import the required Firebase services (e.g., Firestore, Authentication) and inject them into the components where they are needed.

These steps are logically sequenced to properly integrate AngularFire into your Angular application.

For example:

```
@NgModule({
  imports: [
    BrowserModule,
    AngularFireModule.initializeApp(environment.firebaseConfig),
    AngularFireAuthModule
  ],
  bootstrap: [AppComponent]
})
export class AppModule {}
```

In this example, the **AngularFireAuthModule** is included in the **AppModule**, and Firebase configuration is initialized.

Real-world use cases and migration

Question 41. When should you still use NgModules instead of standalone components?

Answer: You might still use NgModules in the following scenarios:

- **Legacy projects**: Existing projects heavily dependent on NgModules will continue to use them for compatibility and to avoid large-scale refactoring.
- **Large-scale applications**: In some cases, especially with complex routing and shared services, NgModules might provide better separation of concerns and organization.
- **Third-party integrations**: Some third-party libraries may still require the use of NgModules.
- **Feature organization**: NgModules are a better choice for organizing features into cohesive, reusable parts that encapsulate components, services, and other resources.

Question 42: How do you gradually migrate an existing NgModule-based project to a standalone API?

Answer: When migrating from NgModules to standalone components, you can do so incrementally as follows:

1. **Start with components**: Convert individual components to stand-alone by using the standalone: true property in their metadata. Test each component independently before proceeding.
2. **Gradually migrate services**: Move services used within the components to standalone services. This avoids breaking the existing structure.
3. **Lazy loading**: Use the **loadComponent** method to load standalone components lazily, just like NgModules.
4. **Update routing**: Change your routes to support standalone components, adjusting the routing configuration to accommodate them.
5. **Mix NgModules and standalone components**: During the migration phase, you can use both NgModules and standalone components in the same application.

Question 43: What is the best approach for handling dependency injection when migrating from NgModules?

Answer: When migrating to standalone components, you need to handle DI as follows:

- **Injectable services**: Services can still be injected into standalone components, but they need to be provided explicitly. If migrating from NgModules, replace the providers array in the NgModule with providedIn in the service.
- **Singleton services**: Use Angular's DI system to ensure services remain singletons by marking services with `providedIn: 'root'`.
- **Providers in standalone components**: You can provide dependencies directly in standalone components via the providers array.
- **Shared modules**: You can still use NgModules for shared services and other dependencies, but as you migrate to standalone, start providing services in individual components as needed.

Question 44: **How do you structure an Angular enterprise application using both standalone and NgModules?**

Answer: For an enterprise application, you can combine both standalone components and NgModules as follows:

- **Feature modules (NgModules)**: For organizing major features and maintaining backward compatibility, continue using NgModules.
- **Standalone components**: For reusable components or smaller features that do not require a lot of infrastructure, use standalone components.
- **Shared module**: Create a shared module that exports common components, directives, and pipes for use across both standalone and NgModule-based components.
- **Routing**: Use NgModules for routing setup and lazy loading of larger modules, while standalone components can be routed dynamically.

Question 45: **How do you test modules in Angular, and what are the best practices?**

Answer: Testing NgModules and components is crucial to maintaining code quality. The best practices for the same are as follows:

- **Unit tests**: Use Jasmine, Karma, or Jest for unit testing components, services, and pipes in isolation.
- **TestBed**: Use `TestBed.configureTestingModule()` to set up test modules for unit testing. You can use imports, declarations, and providers in the testing module.
- **Component testing**: Test components by using `fixture.detectChanges()` to trigger change detection and simulate DOM interactions.
- **Mocking dependencies**: Use spies or mocks for external dependencies such as services.
- **Integration testing**: Test interactions between components, services, and NgModules by using Angular's integration testing features with `HttpClientTestingModule` and mock backend services.

Question 46: **How do you handle security concerns (e.g., lazy loading authentication modules)?**

Answer: You can handle security concerns in Angular applications as follows:

- **Lazy loading authentication modules**: Use lazy loaded modules to load authentication and authorization logic only when needed.
- **CanActivate guards**: Use Angular guards to control access to routes, ensuring that unauthenticated users cannot access restricted areas.
- **Http interceptors**: Use HTTP interceptors to attach tokens and handle secure communication with the backend.
- **Role-based access**: Use guards to check user roles before allowing access to certain features or routes.
- **Sanitization**: Angular's built-in sanitization functions (`DomSanitizer`) prevent XSS attacks by sanitizing potentially dangerous values in templates.

Question 47: How do you modularize a complex UI library using NgModules?

Answer: When building a complex UI library with NgModules, ensure the following:

- **Group components**: Organize components based on their functionality or context (e.g., buttons, modals, form controls).
- **Feature modules**: Break the UI library into feature modules, with each module containing related components, directives, and pipes.
- **Shared modules**: Create shared modules that export commonly used UI components (like buttons, inputs, etc.) and import them into other feature modules as needed.
- **Third-party UI libraries**: If integrating with third-party libraries (e.g., Material UI), make sure they are imported into your library's NgModules appropriately.
- **Lazy loading**: If the library is large, consider lazy loading some UI components to optimize performance.

Question 48: What are some real-world challenges when working with multiple NgModules?

Answer: Working with multiple NgModules can introduce the following:

- **Complex dependency management**: Managing imports and dependencies can get complicated, especially when there are circular dependencies or missing imports.
- **Performance issues**: Incorrect module structure or lack of lazy loading can increase the application's initial loading time.
- **Overloaded modules**: Too many components or services in a single module can make it harder to maintain and scale.
- **Versioning**: If multiple modules are being used across the app, version mismatches between different feature modules can cause conflicts.
- **Testing**: Testing modules with many interdependencies can become challenging, requiring careful setup in test beds.

Question 49: How do NgModules interact with web components in Angular?

Answer: NgModules and Web Components can work together in Angular as follows:

- **Encapsulating web components**: You can use Angular components to encapsulate web components and use them inside Angular templates.
- **Custom elements**: Angular allows you to define Angular components as custom elements, which can be used as web components in other applications.
- **Modules and web components**: You may need to import Angular modules (for services or other components) to use web components within Angular components.
- **Example**: Using `CUSTOM_ELEMENTS_SCHEMA` in NgModules to allow non-Angular elements (web components) to be used in templates.

Question 50: How does Angular's new compiler handle module-based applications differently in recent versions?

Answer: Angular's new Ivy compiler and Angular 18+ compilers have improved how modules are handled in the following ways:

- **Smaller bundles**: Ivy makes it possible to generate smaller, more efficient bundles by using better tree-shaking, meaning unused modules are excluded from the build.
- **Dynamic module loading**: The compiler can optimize lazy loaded modules by only loading them when required, reducing the initial payload.
- **Better dependency resolution**: Ivy's enhanced dependency resolution ensures that Angular can

detect and resolve module dependencies more efficiently, leading to faster builds and better runtime performance.

- **View engine compatibility**: Angular's Ivy compiler, introduced in Angular 9, initially offered backward compatibility with the older View Engine, allowing mixed-mode applications and libraries to coexist. However, starting from Angular 13, the View Engine was fully removed. From Angular 13 onward, and especially in Angular 18+, all applications and libraries must be compiled with Ivy. This means Ivy is now the only supported rendering engine, offering better performance, smaller bundles, and more advanced features (like standalone components and signals).

Conclusion

In this chapter, we explored key concepts related to NgModules, their structure, and how they contribute to Angular's modularity. We also discussed how to manage dependencies effectively, optimize performance, and leverage lazy loading for better resource management. While NgModules remain important for legacy applications, the transition to standalone components marks a new era of flexibility and modularity in Angular. Understanding these concepts equips developers with the knowledge to navigate both older and newer approaches in Angular development.

The next chapter will explore **internationalization (i18n)**, a critical aspect of modern web applications that enables them to be adapted to different languages and regions. We will explore the tools, techniques, and best practices for localizing an Angular application, ensuring that it is accessible and usable by a global audience. This chapter will focus on understanding internationalization concepts, Angular's built-in i18n support, and how to implement localization effectively across multiple languages and regions.

CHAPTER 13
Concepts of Internationalization

Introduction

Internationalization (**i18n**) is the process of designing software applications in a way that allows them to be easily adapted to various languages, regions, and cultures. The goal of internationalization is to ensure that the application can be **localized** (**l10n**) without requiring significant changes to the underlying code. This chapter introduces the concepts and best practices for implementing internationalization in software development, particularly focusing on Angular.

Structure

This chapter covers the following topics:

- Basics of internationalization
- Advanced internationalization concepts
- Latest i18n features

Objectives

By the end of this chapter, you will have a solid understanding of the core concepts of i18n and its relationship to l10n, enabling you to implement effective internationalization strategies in Angular applications using built-in tools and libraries. You will learn to manage text translations, as well as format dates, numbers, and currencies across multiple locales. Additionally, you will be able to set up your application to handle user-specific language preferences and fallback mechanisms efficiently. The chapter will also help you identify common challenges in building globally adaptable software and provide strategies to overcome these obstacles, ensuring your applications are ready for diverse global markets.

Basics of internationalization

Question 1: What is internationalization in Angular, and why is it important?

Answer: i18n in Angular refers to the process of designing and developing applications in such a way that they can be easily adapted to different languages and regions without changing the core functionality of the app. It ensures that an application can support multiple languages, date formats, currency symbols, and other locale-specific features to provide a localized user experience for users around the world.

The following figure illustrates i18n flow in Angular, showing how translation files and locale configurations work together to support multilingual applications:

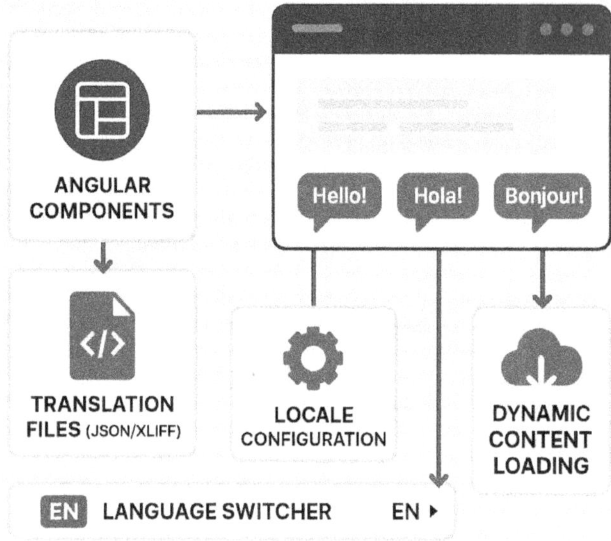

Figure 13.1: Internationalization flow

i18n has the following benefits:

- **Global reach**: Enables you to create applications that are accessible to users from different regions, making your product usable internationally.
- **Localization support**: It provides an easy way to localize text and other region-specific features (like date, time, and currency formatting).
- **Scalability**: Once set up, the application can easily be extended to support additional languages without significant code changes.

For example:

- **Marking translatable content**: In your Angular component, use the i18n attribute to mark content for translation as follows:

  ```
  <!-- app.component.html -->
  <h1 i18n="@@homeTitle">Welcome to our Application!</h1>
  ```

- **Extracting translatable content**: Run the following command to extract the marked content into a translation file:

  ```
  ng xi18n --output-path src/locale
  ```

  This will create a **`messages.xlf`** file, which you can translate into other languages.

- **Using translation files**: Once you have the translation files (e.g., **`messages.fr.xlf`** for French), you can build your application for different locales using the following:

  ```
  ng build --localize
  ```

  Now, the text in the application will be displayed in the user's preferred language.

The benefits of i18n are as follows:

- Reusable, centralizes text to be translated.
- No need to change the application code for every language.
- Helps in maintaining scalable and accessible applications.

Angular handles untranslated content in the following manner:

- If a translation is missing, Angular can:
    - Show the original (source) text (default behavior).
    - Throw a build-time error (if strict mode is enabled).
- You can control this behavior using the **`--missing-translation`** flag:
    - **warning**: Show a warning.
    - **error**: Fail the build.
    - **ignore**: Use original text silently.

  For example:

```
ng build --localize --missing-translation=warning
```

Question 2: What is the difference between i18n and l10n?

Answer: To better understand the differences between i18n and l10n, it is important to distinguish the roles each plays in the global software development process. The following is a breakdown of how these two concepts work together:

- **Internationalization (i18n)**: Refers to the design and development of an application that allows it to be adapted to various languages and regions. It is about preparing your app to support multiple locales and languages without requiring changes to the underlying codebase.
- **Localization (l10n)**: Refers to the actual adaptation of the application to a specific locale by translating content, adjusting formats for dates, numbers, and currencies, and ensuring that cultural preferences are respected.

In summary, internationalization is the process of preparing an application for multiple languages, while localization is the process of translating and adapting the content for a particular language and region.

Question 3: How do you enable i18n support in an Angular application?

Answer: To enable i18n support in an Angular application, complete the following steps:

1. Install the **`@angular/localize`** package with the following command:

```
ng add @angular/localize
```

2. Mark translatable content in your templates using the i18n attribute as follows:

```
<h1 i18n="@@homeTitle">Welcome</h1>
```

3. Run the following command to configure the build system to extract and compile translations:

```
ng build --localize
```

   You can now create different translation files and use Angular CLI to build the application for different languages.

Question 4: What is the purpose of the @angular/localize package in Angular?

Answer: The **`@angular/localize`** package provides the necessary tools and utilities to implement internationalization in an Angular app. It supports the extraction of translatable content from templates, compilation of translations, and generation of locale-specific bundles for different languages. It includes tools such as the following:

- **`localize`** function for marking content to be translated.
- CLI commands to extract and compile translation files.
- Support for working with translation files like XLIFF and XMB formats.

When choosing between formats for Angular translation files (i18n), the decision depends on your use case and tooling needs. Here is a clear comparison to help you decide which is better and why:

- **XML Localization Interchange File Format (XLIFF)**: Recommended for most modern applications and widely supported by **Translation Management Systems** (**TMS**) like POEditor, Lokalise, Crowdin, Phrase, etc.
- **XML Message Bundle (XMB)**: Older format; used in some Google-internal projects. Use XMB if you want a very lightweight format. Also, your project is internal, small, and you do not plan to use third-party translation tools.

Question 5: How does Angular extract translatable content from a project?

Answer: Angular uses the Angular CLI to extract translatable content from your templates and code. The ng xi18n command generates a translation source file (e.g., **`messages.xlf`** or **`messages.xmb`**) that contains all the text marked for translation.

For example:

```
ng xi18n --output-path src/locale
```

The preceding command will extract all the text wrapped in the i18n attribute into the specified src/locale folder. The generated file can be shared with translators for localization.

Question 6: How do you generate a translation file (messages.xlf) in Angular?

Answer: To generate a translation file, use the **`ng xi18n`** command. This command extracts all translatable content from an Angular app and generates a translation file (e.g., **`messages.xlf`**).

For example:

```
ng xi18n --output-path src/locale
```

This will create a **`messages.xlf`** file in the src/locale folder, which can be translated into various languages. You can then compile these translations into the application.

Question 7: What are the different file formats supported for translation in Angular (XLIFF, XMB, etc.)?

Answer: Angular supports the following translation file formats:

- **XML Localization Interchange File Format (XLIFF)**: This is a popular open standard format used for translation files. The file extension is typically **`.xlf`**.
- **XML Message Bundle (XMB)**: An older format that Angular used for translations. It is still supported, but is less common now compared to XLIFF.
- **JSON**: Angular supports using JSON files for translations, which might be useful when integrating with other localization systems or for runtime translation handling.

Question 8: How do you implement runtime translations using Angular's i18n module?

Answer: For runtime translations in Angular, you can use the **`@angular/localize`** package, which supports dynamic translations. You load translations at runtime based on the user's language preferences and inject them into your application. This is typically done using the **`TranslateService`** in an external library like **`@ngx-translate/core`**.

For example:

```
import { TranslateService } from '@ngx-translate/core';
constructor(private translate: TranslateService) {
  translate.setDefaultLang('en');
}
switchLanguage(language: string) {
  this.translate.use(language);
}
```

Question 9: What are the different ways to translate content dynamically in Angular?

Answer: The following are the different ways to translate content dynamically:

- Use Angular i18n with services that load translation files at runtime.
- Use **ngx-translate** library, which provides a flexible and scalable way to manage translations, shown as follows:

  ```
  npm install @ngx-translate/core @ngx-translate/http-loader
  ```

  Then, configure the module and use the service to translate text dynamically.
- Use HTTP requests to load translation files from a server and switch between languages at runtime.

Question 10: How do you handle pluralization and gender-specific translations in Angular?

Answer: Angular i18n supports handling pluralization and gender-specific translations using the **International Components for Unicode** (**ICU**) message format. You can define plural and gender rules directly in the translation file.

Refer to the following example for pluralization:

```
<p i18n="@@message" [i18nPlural]="itemCount">
  { itemCount, plural,
    =0 {No items}
    =1 {One item}
    other {# items}
  }
</p>
```

In an **.xlf** translation file, pluralization is handled through the use of ICU syntax to manage varying translations based on different numeric values. For example, the following code demonstrates how plural forms are defined for the "**itemCount**" variable:

```
<trans-unit id="message">
  <source>{ itemCount, plural, =0 {No items} =1 {One item} other {# items} }</source>
  <target>{ itemCount, plural, =0 {No items} =1 {One item} other {# items} }</target>
</trans-unit>
```

For gender-specific translations, use the same ICU syntax but with gender rules as follows:

```
<p i18n="@@greeting">
  {gender, select,
    male {Hello, Sir}
    female {Hello, Ma'am}
    other {Hello}
  }
</p>
```

These methods ensure that your application can provide proper translations based on context, such as different plural forms or gender-specific translations.

Advanced internationalization concepts

Question 11: How does Angular support multiple languages in an application?

Answer: Angular supports multiple languages using the i18n module, which allows you to mark translatable content in your templates and extract it into translation files. It also provides a mechanism for building your app in different languages. Angular enables the use of localization by creating different bundles for each supported language and loading the correct bundle at runtime based on the user's locale.

For example: You can define text in templates as follows:

```
<h1 i18n="@@homeTitle">Welcome</h1>
```

Then, Angular's build process compiles these translations for different languages into separate bundles.

Question 12: What is the difference between compile-time and runtime translation in Angular?

Answer: To understand the differences between compile-time and runtime translation in Angular, it is important to recognize how and when translation files are processed and applied. The following is a comparison of the two approaches:

- **Compile-time translation**: This occurs during the build process, where Angular compiles the translation files (e.g., **`messages.xlf`**) and generates language-specific bundles. These translations are part of the final build and are ready when the application is deployed.
- **Runtime translation**: This allows you to dynamically load translation files (e.g., JSON or XLF) based on the user's preferences or locale settings during runtime, without rebuilding the application.
- **AOT compilation impact (in compile-time translation)**: AOT compiles templates to highly optimized JavaScript before runtime. It improves app startup time, smaller bundle size, and early error detection. Also, works best with static i18n translations (i.e., compile-time translation).

For example:

- **Compile-time**: **`ng build --localize`**
- **Runtime**: Using libraries like **`ngx-translate`** to load translation files dynamically.

Question 13: How do you switch languages dynamically in an Angular application?

Answer: To switch languages dynamically in Angular, you can use the **`ngx-translate`** library, which provides an easy way to load translation files at runtime.

For example: To implement dynamic language switching in an Angular application using the **`@ngx-translate/core`** library, follow these steps:

1. **Install the necessary library**:

   ```
   npm install @ngx-translate/core @ngx-translate/http-loader
   ```

2. **Configure the TranslateModule in your AppModule**:

   ```
   // Import and configure the TranslateModule in your application's main module
   import { TranslateModule, TranslateService } from '@ngx-translate/core';
   import { HttpClientModule } from '@angular/common/http';
   @NgModule({
     imports: [TranslateModule.forRoot(), HttpClientModule],
     providers: [TranslateService]
   })
   export class AppModule { }
   ```

3. **Switch languages in your component**:

   ```
   // In your component, inject the TranslateService and set the default language. You can then create a method to switch languages dynamically
   constructor(private translate: TranslateService) {
     this.translate.setDefaultLang('en');
   }
   switchLanguage(language: string) {
   ```

```
    this.translate.use(language);
  }
```

In the preceding example, the setup enables the dynamic loading and switching of languages at runtime, allowing an application to adapt to different user preferences or locale settings without the need for a rebuild. By utilizing the **@ngx-translate/core** library, you can easily manage language files and seamlessly provide a localized experience for users.

Question 14: How do you handle i18n for dynamic content (e.g., data from APIs)?

Answer: In Angular applications, static content (like labels and headings) can be easily internationalized using Angular's built-in i18n tools and translation files. However, dynamic content, such as data fetched from APIs or user-generated content, requires additional strategies. The following list explains how to handle such scenarios effectively:

- **Backend-translated content (recommended for CMS-driven or content-rich apps)**: The most robust approach is to have the backend or **content management system** (**CMS**) return translated content based on the requested locale. The Angular frontend simply renders the localized data.

  For example:

  ```
  GET /api/products?lang=fr
  ```

  Response:

  ```
  {"name": "Ordinateur portable", "description": "Ultrabook."}
  ```

  This approach simplifies frontend logic and ensures accurate translations are managed centrally.

- **Using runtime translation libraries (e.g., @ngx-translate/core)**: For frontend-based dynamic translation, libraries like **@ngx-translate/core** are ideal. These libraries allow developers to translate dynamic keys or API-driven values at runtime.

  For example:

  ```
  this.translate.get('WELCOME_USER', {name: user.name}).subscribe(msg => {
    this.welcomeMessage = msg; // "Welcome, Anil"
  });
  ```

  This method supports language switching at runtime and works well for dynamic UI content.

- **Manual translation mapping**: For simple applications with limited dynamic content, developers can define manual translation maps in the frontend and use them to display localized content based on the current language.

  For example:

  ```
  const statusMap = {
    en: { APPROVED: 'Approved', REJECTED: 'Rejected' },
    fr: { APPROVED: 'Approuvé', REJECTED: 'Rejeté' }
  };
  this.statusText = statusMap[this.language][apiStatus];
  ```

  While quick to implement, this method does **not scale well** for large applications or multiple locales.

- **Custom pipes or services**: To simplify translation of dynamic values in templates, you can implement a custom Angular Pipe or a **TranslationService** that wraps the runtime library.

  For example:

  ```
  @Pipe({ name: 'translateKey' })
  export class TranslateKeyPipe implements PipeTransform {
    constructor(private translate: TranslateService) {}
    transform(key: string): string {
  ```

```
    return this.translate.instant(key);
  }
}
```

Usage in template:

```
<span>{{ 'LOGOUT_MESSAGE' | translateKey }}</span>
```

The best practices are as follows:

- **CMS or content-driven apps**: API should return localized data directly.
- **Dynamic UI labels or messages**: Use **`@ngx-translate/core`** or similar runtime translation libraries.
- **Status fields or short values**: Use a manual translation map or a custom pipe.
- **Large-scale multilingual systems**: Combine compile-time i18n (Angular built-in) with runtime translation for flexibility and performance.

Question 15: What is the purpose of LOCALE_ID, and how do you use it in Angular?

Answer: **`LOCALE_ID`** is a token provided by Angular's dependency injection system that allows you to define the current locale (language and region) for your application. This is used for date, number, and currency formatting.

For example:

```
import { LOCALE_ID, NgModule } from '@angular/core';
import { CommonModule } from '@angular/common';
@NgModule({
  providers: [
    { provide: LOCALE_ID, useValue: 'en-US' }
  ],
  imports: [CommonModule]
})
export class AppModule { }
```

Question 16: What is a pipe in Angular? How do you implement currency, date, and number formatting based on locale settings?

Answer: A pipe in Angular is a feature that allows developers to transform values directly within HTML templates. It provides a clean and declarative way to format or manipulate data for display purposes, without altering the underlying data in the component.

Pipes use the `|` (pipe) symbol and follow the syntax:

```
{{ value | pipeName[:arg1][:arg2] }}
```

The following are the types of pipes:

- **Built-in pipes**: Provided by Angular, e.g., **`date`**, **`currency`**, **`percent`**, **`number`**, **`uppercase`**, **`json`**, etc.
- **Custom pipes**: User-defined for specific formatting or logic.

Let us look at locale-based formatting with built-in pipes. Angular's built-in pipes, like currency, date, and number, are locale-aware, which means their output automatically adjusts based on the current locale settings. Consider the following examples:

- **Currency pipe**: Formats numbers as currency based on the active locale. Refer to the following:

  ```
  {{1234.56 | currency:'INR':'symbol':'1.2-2'}}
  ```

  Here:

  - **`'INR'`** is the currency code.

   - For **'symbol'**, use ₹ instead of *INR*.
   - **'1.2-2'** represents a minimum of one digit before the decimal, and two digits after the decimal.

  Output for locale en-IN: **₹1,234.56**

- **Date pipe**: Formats a date object into a locale-aware string, shown as follows:

```
{{today | date:'fullDate'}}
```

  Output: **Wednesday, July 2, 2025**

  Other formats: **'short'**, **'mediumDate'**, **'yyyy-MM-dd'**, etc.

- **Number pipe**: Formats plain numbers with decimal and grouping rules based on locale, shown as follows:

```
{{ 98765.4321 | number:'1.1-3' }}
```

  Output (in en-US): **98,765.432**

  Here, **'1.1-3'** means at least one digit before the decimal, and a minimum of one and a maximum of three digits after the decimal.

Let us look at how to set the locale in Angular. To ensure correct formatting, set the locale when bootstrapping your app as follows:

- **Import locale data**:

```
import { registerLocaleData } from '@angular/common';
import localeFr from '@angular/common/locales/fr';
registerLocaleData(localeFr);
```

- **Provide the locale**:

```
providers: [{ provide: LOCALE_ID, useValue: 'fr' }]
```

  This sets the application-wide locale to **French (France)**.

Other built-in pipes like **DatePipe**, **CurrencyPipe**, and **DecimalPipe** can be used to format currency, dates, and numbers based on the locale, shown as follows:

```
<p>{{ amount | currency:'USD' }}</p>
<p>{{ today | date:'fullDate' }}</p>
<p>{{ amount | number:'1.2-2' }}</p>
```

Angular automatically formats the currency, date, and number according to the specified locale if you set **LOCALE_ID** appropriately.

Question 17: How can you use Angular pipes like DatePipe, CurrencyPipe, and DecimalPipe for localization?

Answer: You can use **DatePipe**, **CurrencyPipe**, and **DecimalPipe** for locale-sensitive formatting by ensuring the correct locale is set using **LOCALE_ID**.

For example:

```
<!-- Date formatting -->
<p>{{ currentDate | date:'fullDate' }}</p>
<!-- Currency formatting -->
<p>{{ amount | currency:'USD' }}</p>
<!-- Number formatting -->
<p>{{ numberValue | number:'1.0-3' }}</p>
```

These pipes automatically format values based on the current locale, which you can adjust at runtime.

Question 18: How do you optimize performance when using i18n in Angular?

Answer: Optimize performance in Angular with i18n as follows:

- **Lazy load language files**: Instead of loading all translations at once, only load the required language at runtime.
- **Use efficient translation management**: Minimize the number of translations by reusing common translation keys.
- **Use OnPush change detection**: This reduces unnecessary checks for changes in templates that contain translated content.

Question 19: How does lazy loading affect i18n in Angular applications?

Answer: Lazy loading can affect i18n by allowing you to load language-specific modules or components only when needed, which reduces the initial loading time. You can configure your app to load only the necessary translation files based on the user's selected language.

Lazy loading can significantly improve the performance of internationalized applications by loading translation files only when needed. The following is how it affects i18n:

- **Reduced initial load time**: Translation files are loaded on demand based on the user's language preference, instead of being included in the initial bundle. This leads to faster initial loading.
- **Improved memory usage**: By loading translations only for the currently active language, memory consumption is reduced, as unused language files are not loaded.
- **On-demand language switching**: Lazy loading enables language switching without requiring a full page reload. Only the necessary translation files for the selected language are loaded dynamically.
- **Better scalability**: For large applications with many languages, lazy loading helps manage translation files more efficiently, ensuring that the app scales better without becoming bloated.

This technique is key for optimizing both performance and user experience in multilingual Angular applications.

Question 20: What are the best practices for organizing and maintaining translation files in Angular projects?

Answer: The best practices for organizing and maintaining translation files include:

- **Use one file per language**: Create separate translation files for each language, such as **`messages.en.xlf`** or **`messages.fr.xlf`**.
- **Organize keys logically**: Structure your translation keys hierarchically, e.g., **`home.title`**, **`home.description`**, to keep it easy to manage.
- **Use external translation tools**: Leverage tools like **`Crowdin`** or **`Lokalise`** to handle translation workflows and collaborate with translators efficiently.

Latest i18n features

Question 21: What are the latest improvements in i18n in Angular 18, 19, and 20?

Answer: Angular has introduced several improvements in i18n, including better SSR support, automatic translation updates, and enhanced performance with large translation files.

The latest improvements in Angular 18 are as follows:

- **Inline translation support**: Translations can be directly added in templates using i18n attributes.
- **Improved localization API**: Better flexibility for switching locales at runtime.

The latest improvements in Angular 19 are as follows:

- **Dynamic locale switching**: Allows changing languages dynamically without page reloads.

- **Lazy loading of translations:** Only loads translations for the active language to improve performance.
- **Pluralization and gender-specific support**: Enhanced handling of complex translation scenarios like plurals and gender.

The latest improvements in Angular 20 are as follows:

- **SSR with i18n**: SSR fully supports translations, improving **search engine optimization** (**SEO**) and initial page load.
- **Automatic translation updates**: Translations can be updated without re-compilation, ensuring real-time updates.
- **Optimized large translation files**: Improved performance for apps with large translation files.
- **Artificial intelligence (AI) powered translation integration**: Integrates with AI translation services for automatic translation management.
- **Better tooling and debugging**: Enhanced tooling for easier translation management and error handling.

These improvements enhance Angular's internationalization capabilities, focusing on performance, flexibility, and easier integration with modern translation tools.

Question 22: How does Angular 20 handle SSR with i18n?

Answer: Angular 20 improves SSR by ensuring that translated content is rendered on the server side, reducing the need for client-side translation processing.

For example: Server-side rendering now ensures that language-specific content is displayed correctly before the client-side app takes over.

Question 23: What are the new optimizations in Angular 20 for handling large translation files?

Answer: Angular 20 optimizes large translation files by allowing lazy loading of specific language files at runtime, which reduces initial load times. The optimizations in Angular 20 for handling large translation files aim to improve performance through the following:

- Lazy loading translations.
- Splitting translation files.
- Efficient caching.
- Optimized compilation and incremental updates.

These changes provide developers with more efficient ways to manage internationalization in large-scale applications.

For example: Instead of loading all language files at once, only the selected language is loaded when needed.

Question 24: How does Angular handle automatic translation updates in the latest versions?

Answer: In the latest versions of Angular, automatic translation updates have been significantly enhanced, providing a more seamless and efficient experience for multilingual users. The following list demonstrates how Angular handles translation updates without the need for re-compilation or redeployment:

- **Dynamic translation loading**: Translations are fetched from external resources (e.g., APIs) based on the user's language selection, reducing the need for a full re-deployment.
- **Lazy loading translations**: Translation files are loaded on demand, improving initial load times and performance.
- **Translation file versioning**: Updated translations are fetched automatically using versioning or cache-busting, ensuring the latest translations are always loaded.
- **Automatic translation updates without re-compilation**: Angular 20 allows for hot-reload-like functionality, enabling the application to pick up updated translations without a full re-deployment.

- **AI-powered integration**: AI translation services (e.g., Google Translate) can automatically update translations when new content is added, keeping the app up-to-date.

These features streamline the process of maintaining up-to-date translations, improving performance and flexibility in multilingual applications.

For example: New translations can be added to existing files, and the app will automatically load the updated translations.

Question 25: How can AI-powered translation tools be integrated with Angular i18n workflows?

Answer: AI-powered tools like Google Translate or DeepL can be used to automatically generate translations for Angular applications, which can then be imported into the translation files. To integrate AI-powered translation tools with Angular i18n workflows, complete the steps as follows:

1. **Choose a translation service**: Use services like Google Translate API, Microsoft Translator, or DeepL.
2. **Extract translatable content**: Use Angular's ng extract-i18n to gather translatable text into an XLIFF or JSON file.
3. **Send content for translation**: Use the chosen AI translation API to send the extracted strings for translation.
4. **Save translations**: After receiving the translated content, save it into language-specific translation files (e.g., `messages.es.xlf`).
5. **Load translations in Angular**: Use Angular's i18n to load these translations dynamically based on the user's selected language.
6. **Dynamic language switching**: Implement language switching functionality in the app to allow users to choose their preferred language.

The integration of automated translation tools offers several key benefits, enhancing both the efficiency and scalability of managing multilingual content. Some of the advantages of using automated translation systems in modern applications are as follows:

- **Automated translations**: Reduce manual translation efforts.
- **Efficiency**: Automating translation reduces manual effort and time spent on translation tasks.
- **Scalability**: Easily supports adding more languages.
- **Real-time updates**: Translations are updated automatically as the content changes.
- **Accuracy and contextual translations**: AI-powered tools can provide more accurate translations, taking into account context, tone, and cultural nuances.

This workflow simplifies multi-language support in Angular applications and improves translation accuracy with AI assistance.

For example: Use an API to fetch translations and update `messages.xlf` files automatically during the build process.

Question 26: How has Angular 18 improved support for inline translations?

Answer: Angular 18 introduced better handling of inline translations, allowing developers to write translations directly in templates and use i18n attributes.

Consider the following example:

```
<h1 i18n="@@title">Welcome to our site</h1>
```

This allows inline translations without extra extraction steps.

Question 27: What changes have been introduced in Angular 19 for handling locale-based content dynamically?

Answer: Angular 19 improved dynamic locale-based content handling by allowing runtime locale switching and automatic loading of translated content.

For example: The app can switch languages based on user preference by setting the locale dynamically, shown as follows:

```
import { LOCALE_ID } from '@angular/core';
@NgModule({
  providers: [{ provide: LOCALE_ID, useValue: 'fr' }],
})
```

Question 28: **How does Angular 20 enhance performance for applications with large translation files?**

Answer: Angular 20 optimizes large translation files by enabling faster load times through selective loading and caching of translations, which helps apps with multiple languages run smoothly.

For example: Use **`loadTranslations()`** to load only the language needed by the user.

Question 29: **What improvements have been made in lazy loading translations in Angular 19 and 20?**

Answer: Angular 19 and 20 improve lazy loading translations by allowing language files to be loaded only when required, enhancing app performance by reducing the initial bundle size.

For example:

```
import { NgModule } from '@angular/core';
import { TranslateService } from '@ngx-translate/core';
@NgModule({
  providers: [TranslateService]
})
export class AppModule {
  constructor(private translate: TranslateService) {
    this.translate.use('en').subscribe();
  }
}
```

Question 30. How does the new Angular SSR feature work with i18n?

Answer: Angular SSR now works seamlessly with i18n by ensuring localized content is rendered on the server, improving performance and SEO. The new Angular SSR feature works with i18n by pre-rendering the localized content on the server based on the user's selected language. This allows for the following:

- **Pre-rendered language-specific content**: Content is rendered in the correct language before being sent to the browser, improving SEO and load times.
- **Efficient language handling**: Angular loads the appropriate translation files on the server, ensuring users receive the correct localized content immediately.
- **Enhanced performance**: SSR reduces the need for client-side language switching, providing faster rendering for multilingual applications.

This approach streamlines the rendering process, delivering localized pages with minimal delay.

For example: The app's language is detected server-side, and the correct language is rendered before the client-side application takes over.

Question 31. What are the enhancements in the @angular/localize package in the latest versions?

Answer: In Angular 20, the **`@angular/localize`** package received improvements that streamline the translation process and integrate better with the build pipeline.

In the latest Angular versions, the **`@angular/localize`** package has seen several key enhancements, which are as follows:

- **Improved translation extraction**: Enhanced tooling for extracting and managing translation files, making the process smoother and more efficient.
- **Better locale handling**: Angular 20 improves the support for locale-based content, allowing easier management of translations across different locales.
- **Runtime translation support**: Better runtime translation handling, allowing for dynamic loading and updating of translations without recompilation.
- **Performance optimizations**: Optimized translation loading, reducing overhead when working with large translation files in multilingual applications.

These improvements help streamline i18n workflows, making translation management and application performance more efficient.

For example: It simplifies the process of extracting and merging translations during build and runtime.

Question 32: How does Angular 20 support automatic translation updates without re-compilation?

Answer: Angular 20 enables automatic translation updates by detecting changes in translation files during runtime and updating the UI accordingly without needing recompilation.

For example: Translations updated via an external source (like an API) are reflected in the app without a new build.

Question 33. How can AI and machine learning (ML)-powered translation services be integrated with Angular i18n?

Answer: AI and ML-powered translation services can be integrated with Angular i18n by using APIs such as Google Cloud, Google Translate, DeepL, or Microsoft Translator, as follows:

- **API integration**: Use the translation service's API to send untranslated content and receive translations dynamically.
- **Automated translation updates**: AI can automatically detect and translate new content in the application, keeping translations up-to-date without manual intervention.
- **Dynamic translation loading**: Fetch translations from AI-powered services on-demand, improving flexibility and reducing the need for manual translation file updates.
- **Integration with Angular i18n**: AI translations can be integrated into Angular's i18n system by mapping dynamic translations to Angular's `@angular/localize` tools for runtime localization.

This integration ensures continuous translation updates and can streamline localization workflows.

For example: Use API calls to translate strings and update the translation files dynamically.

Question 34: What new tooling or debugging support has Angular introduced for i18n in recent versions?

Answer: Angular now offers better tooling for managing and debugging translations, such as improved error messages when translations are missing and more powerful build-time diagnostics.

In recent Angular versions, several new tooling and debugging features have been introduced for i18n, which are as follows:

- **Improved translation extraction tools**: Enhanced CLI commands for extracting translatable content, making it easier to generate and update translation files.
- **i18n debugging tools**: Angular now provides better error messages and warnings for missing translations, improving debugging for i18n-related issues.
- **Translation file management**: Improved tooling for managing and merging translation files, helping developers keep translations synchronized.
- **Locale switching support**: New utilities to easily switch between locales during development, simplifying testing of localized content.

These tools help streamline the i18n workflow, making it easier to manage, debug, and test multilingual applications.

For example: During build, the CLI shows warnings if any translations are missing or incorrectly formatted.

Question 35: How does Angular handle language detection and automatic redirection based on the user's locale in the latest versions?

Answer: Angular provides robust support for i18n, and while it does not include out-of-the-box automatic language redirection, it offers all the tools needed to implement it effectively in localized applications. This includes manual language detection, route-based localization, and redirection logic during the application bootstrap phase:

- **Language detection using browser settings**: To detect the user's preferred language, Angular applications can access the browser's language settings via:

  ```
  const userLang = navigator.language || navigator.languages[0]; // e.g., "en-US"
  ```

  Typically, developers extract the language code (`en`, `fr`, etc.) and match it against a list of supported locales:

  ```
  const supportedLocales = ['en', 'fr'];
  const lang = supportedLocales.includes(userLang.slice(0, 2)) ? userLang.slice(0, 2) : 'en';
  ```

- **Route-based localization**: Angular supports route-based localization, where each language version of the app is served from a distinct URL path such as `/en`, `/fr`, etc.

  To enable this, define multiple locales in **`angular.json`**:

  ```
  "localize": ["en", "fr"]
  ```

  When you build the application using:

  ```
  ng build -localize
  ```

  Angular generates separate localized bundles in directories like `/en/` and `/fr/`.

- **Implementing automatic redirection**: To automatically redirect users to the appropriate locale during app startup, you can use an **`APP_INITIALIZER`**. This runs before the application is bootstrapped.

  An example of a locale redirection service is as follows:

  ```
  @Injectable({ providedIn: 'root' })
  export class LocaleRedirectService {
    constructor(@Inject(DOCUMENT) private document: Document) {}
    detectAndRedirect(): Promise<void> {
      const lang = navigator.language.slice(0, 2);
      const supported = ['en', 'fr'];
      const selectedLang = supported.includes(lang) ? lang : 'en';
      const path = this.document.location.pathname;
      if (!path.startsWith(`/${selectedLang}/`)) {
        this.document.location.href = `/${selectedLang}${path}`;
      }
      return Promise.resolve();
    }
  }
  ```

  Registering the initializer is done in the following manner:

  ```
  providers: [
  ```

```
    {
      provide: APP_INITIALIZER,
      useFactory: (localeService: LocaleRedirectService) => () => localeService.
detectAndRedirect(),
      deps: [LocaleRedirectService],
      multi: true
    }
  ]
```

- **Setting the locale dynamically**: To make sure Angular's internal formatters (like date, number, and currency pipes) use the correct locale, bind the **`LOCALE_ID`** dynamically:

```
export function getCurrentLocale(): string {
  const pathLang = window.location.pathname.split('/')[1];
  return ['en', 'fr'].includes(pathLang) ? pathLang : 'en';
}
providers: [
  { provide: LOCALE_ID, useFactory: getCurrentLocale }
]
```

Thus, to handle language detection and automatic redirection based on the user's locale in the latest versions, Angular does the following:

- **Locale detection**: Use **`navigator.language`** to detect the user's preferred browser language.
- **Localized routing**: Define supported locales in **`angular.json`** and build using the **`--localize`** flag.
- **Automatic redirection**: Use **`APP_INITIALIZER`** to perform redirection to the correct locale before the app initializes.
- **Locale formatting**: Dynamically provide **`LOCALE_ID`** based on the detected or route-based locale for correct formatting of dates, numbers, and currency.

Conclusion

In this chapter, we explored the core concepts of i18n and how it helps in making applications adaptable to different languages and regions. We discussed the tools and strategies available in Angular for effective translation management, handling dynamic content, and supporting various locales. By mastering these techniques, you can ensure that your applications provide a seamless and personalized experience for users worldwide, regardless of their language or cultural background.

The next chapter will explore Angular security. With the increasing number of cyber threats, understanding how to safeguard your Angular applications is crucial. We will cover key security concepts, best practices for protecting user data, and methods to mitigate common vulnerabilities like **cross-site scripting** (**XSS**), **cross-site request forgery** (**CSRF**), and others. This will help you build secure, robust applications that protect both your users and your data.

CHAPTER 14
Angular Security

Introduction

Security is a critical aspect of any web application, ensuring the protection of user data, preventing unauthorized access, and mitigating potential threats. Angular provides built-in security mechanisms and best practices to safeguard applications against vulnerabilities, such as **cross-site scripting** (**XSS**), **cross-site request forgery** (**CSRF**), SQL injection, and more. This chapter explores key security features in Angular, including authentication, authorization, secure data handling, and secure coding techniques. Understanding these security principles will help developers build robust and resilient applications.

Structure

This chapter covers the following topics:

- Authentication and authorization
- Security vulnerabilities and prevention
- Secure HTTP and API communication
- Advanced security and latest features
- AI and next-gen security
- Secure Angular code and deployment

Objectives

By the end of this chapter, you will understand common security threats in web applications and how they affect Angular apps. You will learn about Angular's built-in security mechanisms, best practices, and methods for implementing secure authentication and authorization using **JSON Web Token** (**JWT**) and role-based access control. Additionally, you will gain insights into preventing XSS, CSRF, and injection attacks while ensuring secure data communication through HTTPS, security headers, and encryption. Ultimately, this chapter provides the knowledge and tools to develop robust, secure Angular applications that adhere to industry standards and best practices.

Authentication and authorization

Question 1: What are the best authentication strategies in Angular for securing application programming interfaces (API)?

Answer: Securing APIs in Angular applications is a critical aspect of web application development. A well-structured authentication strategy ensures that only authorized users can access protected endpoints. Depending on the complexity and security requirements of your application, you can choose from several robust methods.

The following are the most effective and widely adopted authentication strategies in Angular for securing APIs:

- **OAuth 2.0**: OAuth 2.0 is an industry-standard protocol for delegated authorization. It enables applications to access user data on other services (like Google, Microsoft, etc.) without exposing user credentials.
    - Commonly used for third-party login (SSO).
    - Supports access tokens, refresh tokens, and scopes to control API access.
    - Ideal for enterprise and cloud-integrated apps.

  Example use case: Login via Google or Microsoft and access APIs with granted scopes.
- **JSON Web Tokens (JWT)**: JWT is one of the most popular methods for stateless authentication in Angular.
    - After login, the server returns a signed token containing user identity and roles.
    - Angular stores the token (typically in localStorage or cookies) and sends it with each API request.
    - The backend verifies the token's signature and expiry to authorize requests.

  Benefits include:
    - Stateless, i.e., no session is stored on the server.
    - Lightweight and easy to decode.
    - Can include claims (e.g., roles, permissions, user ID).

  Example header in Angular:

  ```
  const headers = new HttpHeaders({
    'Authorization': `Bearer ${jwtToken}`
  });
  ```
- **Bearer tokens in HTTP headers**: Bearer tokens are a standard way of passing credentials in an HTTP header.
    - Token is attached in the authorization header as:

      ```
      Authorization: Bearer <token>
      ```
    - Angular interceptors can automatically attach tokens to every HTTP request.

      HTTP interceptor example:

      ```
      intercept(req: HttpRequest<any>, next: HttpHandler):
      Observable<HttpEvent<any>> {
        const token = authService.getToken();
        const authReq = req.clone({
          headers: req.headers.set('Authorization', `Bearer ${token}`)
        });
      ```

```
        return next.handle(authReq);
    }
```

- **Role-based authentication**: In this strategy, user roles (e.g., admin, user, editor) are embedded into the JWT or fetched from the server.
    - Angular can restrict route access using guards based on roles.
    - The backend also uses roles to authorize API endpoints.

  For example:

```
if (userRole === 'admin') {
  // allow access to admin features
}
```

Additional practices for securing APIs:

- Always use HTTPS to encrypt token transmission.
- Validate tokens on the server side using a public key or shared secret.
- Set short token expiration times and use refresh tokens.
- Avoid storing sensitive tokens in localStorage for high-security apps. Instead, prefer HttpOnly cookies where applicable.

Question 2: How does Angular handle JWT securely in SPAs?

Answer: Angular stores JWTs securely using HttpOnly cookies or sessionStorage to prevent XSS attacks, while ensuring tokens are included in API requests using an authorization header.

For example:

```
this.http.get('/api/data', { headers: { Authorization: `Bearer ${token}` } });
```

Question 3: What are the best practices for storing JWT tokens in an Angular application?

Answer: To ensure secure storage of JWT tokens in an Angular application and prevent security vulnerabilities, follow these best practices:

- Use HttpOnly cookies to avoid client-side access.
- Use sessionStorage or localStorage for token storage, but ensure proper security mechanisms are in place.
- Secure flag should be set for cookies to ensure they are sent over HTTPS.

Question 4: How do you implement role-based access control (RBAC) in Angular applications?

Answer: RBAC is a security design pattern that restricts access to features or routes based on a user's assigned role (e.g., admin, editor, viewer). In Angular applications, RBAC is most commonly implemented using route guards, services, and role metadata.

Working of RBAC in Angular:

1. After user login, the server returns a JWT token that includes the user's roles in its payload.
2. The Angular application stores the token (typically in localStorage or cookies).
3. Route guards check the decoded token to determine if the user has the required role to access the route.
4. If the role matches, access is granted; otherwise, the user is redirected (e.g., to an **Access Denied** page).

The step-by-step RBAC implementation is given as follows:

1. **Store roles on login**: After login, store the JWT and extract roles:

```
this.authService.login(username, password).subscribe(res => {
```

```
    localStorage.setItem('access_token', res.token);
    const decoded = this.jwtHelper.decodeToken(res.token);
    this.userRoles = decoded.roles; // e.g., ['admin', 'editor']
  });
```

2. **AuthService to check roles**:

```
@Injectable({ providedIn: 'root' })
export class AuthService {
  getRoles(): string[] {
    const token = localStorage.getItem('access_token');
    if (!token) return [];
    const decoded = JSON.parse(atob(token.split('.')[1]));
    return decoded.roles || [];
  }
  hasRole(expectedRole: string): boolean {
    return this.getRoles().includes(expectedRole);
  }
}
```

3. **Create a role-based route guard**:

```
@Injectable({ providedIn: 'root' })
export class RoleGuard implements CanActivate {
  constructor(private auth: AuthService, private router: Router) {}
  canActivate(route: ActivatedRouteSnapshot): boolean {
    const expectedRole = route.data['role'];
    if (this.auth.hasRole(expectedRole)) {
      return true;
    }
    this.router.navigate(['/access-denied']);
    return false;
  }
}
```

4. **Protect routes with role metadata**:

```
const routes: Routes = [
  {
    path: 'admin',
    component: AdminComponent,
    canActivate: [RoleGuard],
    data: { role: 'admin' }
  },
  {
    path: 'user',
    component: UserComponent,
    canActivate: [RoleGuard],
```

```
        data: { role: 'user' }
      }
    ];
```

Best practices for RBAC in Angular:

- Use JWT tokens with embedded roles to keep the frontend stateless.
- Always enforce roles on the backend as well; frontend RBAC is for UX, not security.
- Centralize role-check logic inside a service or utility function for maintainability.
- Provide a default fallback route like **`/access-denied`**.

Question 5: How does OAuth 2.0 work in Angular applications, and how is it implemented?

Answer: OAuth 2.0 allows secure authorization by delegating user authentication to a trusted identity provider, issuing tokens for API access. Angular implements OAuth using libraries like **`angular-oauth2-oidc`**.

For example:

```
import { OAuthService } from 'angular-oauth2-oidc';
this.oauthService.initCodeFlow();
```

Question 6: How can OpenID Connect (OIDC) be integrated with Angular for secure authentication?

Answer: OIDC, an identity layer on top of OAuth 2.0, is used for user authentication. Angular integrates it using libraries like **`angular-oauth2-oidc`** for authentication and token management.

For example:

```
this.oauthService.configure(authConfig);
this.oauthService.loadDiscoveryDocumentAndTryLogin();
```

Question 7: What is the role of refresh tokens in Angular authentication, and how can they be secured?

Answer: Refresh tokens are used to obtain new access tokens after expiration. They should be securely stored (preferably in HttpOnly cookies) and exchanged on the server for a new JWT.

For example:

```
this.http.post('/auth/refresh-token', { refreshToken: storedRefreshToken });
```

Question 8: How can AI-powered authentication improve security in Angular applications?

Answer: AI can enhance security by detecting unusual login patterns, automating anomaly detection, and implementing adaptive authentication mechanisms based on user behavior.

For example: Using AI-driven CAPTCHA or biometric verification for added security in the login flow.

Question 9: What are the new authentication enhancements introduced in Angular 20?

Answer: Angular 20 introduces:

- Improved authentication guard handling with more flexibility.
- Enhanced support for OAuth2 and OIDC in built-in modules.
- New utilities for securely managing JWT tokens and refresh tokens.

Security vulnerabilities and prevention

Question 10: What is XSS in Angular, and how can it be prevented?

Answer: XSS is a security vulnerability where an attacker injects malicious scripts into web pages viewed by users. Angular prevents XSS by using automatic escaping of data interpolated into templates, ensuring user input is treated as data and not executable code.

Question 11: How does Angular automatically protect against XSS attacks?

Answer: Angular automatically escapes any untrusted data injected into the DOM using interpolation (`{{data}}`) and property binding (`[src]`). Angular sanitizes content using the **`DomSanitizer`** to prevent malicious code execution.

Question 12: What is CSRF, and how can it be mitigated in Angular?

Answer: CSRF is an attack where a malicious user sends unauthorized requests to a site where the user is authenticated. To mitigate it in Angular, you can use tokens (CSRF tokens) sent in HTTP headers to validate requests on the server-side.

For example:

```
const headers = new HttpHeaders().set('X-CSRF-Token', csrfToken);
```

Question 13: What are content security policies (CSP), and how do they enhance Angular security?

Answer: CSP is a security feature that restricts the sources from which content can be loaded. In Angular, CSP prevents the execution of untrusted scripts, making it harder for attackers to inject malicious scripts.

For example:

```
<meta http-equiv="Content-Security-Policy" content="default-src 'self'; script-src 'self'">
```

Question 14: How can Angular prevent SQL injection attacks when working with APIs?

Answer: Angular itself cannot prevent SQL injection on the client side. However, it can mitigate risk by validating and sanitizing user input and by using prepared statements and parameterized queries on the server-side.

Question 15: What are the common security misconfigurations in Angular applications?

Answer: Security misconfigurations can expose Angular applications to various vulnerabilities. Some of the most common security misconfigurations include:

- Not securing API endpoints properly.
- Improper handling of JWT tokens or sensitive data storage.
- Lack of CORS configuration on the server.
- Using unsafe third-party libraries or insecure HTTP instead of HTTPS.

Question 16: How does Angular prevent DOM-based XSS vulnerabilities?

Answer: Angular uses automatic sanitization of potentially dangerous content inserted into the DOM through methods like **`innerHTML`** or **`src`**. The **`DomSanitizer`** class is also used to clean content before it is rendered.

Question 17: What are Angular sanitization and DomSanitizer, and how do they work?

Answer: **Sanitization** is the process of cleaning data to ensure it is safe to insert into the DOM. **`DomSanitizer`** is an Angular service that helps sanitize untrusted values to prevent XSS.

For example:

```
constructor(private sanitizer: DomSanitizer) {}
sanitizedUrl = this.sanitizer.bypassSecurityTrustUrl(url);
```

Question 18: What is clickjacking, and how can it be prevented in Angular applications?

Answer: Clickjacking is an attack where an attacker tricks users into clicking something different from what they think they are clicking. To prevent it, you can use the X-Frame-Options header to prevent your app from being embedded in a frame.

For example:

```
X-Frame-Options: DENY
```

Question 19: **How do Angular's built-in security mechanisms compare with other frontend frameworks?**

Answer: Angular's security mechanisms, like XSS protection, CSRF token handling, CSP, and built-in sanitization, are robust and integrated into the framework. Other frameworks, such as React and Vue, offer similar protection, but Angular's built-in DOM sanitization and automatic data escaping give it an edge in preventing XSS out of the box.

Secure HTTP and API communication

Question 20: **What are the best security practices for handling HTTP requests in Angular applications?**

Answer: To enhance the security of HTTP requests in an Angular application, consider implementing the following best practices:

- Use HTTPS for secure communication.
- Sanitize input to prevent injection attacks.
- Implement JWT or OAuth2 for secure authentication.
- Use **`HttpInterceptors`** for adding security tokens to requests.
- Implement CORS policies on the server.

Question 21: **How does Angular's HttpClient module prevent security vulnerabilities?**

Answer: Angular's **`HttpClient`** module automatically handles CSRF by sending anti-CSRF tokens with each request if the backend supports it. It also automatically serializes and sanitizes request payloads to prevent injection attacks.

Question 22: **How do Angular Interceptors enhance security in API requests?**

Answer: **`HttpInterceptors`** allow you to modify requests and responses globally. They can be used to do the following:

- Attach security tokens (e.g., JWT) to outgoing requests.
- Handle unauthorized access (e.g., by redirecting to a login page).
- Catch and handle errors (e.g., server errors or security issues).

For example:

```
@Injectable()
export class AuthInterceptor implements HttpInterceptor {
  intercept(req: HttpRequest<any>, next: HttpHandler) {
    const token = localStorage.getItem('auth_token');
    const cloned = req.clone({
      setHeaders: { Authorization: `Bearer ${token}` }
    });
    return next.handle(cloned);
  }
}
```

Question 23: **How can you implement secure CORS policies in an Angular application?**

Answer: While Angular does not directly handle CORS, you can configure it on the server to control which domains are allowed to access resources. The Angular app should ensure that CORS headers are correctly set on the backend.

Example on the server side:

```
Access-Control-Allow-Origin: https://your-angular-app.com
```

Question 24: What are the best practices for handling user credentials securely in Angular?

Answer: To protect user credentials and prevent security breaches in an Angular application, follow these best practices:

- Never store sensitive information (like passwords or tokens) in localStorage or sessionStorage.
- Use **`HttpOnly`** cookies for storing JWTs securely.
- Ensure that credentials are sent over HTTPS.
- Use two-factor authentication for additional security.

Question 25: How can Angular prevent API key exposure in frontend applications?

Answer: Never expose sensitive API keys directly in the frontend code. Instead, do the following:

- Store them securely on the server-side and use server-to-server communication.
- Use proxy servers to hide the API key from the client.
- For public APIs, consider API key restrictions based on IP or domain.

Question 26: What is the difference between cookies and internal storage in frontend applications?

Answer: In Angular applications, both cookies and internal storage mechanisms like localStorage and sessionStorage are used to store client-side data. However, they differ significantly in their behavior, security, and use cases. Understanding these differences is critical when implementing authentication, personalization, and data caching strategies in modern web applications.

Cookies are small key-value pairs that are stored in the browser and automatically sent to the server with every HTTP request. They are often used for session management, especially in server-side authentication mechanisms.

The characteristics of cookies are:

- **Size limit**: ~4KB
- **Automatic transmission**: Sent with every HTTP request (if not restricted)
- **Expiration**: Can be configured via Expires or Max-Age
- **Security options**: Can be marked HttpOnly, Secure, and SameSite to protect against XSS and CSRF attacks
- **Accessibility**: Must be accessed manually via **`document.cookie`** or through Angular libraries like **`ngx-cookie-service`**

Use cases of cookies are as follows:

- Server-side session tokens
- CSRF protection using same-origin cookies
- Authentication via HttpOnly cookies

Internal storage (localStorage and sessionStorage) is part of the Web Storage API, providing a simple way to store larger amounts of data directly in the browser, and is not automatically sent to the server.

The characteristics of internal storage are:

- **Size limit**: ~5MB to 10MB
- **Manual access**: Only accessible via JavaScript (**`window.localStorage`**)
- **Persistence**:
    - **localStorage**: Persists even after browser restart
    - **sessionStorage**: Persists only until the browser tab is closed
- **Security**: Vulnerable to XSS attacks if the application is not properly secured

Use cases of internal storage are as follows:

- Storing JWT tokens in SPAs
- Caching UI preferences (theme, layout)
- Retaining user filters or form state

Advanced security and latest features

Question 27: What is subresource integrity (SRI), and how does it improve Angular security?

Answer: SRI ensures that the resources (like scripts or styles) loaded from a CDN have not been tampered with. By using a cryptographic hash, SRI helps prevent malicious changes to third-party resources.

For example:

```
<script src="https://example.com/script.js" integrity="sha384-..." crossorigin="anonymous"></
script>
```

Question 28: How do trusted types enhance security in Angular applications?

Answer: Trusted types is a security feature that helps prevent XSS by ensuring that only trusted code can execute potentially dangerous operations (like DOM manipulation).

For example:

```
const policy = window.trustedTypes.createPolicy('angular', {
  createHTML: (input) => input, // Sanitizing the HTML input before adding it to the DOM
});
```

Question 29: What security improvements were introduced in Angular 18, 19, and 20?

Answer: Angular has introduced improvements like enhanced CSP, XSS protections, and stricter input sanitization. These versions also bring better SSR security and automated updates for vulnerabilities.

Question 30: How does Angular handle security in SSR and hybrid rendering?

Answer: Angular SSR mitigates risks by ensuring that server-side templates are rendered securely, using sanitization to protect against XSS. In hybrid rendering, Angular dynamically manages rendering both on the client and server to ensure security during both processes.

Question 31: How can Angular applications detect and mitigate supply chain attacks?

Answer: Angular apps can use package auditing tools like `npm audit` to detect vulnerabilities in dependencies and apply patches. Additionally, ensuring dependencies are from trusted sources and verifying the integrity of packages can help mitigate attacks.

Question 32: What role does AI play in real-time security threat detection in Angular applications?

Answer: AI can analyze real-time traffic, identify anomalous patterns (e.g., brute force attacks, **distributed denial-of-service (DDoS)**), and trigger alerts or mitigation actions, making security proactive rather than reactive.

Question 33: How can machine learning models be used to detect fraudulent activities in Angular applications?

Answer: Machine learning models can analyze user behavior patterns in real-time, detecting fraud like login anomalies, transaction irregularities, or identity theft based on historical data.

Question 34: What are the best practices for securing third-party dependencies in Angular projects?

Answer: To minimize security risks associated with third-party dependencies in an Angular project, follow these best practices:

- Regularly audit dependencies with tools like **`npm audit`**.
- Ensure dependencies come from trusted sources.
- Use lock files (**`package-lock.json`**) to prevent unintentional version upgrades.
- Opt for minimal dependencies and secure versions.

Question 35: How can Angular applications enforce stricter security headers for better protection?

Answer: Angular applications can enforce security headers like X-Content-Type-Options, Strict-Transport-Security (HSTS), and CSP through the server configuration (e.g., in Express or NGINX).

Example for express server:

```
app.use((req, res, next) => {
  res.setHeader('Content-Security-Policy', "default-src 'self'");
  next();
});
```

Question 36: How does Angular manage security for Progressive Web Apps (PWAs)?

Answer: Angular PWAs manage security by enforcing HTTPS for service worker communication, content caching, and ensuring service worker updates are handled securely with validation.

Question 37: What new security improvements were introduced in Angular 20 for hybrid and server-side rendering?

Answer: Angular 20 focuses on secure SSR by improving input sanitization and making it easier to integrate CSP policies into SSR. It also ensures cross-platform security when rendering content both on the client and server.

Question 38: How do Angular signals impact security when managing real-time data flow?

Answer: Angular signals manage data reactively, ensuring that sensitive data updates are securely handled without exposing it unnecessarily in the template. signal-based state management reduces the risk of exposing outdated or incorrect data.

Question 39: How does Angular ensure safe dependency injection (DI) to prevent supply chain attacks?

Answer: Angular's DI system ensures that services are loaded from trusted sources. By enforcing strict typing and controlled service providers, it minimizes the risk of introducing malicious dependencies.

AI and next-gen security

Question 40: How can AI-powered anomaly detection be used to identify security threats in Angular applications?

Answer: AI-powered anomaly detection analyzes user behavior to identify suspicious activities, such as unusual access patterns or excessive API requests, indicating potential threats like unauthorized access or brute-force attempts.

For example: Implement a login anomaly detection system that uses AI to track failed login attempts. If a user from a new location or IP address attempts multiple failed logins, the system triggers an alert or locks the account temporarily.

Consider the following example of anomaly detection on failed login attempts:

```
const failedLoginAttempts = [/* store failed attempts info */];
function detectAnomaly(user) {
  // Detect login anomalies based on patterns
  if (user.failedAttempts > 5) {
    lockAccount(user.id); // Trigger lock for suspicious behavior
```

```
  }
}
```

Question 41: What is Zero Trust security, and how can it be applied to Angular applications?

Answer: Zero Trust security assumes that every request, even from trusted internal networks, needs to be authenticated and authorized. In Angular, this can be applied by using JWTs, ensuring every API call is verified regardless of source.

For example: Implement JWT authentication for all API requests, ensuring that the backend verifies the token before proceeding.

Consider the following example of using a JWT token in an HTTP request:

```
import { HttpClient, HttpHeaders } from '@angular/common/http';
const token = localStorage.getItem('auth_token');
const headers = new HttpHeaders().set('Authorization', `Bearer ${token}`);
this.http.get('/api/data', { headers }).subscribe(response => {
  console.log(response);
});
```

Question 42: How does AI-driven behavior analysis help prevent brute-force attacks in Angular authentication?

Answer: AI-driven behavior analysis can detect brute-force attacks by analyzing login patterns. For example, multiple failed login attempts within a short period can trigger additional security measures, such as CAPTCHA or MFA.

For example: Use an AI model to track failed login attempts and introduce a CAPTCHA challenge after a set number of failed logins.

The following is an example command to trigger CAPTCHA after multiple failed login attempts:

```
if (failedAttempts > 3) {
  triggerCaptcha(); // Show CAPTCHA after multiple failed logins
}
```

Question 43: How can federated authentication improve security in large-scale Angular applications?

Answer: Federated authentication uses third-party identity providers (e.g., Google, Facebook) to authenticate users. It helps in reducing the risks of password fatigue and credential theft by relying on trusted identity systems.

For example: Use OAuth 2.0 with Google authentication in an Angular app, shown as follows:

```
import { OAuthService } from 'angular-oauth2-oidc';
this.oauthService.configure(authConfig);
this.oauthService.loadDiscoveryDocumentAndTryLogin().then(() => {
  console.log('Logged in');
});
```

Question 44: How can AI-driven fraud detection be implemented in Angular applications to identify suspicious user behavior?

Answer: AI models can detect fraudulent behavior by analyzing user actions, such as sudden high-value transactions or logins from unusual locations.

For example: Use an AI-based fraud detection system to flag transactions from new devices or locations and trigger an additional email confirmation, shown as follows:

```
function detectFraud(userTransaction) {
```

```
  if (userTransaction.isHighValue && userTransaction.isFromNewLocation) {
    sendConfirmationEmail(userTransaction.userId);
  }
}
```

Question 45: What are AI-powered CAPTCHAs, and how can they enhance authentication security in Angular apps?

Answer: AI-powered CAPTCHAs are more dynamic than traditional CAPTCHAs, adapting to different behaviors. They provide better security by challenging bots with tasks like identifying objects in images.

For example: Implement Google reCAPTCHA v3 in an Angular app:

```
import { ReCaptchaV3Service } from 'ng-recaptcha';
this.recaptchaV3Service.execute('action_name').subscribe((token) => {
  console.log('reCAPTCHA Token:', token);
});
```

Question 46: How can machine learning models be used to prevent phishing attacks in Angular-based applications?

Answer: ML models can analyze URLs and email patterns to detect phishing attempts. The system can flag suspicious URLs or email addresses before they can impact users.

For example: Use ML to check URLs for suspicious patterns and warn users when visiting potentially fraudulent sites:

```
function isPhishing(url) {
  // AI-based model checks for suspicious patterns in URL
  if (url.includes('phishing')) {
    showWarning('Suspicious website detected!');
  }
}
```

Question 47: How can AI enhance Angular's logging and monitoring for proactive security threat detection?

Answer: AI can enhance logging and monitoring by analyzing real-time logs for unusual patterns and identifying potential security threats like unauthorized access.

For example: Use AI-powered log analysis tools, like ELK Stack, combined with machine learning to detect anomalies in real-time:

```
import { LogService } from './log.service';
logService.monitorLogs().subscribe(log => {
  if (isAnomalous(log)) {
    alertAdmin('Suspicious activity detected!');
  }
});
```

Question 48: How can Angular applications leverage AI for adaptive security policies based on user behavior analysis?

Answer: AI models can continuously analyze user behavior and adapt security policies, such as requiring MFA for unusual activities like logins from new devices.

An example of adaptive security based on behavior is as follows:

```
function adjustSecurityPolicy(user) {
```

```
  if (user.loginFromNewDevice) {
    requireMFA(user.id); // Trigger MFA for new device logins
  }
}
```

Question 49: How does AI help mitigate API abuse and bot-driven attacks in Angular applications?

Answer: AI can detect bot-driven API requests and mitigate attacks like scraping or **denial-of-service (DoS)** by analyzing traffic patterns and blocking suspicious IPs.

For example: Use AI models to block traffic from known bot IPs, shown as follows:

```
function isBotTraffic(request) {
  if (isKnownBotIP(request.ip)) {
    blockRequest(request); // Block bot requests
  }
}
```

Question 50: What role does AI play in real-time DDoS attack prevention for Angular applications?

Answer: AI can detect traffic spikes and patterns indicative of DDoS attacks, automatically triggering rate-limiting or rerouting traffic to mitigate the attack.

For example: Use AI-driven traffic analysis to detect and block DDoS attacks:

```
function monitorTraffic(traffic) {
  if (traffic.spikeDetected()) {
    triggerDDoSDefense(); // Apply DDoS mitigation measures
  }
}
```

Question 51: How can AI-driven biometric authentication be integrated into Angular applications?

Answer: AI-driven biometric authentication (e.g., face recognition or fingerprint scanning) can be integrated with WebAuthn for passwordless login.

For example: Use WebAuthn API in Angular to implement biometric login:

```
navigator.credentials.create({ publicKey: publicKeyCredential }).then((result) => {
  console.log('User authenticated', result);
});
```

Question 52: What are the security risks of AI-generated content in Angular applications, and how can they be managed?

Answer: AI-generated content could be used for phishing or misleading users. Implement content verification tools to ensure content is legitimate.

For example: Use content moderation tools to filter AI-generated messages:

```
function filterContent(content) {
  if (isSuspicious(content)) {
    flagContent(content); // Flag suspicious content
  }
}
```

Question 53: How can federated learning be used to enhance security in distributed Angular applications?

Answer: Federated learning allows for decentralized AI training, where data remains on the client side, improving privacy while enhancing security models across multiple clients.

For example: Train a fraud detection model on distributed client devices without transmitting sensitive user data:

```
const modelUpdates = trainModelLocally(userData); // Model training occurs on client side
syncModelUpdatesToServer(modelUpdates); // Send only model updates, not raw data
```

Secure Angular code and deployment

Question 54: **What are the best practices for securing WebSockets in Angular applications?**

Answer: To secure WebSockets, use **wss://** (secure WebSocket) instead of **ws://**, authenticate connections, and validate messages.

For example: Ensure WebSocket connection is secure by using **wss://** and add a token for authentication:

```
const socket = new WebSocket('wss://example.com/socket');
socket.onopen = () => {
  socket.send(JSON.stringify({ token: 'user-token' }));
};
```

Question 55: **How can Angular applications be hardened against man-in-the-middle (MITM) attacks?**

Answer: Use HTTPS to encrypt all communications, implement SSL/TLS for secure data transmission, and ensure server certificates are valid.

For example: Always ensure requests use the HTTPS protocol:

```
// Ensure API calls are made over HTTPS
this.httpClient.get('https://api.example.com/data');
```

Question 56: **What are the security risks of using third-party Angular components, and how can they be mitigated?**

Answer: Risks include malicious code, vulnerabilities, or supply chain attacks. Mitigate by reviewing source code, using trusted sources (e.g., **npm**), and keeping dependencies up to date.

For example: Regularly run **npm audit** to check for vulnerabilities:

```
npm audit fix
```

Question 57: **How can static code analysis tools like SonarQube be used to identify security vulnerabilities in Angular applications?**

Answer: SonarQube scans the source code for security flaws and potential vulnerabilities. Integrate it into CI/CD pipelines to automatically identify issues.

For example: Set up SonarQube in the CI pipeline:

```
# Example: SonarQube configuration in CI
- name: SonarQube Analysis
  run: sonar-scanner
```

Question 58: **What are the best practices for securing environment variables and sensitive data in Angular applications?**

Answer: Use environment variables for storing sensitive data, avoid hardcoding secrets in source code, and leverage services like Azure Key Vault or AWS Secrets Manager.

For example: Store API keys in **environment.ts**, and use Angular's build process for each environment:

```
// environment.ts
export const environment = {
  production: false,
```

```
  apiKey: process.env.API_KEY,
};
```

Question 59: **How can Angular applications prevent reverse tabnabbing attacks?**

Answer: To prevent reverse tabnabbing, always use **`rel="noopener noreferrer"`** in links opening in a new tab (**`target="_blank"`**).

For example: Use **`rel="noopener noreferrer"`** in anchor tags as follows:

```
<a href="https://example.com" target="_blank" rel="noopener noreferrer">Link</a>
```

Question 60: **What are the risks of using innerHTML in Angular, and how can it be mitigated?**

Answer: Using innerHTML exposes the app to **XSS** attacks. Use Angular's **`sanitization`** service (**`DomSanitizer`**) to sanitize any dynamic HTML content.

For example: Use **`DomSanitizer`** to safely bind HTML:

```
import { DomSanitizer } from '@angular/platform-browser';
constructor(private sanitizer: DomSanitizer) {}
getSafeHTML() {
  return this.sanitizer.bypassSecurityTrustHtml('<b>Safe HTML</b>');
}
```

Question 61: **How can content security policy (CSP) be configured to improve Angular application security?**

Answer: CSP mitigates XSS by specifying allowed sources for content. Set a strong CSP header to restrict the execution of malicious scripts.

For example: Configure CSP header in server response:

```
# Example: Configure CSP in HTTP headers
Content-Security-Policy: default-src 'self'; script-src 'self' https://trusted-source.com;
```

Question 62: **What are the security best practices for deploying Angular applications on cloud platforms (AWS, Azure, GCP)?**

Answer: Use HTTPS, configure proper IAM roles, secure APIs, and ensure only necessary services are exposed.

For example: In AWS, restrict API access using IAM policies and deploy behind CloudFront for added security:

```
aws iam create-policy --policy-name RestrictApiAccess --policy-document file://policy.json
```

Question 63: **How can DevSecOps practices be integrated into the CI/CD pipeline for Angular applications?**

Answer: Integrate security tools like SonarQube, OWASP Dependency-Check, and **Static Application Security Testing** (**SAST**) into the CI/CD pipeline to automatically scan code and dependencies.

For example: Add security scans in CI pipeline:

```
- name: Dependency Vulnerability Scan
  run: npx snyk test
```

Question 64: **How can Angular applications be protected against dependency hijacking and supply chain attacks?**

Answer: Use **`npm audit`** regularly, avoid using packages with critical vulnerabilities, and lock package versions using **`package-lock.json`**.

For example: Regularly audit dependencies:

```
npm audit
npm audit fix
```

Question 65: **How can server-side rendering (SSR) in Angular Universal be secured against SSRF and data leaks?**

Answer: Use proper input validation, output sanitization, and avoid exposing internal services or URLs to prevent SSRF.

For example: In SSR, validate any URLs before making requests:

```
// Example: SSR URL validation
const isValidUrl = (url) => /^https?:\/\//.test(url);
```

Question 66: **What security headers should be configured for production Angular deployments to prevent attacks?**

Answer: Configure headers like Strict-Transport-Security, X-Content-Type-Options, X-Frame-Options, and X-XSS-Protection to enhance security.

For example: Configure headers on the server:

```
# Example: HTTP security headers
Strict-Transport-Security: max-age=31536000; includeSubDomains
X-Content-Type-Options: nosniff
```

Conclusion

Securing an Angular application is a continuous process that involves implementing best practices at every layer, from authentication and authorization to handling HTTP requests and securing third-party dependencies. By following industry standards such as OAuth 2.0, JWT, HTTPS, and proper API security configurations, developers can safeguard their applications from common vulnerabilities. Additionally, regular security audits, input sanitization, and secure data storage mechanisms play a vital role in maintaining a robust and secure application.

By integrating these security measures, developers can build resilient applications that protect user data and ensure a seamless, secure experience.

In the next chapter, we will explore **Reactive Extensions for JavaScript** (**RxJS**) and its integration with Angular. RxJS provides powerful tools for handling asynchronous data streams, state management, and event-driven programming. We will cover key concepts such as observables, operators, Subjects, and how they enhance Angular applications' reactivity and performance.

Join our Discord space

Join our Discord workspace for latest updates, offers, tech happenings around the world, new releases, and sessions with the authors:

https://discord.bpbonline.com

Chapter 15
RxJS Concepts with Angular

Introduction

Reactive programming is a fundamental paradigm in modern web development, especially in Angular applications, where handling asynchronous operations efficiently is crucial. **Reactive Extensions for JavaScript (RxJS)** is a powerful library that provides observable-based programming to handle events, data streams, and asynchronous operations effectively. Angular integrates deeply with RxJS to manage everything from HTTP requests to UI interactions, making it an essential concept for developers.

Structure

This chapter covers the following topics:

- Core concepts and fundamentals
- Operators and transformations
- RxJS with HTTP and API calls
- State management and signals integration
- Lifecycle management and performance optimization
- Advanced topics and latest RxJS features
- Security-related RxJS in Angular

Objectives

By the end of this chapter, you should have a strong understanding of RxJS and its role in Angular. You will be able to work with observables, Subjects, and operators to efficiently manage asynchronous data. You will gain hands-on experience implementing RxJS in Angular applications for HTTP requests, event handling, and state management. Additionally, you will learn to use key operators like map, filter, mergeMap, and switchMap to optimize data flow. Finally, you will be able to handle errors effectively and apply best practices to improve performance, making your applications more scalable and maintainable.

Core concepts and fundamentals

Question 1: What is RxJS, and why is it used in Angular?

Answer: RxJS is a powerful library for reactive programming using observables. It provides a way to handle asynchronous operations, such as HTTP requests, user inputs, or real-time events, in a clean, declarative, and efficient manner. It enables Angular applications to manage complex asynchronous data streams with operators like map, filter, merge, switchMap, etc.

Key concepts in RxJS are as follows:

- **Observable**: Represents a data stream that can emit multiple values over time (e.g., HTTP response, user input).
- **Observer**: An object that reacts to data from an observable, with handlers for next, error, and complete events.
- **Operators**: Functions like map, filter, merge, etc., that transform, combine, and manipulate the data emitted by observables.
- **Subscription**: A mechanism for executing the observable and receiving its emitted values. You subscribe to an observable to start receiving values.

RxJS has the following benefits:

- **Asynchronous data management**: RxJS simplifies handling multiple asynchronous operations such as HTTP requests, user events, or WebSocket messages by representing them as streams that emit values over time.
- **Composability**: RxJS operators allow developers to compose complex asynchronous workflows using simple, declarative syntax.
- **Declarative syntax**: Instead of writing complex callback-based logic for asynchronous tasks, RxJS allows developers to use operators that make asynchronous code more readable and maintainable.
- **Error handling**: RxJS provides built-in error handling capabilities using catchError and retry operators, which are easier to manage than traditional callback-based error handling.
- **Cancellation**: RxJS makes it easier to cancel ongoing asynchronous tasks using operators like takeUntil or unsubscribe, making it particularly useful in Angular to avoid memory leaks when dealing with components and services.
- **Reacting to multiple streams**: RxJS is perfect for cases where multiple asynchronous events need to be handled together, like user input, HTTP requests, and WebSocket events.
- **Streamlining asynchronous programming**: RxJS allows you to handle complex asynchronous logic in a clean and manageable way, making Angular applications more efficient and maintainable.
- **Better UI/UX**: You can create interactive, real-time features like live search, form validation, and notifications easily using RxJS.
- **State management**: In Angular, managing state can be easier with RxJS, especially for handling complex or shared application states across multiple components or services.
- **Concurrency handling**: RxJS provides operators like mergeMap, switchMap, and concatMap to control how multiple asynchronous operations are executed concurrently or in sequence.

For example:

```
import { of } from 'rxjs';
const observable = of(1, 2, 3);
observable.subscribe(value => console.log(value)); // Output: 1, 2, 3
```

The following is an example of an HTTP request with RxJS in Angular:

```
import { Injectable } from '@angular/core';
```

```
import { HttpClient } from '@angular/common/http';
import { Observable } from 'rxjs';
@Injectable({
  providedIn: 'root',
})
export class DataService {
  constructor(private http: HttpClient) {}
  getData(): Observable<any> {
    return this.http.get('https://api.example.com/data');
  }
}
```

The following example illustrates the handling of user input with RxJS:

```
import { Component, OnInit } from '@angular/core';
import { fromEvent } from 'rxjs';
import { debounceTime, map } from 'rxjs/operators';
@Component({
  selector: 'app-keyboard-input',
  template: `<input id="search" placeholder="Type to search" />`,
})
export class KeyboardInputComponent implements OnInit {
  ngOnInit() {
    const inputElement = document.getElementById('search') as HTMLInputElement;
    fromEvent(inputElement, 'input').pipe(
      map((event: any) => event.target.value),
      debounceTime(300)  // Avoid multiple API calls
    ).subscribe(value => {
      console.log('User input:', value);
    });
  }
}
```

Question 2: What are observables in RxJS, and how do they work in Angular?

Answer: Observables represent a stream of values over time, enabling asynchronous programming in Angular. You use them to handle asynchronous events like HTTP requests and user interactions.

For example:

```
import { Observable } from 'rxjs';
const observable = new Observable(subscriber => {
  subscriber.next('Hello');
  subscriber.next('RxJS');
  subscriber.complete();
});
observable.subscribe({
  next: value => console.log(value),
```

```
  complete: () => console.log('Done'),
});
```

Question 3: What is the difference between observables and promises in Angular?

Answer: Observables and promises are both used to handle asynchronous operations in Angular, but they differ in key aspects:

- **Observables** are more powerful, can emit multiple values over time, and support operators for data manipulation.
- **Promises** handle a single asynchronous result, which resolves or rejects.

For example:

```
// Observable
const observable = new Observable(observer => {
  observer.next('Hello');
  observer.complete();
});
observable.subscribe(value => console.log(value));  // Can emit multiple values
// Promise
const promise = new Promise((resolve, reject) => resolve('Hello'));
promise.then(value => console.log(value)); // Single value
```

Use an observable when:

- You expect multiple values over time (stream-based).
- You need to cancel the request (e.g., on component destroy).
- You want operators like map, filter, retry, or debounceTime (RxJS power).
- You are handling real-time data, such as websockets or user input streams.
- You are working with Angular's HttpClient, which returns observables by default.

Use a promise when:

- You expect only a single value or result.
- You do not need to cancel or unsubscribe from the operation.
- You are dealing with simple async logic, like reading local data or a one-time API call.
- You want simpler syntax with async or await.

Question 4: What are Subjects in RxJS, and how do they differ from observables?

Answer: Subjects are both observable and observer, meaning they can emit and subscribe to values. Unlike regular observables, Subjects allow multicasting, where multiple subscribers can listen to the same data stream.

For example:

```
import { Subject } from 'rxjs';
const subject = new Subject();
subject.subscribe(value => console.log('Subscriber 1:', value));
subject.subscribe(value => console.log('Subscriber 2:', value));
subject.next('Hello'); // Both subscribers will receive 'Hello'
```

A Subject in RxJS is both an observable and an observer if:

- It can emit values (observer part).
- It can be subscribed to like an observable.

There are several types of Subjects (Subject, BehaviorSubject, ReplaySubject, AsyncSubject), each with different behavior.

Subjects in Angular (RxJS):

- A Subject is both an observable (you can subscribe to it) and an observer (you can emit values with `.next()`).
- Useful for bridging manual event emission with reactive streams.

Use a Subject when:

- **Cross-component communication** via a shared service (e.g., broadcasting data updates).
- **Manual triggering of events** such as refreshes or user actions outside Angular events.
- **Reactive form or UI input streaming**, combined with RxJS operators like debounceTime.
- **Imperative control over data emission** when needed in business logic.

Use BehaviorSubject when:

- When you need to store and emit the latest value to new subscribers immediately.
- Common for authentication state, user session, or theme preferences.
- Works well for state management scenarios (alternative to NgRx for simple apps).

Use a regular observable when:

- For one-time async operations, like HTTP calls (`HttpClient.get()`).
- When you want lazy execution, the stream activates only when subscribed.
- For read-only streams with no need for manual `.next()` emission.

Question 5: What are the different types of Subjects in RxJS, and when should you use them?

Answer: The different types of Subjects in RxJS are:

- **Subject**: Basic multicast observable.
- **BehaviorSubject**: Stores the last emitted value and provides it to new subscribers immediately.
- **ReplaySubject**: Records the emitted values and replays them to new subscribers.
- **AsyncSubject**: Emits only the last value when the observable completes.

The use cases are as follows:

- **BehaviorSubject** for state management, where you need to retain the last value.
- **ReplaySubject** for buffering multiple values.
- **AsyncSubject** for sending the final value after completion.

Question 6: What is an AsyncSubject, and how does it behave in Angular applications?

Answer: An `AsyncSubject` only emits the last value when the observable completes. It is useful when you only care about the final outcome.

For example:

```
import { AsyncSubject } from 'rxjs';
const asyncSubject = new AsyncSubject();
asyncSubject.subscribe(value => console.log('Subscriber:', value));
asyncSubject.next(1);
asyncSubject.next(2);
asyncSubject.complete(); // Output: 'Subscriber: 2'
```

Question 7: How does a BehaviorSubject work, and how is it used for state management in Angular?

Answer: A **`BehaviorSubject`** retains the last emitted value and provides it to new subscribers immediately. It is often used in Angular for managing application state.

For example:

```
import { BehaviorSubject } from 'rxjs';
const behaviorSubject = new BehaviorSubject('Initial value');
behaviorSubject.subscribe(value => console.log('Subscriber 1:', value));
behaviorSubject.next('New value');  // Subscriber 1: New value
behaviorSubject.subscribe(value => console.log('Subscriber 2:', value));  // Subscriber 2: 
New value
```

Question 8: What is a ReplaySubject, and how does it differ from a BehaviorSubject?

Answer: A **`ReplaySubject`** records multiple emitted values and replays them to new subscribers. It is different from a **`BehaviorSubject`**, which only retains the last emitted value.

For example:

```
import { ReplaySubject } from 'rxjs';
const replaySubject = new ReplaySubject(2); // Buffer size is 2
replaySubject.next(1);
replaySubject.next(2);
replaySubject.next(3);  // Last 2 values (2, 3) will be replayed
replaySubject.subscribe(value => console.log(value));  // Output: 2, 3
```

Question 9: What is the purpose of the subscribe method in RxJS, and what are its parameters?

Answer: The subscribe method in RxJS is used to start receiving data from an observable. Its parameters can be:

- **next**: Handles each emitted value.
- **error**: Handles errors.
- **complete**: Handles completion.

For example:

```
import { of } from 'rxjs';
const observable = of(1, 2, 3);
observable.subscribe({
  next: value => console.log(value),
  complete: () => console.log('Completed'),
});
```

Question 10: What are Operators in RxJS, and why are they important?

Answer: Operators in RxJS are functions that allow you to transform, filter, and manipulate observables. They are crucial for composing complex asynchronous workflows.

For example:

```
import { of } from 'rxjs';
import { map, filter } from 'rxjs/operators';
of(1, 2, 3, 4, 5)
  .pipe(
    filter(value => value > 2),
```

```
    map(value => value * 2)
  )
  .subscribe(value => console.log(value)); // Output: 6, 8, 10
```

Operators and transformations

Question 11: What are pipeable operators in RxJS, and how are they used in Angular?

Answer: **Pipeable operators** are functions that can be used to transform or combine observables in RxJS. They are used within the **.pipe()** method to chain multiple operations on an observable.

For example:

```
import { of } from 'rxjs';
import { map, filter } from 'rxjs/operators';
const data = of(1, 2, 3, 4, 5);
data.pipe(
  filter(value => value % 2 === 0),
  map(value => value * 2)
).subscribe(console.log);
```

Output: **4, 8**

Question 12: What is the difference between map, mergeMap, switchMap, and concatMap in RxJS?

Answer: These RxJS operators are used to transform or manage nested or dependent observables, each with different behavior for handling emissions and subscriptions:

- map:
  - **What it does**: Transforms each emitted value into a new value. It does not handle inner observables.
  - **Use case**: Convert raw API data into a new shape or format.

    Example: **source$.pipe(map(value => value * 2))**
- mergeMap:
  - **What it does**: It projects each value to an inner observable and merges all outputs concurrently. All inner subscriptions are active simultaneously.
  - **Use case**: Fire multiple HTTP requests in parallel, like uploading multiple files at once.

    Example: **from(files).pipe(mergeMap(file => upload(file)))**
- switchMap:
  - **What it does**: Switches to a new inner observable and cancels the previous one.
  - **Use case**: Handle live search or autocomplete, where only the latest input matters.

    Example: **searchInput$.pipe(switchMap(query => search(query)))**
- concatMap:
  - **What it does**: Projects each value to an inner observable and queues them, executing one after the other.
  - **Use case**: Sequential HTTP calls, like form steps or API workflows that must run in order.

    Example: **from(tasks).pipe(concatMap(task => run(task)))**

For example:

```
import { from, of, timer } from 'rxjs';
```

```
import { map, mergeMap, switchMap, concatMap } from 'rxjs/operators';
import { HttpClient } from '@angular/common/http';
export class RxjsExampleComponent {
  constructor(private http: HttpClient) {
    this.runExample();
  }
  runExample() {
    const userIds = [1, 2, 3];
    // Step 1: Use `map` to double each user ID
    from(userIds).pipe(
      map(id => id * 2), // map: Transform values
      // Step 2: Use `mergeMap` to fetch user details in parallel
      mergeMap(id => this.http.get(`/api/users/${id}`))
    ).subscribe(user => {
      console.log('User data (parallel):', user);
    });
    // Step 3: Use `switchMap` for live user selection (e.g., dropdown)
    const userSelection$ = timer(0, 3000); // Emits every 3 seconds (simulate user
selection)
    userSelection$.pipe(
      switchMap(id => this.http.get(`/api/users/${id}`)) // switchMap: cancels previous
    ).subscribe(user => {
      console.log('Latest selected user:', user);
    });
    // Step 4: Use `concatMap` to update users sequentially
    const updatedUsers = [
      {id: 1, name: 'Aradhya Singh'},
      {id: 2, name: 'Shiva Singh'},
    ];
    from(updatedUsers).pipe(
      concatMap(user => this.http.put(`/api/users/${user.id}`, user)) // concatMap: runs in
order
    ).subscribe(result => {
      console.log('Update result:', result);
    });
  }
}
```

As per the preceding example:

- **map**: Doubles each ID before calling the API.
- **mergeMap**: Makes parallel API calls to get user data.
- **switchMap**: Simulates user selection (e.g., dropdown) and always keeps only the latest request.
- **concatMap**: Updates each user one after another, ensuring order.

Question 13: How does the filter operator work, and when should it be used?

Answer: The `filter` operator filters values from an observable stream based on a predicate condition. An example is given as follows:

```
import { of } from 'rxjs';
import { filter } from 'rxjs/operators';
const data = of(1, 2, 3, 4, 5);
data.pipe(
  filter(value => value % 2 === 0)
).subscribe(console.log);  // Output: 2, 4
```

The filter operator can be used when you need to filter out specific values from a stream.

Question 14: How does the debounceTime operator help in performance optimization?

Answer: `debounceTime` delays the emission of values from an observable until a specified amount of time has passed without any new emissions. It is useful for reducing the number of requests triggered by user input (e.g., typing).

For example:

```
import { fromEvent } from 'rxjs';
import { debounceTime, map } from 'rxjs/operators';
const searchBox = document.getElementById('search');
fromEvent(searchBox, 'input').pipe(
  map((event: any) => event.target.value),
  debounceTime(300)
).subscribe(console.log);
// Delay API calls while typing stops for 300ms
```

Question 15: What is the difference between take, takeUntil, and takeWhile in RxJS?

Answer: The difference between `take`, `takeUntil`, and `takeWhile` is outlined as follows:

- **take**: Emits only the first n values and then completes.
- **takeUntil**: Emits values until a second observable emits a value.
- **takeWhile**: Emits values as long as the predicate is true.

For example:

```
import { interval } from 'rxjs';
import { take, takeUntil } from 'rxjs/operators';
const stop$ = interval(5000);
interval(1000).pipe(takeUntil(stop$)).subscribe(console.log);
// Stop after 5 seconds
```

Question 16: How does the combineLatest operator work, and how is it useful?

Answer: `combineLatest` combines the latest emitted values from multiple observables and emits a new value when any observable emits a value.

For example:

```
import { of } from 'rxjs';
import { combineLatest } from 'rxjs/operators';
const obs1 = of(1, 2, 3);
```

```
const obs2 = of('A', 'B', 'C');
combineLatest([obs1, obs2]).subscribe(console.log);
// Output: [3, 'C']
```

Question 17: How do you use the forkJoin operator, and when is it preferable over combineLatest?

Answer: `forkJoin` waits for all observables to complete and then emits the last value from each observable.

For example:

```
import { forkJoin } from 'rxjs';
import { of } from 'rxjs';
forkJoin([of(1, 2), of('A', 'B')]).subscribe(console.log);
// Output: [2, 'B']
```

Use `forkJoin` when you need the result of multiple observables after all have completed (e.g., for multiple API requests).

Question 18: What is the difference between merge, concat, and zip operators?

Answer: The difference between `merge`, `concat`, and `zip` operators is as follows:

- **merge**: Merges multiple observables and emits values as they arrive.
- **concat**: Concatenates observables, emitting values sequentially.
- **zip**: Combines values from multiple observables pairwise and emits them together.

Question 19: What does the throttleTime operator do, and how does it differ from debounceTime?

Answer: `throttleTime` limits the frequency of emitted values by emitting a value once every specified interval. Unlike `debounceTime`, it does not wait for silence; it emits at a fixed rate.

Question 20: How does the distinctUntilChanged operator help in optimizing API calls?

Answer: `distinctUntilChanged` ensures that only distinct consecutive values are emitted, preventing unnecessary API calls when the value has not changed.

For example:

```
import { of } from 'rxjs';
import { distinctUntilChanged } from 'rxjs/operators';
const data = of(1, 1, 2, 2, 3);
data.pipe(
  distinctUntilChanged()
).subscribe(value => console.log(value));
```

RxJS with HTTP and API calls

Question 21: How do you use RxJS to handle HTTP requests in Angular?

Answer: In Angular, RxJS is used to handle HTTP requests with the `HttpClient` service. The `HttpClient` methods return observables, allowing the use of RxJS operators to manipulate responses.

For example:

```
import { HttpClient } from '@angular/common/http';
import { catchError } from 'rxjs/operators';
import { of } from 'rxjs';
constructor(private http: HttpClient) {}
getData() {
```

```
  this.http.get('https://api.example.com/data')
    .pipe(
      catchError(error => of(`Error: ${error}`))
    )
    .subscribe(response => console.log(response));
}
```

Question 22: What is the difference between HttpClient.get() returning an observable and a promise?

Answer: When using **`HttpClient.get()`** in Angular, it can return either an observable or a promise, each with distinct characteristics:

- **Observable**: Supports multiple values over time, allows operators for transforming streams, and can be cancelled.
- **Promise**: Resolves a single value but cannot be cancelled or transformed easily.

The following example illustrates this difference:

```
// Observable
this.http.get('https://api.example.com/data').subscribe(data => console.log(data));
// Promise
this.http.get('https://api.example.com/data').toPromise().then(data => console.log(data));
```

Question 23: How do you cancel an ongoing HTTP request using RxJS?

Answer: You can cancel an HTTP request by unsubscribing from the observable, illustrated as follows:

```
import { Subscription } from 'rxjs';
let subscription: Subscription;
subscription = this.http.get('https://api.example.com/data').subscribe();
// To cancel:
subscription.unsubscribe();
```

Question 24: How do you implement exponential backoff retries with RxJS in Angular?

Answer: You can use the **`retryWhen`** operator combined with **`delayWhen`** and **`exponentialBackoff`** logic to implement retries with increasing intervals.

This can be demonstrated by the following example:

```
import { of } from 'rxjs';
import { delayWhen, retryWhen, take, map } from 'rxjs/operators';
this.http.get('https://api.example.com/data')
  .pipe(
    retryWhen(errors => errors.pipe(
      delayWhen(() => of(1).pipe(map(n => Math.pow(2, n) * 1000))),
      take(3)
    ))
  )
  .subscribe();
```

Question 25: How does RxJS handle API polling, and which operator is best suited for it?

Answer: For API polling, the interval operator is commonly used to emit values at specified intervals, and the **`switchMap`** operator is used to make API calls.

For example:

```
import { interval } from 'rxjs';
import { switchMap } from 'rxjs/operators';
interval(5000) // poll every 5 seconds
  .pipe(
    switchMap(() => this.http.get('https://api.example.com/data'))
  )
  .subscribe(response => console.log(response));
```

Question 26: **What are the best practices for handling errors in RxJS-based HTTP requests?**

Answer: Use operators like **`catchError`** and **`retryWhen`** to handle errors gracefully, as illustrated in the following example:

```
this.http.get('https://api.example.com/data')
  .pipe(
    catchError(error => {
      console.error('Error:', error);
      return of([]); // Return fallback value
    })
  )
  .subscribe(response => console.log(response));
```

Question 27: **How do you retry failed API requests using the retryWhen operator?**

Answer: The **`retryWhen`** operator allows you to control how retries are handled after a failure.

For example:

```
import { timer } from 'rxjs';
import { retryWhen, switchMap } from 'rxjs/operators';
this.http.get('https://api.example.com/data')
  .pipe(
    retryWhen(errors => errors.pipe(
      switchMap((error, count) => (count < 3 ? timer(1000 * count) : throwError(error)))
    ))
  )
  .subscribe();
```

Question 28: **How do you chain multiple API calls sequentially using RxJS?**

Answer: You can chain multiple API calls using operators like **`concatMap`** or **`switchMap`**, shown as follows:

```
this.http.get('https://api.example.com/data1')
  .pipe(
    concatMap(data1 => this.http.get('https://api.example.com/data2')),
    concatMap(data2 => this.http.get('https://api.example.com/data3'))
  )
  .subscribe(response => console.log(response));
```

Question 29: **How do you execute multiple API calls in parallel using RxJS?**

Answer: Use **`forkJoin`** to execute multiple API calls in parallel and wait for all to complete.

For example:

```
import { forkJoin } from 'rxjs';
forkJoin([
  this.http.get('https://api.example.com/data1'),
  this.http.get('https://api.example.com/data2')
]).subscribe(([data1, data2]) => {
  console.log(data1, data2);
});
```

Question 30: How does RxJS improve real-time data fetching using WebSockets in Angular?

Answer: RxJS integrates well with WebSockets by using the **`webSocket`** operator to create an observable stream of messages.

In the following example, RxJS provides real-time handling of WebSocket messages:

```
import { webSocket } from 'rxjs/webSocket';
const socket$ = webSocket('ws://localhost:8080');
socket$.subscribe(
  msg => console.log(msg),
  err => console.error(err),
  () => console.log('WebSocket closed')
);
```

State management and signals integration

Question 31. How can RxJS be used for state management in an Angular application?

Answer: RxJS can manage application state by using **`BehaviorSubject`** to store the current state and expose it as an observable, to which components can subscribe. This provides an easy way to react to state changes and keep components in sync.

For example:

```
import { BehaviorSubject } from 'rxjs';
export class AppStateService {
  private state = new BehaviorSubject<number>(0); // initial state
  state$ = this.state.asObservable();
  updateState(value: number) {
    this.state.next(value); // updates the state
  }
}
```

In a component:

```
this.appStateService.state$.subscribe(state => {
  console.log(state); // react to state changes
});
```

Question 32: What is the best way to manage global application state with RxJS?

Answer: To manage global state, you can create a service that holds the state in a **`BehaviorSubject`** or **`ReplaySubject`**, and then expose the state as an observable. Components can subscribe to this observable to get updates and modify the state.

For example:

```
import { Injectable } from '@angular/core';
import { BehaviorSubject } from 'rxjs';
@Injectable({
  providedIn: 'root'
})
export class GlobalStateService {
  private globalState = new BehaviorSubject<any>({ user: null });
  globalState$ = this.globalState.asObservable();
  updateUser(user: any) {
    this.globalState.next({ user });
  }
}
```

In the component:

```
this.globalStateService.globalState$.subscribe(state => {
  console.log(state.user); // react to global state changes
});
```

Question 33: **How do you share data between components using RxJS?**

Answer: You can use a shared service with a Subject or **`BehaviorSubject`** to emit data to multiple components. Components subscribe to the observable provided by the service.

For example:

```
import { Injectable } from '@angular/core';
import { BehaviorSubject } from 'rxjs';
@Injectable({
  providedIn: 'root'
})
export class DataService {
  private dataSource = new BehaviorSubject<string>('initial data');
  data$ = this.dataSource.asObservable();
  updateData(newData: string) {
    this.dataSource.next(newData);
  }
}
```

In component 1 (sending data):

```
this.dataService.updateData('new data');
```

In component 2 (receiving data):

```
this.dataService.data$.subscribe(data => {
  console.log(data); // 'new data'
});
```

Question 34: How does Angular 20 integrate RxJS with the new signals feature?

Answer: In Angular 20, signals are introduced as a new reactivity model. While signals are a simpler and more direct way to manage state, you can still use RxJS within Angular components to work with more complex, stream-based data or interactions alongside signals.

For example: Integration with signals and RxJS:

```
import { signal } from '@angular/core';
export class MyComponent {
  signalState = signal('Initial state'); // Angular signal
  constructor(private dataService: DataService) {
    // Using RxJS to react to data service changes
    this.dataService.data$.subscribe(data => {
      this.signalState.set(data); // Update signal based on RxJS data
    });
  }
}
```

In the preceding example, the **`signalState`** is updated with data received from an RxJS-based observable (**`data$`**).

Question 35: What are the key advantages of using RxJS over signals in Angular 20?

Answer: While Angular 20 introduces signals for reactive state management, RxJS remains advantageous in several scenarios:

- **Complexity handling**: RxJS is better suited for complex asynchronous workflows like handling HTTP requests, event streams, and WebSocket connections.
- **Declarative composition**: RxJS allows complex transformations and compositions of streams using operators like **`map`**, **`mergeMap`**, **`switchMap`**, etc.
- **Backpressure handling**: RxJS provides built-in backpressure management (e.g., **`throttleTime`**, **`debounceTime`**) for handling large data streams.
- **Cancellation**: RxJS streams can be easily cancelled, whereas signals do not offer built-in cancellation or cancellation logic for complex asynchronous operations.

Consider the following example of RxJS advantage:

```
this.http.get('https://api.example.com/data')
  .pipe(
    debounceTime(300), // debouncing the requests
    catchError(err => of('Error occurred'))
  )
  .subscribe(response => console.log(response));
```

Signal would not easily manage debounce time or HTTP-specific behaviors as efficiently as RxJS.

Lifecycle management and performance optimization

Question 36: How do you prevent memory leaks in Angular using RxJS?

Answer: Memory leaks in Angular applications often occur when observables are not unsubscribed. To prevent memory leaks with RxJS, use operators like **`takeUntil`** or the async pipe to manage subscriptions efficiently.

Example using **`takeUntil`**:

```
import { Subject } from 'rxjs';
export class MyComponent implements OnInit, OnDestroy {
  private destroy$ = new Subject<void>();
  ngOnInit() {
    this.dataService.getData()
      .pipe(takeUntil(this.destroy$))
      .subscribe(data => {
        console.log(data);
      });
  }
  ngOnDestroy() {
    this.destroy$.next();
    this.destroy$.complete(); // Unsubscribes from the observable
  }
}
```

In the aforementioned example, **takeUntil** ensures that the subscription is automatically unsubscribed when the component is destroyed.

Question 37: What is the takeUntil pattern, and how does it help in unsubscribing from observables?

Answer: The **takeUntil** operator automatically unsubscribes from an observable when a certain condition is met (typically when a **Subject** emits a value). It is commonly used in conjunction with **ngOnDestroy** to prevent memory leaks.

For example:

```
import { takeUntil } from 'rxjs/operators';
import { Subject } from 'rxjs';
class MyComponent {
  private unsubscribe$ = new Subject<void>();
  ngOnInit() {
    this.myService.getData()
      .pipe(takeUntil(this.unsubscribe$)) // Will unsubscribe when unsubscribe$ emits
      .subscribe(data => console.log(data));
  }
  ngOnDestroy() {
    this.unsubscribe$.next(); // Triggers unsubscription
    this.unsubscribe$.complete(); // Complete the subject
  }
}
```

In the preceding pattern, **takeUntil** listens for a signal from unsubscribe$ to trigger the **unsubscription**, ensuring proper cleanup.

Question 38: How does the unsubscribe method work, and when should it be called?

Answer: The **unsubscribe()** method manually stops the subscription to an observable. You should call **unsubscribe()** when you are done with the observable (e.g., in **ngOnDestroy** for Angular components) to avoid memory leaks.

For example:

```
export class MyComponent implements OnInit, OnDestroy {
  private subscription: Subscription;
  ngOnInit() {
    this.subscription = this.dataService.getData().subscribe(data => {
      console.log(data);
    });
  }
  ngOnDestroy() {
    if (this.subscription) {
      this.subscription.unsubscribe(); // Manually unsubscribe when component is destroyed
    }
  }
}
```

You should call **unsubscribe()** when you no longer need to listen to the observable to prevent lingering subscriptions.

Question 39: What is the async pipe in Angular, and how does it help with RxJS?

Answer: The async pipe in Angular automatically subscribes to an observable and updates the view whenever the observable emits a new value. It also unsubscribes when the component is destroyed, preventing memory leaks.

For example:

```
<div *ngIf="dataService.data$ | async as data">
  <p>{{ data }}</p>
</div>
```

Here, the async pipe subscribes to **data$** and updates the DOM automatically whenever a new value is emitted. No manual subscription or unsubscription is required.

Question 40: How can you optimize performance when working with large data streams in RxJS?

Answer: To optimize performance with large data streams in RxJS, use operators like **debounceTime**, **throttleTime**, **bufferTime**, **auditTime**, and **distinctUntilChanged** to control the rate at which data is emitted or processed.

Example using **debounceTime** and **distinctUntilChanged**:

```
this.searchInput$
  .pipe(
    debounceTime(300), // Wait for the user to stop typing for 300ms
    distinctUntilChanged(), // Only emit when the value changes
    switchMap(query => this.apiService.search(query)) // Trigger search
  )
  .subscribe(results => {
    this.results = results;
  });
```

In this example:

- **debounceTime** ensures that only one request is made after the user stops typing.

- **distinctUntilChanged** prevents multiple requests with the same value, reducing unnecessary API calls.

You can also use **takeWhile** to limit data processing to certain conditions and improve efficiency.

Advanced topics and latest RxJS features

Question 41: How does RxJS help in optimizing SSR in Angular?

Answer: RxJS can be used to handle data streams asynchronously in SSR applications, enabling better control over the sequence of API calls and data loading. By using operators like **mergeMap** or **switchMap**, RxJS ensures that data is fetched in a controlled and non-blocking manner, improving SSR performance.

Example of SSR optimization:

```
this.httpClient.get('/api/data')
  .pipe(
    switchMap(data => this.httpClient.get(`/api/details/${data.id}`))
  )
  .subscribe(result => this.processData(result));
```

In SSR, RxJS helps ensure non-blocking API calls that can be managed and ordered effectively, allowing the server to send a fully rendered page with data quickly.

Question 42: What are the new performance optimizations in RxJS 7+ that impact Angular applications?

Answer: RxJS 7+ introduced several performance improvements:

- **Optimized operators** like **switchMap**, **mergeMap**, and **concatMap** to reduce overhead.
- **Better memory management** and faster garbage collection.
- **Improved scheduling** with **asyncScheduler** optimizations. These changes reduce CPU load and improve the responsiveness of Angular applications.

For example:

```
import { from } from 'rxjs';
import { observeOn } from 'rxjs/operators';
import { asyncScheduler } from 'rxjs';
from([1, 2, 3])
.pipe(observeOn(asyncScheduler))  // Improved scheduling for async tasks
.subscribe(console.log);
```

Question 43: How does RxJS handle backpressure, and what strategies can be used to manage it?

Answer: RxJS handles backpressure by using operators like **throttleTime**, **debounceTime**, and **bufferTime**. These operators help manage large amounts of data by controlling the flow of emissions, ensuring that the consumer is not overwhelmed.

Example with **throttleTime**:

```
this.searchInput$
  .pipe(throttleTime(300)) // Only allow one emission per 300ms
  .subscribe(query => this.search(query));
```

throttleTime can be used to manage excessive rapid emissions, helping avoid backpressure in scenarios like search input.

Question 44: What are multicasting observables, and how do they improve performance?

Answer: Multicasting allows an observable to emit the same values to multiple subscribers without re-executing the source observable. Operators like share and publish are used for multicasting in RxJS, reducing unnecessary computation and improving performance.

Example with share:

```
const source$ = this.httpClient.get('/api/data').pipe(share());
source$.subscribe(data => console.log('Subscriber 1:', data));
source$.subscribe(data => console.log('Subscriber 2:', data));
```

The source observable is executed once, and the result is shared across multiple subscribers, reducing unnecessary API calls.

Question 45: What is the shareReplay operator, and how does it optimize caching in Angular?

Answer: The `shareReplay` operator allows an observable to replay the last emitted value to new subscribers. It can be used to cache the result of an observable, improving performance by preventing repeated network requests.

For example:

```
const cachedData$ = this.httpClient.get('/api/data').pipe(shareReplay(1));
cachedData$.subscribe(data => console.log('Subscriber 1:', data));
cachedData$.subscribe(data => console.log('Subscriber 2:', data)); // Replays the cached
value
```

This operator helps in caching the latest emitted value, avoiding the need to re-fetch the same data for subsequent subscribers.

Question 46: How does the RxJS tap operator help with debugging and logging?

Answer: The tap operator allows you to perform side effects without modifying the stream. It is useful for debugging, logging, or inspecting the values flowing through an observable.

For example:

```
this.dataService.getData()
  .pipe(
    tap(data => console.log('Data:', data)) // Log the data without affecting the flow
  )
  .subscribe();
```

In this example, tap is used to log the data, helping with debugging while preserving the observable's original behavior.

Question 47: What are cold and hot observables in RxJS, and how do they impact Angular performance?

Answer: Observables in RxJS can be classified as cold or hot, affecting how data is produced and shared among subscribers:

- **Cold observables**: Start execution when subscribed to, meaning each subscriber triggers the execution.
- **Hot observables**: Share a single execution for multiple subscribers, reducing redundancy.

An example of each is given as follows:

- **Cold observable**: `httpClient.get()` is a cold observable; it triggers a new HTTP request for every subscriber.
- **Hot observable**: Using `Subject` or `BehaviorSubject` to share data among multiple subscribers can create hot observables.

Cold observables can increase performance overhead when multiple subscriptions are involved, while hot observables optimize shared data flow.

Question 48: What is the exhaustMap operator, and how does it help in handling user interactions?

Answer: The **`exhaustMap`** operator helps handle user interactions by ignoring incoming emissions when a previous one is still in progress. It is useful for preventing race conditions or overloading systems, particularly in scenarios like submitting forms.

In the following example, **`exhaustMap`** ensures that new form submissions are ignored while a previous submission is still processing:

```
this.formSubmit$
  .pipe(
    exhaustMap(data => this.apiService.submitForm(data))
  )
  .subscribe(response => console.log(response));
```

Question 49: How can RxJS be used for real-time applications like chat apps or live-stock updates?

Answer: RxJS is ideal for handling real-time data streams like WebSockets or server-sent events. You can use operators like map, **`switchMap`**, and **`mergeMap`** to process the stream efficiently.

Example using WebSocket:

```
import { webSocket } from 'rxjs/webSocket';
const socket$ = webSocket('ws://chat.example.com');
socket$.pipe(map(message => `Received: ${message}`)).subscribe(console.log);
```

This example sets up a WebSocket connection to receive real-time chat messages and processes them using RxJS.

Question 50: What are the best practices for using RxJS with Angular in enterprise applications?

Answer: Best practices for using RxJS with Angular include:

- **Use operators for efficient data flows**: Prefer **`switchMap`** for API calls, **`debounceTime`** for search inputs, and **`takeUntil`** for unsubscribing.
- **Leverage the async pipe**: Use the async pipe to manage subscriptions and avoid memory leaks.
- **Keep observables declarative**: Use operators to transform and manage streams declaratively, avoiding imperative logic.
- **Use caching**: Use operators like **`shareReplay`** to cache API responses and prevent unnecessary re-fetching.
- **Error handling**: Always handle errors with operators like **`catchError`** or retry.

For example:

```
this.httpClient.get('/api/user')
  .pipe(
    catchError(err => of([])), // Handle errors gracefully
    shareReplay(1) // Cache the result for future subscribers
  )
  .subscribe(user => console.log(user));
```

By following these practices, RxJS helps ensure a scalable and maintainable Angular application.

Security-related RxJS in Angular

51. How can RxJS be used to securely manage user authentication and session handling in Angular?

Answer: RxJS can be used to manage authentication and session handling by using observables for token management, secure API calls, and session expiration handling. By subscribing to authentication observables and securely storing the JWT, the application can react to changes in the user session, automatically refreshing the token if necessary.

In the following example, **authStatus$** triggers further requests only if the user is authenticated:

```
// Authentication service
this.authService.authStatus$.pipe(
  switchMap(isAuthenticated => {
    if (isAuthenticated) {
      return this.httpClient.get('/api/protected', { headers: this.authHeaders() });
    } else {
      return throwError('Not authenticated');
    }
  })
).subscribe(data => console.log(data), error => console.error(error));
```

Question 52: How do you prevent memory leaks in RxJS to avoid potential security vulnerabilities?

Answer: Memory leaks in RxJS can occur if subscriptions are not properly unsubscribed, potentially leaving sensitive data in memory or causing unexpected behavior. To avoid leaks, use **takeUntil** or the async pipe to automatically manage subscriptions.

Example with **takeUntil**:

```
const destroy$ = new Subject();
this.dataService.getData().pipe(
  takeUntil(destroy$)
).subscribe(data => console.log(data));
// On component destruction, trigger destroy$
ngOnDestroy() {
  destroy$.next();
  destroy$.complete();
}
```

This ensures that subscriptions are cleaned up when the component is destroyed, avoiding memory leaks.

Question 53: What are the risks of using shareReplay incorrectly in RxJS, and how can it expose sensitive data?

Answer: Using **shareReplay** incorrectly can cause sensitive data to be exposed if the observable is shared among multiple subscribers, especially if the observable emits sensitive information like tokens or user data. This could allow unauthorized users to access cached data.

Example of risky use:

```
const sharedData$ = this.httpClient.get('/api/user').pipe(shareReplay(1));
sharedData$.subscribe(data => console.log('Subscriber 1:', data));
sharedData$.subscribe(data => console.log('Subscriber 2:', data)); // Caches and shares data
```

In this case, if sensitive user information is returned, multiple subscribers might receive the cached result, potentially violating security principles.

The solution is to use proper cache invalidation strategies and only share non-sensitive data or sensitive data after proper authorization checks.

Question 54: How do you securely handle and refresh JWT tokens using RxJS in Angular?

Answer: You can use RxJS to refresh JWT tokens by monitoring token expiry and making a request to refresh the token automatically. The refresh request should only be made securely and never expose the refresh token in public-facing components.

Example of JWT refresh:

```
this.httpClient.get('/api/token/refresh').pipe(
  switchMap((response: any) => {
    const newToken = response.token;
    localStorage.setItem('authToken', newToken);
    return this.httpClient.get('/api/protected', { headers: { Authorization: `Bearer ${newToken}` } });
  })
).subscribe(data => console.log(data), error => console.error(error));
```

This flow ensures that tokens are refreshed securely before making protected API calls.

Question 55: What are the best practices for securing API calls made using RxJS observables?

Answer: To secure API calls follow the given best practices:

- Use HTTPS for secure data transmission.
- Use the Authorization header to pass secure tokens.
- Handle errors gracefully with **`catchError`**.
- Secure token storage (avoid localStorage for sensitive tokens).
- Apply rate-limiting using RxJS operators like **`debounceTime`** or **`throttleTime`**.

For example:

```
this.httpClient.get('/api/data', { headers: this.authHeaders() })
  .pipe(catchError(error => of('Error occurred')))
  .subscribe(data => console.log(data));
```

Question 56: How do you prevent race conditions and unauthorized API calls in an Angular RxJS-based application?

Answer: To prevent race conditions, use operators like **`exhaustMap`** or **`switchMap`** to handle user input or multiple API calls, ensuring that only the last valid request is processed, and others are ignored until the previous one completes.

Example using **`exhaustMap`**:

```
this.buttonClick$.pipe(
  exhaustMap(() => this.apiService.makeRequest())
).subscribe(response => console.log(response));
```

`exhaustMap` ensures only one API call is made at a time, even if the button is clicked multiple times in quick succession.

Question 57: What is the risk of over-subscribing to an observable, and how does it impact security?

Answer: Over-subscribing can lead to unnecessary executions of side-effects, such as multiple HTTP requests, leading to performance issues and possibly exposing sensitive data. Proper management of subscriptions with operators like **takeUntil** or async pipe can mitigate risks.

For example:

```
const api$ = this.httpClient.get('/api/data');
api$.subscribe(data => console.log('Request 1', data)); // Over-subscribing
api$.subscribe(data => console.log('Request 2', data)); // Over-subscribing again
```

This example could trigger two requests for the same data unnecessarily, potentially causing performance and security issues.

Question 58: How can you prevent unauthorized state changes when using RxJS for global state management?

Answer: To prevent unauthorized state changes, use operators like filter to ensure only authorized actions are allowed, and use **BehaviorSubject** to track state changes in a controlled manner.

The following ensures that only authorized users can modify or subscribe to the state:

```
const state$ = new BehaviorSubject(initialState);
state$.pipe(
  filter(state => state.isAuthorized)
).subscribe(state => console.log(state));
```

Question 59: How do you securely handle and log errors in RxJS-based Angular applications without exposing sensitive data?

Answer: Use the **catchError** operator to handle errors securely, logging the error in a way that does not expose sensitive information. Errors can be logged for debugging, but should be masked for production environments.

Refer to the following example:

```
this.httpClient.get('/api/data').pipe(
  catchError(error => {
    console.error('Logging error:', error.message); // Mask sensitive error details
    return of([]);
  })
).subscribe();
```

Question 60: What are the security implications of using Subject and BehaviorSubject for data sharing in Angular?

Answer: Both **Subject** and **BehaviorSubject** are hot observables, meaning data is shared across multiple subscribers. If sensitive data is emitted, unauthorized subscribers could access it. To mitigate risks, ensure proper authorization checks are applied before emitting sensitive data.

For example:

```
// Sensitive data being shared
const userSubject = new BehaviorSubject<User>(null);
userSubject.next(authenticatedUser);
// Unauthorized subscriber access
userSubject.subscribe(user => console.log(user)); // Could expose sensitive user data
```

To prevent this, sensitive data should be filtered or guarded using proper authentication and authorization mechanisms.

Conclusion

RxJS provides a powerful and flexible way to handle asynchronous operations, event streams, and complex data transformations in Angular. By leveraging observables, operators, and various stream-handling techniques, developers can efficiently manage data flow and improve application performance. Understanding the differences between observables and promises, as well as the nuances of operators like map, mergeMap, switchMap, and concatMap, is crucial for building robust and scalable Angular applications.

In the next chapter, we will explore **artificial intelligence** (**AI**) experimental features, looking into how AI-driven enhancements can be integrated into Angular applications to improve automation, decision-making, and user experience.

CHAPTER 16
AI Experimental Features

Introduction

Artificial intelligence (AI) is rapidly evolving, with new experimental features constantly emerging to enhance automation, decision-making, and predictive analytics. These experimental features aim to improve AI-driven applications by optimizing performance, increasing adaptability, and refining human-machine interactions. This chapter explores the experimental AI features that are shaping the future of software applications, with a focus on their practical applications and implications.

Structure

This chapter covers the following topics:

- AI in Angular development and optimization
- AI in testing, security, and automation
- AI in Angular UI, UX, and personalization

Objectives

By the end of this chapter, readers will understand the significance of experimental AI features in driving technological innovation and their role in improving automation and decision-making. They will learn how to effectively integrate these capabilities into their projects while recognizing potential risks and limitations associated with emerging AI technologies. Additionally, they will explore real-world applications demonstrating the impact of experimental AI features across various industries. Finally, readers will gain insights into the future trajectory of AI and how they can leverage these advancements for business and technical growth.

AI in Angular development and optimization

Question 1: How is AI being integrated into Angular for automated code optimizations?

Answer: AI in Angular is used to analyze and optimize code by identifying patterns and suggesting refactors. It can recommend changes that enhance performance, reduce complexity, and improve maintainability.

The following is a visual overview illustrating how AI tools enhance productivity, code generation, and debugging within the Angular ecosystem:

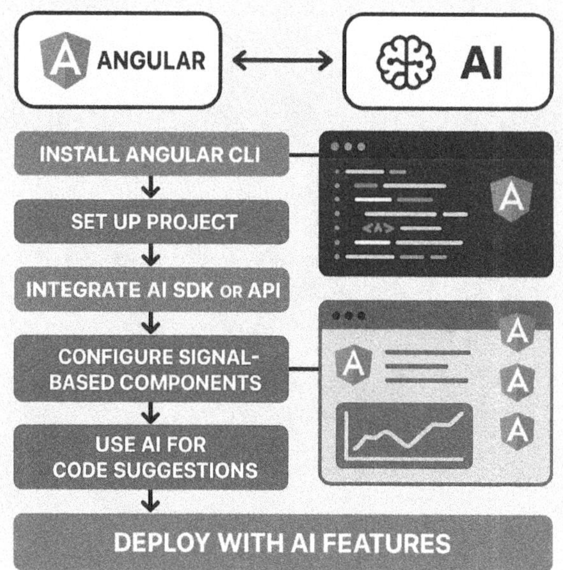

Figure 16.1: Integrating AI Tools in Angular development workflow

For example: AI tools can suggest refactoring a component to use **`ChangeDetectionStrategy.OnPush`**, shown as follows:

```
@Component({
  selector: 'app-example',
  changeDetection: ChangeDetectionStrategy.OnPush
})
export class ExampleComponent {}
```

Question 2: What are the latest AI-powered experimental features introduced in Angular 20?

Answer: Angular 20 includes experimental AI tools (Angie AI assistant, **`llms.txt`** or **`llms-full.txt`**, AI app integrations) that offer real-time suggestions for code optimization and performance enhancements based on usage patterns and performance profiling:

- **Angie AI assistant**:
    - **Offers inline AI help**: Code completion, doc lookup, and optimization tips.
    - **Built-in assistant**: Angie is Angular's built-in AI assistant that provides real-time, in-editor suggestions, similar to GitHub Copilot but Angular-aware.
    - **Still experimental**: Some features may need enabling in **`angular.json`** under **`"angularCompilerOptions": { "aiAssistance": true }`**.
    - **Enabling Angie**: Available in Angular DevTools or VS Code via Angular Language Service (latest).
    - Make sure you are using:
        - Angular 20+
        - **`@angular/language-service@20.x`**
        - Latest version of **Angular DevTools** (Chrome extension or standalone)
    - **How it works**: Offers intelligent suggestions for:
        - Fixing common errors

    - Optimizing component structure
    - Converting old code (e.g., from NgModules to standalone)
    - Improving change detection strategies
- **llms.txt or llms-full.txt**:
    - These files guide **large language models (LLMs)** like ChatGPT, Copilot, and others on how to best generate Angular code.
    - **Included in Angular CLI (v20+)**:
        - **llms.txt**: Prioritizes stable APIs and modern patterns (e.g., signals, standalone components).
        - **llms-full.txt**: Covers more experimental or internal APIs.
    - **Auto inclusion**: You do not need to configure anything; these are auto-included in your project root and used by LLM-aware tools.
    - **Benefit**: AI tools generate better Angular code (fewer NgModules, more **`@Component-only`** patterns, etc.)
- **AI app integrations**: **GenAI Tools (e.g., Genkit, Vertex AI)**:
    - Angular-provided examples (e.g., Genkit, Vertex AI) for building AI-driven apps.
    - Angular now offers recipes for GenAI integration. Here is how to try it out:
        1. **Set up with Genkit (by Firebase or Google)**: Install Genkit:
        ```
        npm create genkit
        cd my-ai-project
        ```
        2. **Use Genkit SDK in Angular**:
        ```
        import { useGenkit } from '@genkit/angular';
        const ai = useGenkit();
        ai.chat({ prompt: 'Suggest blog title for Angular Signals'
        }).subscribe(console.log);
        ```

Question 3: **How does AI assist in performance monitoring and optimizations in Angular applications?**

Answer: AI tools (Angie AI assistant, **`llms.txt`** or **`llms-full.txt`**, AI app integrations) monitor application performance in real time, analyzing API response times, DOM rendering speeds, and change detection cycles to suggest optimizations.

For example: AI recommends optimizing change detection, shown as follows:

```
@Component({
  selector: 'app-example',
  changeDetection: ChangeDetectionStrategy.OnPush
})
export class ExampleComponent {}
```

Question 4: **Can AI be used to improve Angular's change detection mechanism?**

Answer: AI helps optimize the change detection process by suggesting strategies like `OnPush` or detach based on component behavior.

For example: An AI tool suggests using **`OnPush`** for components with minimal state changes:

```
@Component({
  selector: 'app-user',
  changeDetection: ChangeDetectionStrategy.OnPush
```

```
})
export class UserComponent {}
```

Question 5: How can AI-driven tools help in analyzing and refactoring large Angular codebases?

Answer: AI tools can refactor Angular applications by identifying patterns in large codebases and suggesting modularization and simplification.

For example: AI can suggest refactoring a service to reduce redundancy:

```
@Injectable({
  providedIn: 'root'
})
export class UserService {
  getUser() {
    return this.http.get('api/user');
  }
}
```

Question 6: What AI-based debugging tools are available for Angular applications?

Answer: AI-based debugging tools like *Sentry* and *Raygun* provide real-time error tracking and categorize issues to predict and recommend fixes.

For example: Sentry automatically tracks errors and groups them, making it easier to fix similar issues at once.

Question 7: How can AI be used to predict and prevent runtime errors in Angular?

Answer: AI predicts runtime errors by analyzing app logs and interactions, identifying risky areas in the code, and suggesting preventive measures.

For example: AI may flag unhandled promises and suggest handling errors:

```
this.http.get('api/data').subscribe(
  (data) => this.handleData(data),
  (error) => this.handleError(error)
);
```

Question 8: How does AI improve dependency injection efficiency in Angular applications?

Answer: AI optimizes dependency injection by detecting unused services and recommending lazy loaded modules to improve performance.

For example: AI can recommend lazy loading a service:

```
@NgModule({
  imports: [RouterModule.forChild(routes)],
  providers: [MyLazyLoadedService]
})
export class LazyLoadedModule {}
```

Question 9: How do AI-powered linters enhance Angular coding standards and best practices?

Answer: AI-powered linters not only check for syntax errors but also ensure the code follows best practices, such as Angular-specific optimizations.

For example: AI can suggest using **`async/await`** instead of **`setTimeout`**:

```
async ngOnInit() {
  const data = await this.dataService.getData();
}
```

Question 10: What are the benefits of AI-powered predictive caching in Angular applications?

Answer: AI-powered predictive caching helps Angular applications by intelligently preloading data or assets that are likely to be requested next, based on user behavior and patterns. This can improve performance, reduce latency, and provide a smoother user experience. The key benefits of AI-powered predictive caching are:

- **Faster response times**: Predictive caching reduces wait times by loading data before it is requested.

  For example: AI can predict which data is likely to be used on the next screen and pre-fetch it in the background.

- **Improved user experience**: It minimizes the delay in loading content and assets.

  For example: a user scrolling through a list of items might have the next set of items already cached, improving fluidity.

- **Reduced network traffic**: By caching frequently accessed data, AI minimizes unnecessary API calls.

  For example: AI can identify repeated requests to the same API endpoints and store results locally.

- **Optimized resource usage**: Caching helps reduce the load on backend servers by serving data from the cache.

  For example: AI predicts which pages are frequently accessed and keeps their content in memory to reduce load on the server.

- **Adaptive caching strategy**: AI adjusts the caching strategy based on user interaction patterns, ensuring the cache is updated with the most relevant data.

  For example: for an e-commerce app, AI could prioritize caching products that a user has previously viewed or interacted with.

- **Example implementation**: In an Angular service, predictive caching can be used by pre-fetching data based on user navigation:

  ```
  @Injectable({
    providedIn: 'root'
  })
  export class PredictiveCacheService {
    private cache = new Map();
    constructor(private http: HttpClient) {}
    getData(url: string) {
      if (this.cache.has(url)) {
        return of(this.cache.get(url)); // Serve from cache
      } else {
        return this.http.get(url).pipe(
          tap((data) => this.cache.set(url, data)) // Predictively cache data
        );
      }
    }
  }
  ```

In the preceding example, data is cached when it is fetched and served from the cache on subsequent requests, improving response times. AI could enhance this by learning which URLs are most likely to be requested next and preloading them.

AI in testing, security, and automation

Question 11: How can AI improve test case generation and coverage in Angular applications?

Answer: AI analyzes Angular code to generate test cases automatically, covering critical paths and edge cases.

For example: AI generates unit tests for a component's **`ngOnInit()`** lifecycle hook by analyzing its dependencies and interactions.

Question 12: How does AI help in automating end-to-end (E2E) testing in Angular?

Answer: AI can simulate real user behavior, automatically generating E2E test scripts based on code changes and user flows.

For example: AI can create an E2E test script that simulates logging in, navigating the dashboard, and making a transaction.

Question 13: Can AI assist in auto-generating unit tests for Angular components?

Answer: AI examines Angular components, generating unit tests that cover various scenarios, including edge cases.

For example: For an HTTP service method, AI generates tests to check success and error scenarios.

Question 14: How does AI enhance security vulnerability detection in Angular applications?

Answer: AI identifies security risks like XSS and injection flaws by scanning the code for patterns and vulnerabilities.

For example: AI flags missing input sanitization, suggesting the use of Angular's DomSanitizer to prevent XSS.

Question 15: How does AI help in analyzing API request patterns to optimize Angular HTTP client performance?

Answer: AI analyzes API requests and suggests optimizations like caching or request batching based on patterns.

For example: AI detects frequent API calls and suggests caching results locally to reduce redundant network calls.

Question 16: What AI-driven tools can be used for real-time security threat detection in Angular applications?

Answer: AI tools like Snyk and Dependabot analyze code and dependencies for vulnerabilities, providing real-time alerts.

For example: Snyk detects a vulnerable library in an Angular project and suggests an upgrade to a secure version.

Question 17: How can AI help in automatic bug fixing in Angular applications?

Answer: AI analyzes error logs and stack traces to propose fixes for common bugs in Angular applications.

For example: AI detects an undefined error and suggests adding a null check before accessing the property.

Question 18: How can machine learning be integrated into Angular forms for predictive input validation?

Answer: ML analyzes past form submissions to predict input patterns, offering real-time suggestions and validation.

For example: For a phone number field, AI predicts the most common format and provides real-time formatting assistance.

Question 19: How do AI-powered accessibility tools improve Angular applications for a diverse user base?

Answer: AI tools analyze an app's accessibility and suggest improvements such as proper alt text or contrast adjustments.

For example: AI detects missing ARIA labels in an Angular component and suggests adding them to improve screen reader compatibility.

Question 20: How does AI improve state management in Angular applications?

Answer: AI optimizes state management by predicting and recommending efficient state handling strategies based on app complexity. ARIA labels AI suggests using `ngrx` for managing complex application states based on the app's structure and size.

AI in Angular UI, UX, and personalization

Question 21: How can AI be used to enhance the user experience in Angular applications?

Answer: AI can adapt the UI based on user behavior, providing personalized recommendations or content. ARIA labels AI analyzes user behavior and displays a personalized homepage with frequently visited items.

Question 22: How does AI-driven dynamic theming work in Angular applications?

Answer: AI selects the most appropriate theme for the user based on environmental factors or preferences.

For example: Based on the time of day, AI automatically switches to a dark theme at night for better readability.

Question 23: What role does AI play in personalizing content and UI elements in Angular applications?

Answer: AI customizes content and UI elements by analyzing user preferences and interaction history.

For example: AI shows product recommendations based on a user's past browsing and shopping behavior.

Question 24: How can AI-powered voice assistants be integrated into Angular applications?

Answer: AI voice assistants process user voice commands and perform tasks such as navigation or content retrieval.

For example: An AI-powered voice assistant allows users to ask for weather updates or search for products using voice commands.

Question 25: How does AI-driven real-time translation improve internationalization (i18n) in Angular?

Answer: AI translates content on the fly, allowing Angular apps to dynamically change languages without requiring full page reloads.

For example: AI detects a user's preferred language and translates the UI content into Spanish.

Question 26: How does AI improve lazy loading and module preloading strategies in Angular applications?

Answer: AI predicts which modules are likely to be needed next and preloads them, reducing load times.

For example: AI predicts the next screen the user will visit and starts loading the associated module in the background.

Question 27: What are the AI-powered enhancements in Angular Ivy and its rendering performance?

Answer: AI optimizes change detection and component rendering, improving Angular Ivy's performance by reducing unnecessary operations.

For example: AI dynamically adjusts rendering strategies to only update components that have changed, improving rendering speed.

Question 28: How does AI help in optimizing Angular's hydration process in server-side rendering (SSR)?

Answer: AI adjusts the hydration strategy by analyzing the initial load and deferring non-essential scripts for faster page rendering.

For example: AI only hydrates critical parts of the app initially and delays less important features until after the page is fully loaded.

Question 29: Can AI be used to analyze user interactions and dynamically adjust Angular application behavior?

Answer: AI can analyze user interactions and adjust the app behavior in real-time, optimizing engagement.

For example: AI detects that a user often interacts with a specific feature and dynamically displays it more prominently in the UI.

Question 30: How can AI predict and optimize Angular component lifecycles for better performance?

Answer: AI can predict when components will be used based on user behavior and optimize lifecycle hooks for better performance.

For example: AI delays component initialization for parts of the UI that are less likely to be used immediately, reducing initial load time.

Question 31: What are the best AI-driven tools to generate real-time analytics in Angular dashboards?

Answer: AI tools analyze user interactions and data, generating real-time insights for dynamic dashboard updates.

For example: AI detects trending metrics and updates the dashboard in real-time with graphs reflecting the latest data.

Question 32: How can AI improve Angular's error handling by providing automated fix recommendations?

Answer: AI analyzes error logs and provides suggestions for automated fixes based on known patterns and best practices.

For example: AI detects a recurring null pointer exception and suggests adding null checks to prevent the error.

Question 33: How does AI enhance Angular's signals system for real-time data streaming and reactivity?

Answer: AI optimizes the signals system by predicting data changes and updating only necessary components.

For example: AI detects frequent changes in user preferences and updates the UI in real-time using Angular signals.

Question 34: How can AI assist in automatic migration from older Angular versions to the latest versions?

Answer: AI analyzes the existing codebase and automates migration by refactoring and updating deprecated features.

For example: AI automatically updates Angular CLI configurations and replaces deprecated lifecycle hooks when upgrading to the latest Angular version.

Question 35: What AI-powered tools can be used for real-time threat monitoring and mitigation in Angular applications?

Answer: AI tools like Snyk and DeepCode detect vulnerabilities in real-time, providing suggestions to mitigate threats.

For example: AI alerts developers of new vulnerabilities in third-party libraries and suggests patches or updates to prevent security breaches.

Conclusion

The integration of AI experimental features in modern development has brought significant improvements in automation, predictive analytics, and intelligent assistance. These advancements have enhanced code efficiency, debugging, and performance optimization, making software development more streamlined. However, despite these benefits, challenges such as accuracy, ethical concerns, and dependency on AI-driven decisions remain key considerations. As AI continues to evolve, developers must strike a balance between automation and manual oversight, ensuring that AI complements rather than replaces human expertise. The adoption of AI-powered tools should be approached with a strategic mindset, leveraging their capabilities while maintaining control over the development process.

The next chapter focuses on compilers and build tools, which play a fundamental role in transforming source code into executable applications. The chapter will explore the working principles of compilers, interpreters, and linkers, along with modern build automation techniques. It will also cover optimization strategies that enhance application efficiency and ensure seamless deployment.

CHAPTER 17
Compiler and Build Tools

Introduction

The Angular compiler and build tools are essential components that transform TypeScript and HTML templates into highly optimized JavaScript code, ensuring efficient execution in the browser. Angular provides a powerful compilation pipeline, including **ahead-of-time** (AOT) compilation, **just-in-time** (JIT) compilation, and tree-shaking mechanisms to eliminate unused code. Additionally, modern build tools like Webpack, esbuild, and caching strategies help improve build performance and application efficiency. This chapter explores the inner workings of Angular's compiler, various build processes, and key optimizations that enhance both development and production workflows.

Structure

This chapter covers the following topics:

- Compiler core concepts and fundamentals
- Compiler build process and optimization
- Advanced compilation and latest enhancements
- Dependency management and build tools
- Performance, debugging, and deployment

Objectives

By the end of this chapter, you will understand the object of the Angular Compiler in transforming TypeScript into JavaScript, differentiate between JIT and AOT compilation, and know when to use each, learn about modern build tools like Webpack, esbuild, and Vite, and gain insights into optimizing application performance through tree shaking and lazy loading. You will also be able to configure and customize Angular's build system for various environments, implement best practices to reduce build time and improve runtime efficiency, and understand debugging and source map strategies for troubleshooting. With a solid grasp of these concepts, you will be equipped to build scalable, high-performance Angular applications using the most effective compilation and build strategies.

Compiler core concepts and fundamentals

Question 1: What is the Angular compiler, and how does it work?

Answer: The Angular compiler (**ngc**) converts TypeScript and HTML templates into efficient JavaScript code that the browser can understand. It processes components, templates, and services, transforming them into a format that Angular can run in the browser.

For example: In Angular, the **ngc** command compiles a component template along with its TypeScript code into JavaScript code:

```
@Component({
  selector: 'app-hello',
  template: '<h1>Hello World</h1>',
})
export class HelloComponent {}
```

The Angular compiler (**ngc**) transforms this TypeScript and HTML template into efficient JavaScript code that the browser can understand and execute. This is essential because JavaScript is the only programming language natively understood and executed by all modern web browsers.

Question 2: What are the differences between the view engine and Ivy in Angular?

Answer: The view engine is the old rendering engine in Angular, while Ivy is the new rendering engine introduced in Angular 9. Ivy improves bundle size, compilation speed, and provides a more flexible and faster change detection mechanism.

Angular has evolved from the view engine to the Ivy rendering engine, bringing significant improvements in performance and bundle optimization. The following are key differences between the two:

- **View engine**: Uses a global bundle for each component.
- **Ivy**: Produces smaller, more efficient bundles, and tree-shakes unused code more effectively.

For example: In Angular 9 and above, Ivy allows Angular applications to be smaller and load faster due to improved tree-shaking and a smaller runtime bundle.

Question 3: How does the AOT compiler improve performance?

Answer: AOT pre-compiles the Angular app during build time, reducing the amount of work the browser has to do at runtime. This results in faster page loads and fewer runtime errors.

For example: With AOT enabled, the Angular template is compiled during the build process, leading to faster startup time and fewer issues in production, shown as follows:

```
ng build --prod
```

The AOT compiler creates optimized JavaScript that runs efficiently in the browser.

Question 4: What is JIT compilation, and when should it be used?

Answer: JIT compiles Angular components and templates in the browser at runtime. It is useful for development since it provides faster iteration times, but is less efficient for production due to the extra work done in the browser.

For example: In development, you might use JIT compilation:

```
ng serve
```

This compiles the code in the browser, which is slower for large apps but useful for fast development iterations.

Question 5: What is the purpose of the ngc command?

Answer: The **ngc** command compiles Angular TypeScript and HTML templates into optimized JavaScript code. It is mainly used for AOT compilation during the build process.

For example: Running **ngc** in the terminal will compile the Angular app with AOT:

```
ngc --project tsconfig.app.json
```

This generates compiled JavaScript code from the TypeScript and template files.

Question 6: What is the difference between the Angular compiler and the TypeScript compiler (tsc)?

Answer: The ngc processes Angular-specific features such as templates, decorators, and metadata to generate highly optimized JavaScript code tailored for Angular applications. In contrast, the TypeScript compiler (**tsc**) only transpiles plain TypeScript code to JavaScript and is unaware of Angular's structure or templates.

You typically use **tsc** for general TypeScript projects or libraries, while **ngc** is required when building Angular applications or libraries that include Angular decorators, templates, and dependency injection.

For example::

- **tsc**: Compiles TypeScript files into JavaScript.
- **ngc**: Compiles both TypeScript and Angular-specific metadata, such as templates and decorators, into optimized JavaScript.

Question 7: How does the Angular Ivy compiler improve application performance?

Answer: Ivy compiles code in a more efficient and granular manner, resulting in smaller bundles, better tree-shaking, and faster change detection. It also improves the performance of lazy loaded modules and reduces the initial bundle size.

For example: With Ivy, Angular only includes the code that is actually used in the app, reducing the final bundle size significantly:

```
ng build --prod
```

The production build will be optimized using Ivy to create smaller and faster apps.

Here is the difference between AOT and JIT:

- **Ahead-of-time compilation:**
  - Compiles Angular templates and TypeScript at build time.
  - Results in faster app startup since no compilation happens in the browser.
  - Catches template and type errors early during the build.
  - Smaller bundle size because the Angular compiler is excluded from the final output.
  - More secure, as templates are precompiled and sanitized.
  - Recommended for production builds to improve performance and reliability.
- **Just-in-time compilation:**
  - Compiles Angular code in the browser at runtime.
  - Slower startup time, as compilation happens on the client side.
  - Errors may appear at runtime, and are harder to catch during development.
  - Larger bundle size because the compiler is included in the app.
  - Useful in development mode for quick changes and faster rebuilds.
  - Easier for debugging and testing during early development phases.

Question 8: What are the main differences between template compilation and module compilation in Angular?

Answer: Template compilation converts Angular templates (HTML) into JavaScript code, while module compilation compiles metadata about Angular modules and their components. Let us look at the differences between them.

Template compilation:

- Transforms HTML into executable code for rendering the view.
- Converts component HTML templates into JavaScript render functions.
- Needed when using template or **`templateUrl`** in a component.
- Processes Angular syntax like **`*ngIf`**, **`{{ }}`**, **`[input]`**, **`(event)`**, etc.
- Happens during both AOT and JIT builds.
- Essential for rendering the UI.

Template compilation is needed when:

- You use inline or external templates in components (template or **`templateUrl`**).
- During AOT or JIT compilation to pre-process the Angular syntax like **`*ngIf`**, **`*ngFor`**, bindings (**`{{ }}`**, **`[property]`**, **`(event)`**), etc.
- When Angular needs to understand the structure and logic of your view to generate render code.

For example: In the template:

```
<div>{{ user.name }}</div>
```

The template compilation converts this into JavaScript that Angular can execute to render the data.

Module compilation:

- Creates metadata for modules to define the components, directives, and pipes they contain.
- Processes **`@NgModule`** metadata.
- Needed to register components, directives, pipes, and services.
- Resolves dependencies and bootstraps the app.
- Organizes the app into logical units (e.g., **`AppModule`**, **`FeatureModule`**).
- Required in both AOT and JIT to wire everything together.

Module compilation is needed when:

- Whenever you define an **`@NgModule`** to organize and configure your app or feature.
- During AOT or JIT compilation to resolve dependencies and optimize tree shaking.
- Angular uses module metadata to know:
  - Which components to compile
  - Which services to inject
  - What features to include (like routing, forms, etc.)

For example: In the module:

```
@NgModule({
  declarations: [HelloComponent],
  imports: [BrowserModule],
  bootstrap: [HelloComponent]
})
export class AppModule {}
```

This module must be compiled so Angular knows to bootstrap **`HelloComponent`** and load **`BrowserModule`**.

Question 9: What are entry components, and how does the compiler handle them?

Answer: Entry components are components that are not directly referenced in a template but need to be compiled and included in the app's final build, such as components dynamically created by **`ComponentFactoryResolver`**.

For example: If you have a modal component that is dynamically loaded:

```
@Component({
  selector: 'app-modal',
  template: '<div>Modal content</div>',
})
export class ModalComponent {}
```

The compiler ensures this component is included in the final build, even though it is not statically referenced in templates.

Question 10: How does the Angular compiler optimize template expressions?

Answer: The Angular compiler optimizes template expressions by analyzing bindings and reducing unnecessary computations. For example, Angular avoids recalculating bindings that have not changed, making template rendering more efficient.

For example: In a template:

```
<div>{{ user.name.toUpperCase() }}</div>
```

The compiler optimizes it by ensuring that user.name is only recalculated when it changes, rather than re-running the `toUpperCase()` method on every change detection cycle.

Compiler build process and optimization

Question 11: What happens internally when we run ng build in an Angular project?

Answer: When you run ng build, Angular executes a series of steps:

1. **Compilation**: The Angular compiler (`ngc`) compiles the TypeScript files and templates into JavaScript.
2. **Bundling**: Webpack bundles the compiled JavaScript code, CSS, HTML, and assets into a smaller, optimized output.
3. **Minification**: The output files are minified, removing unnecessary whitespace and shortening variable names to reduce size.
4. **Tree-shaking**: Unused code (dead code) is eliminated, making the final bundle smaller.
5. **Output**: The final output is stored in the `dist/` folder.

For example: `ng build -prod` will build the production-ready version of the Angular app, enabling optimizations like minification, tree-shaking, and AOT compilation.

Question 12: What are Angular build artifacts, and where are they stored?

Answer: Build artifacts are the output files generated during the Angular build process, such as JavaScript bundles, CSS files, and assets. These artifacts are typically stored in the `dist/` directory.

For example: After running `ng` build, you can find the build artifacts in the `dist/` folder:

```
/dist/
  /your-app/
    /index.html
    /main.js
    /styles.css
    /assets/
```

Question 13: What are the differences between production and development builds in Angular?

Answer: In Angular, production and development builds serve different purposes, each optimized for specific scenarios. The key differences between them are:

- **Development build**: Includes debugging tools, sourcemaps, unminified code, and is not optimized for performance. It is meant for development environments.
- **Production build**: Optimized for performance, with code minified, AOT compiled, and dead code eliminated.

For example:

```
ng build --prod  # Production build
ng build          # Development build
```

The production build is smaller, faster, and ready for deployment.

Question 14: How does the Angular build process leverage esbuild for faster compilation? (Angular 16+)

Answer: esbuild is a modern bundler and minifier that Angular started using for faster build performance in Angular 16. It replaces Webpack for parts of the build process, improving build times, especially for large applications.

For example: In Angular 16+, when you run `ng build --prod`, esbuild takes over tasks like TypeScript compilation and minification, significantly speeding up the build.

Question 15: How can we analyze the Angular build size and optimize it?

Answer: Angular CLI provides tools to analyze the build size, like `source-map-explorer` or `webpack-bundle-analyzer`. You can visualize the size of different modules in your app and identify large dependencies.

For example: Run the following command to generate the `build` stats:

```
ng build --prod --stats-json
```

Then, use `webpack-bundle-analyzer` to visualize the bundle:

```
webpack-bundle-analyzer dist/your-app/stats.json
```

Question 16: What is dead code elimination, and how does Angular's build process utilize it?

Answer: Dead code elimination removes code that is not used in the application. Angular uses tree-shaking during the build process to eliminate unused code from the final bundle.

For example: If you have a function that is not called anywhere in the code, it will be eliminated during the build process:

```
// Unused function (dead code)
function unusedFunction() {
  console.log("This will be removed in production.");
}
```

The Angular build process removes such code in production builds to reduce bundle size.

Question 17: What is differential loading, and how does it improve performance?

Answer: Differential loading creates two sets of bundles: one for modern browsers (ES2015+) and one for older browsers (ES5). This improves performance by loading optimized JavaScript for modern browsers, while still supporting older ones.

For example: Differential loading automatically creates both ES2015 and ES5 bundles:

```
ng build --prod
```

This ensures users with modern browsers download smaller, faster ES2015 code, while legacy browsers fall back to ES5 code.

Question 18: How does the Angular linker work in the build process?

Answer: The Angular linker (available in Angular 13+) processes the generated JavaScript code to ensure that only the necessary parts of the Angular framework are included in the final build. It also optimizes the use of services, modules, and components.

For example: The linker ensures that only the parts of Angular that are used in the app are included in the final build, reducing the size of the application.

Question 19: What is the purpose of the angular.json file in the build process?

Answer: The `angular.json` file defines the configuration settings for an Angular project, such as build options, file paths, and environments. It specifies how the project should be built, including settings for AOT, optimization, and file replacements.

For example: In the `angular.json`, you can configure the build settings:

```
{
  "projects": {
    "your-app": {
      "architect": {
        "build": {
          "configurations": {
            "production": {
              "fileReplacements": [
                {
                  "replace": "src/environments/environment.ts",
                  "with": "src/environments/environment.prod.ts"
                }
              ]
            }
          }
        }
      }
    }
  }
}
```

Question 20: What role does Webpack play in the Angular build system?

Answer: Webpack is the default bundler used by Angular CLI. It processes and bundles the application's code, CSS, HTML, and assets into optimized files for deployment. Webpack handles tasks like bundling, minification, and file transformations.

For example: When running ng build, Webpack is used to bundle and optimize the app:

```
ng build --prod
```

Webpack will process and bundle the app for production, applying optimizations like minification and tree-shaking.

Advanced compilation and latest enhancements

Question 21: What is the role of partial compilation in Angular libraries?

Answer: Partial compilation refers to compiling only the code that has changed instead of recompiling the entire Angular application or library. This approach helps in optimizing the build process, making it faster and more efficient, especially for large libraries.

For example: When you make changes to a component in a library, Angular compiles only that specific component instead of the whole library, reducing the compilation time.

Question 22: How does Angular's new build optimizer reduce bundle size?

Answer: The Angular build optimizer removes unnecessary code from production builds, such as unused Angular decorators, and optimizes the internal code to reduce the final bundle size. It also helps with tree-shaking and other optimizations.

For example: When running `ng build --prod`, the build optimizer removes unused code from the final bundle, helping reduce its size.

Question 23: How do source maps help in debugging Angular applications?

Answer: Source maps map the minified and compiled JavaScript code back to the original TypeScript or source code. They allow developers to debug the application in the browser as if they were working with the original, untranspiled source code.

For example: In the browser's developer tools, you can see and debug TypeScript code even in production because of the source maps:

```
ng build --source-map
```

Question 24: How can lazy loading be optimized in the Angular build process?

Answer: Lazy loading optimizes the build process by splitting the application into smaller chunks that are loaded only when needed. This can be achieved using Angular's `loadChildren` feature in routing, which reduces the initial bundle size and improves the loading speed.

For example:

```
const routes: Routes = [
  { path: 'feature', loadChildren: () => import('./feature/feature.module').then(m =>
m.FeatureModule) }
];
```

This ensures that the `FeatureModule` is loaded only when the user navigates to the `/feature` route.

Question 25: What is inline critical CSS, and how does it affect build performance?

Answer: Inline critical CSS refers to embedding the essential styles directly into the HTML file, rather than loading them as separate CSS files. This reduces the number of requests made by the browser and speeds up the rendering of the page.

For example: Angular can automatically inline critical CSS in production builds by using the optimization flag in `angular.json`:

```
"build": {
  "configurations": {
    "production": {
      "optimization": {
        "styles": {
          "inlineCritical": true
        }
      }
    }
```

```
  }
}
```

Question 26: How does esbuild compare to Webpack in Angular's build process?

Answer: esbuild is faster than Webpack in Angular's build process. It replaces certain Webpack tasks (like TypeScript compilation) with a more efficient and faster bundling mechanism, resulting in reduced build times, especially in large projects.

For example: esbuild is used for bundling and minification in Angular 16+, improving build performance significantly compared to Webpack, which was the default bundler in earlier versions.

Question 27: What are incremental builds, and how do they speed up Angular development?

Answer: Incremental builds compile only the files that have changed since the last build, rather than recompiling the entire application. This speeds up the development cycle, allowing developers to see their changes faster.

For example: By using Angular's watch mode (**`ng serve`**), only the modified files are recompiled during development.

Question 28: What are the advantages of using standalone components in the build process? (Angular 17+)

Answer: Standalone components eliminate the need for a module, making them lighter and faster to build. They reduce the complexity of the application structure and improve the modularity and reusability of components. This can speed up the build process by reducing the number of files that need to be compiled and bundled.

For example:

```
@Component({
  selector: 'app-standalone',
  template: `<h1>Standalone Component</h1>`,
  standalone: true
})
export class StandaloneComponent {}
```

This component can be used without the need for an Angular module.

Question 29: How does the hydration feature improve SSR performance (Angular 17+)?

Answer: Hydration refers to the process of loading the server-rendered content and making it interactive by attaching Angular's client-side logic to the static HTML. It reduces the time to interactivity by reusing the server-rendered content instead of rebuilding it entirely.

For example: When Angular 17+ server-side renders a page, the client-side application can hydrate the pre-rendered HTML to make it fully interactive without reloading all content:

```
// Server-side rendering + hydration in Angular Universal
```

Question 30: How does the Angular compiler handle signals in templates (Angular 18+)?

Answer: In Angular 18+, the signals feature introduces reactive data binding, where changes to data can automatically trigger updates in the DOM. The Angular compiler works with signals to optimize change detection by directly binding components to reactive signals instead of relying on Angular's traditional zone-based change detection.

For example:

```
import { signal } from '@angular/core';
@Component({
  selector: 'app-signal-example',
  template: `<div>{{ count() }}</div>`,
```

```
})
export class SignalExampleComponent {
  count = signal(0);  // Signal to track a count value
}
```

The preceding example demonstrates how count is a reactive signal, automatically updating the DOM whenever its value changes.

Dependency management and build tools

Question 31: What is the difference between ng build --prod and ng serve?

Answer: In Angular, **`ng build --prod`** and **`ng serve`** are two commonly used commands, each serving a distinct purpose. The key differences between them are:

- **ng build --prod**: This command builds the Angular application for production, optimizing it by applying AOT compilation, tree-shaking, minification, and other optimizations to reduce the final bundle size and improve performance.
- **ng serve**: This command is used for local development, providing a development server. It compiles the application in JIT mode for faster builds, but does not perform production-level optimizations like AOT or minification.

For example:

```
# Production build
ng build --prod
# Local development server
ng serve
```

Question 32: How does Angular's CLI optimize third-party dependencies in production builds?

Answer: Angular's CLI optimizes third-party dependencies by using tree-shaking to remove unused code from libraries and bundling only the necessary parts. It also minifies JavaScript files and uses differential loading to serve modern JavaScript to compatible browsers, reducing the bundle size.

For example: In production builds, Angular automatically removes unused parts of third-party libraries:

```
ng build --prod
```

Question 33: What are package.json dependencies, and how do they affect the build process?

Answer: **`package.json`** dependencies are external libraries or packages that the application relies on. They can be categorized into dependencies (runtime dependencies) and **`devDependencies`** (development-time dependencies). These dependencies are installed via **`npm`** or **`yarn`**, and they directly impact the build process by contributing to the final bundle.

For example:

```
{
  "dependencies": {
    "rxjs": "^6.6.3",
    "angular": "^12.0.0"
  },
  "devDependencies": {
    "typescript": "^4.3.5",
    "tslint": "^6.1.0"
```

```
  }
}
```

These dependencies are bundled during the build process (**ng build**), contributing to the final output.

Question 34: How does the Angular compiler work with tree-shaking to remove unused code?

Answer: Tree-shaking is a technique that eliminates unused code from the final bundle by analyzing the source code and identifying parts that are not used. The Angular compiler uses this during the production build to remove unused components, services, or other code from the final application.

For example: In production builds:

```
ng build --prod
```

Unused imports or services are removed from the final bundle due to tree-shaking.

Question 35: What is the purpose of package-lock.json in an Angular project?

Answer: The **package-lock.json** file ensures that the exact same version of dependencies is installed across different machines. It locks the versions of all installed packages and their dependencies to avoid version mismatches or conflicts.

For example: When you run **npm install**, the **package-lock.json** ensures the same versions of dependencies are used, regardless of the environment.

Question 36: How do peer dependencies affect Angular library builds?

Answer: Peer dependencies are packages that a library expects to be provided by the consuming project rather than being bundled with the library itself. If mismatches occur between the expected peer dependency versions and the actual versions in the consuming project, it may lead to build or runtime errors.

For example: A library may require a specific version of Angular:

```
"peerDependencies": {
  "@angular/core": "^12.0.0"
}
```

Question 37: What are monorepos, and how does Angular CLI support them?

Answer: A monorepo is a repository that houses multiple projects, such as applications, libraries, and tools, within a single version-controlled codebase. Angular CLI supports monorepos using the Angular workspace, which allows managing multiple applications and libraries in one repository.

For example:

```
ng new my-workspace --createApplication=false
cd my-workspace
ng generate application my-app
ng generate library my-lib
```

Question 38: How does Angular handle version mismatches between dependencies?

Answer: Angular uses the **npm** package manager to resolve and install dependencies. If there are version mismatches, **npm** will attempt to resolve them by installing compatible versions. Angular CLI may show warnings or errors if dependencies are incompatible.

For example: If two packages require different versions of the same dependency:

```
npm install
# npm will try to resolve the versions for you, but errors may occur if incompatible.
```

Question 39: What is the role of the tsconfig.json file in the Angular build process?

Answer: The `tsconfig.json` file specifies the compiler options for TypeScript, such as the module system, target version of JavaScript, and path mappings. Angular uses this file to configure the TypeScript compiler when building the application.

For example:

```
{
  "compilerOptions": {
    "target": "es2015",
    "module": "es2020",
    "strict": true
  }
}
```

This configuration ensures that TypeScript is compiled correctly for Angular.

Question 40: How does Angular handle polyfills, and how do they impact the build?

Answer: Polyfills are scripts that provide support for newer JavaScript features in older browsers. Angular includes polyfills by default in the `polyfills.ts` file, ensuring the application works across a wide range of browsers. In production, unused polyfills are excluded, optimizing the build size.

For example: Polyfills are automatically added to the `index.html` in production:

```
import 'core-js/es6';
import 'zone.js';
```

This ensures compatibility across older browsers during runtime.

Conclusion

Angular compiler and build tools play a crucial role in optimizing application performance, reducing bundle size, and improving developer efficiency. The transition from view engine to Ivy has significantly enhanced the build process, enabling better tree-shaking, faster compilation, and improved runtime performance. Features like AOT compilation, differential loading, and caching strategies streamline both development and production builds, ensuring a robust and scalable Angular application. Understanding these tools helps developers make informed decisions about build configurations, optimizations, and deployment strategies.

Building efficient Angular applications is not just about writing code; it is also about using the right tools to debug, profile, and optimize performance. The next chapter explores essential utilities like Angular DevTools, Chrome Developer Tools, and third-party debugging extensions. We will also discuss performance monitoring, state inspection, and techniques for enhancing the development experience.

CHAPTER 18
Developer Tools

Introduction

Modern web development requires a robust set of tools to ensure efficiency, performance, and ease of debugging. Angular provides a variety of developer tools that help streamline the development process. These tools assist in debugging, profiling, performance optimization, and state management, making it easier to build, maintain, and scale applications efficiently.

Angular Developer Tools (**Angular DevTools**) enhance the developer experience by providing real-time insights into component structures, change detection, dependency injection, and performance monitoring. In this chapter, we will explore the essential tools available for Angular development and how they can be effectively utilized to optimize application workflows.

Structure

This chapter covers the following topics:

- Angular Command Line Interface
- Angular libraries
- Angular DevTools
- Angular language service

Objectives

By the end of this chapter, readers should be able to effectively utilize Angular DevTools for debugging and performance monitoring, inspect application behavior using Chrome Developer Tools and Augury, and identify and resolve common Angular runtime errors. They will gain the ability to analyze and optimize performance using change detection and lazy loading, implement debugging strategies for both synchronous and asynchronous code, and manage state efficiently using tools like NgRx. Additionally, they will learn to integrate Angular applications with Git and CI/CD pipelines, ensuring a streamlined and efficient development workflow.

Angular Command Line Interface

Question 1: What is Angular CLI, and why is it important for Angular development?

Answer: Angular **Command Line Interface** (**CLI**) is an open-source tool built and maintained by the Angular team at *Google*, integrated with Node.js and **Node Package Manager** (`npm`). It is installed globally on your system via `npm` with the command `npm install -g @angular/cli`, after which you can use the ng command to access its functionality. Once installed, it provides a suite of commands to handle common development tasks, such as creating a new project (`ng new`), generating components (`ng generate`), running the development server (`ng serve`), building the app for production (`ng build`), and running tests (`ng test`).

The CLI is tightly integrated with Angular's ecosystem and follows the framework's conventions and best practices. It leverages tools like TypeScript, Webpack (for bundling), Karma (for testing), and Protractor (for end-to-end testing) under the hood, but abstracts their complexity so developers do not need to configure them manually.

The key features of Angular CLI are as follows:

- **Project initialization**: With a single command (`ng new project-name`), Angular CLI sets up a new Angular project with a predefined folder structure, configuration files (e.g., `angular.json`, `tsconfig.json`), and necessary dependencies. It also includes a basic app module and component to get you started.
- **Code scaffolding**: The `ng generate` (or `ng g`) command allows you to quickly create components, services, modules, pipes, directives, and more. For example:
    - `ng generate` component my-component creates a new component with its HTML, CSS, TypeScript, and test files.
    - This ensures consistency and saves time compared to manually creating files and wiring them up.
- **Development server**: The `ng serve` command launches a local development server with live reloading, so you can see changes in real-time as you edit your code. It also supports options like `--open` to automatically open the app in a browser.
- **Build optimization**: The `ng build` command compiles the application into an optimized bundle for deployment. It supports production builds (`ng build --prod`) with tree-shaking, **ahead-of-time** (**AOT**) compilation, and minification to reduce bundle size and improve performance.
- **Testing support**: Angular CLI integrates testing tools like Jasmine and Karma for unit tests (`ng test`) and Protractor for **end-to-end** (**E2E**) tests (`ng e2e`). It generates test files automatically when creating components or services, encouraging a test-driven development approach.
- **Linting and formatting**: The CLI includes support for code linting (via TSLint or ESLint) and formatting tools to enforce coding standards and maintain code quality.
- **Dependency management**: It handles the installation and updating of project dependencies via npm, ensuring compatibility with Angular's version requirements.
- **Extensibility**: Angular CLI is customizable through schematics and blueprints for generating or modifying code. Developers can create custom schematics or use third-party ones to tailor the CLI to specific needs.

Angular CLI is a cornerstone of Angular development because it significantly enhances productivity, enforces consistency, and reduces the learning curve for new developers. Here is why it is so valuable:

- **Simplifies workflow**: Without the CLI, setting up an Angular project involves manually configuring tools like Webpack, TypeScript, and testing frameworks, a time-consuming and error-prone process. The CLI automates this, allowing developers to start coding immediately.
- **Enforces best practices**: Angular CLI adheres to Angular's official style guide and recommended project structure. This ensures that projects are organized in a way that is maintainable and scalable, even as teams grow or requirements evolve.
- **Reduces boilerplate code**: By generating files with pre-configured code (e.g., component classes, templates, and styles), the CLI eliminates repetitive manual work, letting developers focus on business logic.

- **Consistency across teams**: In collaborative environments, the CLI ensures that all developers use the same conventions and tools, reducing discrepancies and making onboarding easier.
- **Built-in optimization**: Features like AOT compilation, lazy loading, and differential loading (serving modern JavaScript to modern browsers and legacy code to older ones) improve performance and user experience. Tasks that would otherwise require manual configuration are handled seamlessly by the CLI.
- **Time savings**: Automating tasks like testing, building, and deployment cuts down development time, allowing faster iteration and delivery.
- **Community and support**: As an official tool, Angular CLI is well-documented and supported by the Angular team and community, with regular updates to align with new Angular releases.

For example:

```
# Install Angular CLI globally
npm install -g @angular/cli
```

Consider another example. Imagine you are starting a new Angular project:

- Run `ng new my-app --routing --style=scss` to create a project with routing and SCSS support.
- Use `ng generate component` header to add a header component.
- Run `ng serve` to see it live in your browser.
- When ready, `run ng build --prod` to create a production-ready build.

Without CLI, you would need to manually set up TypeScript, configure Webpack, write test setups, etc., a process that could take hours or days. With Angular CLI, it is done in minutes.

Thus, Angular CLI is indispensable for Angular development as it simplifies complex tasks, enforces standards, and accelerates the development process, making it an invaluable tool for both beginners and experienced developers.

Question 2: How do you create a new Angular project using Angular CLI?

Answer: You can create an Angular project using the `ng new` command.

For example:

```
ng new my-angular-app --standalone -strict
```

This does the following:

- **--standalone**: Creates a project using **standalone components** instead of NgModules (introduced in Angular 14).
- **-strict**: Enables strict mode for better type safety and performance.

Once created, navigate into the project and start the development server:

```
cd my-angular-app
ng serve
```

Question 3: What is the difference between ng serve and ng build?

Answer: The main difference between `ng serve` and `ng build` lies in their purpose and output:

- **ng serve**: Compiles the application in memory and serves it locally with **hot-reloading**, making it useful for development.
- **ng build**: Compiles the application and generates static files in the `dist/` directory, which are used for **production deployment**.

For example:

```
ng serve --port 4201 # Run on custom port
ng build --configuration=production # Build optimized production bundle
```

Question 4: What are Angular CLI workspaces, and how are they structured?

Answer: An Angular CLI workspace is a project folder that can contain one or more Angular applications and libraries. The structure is as follows:

```
my-workspace/
|— projects/        # Contains multiple applications/libraries
|— src/             # Main application source code
|— angular.json     # CLI configuration file
|— package.json     # Dependencies
|— tsconfig.json   # TypeScript configuration
|— node_modules/    # Installed dependencies
```

For example: Creating a workspace with multiple projects:

```
ng new my-workspace --create-application=false
cd my-workspace
ng generate application app-one
ng generate library shared-lib
```

Now, **projects/** contains both **app-one** and **shared-lib**.

Question 5: How does the Angular CLI handle environment configurations?

Answer: Angular CLI uses environment-specific TypeScript files (**environment.ts**) to manage settings like API URLs, feature flags, etc.

For example:

```
//src/environments/environment.ts
export const environment = {
  production: false,
  apiUrl: 'https://dev.api.com'
};
//src/environments/environment.prod.ts
export const environment = {
  production: true,
  apiUrl: 'https://prod.api.com'
};
```

The usage in code is as follows:

```
import { environment } from '../environments/environment';
console.log(environment.apiUrl);
```

Switch environments during build with the following command:

```
ng serve --configuration=production
ng build --configuration=staging
```

Question 6: How can you create a multi-project workspace using Angular CLI?

Answer: A multi-project workspace allows managing multiple applications or libraries in a single Angular workspace. The steps are as follows:

1. **Create an empty workspace (no initial app)**:

   ```
   ng new my-workspace --create-application=false
   cd my-workspace
   ```

2. **Generate multiple applications**:

```
ng generate application admin-app
ng generate application user-app
```

3. **Generate a shared library**:

```
ng generate library shared-utils
```

Now, `projects/` contains:

```
projects/
|— admin-app/
|— user-app/
|— shared-utils/   # Can be imported into both apps
```

This approach is useful for monorepos.

Question 7: What is the purpose of the angular.json configuration file?

Answer: The `angular.json` file is the main configuration file for Angular CLI. It manages build options, environments, assets, styles, scripts, and workspace settings. The key sections are:

```
{
  "projects": {
    "my-app": {
      "architect": {
        "build": {
          "options": {
            "outputPath": "dist/my-app",
            "styles": ["src/styles.css"],
            "scripts": ["src/assets/custom-script.js"]
          }
        }
      }
    }
  }
}
```

The usage is as follows:

- Change build output path (outputPath).
- Add global styles/scripts.
- Configure environments.

Question 8: How do you update an existing Angular project to the latest version using CLI?

Answer: To update your Angular project to the latest version, use:

```
ng update @angular/cli @angular/core
```

To check available updates:

```
ng update
```

For a major version upgrade (e.g., Angular 19 to 20):

```
ng update @angular/cli @angular/core --force
```

Use `--force` cautiously to override incompatible dependencies.

Question 9: What are the experimental CLI features introduced in Angular 20+?

Answer: Angular 20+ introduced several experimental CLI features:

- **esbuild default for faster builds**:
  - esbuild replaces Webpack for optimized builds.
  - Faster development builds (**`ng serve`**).

    ```
    ng serve -esbuild
    ```
- **Vite-powered dev server (experimental)**:
  - Vite improves **hot module reloading** (HMR).

    ```
    ng serve --vite
    ```
- **Standalone components by default**:
  - No need for NgModules (**`@NgModule`**), reducing boilerplate.

    ```
    ng new my-app --standalone
    ```
- **Enhanced tree-shaking and optimizations**:
  - Improved dead code elimination.
  - Reduced bundle size in production builds.
  - Dynamic imports for routing (lazy loading optimization)

    ```
    const routes: Routes = [
      { path: 'dashboard', loadComponent: () => import('./dashboard.component').
    then(m => m.DashboardComponent) }
    ];
    ```

Angular libraries

Question 10: What are Angular libraries, and how do they differ from Angular applications?

Answer: An Angular library is a reusable collection of Angular components, directives, services, and other utilities that can be shared across multiple projects. It does not run independently and must be imported into an Angular application.

An Angular application is a fully functional project that can run in a browser and contains essential files like **`main.ts`**.

The key differences are as follows:

- An Angular library cannot run independently, whereas an Angular application can.
- Libraries do not have **`main.ts`**, while applications do.
- Libraries are meant to be reused and often published to npm, whereas applications are typically deployed.

For example: A design system like **`@angular/material`** is an Angular library.

Question 11: How do you create and publish a reusable Angular library?

Answer: Steps to creating an Angular library are as follows:

1. **Generate a library**: **`ng generate library my-lib`**
2. **Build the library**: **`ng build my-lib`**
3. **Publish to npm**:

   ```
   cd dist/my-lib
   npm publish
   ```

Question 12: What is the purpose of the ng-packagr tool in Angular libraries?

Answer: `ng-packagr` is a tool that compiles Angular libraries into the **Angular Package Format** (**APF**), ensuring compatibility with Angular applications and tree-shaking.

For example: It is used internally when running:

```
ng build my-lib
```

Question 13: How do you integrate a third-party library into an Angular project?

Answer: To integrate a third-party library into an Angular project, follow these steps:

1. Install the library: `npm install lodash`
2. Import into the Angular component:
    a. `import _ from 'lodash';`
    b. `console.log(_.chunk([1, 2, 3, 4], 2)); // [[1,2], [3,4]]`

Question 14: How can you optimize Angular libraries for tree shaking?

Answer: Angular libraries can be optimized for tree shaking as follows:

- Use **ES modules (esm2022)** instead of CommonJS.
- Mark unused exports with `sideEffects: false` in `package.json`.
- Use `providedIn: 'root'` for services to prevent redundant injections.

For example:

```
@Injectable({ providedIn: 'root' })
export class MyService {}
```

Question 15: What is the role of peerDependencies in an Angular library?

Answer: `peerDependencies` specify the required dependencies that must be installed by the consumer of the library.

For example: In package.json:

```
"peerDependencies": {
  "@angular/core": "^16.0.0",
  "@angular/common": "^16.0.0"
}
```

This ensures that the consuming project provides compatible versions.

Question 16: How can Angular libraries be used in monorepo architectures?

Answer: In a monorepo architecture, Angular libraries can be efficiently managed and shared across multiple applications using the following approaches:

- Use **Nx** or **Angular CLI workspaces** to manage multiple libraries and applications.
- Define libraries inside libs/ and reference them within the workspace.

For example: Generate a library in a monorepo:

```
ng generate library shared-ui
```

Question 17: How do you test and maintain compatibility of an Angular library with multiple Angular versions?

Answer: To ensure an Angular library remains compatible with multiple Angular versions, follow these best practices:

- Use `ng update` to test with the latest Angular versions.
- Set up multiple CI/CD pipelines for different Angular versions.
- Use Angular CLI's `--create-ivy-entry-points=false` to support older versions.

For example: CI matrix for multiple Angular versions:

```
strategy:
  matrix:
    angular_version: [16, 17, 18]
```

Question 18: How do you use standalone components in Angular libraries?

Answer: Standalone components allow library consumers to use components without requiring an NgModule.

For example:

```
@Component({
  selector: 'my-button',
  standalone: true,
  template: `<button>Click me</button>`,
})
export class MyButtonComponent {}
```

Usage in a consuming application is as follows:

```
import { MyButtonComponent } from 'my-lib/my-button';
```

Question 19: What are the best practices for structuring and maintaining large Angular libraries?

Answer: Managing a large Angular library requires a well-organized structure, modular design, and proper maintenance strategies to ensure scalability and ease of use. Here are some best practices:

- **Modular structure with feature-based organization**:
  - Divide the library into feature-specific modules or standalone components.
  - Group related components, directives, and services into separate folders.
- **Use standalone components for simplicity**:
  - Avoid unnecessary NgModule usage by leveraging standalone components.
  - Simplifies dependency management and improves tree shaking.
- **Follow Angular Package Format (APF)**:
  - Use **`ng-packagr`** to build libraries correctly.
  - Ensure output formats (esm2022, fesm2022) are compatible with Angular applications.
- **Maintain proper public API (index.ts)**:
  - Avoid exposing internal implementation details.
  - Export only what is necessary in **`index.ts`** to prevent breaking changes.
- **Implement versioning and compatibility testing**:
  - Use semantic versioning (**`major.minor.patch`**) to track updates.
  - Test the library against multiple Angular versions using a CI/CD pipeline.
- **Optimize for tree shaking**:
  - Use **`providedIn: 'root'`** for services to prevent unnecessary bundle size increases.
  - Mark unused files as **`"sideEffects": false`** in **`package.json`**.
- **Provide documentation and demo application**:
  - Maintain a **`README.md`** with clear installation and usage examples.
  - Create a demo Angular app showcasing components and services.

Angular DevTools

Question 20: What is Angular DevTools, and how does it help developers?

Answer: Angular DevTools is a Chrome/Edge extension for debugging Angular apps. It provides component tree inspection, change detection profiling, and performance analysis.

For example:

```
# Install Angular DevTools in Chrome/Edge
```

Go to the Chrome Web Store and install Angular DevTools.

Question 21: How does Angular DevTools help in profiling application performance?

Answer: It tracks change detection cycles, helping identify unnecessary re-renders.

For example:

- Open **DevTools** | **Profiler Tab**.
- Click **Record** | **Interact with the app**.
- Check for excessive re-renders.

Question 22: What is the purpose of the component explorer in Angular DevTools?

Answer: It allows inspecting and modifying component states.

For example:

- Open **Angular Tab** in DevTools.
- Click a component | modify `@Input()` values.

Question 23: How does Angular DevTools visualize component change detection cycles?

Answer: It highlights change detection triggers for optimization.

For example:

- Open **Profiler**.
- Click **Record** | **check for unnecessary re-executions**.

Question 24: What are the key debugging features provided by Angular DevTools?

Answer: The key debugging features are:

- Component tree inspection
- Change detection profiling
- State modification

For example:

```
@Component({
  selector: 'app-test',
  template: `<p>{{ count }}</p>`
})
export class TestComponent {
  count = 0;
}
```

Modify count in DevTools and see real-time updates.

Question 25: How can Angular DevTools be used to optimize signals-based applications in Angular 20?

Answer: It helps analyze signal dependencies and optimize computations.

For example:

```
import { signal } from '@angular/core';
const count = signal(0);
```

Check signal debugging in DevTools profiler.

Question 26: How does Angular DevTools compare with Chrome Developer Tools for debugging Angular applications?

Answer: Angular DevTools is framework-specific, providing detailed insights into Angular internals.

For example:

- **Chrome DevTools**: Generic debugging
- **Angular DevTools**: Change detection and signals profiling

Question 27: Can Angular DevTools help in detecting memory leaks? If so, how?

Answer: Yes, it identifies unreleased subscriptions and detached components.

For example:

1. Open **Profiler**.
2. Look for long-running components that should be destroyed.

Question 28: How do you install Angular DevTools, and what browsers support it?

Answer: Angular DevTools is a browser extension that helps in debugging and profiling Angular applications.

For example:

- Supported on Chrome and Edge.
- Install via Chrome Web Store or Edge add-ons store.

Then, open DevTools and click on the Angular tab.

Question 29: What new DevTools improvements were introduced in Angular 19+?

Answer: Angular 19+ brought several enhancements to DevTools, making debugging and performance analysis more efficient:

- Signal debugging support
- Enhanced Profiler tools
- Better visualization for change detection

For example:

```
# Angular 20+
ng update @angular/core @angular/cli
```

Then, use **Profiler** for advanced debugging.

Conclusion

In this chapter, we explored essential developer tools that enhance productivity and efficiency when working with Angular. From debugging applications using Angular DevTools to leveraging the Angular Language Service for improved code intelligence, these tools play a crucial role in streamlining development and maintenance. Understanding how to integrate and utilize these tools effectively can significantly improve the overall development experience.

In the next chapter, we will explore strategies for writing clean, maintainable, and scalable Angular applications. This includes architectural patterns, performance optimizations, and coding standards that help build robust enterprise-level applications.

Chapter 19
Angular Best Practices

Introduction

Angular enables scalable web applications. Following best practices ensures maintainability, performance, and security. A well-structured Angular application enhances development efficiency, simplifies debugging, and promotes reusability. Adopting modular architecture, optimizing change detection, and leveraging AI-powered features can significantly improve application performance. This chapter covers project structure, coding standards, performance tuning, security, and AI-driven enhancements to help developers build robust and maintainable Angular applications.

Structure

This chapter covers the following topics:

- AI-powered Angular features
- Change detection and performance optimization

Objectives

This chapter aims to provide best practices for structuring Angular projects, leveraging AI-powered enhancements, and optimizing change detection and performance. It covers security best practices to prevent vulnerabilities, guidelines for writing clean and reusable code, and strategies for improving maintainability through effective state management. By following these principles, developers can build efficient, scalable, and maintainable Angular applications.

AI-powered Angular features

Question 1: What are some AI-powered optimizations introduced in Angular 19 and 20, and how do they improve development?

Answer: At the time of writing, Angular 19 and 20 have introduced several optimizations aimed at improving developer productivity and application performance, which are as follows:

- **AI-powered optimizations in Angular 19 and 20**: While Angular 19 and 20 have brought significant improvements, there is no official documentation indicating the introduction of AI-powered features in these versions. The enhancements primarily focus on performance and developer experience.
- **Template optimization, build-time performance enhancements, and change detection improvements**:
  - **Template optimization**: Angular 19 introduced built-in deferred loading, allowing developers to load components only when needed. This approach reduces initial load times and enhances application performance. For example, using the ng-defer directive can defer the loading of non-critical components.
  - **Build-time performance enhancements**: Integration with esbuild in Angular 19 has led to faster build and rebuild times. esbuild is a modern bundler that compiles code swiftly, improving the development experience, especially in large projects. Developers can benefit from reduced build times by configuring Angular to use esbuild in their build process.

    For example, a large e-commerce platform experienced slow page loads due to heavy product listings. After upgrading to Angular 19, the enhanced build process reduced the bundle size and improved page load speed by 30%, enhancing the user experience.
- **Change detection improvements**: Angular's change detection mechanism has been fine-tuned in recent versions. By adopting the OnPush change detection strategy, developers can optimize performance by limiting checks to components with changed inputs. This strategy reduces unnecessary change detection cycles, leading to more efficient rendering. Implementing `ChangeDetectionStrategy.OnPush` in a component ensures that Angular only checks for changes when explicitly triggered.

  For example, in a real-time chat application, the improved change detection in Angular 19 ensures that only components with actual data changes are re-rendered, reducing CPU usage and enhancing performance during high message volumes.

These enhancements collectively contribute to building more efficient and high-performing Angular applications.

Question 2: Discuss AI-assisted template optimization, build-time performance enhancements, and smart change detection improvements.

Answer: Angular's latest version introduces several AI-powered optimizations designed to enhance development efficiency and application performance:

- **AI-assisted template optimization**: Angular 19 introduces AI-assisted template optimization, which analyzes component templates to identify and eliminate unnecessary bindings and DOM elements. This results in cleaner templates and improved rendering performance.

  Consider a component template with redundant bindings:

  ```
  <div>
    <span>{{ user.name }}</span>
    <span>{{ user.name }}</span> <!-- Redundant binding -->
  </div>
  ```

  `The AI-assisted optimizer detects the redundancy and refactors the template to:`

  ```
  <div>
    <span>{{ user.name }}</span>
  </div>
  ```

  This reduces unnecessary DOM elements, enhancing rendering efficiency.

  For more details, refer to *Answer 1*.

Change detection and performance optimization

Question 3: What are the best practices for optimizing change d33etection in large-scale Angular applications?

Answer: To optimize change detection in large-scale Angular applications:

- **Use OnPush change detection strategy**: Angular's default change detection checks every component in the tree, but with OnPush, only components with changed inputs or events trigger checks. This reduces unnecessary checks and boosts performance.

  For example:

  ```
  @Component({
    selector: 'app-item',
    changeDetection: ChangeDetectionStrategy.OnPush,
    template: `<div>{{ item.name }}</div>`
  })
  export class ItemComponent {
    @Input() item: { name: string };
  }
  ```

- **Avoid NgZone and setTimeout in critical paths**: Minimize operations that trigger Angular's change detection cycle, such as unnecessary zone operations or **`setTimeout`**.

Question 4: What are the best practices for optimizing change detection in signal-based Angular applications?

Answer: Angular signals are a new way to manage reactive state, introduced to simplify and optimize Angular's change detection mechanism. Unlike RxJS, which is asynchronous and stream-based, signals are synchronous and fine-grained. They automatically track dependencies and update only when the data they rely on changes, resulting in more predictable and performant UI updates.

Optimizing change detection in signal-based Angular applications ensures efficient performance and minimal unnecessary re-renders. Here are some best practices to follow:

- **Use signals efficiently**: Signals (introduced in Angular 18) are more granular and fine-tuned, allowing for minimal updates. Use signals for reactive data instead of traditional state management systems like services.

  For example:

  ```
  import { Signal } from '@angular/core';
  export class AppComponent {
    count: Signal<number> = new Signal(0);
    increment() {
      this.count.set(this.count() + 1);
    }
  }
  ```

- **Isolate signal updates**: Isolate signals to the smallest possible component scope to reduce unnecessary triggers.
- **Reduce component re-renders**: Break down large components into smaller ones with localized signals to limit the scope of updates.
- **Use signalEffect() wisely**: Effects should be used sparingly and only when necessary, such as for side effects like API calls or DOM interactions.
- **Minimize unnecessary reads**: Avoid reading signals inside frequently running functions (like event

handlers or lifecycle hooks) unless necessary, as this can trigger unintended updates.

- **Use untracked() when necessary**: Prevent unnecessary reactivity by wrapping certain reads inside **`untracked()`**, ensuring that those values do not trigger change detection.

Examples of Angular signals using **`signal()`**, **`computed()`**, and **`effect()`** are given as follows:

- **signal()**: Creates a reactive state:

```
import { signal } from '@angular/core';
const count = signal(0);
console.log(count()); // 0
count.set(5);
console.log(count()); // 5
```

- **computed()**: Creates derived values based on other signals:

```
import { computed } from '@angular/core';
const count = signal(2);
const double = computed(() => count() * 2);
console.log(double()); // 4
count.set(3);
console.log(double()); // 6
```

- **effect()**: Triggers side-effects when dependent signals change:

```
import { effect } from '@angular/core';
const count = signal(1);
effect(() => {
  console.log('Count changed to:', count());
});
count.set(2); // Logs: Count changed to: 2
```

Angular signals offer a simpler, faster, and more predictable way to handle reactive state compared to traditional RxJS.

Thus, it can be said that:

- **`signal()`** is a reactive value holder.
- **`computed()`** is a reactive derived value.
- **`effect()`** is a side-effect on change.

Question 5: What are the best ways to avoid unnecessary DOM updates in Angular templates?

Answer: The best ways to avoid unnecessary DOM updates in Angular templates are:

- **Use trackBy with ngFor**: When rendering lists, avoid re-rendering the entire list by using the **`trackBy`** function to track individual items based on a unique identifier.

  For example:

```
<div *ngFor="let item of items; trackBy: trackById">
  {{ item.name }}
</div>
trackById(index: number, item: any) {
  return item.id;
}
```

- **Use ngIf instead of *ngFor with empty lists**: Avoid rendering unnecessary DOM elements when the list is empty.

Question 6: How does Angular 17+ hydration improve performance, and what are the best practices for optimizing it?

Answer: Angular 17+ introduces hydration to optimize **server-side rendering (SSR)** by rehydrating a static page on the client, allowing faster rendering.

Hydration is the process of taking a server-rendered HTML page and attaching client-side JavaScript behavior to make it interactive in the browser.

Best practices include:

- **Use ngAdd for hydration support**: Ensure your Angular project has hydration support enabled during SSR setup.
- **Optimize server rendering**: Hydration speeds up when SSR is optimized and matches the client-side rendered state accurately.

Question 7: How does Angular optimize bundle size, and what are the best practices for reducing it?

Answer: Angular optimizes bundle size through various techniques to enhance performance and reduce load times. Developers can further minimize the bundle size by following these best practices:

- **Tree shaking**: Angular uses tree-shaking to eliminate unused code. Use lazy loading and modularize the application to reduce the size.
- **Use lazy loading for modules**: Break the application into smaller bundles to load them on demand.

For example:

```
const routes: Routes = [
  {
    path: 'feature',
    loadChildren: () => import('./feature/feature.module').then(m => m.FeatureModule)
  }
];
```

Question 8: What are the best practices for optimizing Angular signals to avoid unnecessary re-renders?

Answer: Optimizing Angular signals helps prevent unnecessary re-renders and improves application performance. Here are some best practices to achieve this:

- **Fine-grained signals**: Ensure that only the required components are subscribed to specific signals to avoid redundant re-renders.
- **Use computed properties for derived state** to prevent unnecessary signal updates in multiple places.

Question 9: How can lazy loading improve performance in Angular applications, and what are the best practices for its implementation?

Answer: Lazy loading is an essential optimization technique in Angular that improves performance by loading feature modules only when needed. This reduces the initial bundle size and speeds up application startup. Here are some key benefits and best practices for implementing lazy loading:

- **Reduces initial load time**: By lazy loading feature modules, the application only loads the necessary code, improving initial load times.

  For example:

  ```
  const routes: Routes = [
    { path: 'lazy', loadChildren: () => import('./lazy/lazy.module').then(m =>
  m.LazyModule) }
  ];
  ```

- **Use preloading strategy**: Consider using preloading strategies to load critical modules after the initial load.
- **Use Angular's built-in lazy loading**: Implement lazy loading using the **`loadChildren`** property in the route configuration to ensure efficient module loading.
- **Modularize the application**: Structure the application into feature modules to take full advantage of lazy loading and prevent loading unnecessary code upfront.
- **Optimize dependencies**: Ensure lazy loaded modules only import the dependencies they need to reduce bundle size further.
- **Use standalone components where applicable**: Standalone components (introduced in Angular 14) can help reduce unnecessary module dependencies and streamline lazy loading.

  For example*:*

  ```
  RouterModule.forRoot(routes, { preloadingStrategy: PreloadAllModules })
  ```

Question 10: What are the best practices for managing application state in Angular, and how do signals (Angular 18+) improve state management?

Answer: Effective state management in Angular ensures better maintainability, scalability, and performance. With the introduction of signals in Angular 18+, managing state has become more efficient by reducing unnecessary updates. Here are some best practices for managing application state:

- **Use signals for reactive data**: signals allow for more efficient and declarative state management, ensuring the components update only when necessary.
- **Store state in services**: Use services to manage global application state and inject them where needed.

Question 11: How do standalone components improve Angular application structure, and when should they be used over traditional modules?

Answer: Standalone components, introduced in Angular 14, simplify application structure by removing the dependency on NgModules. They provide a more modular and flexible approach to building Angular applications. Here is how they improve application structure and when to use them:

- **Simplified structure**: Standalone components reduce the need for modules, improving the readability and simplicity of the application.
- **When to use**: Use standalone components when your feature does not require a complex module structure, such as for isolated UI elements or simple views.

Question 12: What are the best practices for handling large and dynamic forms in Angular applications?

Answer: Handling large and dynamic forms efficiently in Angular ensures better performance, maintainability, and user experience. Here are some best practices to follow:

- **Use reactive forms**: For large forms, reactive forms offer better performance and flexibility. Use **`FormArray`** for handling dynamic fields.

  For example*:*

  ```
  this.form = this.fb.group({
    name: [''],
    phones: this.fb.array([this.createPhone()])
  });
  createPhone() {
    return this.fb.group({
      phone: ['']
    });
  }
  ```

- **Lazy load form controls**: Add and remove form controls dynamically only when needed to optimize memory usage.
- **Optimize change detection**: Use OnPush change detection strategy and avoid unnecessary re-renders by limiting reactive updates.
- **Utilize form validation efficiently**: Implement both synchronous and asynchronous validators while keeping validation logic inside services for better reusability.
- **Divide large forms into smaller sections**: Use stepper components or multi-step forms to enhance usability and performance.

Difference between dynamic forms and reactive forms: All dynamic forms are reactive forms, but not all reactive forms are dynamic.

Reactive forms:

- Defined using `FormControl`, `FormGroup`, and `FormArray` in the component class.
- Structure is statically coded (though can be conditionally built).
- Provides strong type safety and predictability.
- Best for forms with a known structure at design time.

Dynamic forms:

- A type of reactive form built dynamically based on metadata or configuration.
- Form structure is generated at runtime (e.g., from JSON or a database).
- Useful when form fields are not known ahead-of-time .
- Enables generic form rendering from a schema.

Question 13: What are the best practices for securing routes and optimizing lazy loaded modules in Angular applications?

Answer: Securing routes and optimizing lazy loaded modules in Angular applications is essential for both performance and security. Implement these best practices to ensure a secure and efficient application:

- **Guard routes with CanActivate**: Protect sensitive routes using `CanActivate` guards to prevent unauthorized access.
- **Lazy load secure modules**: Ensure that sensitive modules are lazy loaded, reducing their footprint on initial loads.
- **Use CanLoad for lazy loaded modules**: Prevent unauthorized users from even loading certain modules by implementing `CanLoad` guards.
- **Restrict access with role-based authentication**: Implement **role-based access control** (RBAC) to allow only authorized users to access specific routes.
- **Optimize lazy loaded modules**: Keep lazy loaded modules lightweight and ensure they import only necessary dependencies to enhance performance.
- **Preload strategic modules**: Use Angular's `PreloadAllModules` strategy selectively to balance performance and security.

Question 14: How do you handle and log errors in an Angular application effectively?

Answer: Effective error handling and logging in Angular applications improve debugging, maintainability, and user experience. Here are some best practices to follow:

- **Use global error handler**: Implement a global error handler to catch unhandled exceptions and log them.

  For example:

  ```
  @Injectable()
  ```

```
export class GlobalErrorHandler implements ErrorHandler {
  handleError(error: any) {
    console.error('An error occurred:', error);
  }
}
```

- **Log errors to a backend**: For better monitoring, send error logs to a backend service.

Question 15: What are the best practices for handling HTTP requests efficiently in Angular applications?

Answer: Effective error handling and logging in Angular applications improve debugging, maintainability, and user experience. Here are some best practices to follow:

- **Use HttpClient interceptors**: Implement interceptors for adding authentication headers, logging requests, or handling errors.
- **Cache responses**: Use caching strategies to reduce unnecessary HTTP requests.
- **Handle HTTP errors with interceptors**: Implement an `HttpInterceptor` to catch and manage API errors globally.
- **Provide user-friendly error messages**: Display meaningful error messages instead of exposing raw system errors.
- **Use try-catch blocks wisely**: Wrap critical logic in try-catch blocks to gracefully handle exceptions.
- **Leverage Angular's error boundary (ngOnError in signals)**: Use Angular's built-in error handling mechanisms for better fault isolation.

Conclusion

In this chapter, we explored essential best practices for building scalable, maintainable, and high-performance Angular applications. By following modular architecture, optimizing rendering strategies, leveraging RxJS effectively, and implementing efficient build and deployment processes, developers can enhance both application performance and user experience. Additionally, adopting structured state management, caching techniques, and zero-downtime deployment ensures robust and seamless Angular applications for enterprise-grade solutions.

With these best practices in place, the next chapter will focus on ensuring application reliability through unit testing, integration testing, and end-to-end testing strategies. We will explore testing frameworks, best practices, and tools to build highly testable Angular applications.

Join our Discord space

Join our Discord workspace for latest updates, offers, tech happenings around the world, new releases, and sessions with the authors:

https://discord.bpbonline.com

CHAPTER 20
Angular Testing

Introduction

Testing is a crucial aspect of Angular application development, ensuring the reliability, maintainability, and performance of the application. This chapter introduces various testing strategies, tools, and best practices used in Angular projects. It covers unit testing, integration testing, and **end-to-end** (**E2E**) testing with frameworks like Jasmine, Karma, and Cypress.

Structure

This chapter covers the following topics:

- Unit testing and component testing
- Integration testing
- End-to-end testing
- Performance, debugging, security-related tests

Objectives

By the end of this chapter, you will understand the significance of testing in Angular applications and how to set up and configure a testing environment. You will learn to write effective unit tests for components, services, and directives using Jasmine and Karma, perform integration testing to validate component interactions, and implement end-to-end testing with Cypress. Additionally, you will explore best practices for writing maintainable and efficient tests, ensuring high code quality and reliability in Angular applications.

Unit testing and component testing

Question 1: How do you write unit tests for Angular components, using Jasmine and Karma?

Answer: To write unit tests for Angular components, you need to use Jasmine for writing the test cases and Karma for running them. Here is an example:

Component:

```
@Component({
  selector: 'app-hello',
  template: `<h1>{{message}}</h1>`
})
export class HelloComponent {
  message = 'Hello, World!';
}
```

Test:

```
import { ComponentFixture, TestBed } from '@angular/core/testing';
import { HelloComponent } from './hello.component';
describe('HelloComponent', () => {
  let component: HelloComponent;
  let fixture: ComponentFixture<HelloComponent>;
  beforeEach(async () => {
    await TestBed.configureTestingModule({
      declarations: [HelloComponent]
    }).compileComponents();
  });
  beforeEach(() => {
    fixture = TestBed.createComponent(HelloComponent);
    component = fixture.componentInstance;
    fixture.detectChanges();
  });
  it('should display the message', () => {
    const compiled = fixture.nativeElement;
    expect(compiled.querySelector('h1').textContent).toContain('Hello, World!');
  });
});
```

Question 2: What is TestBed in Angular, and how does it help in unit testing?

Answer: `TestBed` is a testing utility provided by Angular, which helps configure and initialize the environment for unit tests. It allows you to set up an Angular module in isolation, which is useful for testing components, services, and other Angular elements.

For example:

```
TestBed.configureTestingModule({
  declarations: [MyComponent],
  providers: [MyService]
});
```

It creates a mock environment that enables you to test Angular components or services independently from other parts of the application.

Question 3: How do you test Angular services that depend on HTTPClient?

Answer: To test services that depend on `HttpClient`, you can use the `HttpClientTestingModule` and `HttpTestingController`. This helps mock HTTP requests and test how your service behaves.

For example:

```
import { HttpClientTestingModule, HttpTestingController } from '@angular/common/http/
testing';
import { MyService } from './my-service';
import { TestBed } from '@angular/core/testing';
describe('MyService', () => {
  let service: MyService;
  let httpMock: HttpTestingController;
  beforeEach(() => {
    TestBed.configureTestingModule({
      imports: [HttpClientTestingModule],
      providers: [MyService]
    });
    service = TestBed.inject(MyService);
    httpMock = TestBed.inject(HttpTestingController);
  });
  it('should fetch data', () => {
    const mockData = { name: 'Angular' };
    service.getData().subscribe(data => {
      expect(data.name).toBe('Angular');
    });
    const req = httpMock.expectOne('http://example.com/data');
    expect(req.request.method).toBe('GET');
    req.flush(mockData);
    httpMock.verify();
  });
});
```

Question 4: How do you test Angular pipes and directives effectively?

Answer: Testing pipes and directives in Angular ensures that they function correctly and behave as expected within templates. Pipes transform data in templates, while directives modify the behavior or appearance of elements. Both require different testing approaches:

- **Pipes**: You can test pipes by passing input values to them and checking the output.

  Pipe test:

  ```
  import { MyPipe } from './my-pipe.pipe';
  describe('MyPipe', () => {
    const pipe = new MyPipe();
    it('transforms "hello" to "HELLO"', () => {
      expect(pipe.transform('hello')).toBe('HELLO');
    });
  });
  ```

- **Directives**: Directives are usually tested by checking the element's behavior or properties after applying the directive.

Directive test:

```
import { MyDirective } from './my-directive.directive';
import { ComponentFixture, TestBed } from '@angular/core/testing';
import { ElementRef } from '@angular/core';
describe('MyDirective', () => {
  let fixture: ComponentFixture<any>;
  let el: ElementRef;
  beforeEach(() => {
    TestBed.configureTestingModule({
      declarations: [MyDirective]
    });
    fixture = TestBed.createComponent(MyComponent);
    el = fixture.debugElement.query(By.directive(MyDirective)).nativeElement;
  });
  it('should change background color', () => {
    const directive = new MyDirective(el);
    directive.ngOnInit();
    expect(el.style.backgroundColor).toBe('red');
  });
});
```

Question 5: How do you test asynchronous operations in Angular components and services?

Answer: You can use Jasmine's async and **fakeAsync** utilities to handle asynchronous operations in unit tests. **Tick()** and **flush()** can also be used to simulate time passage in **fakeAsync**.

For example:

```
it('should load data asynchronously', async () => {
  let data;
  service.getData().subscribe(res => {
    data = res;
  });
  fixture.detectChanges();
  await fixture.whenStable();
  expect(data).toBeDefined();
});
```

Question 6: What is the difference between fakeAsync and async in Angular unit tests?

Answer: When testing asynchronous code in Angular, it is important to ensure that tests execute reliably without unexpected delays or race conditions. Angular provides two key utilities for handling asynchronous behavior in unit tests: async and **fakeAsync**, which function as follows:

- **async:** It is used for handling asynchronous code that returns a promise. It allows the test to wait until the promise resolves before proceeding.
- **fakeAsync:** It is used to simulate the passage of time and control asynchronous behavior using **tick()** for time-based operations like **setTimeout()** or **setInterval()**.

  An example with **fakeAsync** is given as follows:

  ```
  it('should simulate a delay', fakeAsync(() => {
  ```

```
    let result = false;
    setTimeout(() => {
      result = true;
    }, 1000);
    tick(1000);
    expect(result).toBeTrue();
  }));
```

Question 7: How do you mock dependencies in Angular unit tests using Jasmine spies?

Answer: Jasmine spies are used to mock functions or methods in your service or component. You can spy on services to prevent actual execution during tests.

For example:

```
import { MyService } from './my-service';
import { TestBed } from '@angular/core/testing';
describe('MyComponent', () => {
  let serviceSpy: jasmine.SpyObj<MyService>;
  beforeEach(() => {
    serviceSpy = jasmine.createSpyObj('MyService', ['getData']);
    TestBed.configureTestingModule({
      providers: [{ provide: MyService, useValue: serviceSpy }]
    });
  });
  it('should call getData', () => {
    serviceSpy.getData.and.returnValue(of('data'));
    // Test component behavior here
    expect(serviceSpy.getData).toHaveBeenCalled();
  });
});
```

Question 8: How do you test change detection in Angular components?

Answer: You can test change detection by triggering **`fixture.detectChanges()`** and checking whether the component's properties are updated correctly.

For example:

```
it('should update the message', () => {
  component.message = 'New message';
  fixture.detectChanges();
  const compiled = fixture.nativeElement;
  expect(compiled.querySelector('h1').textContent).toContain('New message');
});
```

Question 9: How do you write tests for standalone components in Angular 15+?

Answer: Standalone components can be tested like regular components. However, you need to import the necessary dependencies directly in the **`TestBed`** setup.

For example:

```
import { StandaloneComponent } from './standalone.component';
import { TestBed } from '@angular/core/testing';
```

```
describe('StandaloneComponent', () => {
  beforeEach(() => {
    TestBed.configureTestingModule({
      imports: [StandaloneComponent]
    }).compileComponents();
  });
  it('should create the component', () => {
    const fixture = TestBed.createComponent(StandaloneComponent);
    const component = fixture.componentInstance;
    expect(component).toBeTruthy();
  });
});
```

Question 10: How do you handle global services like router or ActivatedRoute in unit tests?

Answer: Global services like router or **ActivatedRoute** can be mocked using Jasmine spies or **RouterTestingModule** for testing components that rely on routing.

Consider the following example with **RouterTestingModule**:

```
import { RouterTestingModule } from '@angular/router/testing';
import { ComponentFixture, TestBed } from '@angular/core/testing';
import { MyComponent } from './my-component';
describe('MyComponent', () => {
  let fixture: ComponentFixture<MyComponent>;
  beforeEach(() => {
    TestBed.configureTestingModule({
      imports: [RouterTestingModule],
      declarations: [MyComponent]
    });
    fixture = TestBed.createComponent(MyComponent);
  });
  it('should create', () => {
    expect(fixture.componentInstance).toBeTruthy();
  });
});
```

Integration testing

Question 11: How do you test Angular modules that use feature modules and lazy loading?

Answer: To test Angular modules that use feature modules and lazy loading, you must mock the lazy loaded module and ensure it is correctly imported and initialized. You can do this by using **RouterTestingModule** to test routes with lazy loaded feature modules.

For example:

```
import { TestBed } from '@angular/core/testing';
import { RouterTestingModule } from '@angular/router/testing';
import { AppComponent } from './app.component';
import { MyFeatureModule } from './feature/feature.module';
```

```
describe('AppComponent with Lazy Loaded Module', () => {
  beforeEach(() => {
    TestBed.configureTestingModule({
      imports: [
        RouterTestingModule.withRoutes([
          { path: 'feature', loadChildren: () => import('./feature/feature.module').then(m
=> m.MyFeatureModule) }
        ]),
        MyFeatureModule
      ],
      declarations: [AppComponent]
    });
  });
  it('should create the app', () => {
    const fixture = TestBed.createComponent(AppComponent);
    const app = fixture.componentInstance;
    expect(app).toBeTruthy();
  });
});
```

In this example, **`RouterTestingModule.withRoutes`** is used to simulate the routing behavior of lazy loaded modules in the test environment.

Question 12: How do you write tests for Angular components that interact with child components?

Answer: When testing components that interact with child components, you must create instances of both parent and child components, and simulate interactions like input/output bindings and events.

For example:

```
import { ComponentFixture, TestBed } from '@angular/core/testing';
import { ParentComponent } from './parent.component';
import { ChildComponent } from './child.component';
describe('ParentComponent', () => {
  let fixture: ComponentFixture<ParentComponent>;
  let component: ParentComponent;
  beforeEach(() => {
    TestBed.configureTestingModule({
      declarations: [ParentComponent, ChildComponent]
    });
    fixture = TestBed.createComponent(ParentComponent);
    component = fixture.componentInstance;
  });
  it('should pass input data to child component', () => {
    component.parentData = 'Test Data';
    fixture.detectChanges();
    const childComponent = fixture.debugElement.query(By.directive(ChildComponent)).
componentInstance;
    expect(childComponent.childData).toBe('Test Data');
```

```
  });
  it('should listen to child component event', () => {
    spyOn(component, 'onChildEvent');
    const childComponent = fixture.debugElement.query(By.directive(ChildComponent)).
componentInstance;
    childComponent.childEvent.emit('Child Event');
    expect(component.onChildEvent).toHaveBeenCalledWith('Child Event');
  });
});
```

In this example, **parentData** is passed to the child component via an input binding, and an event emitted by the child is captured by the parent.

Question 13: How do you mock HTTP requests in integration tests using HttpTestingController?

Answer: In integration tests, you can mock HTTP requests using **HttpTestingController** provided by Angular's **HttpClientTestingModule**. You simulate HTTP calls and control their responses. An example is given as follows:

```
import { TestBed } from '@angular/core/testing';
import { HttpClientTestingModule, HttpTestingController } from '@angular/common/http/
testing';
import { MyService } from './my-service';
import { HttpClient } from '@angular/common/http';
describe('MyService with HTTP', () => {
  let service: MyService;
  let httpMock: HttpTestingController;
  beforeEach(() => {
    TestBed.configureTestingModule({
      imports: [HttpClientTestingModule],
      providers: [MyService]
    });
    service = TestBed.inject(MyService);
    httpMock = TestBed.inject(HttpTestingController);
  });
  it('should fetch data', () => {
    const mockData = { name: 'Angular' };
    service.getData().subscribe(data => {
      expect(data.name).toBe('Angular');
    });
    const req = httpMock.expectOne('http://example.com/data');
    expect(req.request.method).toBe('GET');
    req.flush(mockData);
    httpMock.verify();
  });
});
```

Here, **expectOne()** checks for a specific HTTP request, and **flush()** is used to provide a mock response.

Question 14: How do you test an Angular component that makes API calls on initialization?

Answer: To test a component that makes API calls on initialization, you can mock the API service and verify that the component responds correctly. Use **`TestBed`** to configure the component with the necessary service mocks.

For example:

```
import { ComponentFixture, TestBed } from '@angular/core/testing';
import { MyComponent } from './my-component';
import { MyService } from './my-service';
import { of } from 'rxjs';
describe('MyComponent', () => {
  let fixture: ComponentFixture<MyComponent>;
  let component: MyComponent;
  let service: MyService;
  beforeEach(() => {
    TestBed.configureTestingModule({
      declarations: [MyComponent],
      providers: [
        {
          provide: MyService,
          useValue: { getData: () => of({ name: 'Angular' }) }
        }
      ]
    });
    fixture = TestBed.createComponent(MyComponent);
    component = fixture.componentInstance;
    service = TestBed.inject(MyService);
  });
  it('should fetch data on init', () => {
    fixture.detectChanges();
    expect(component.data.name).toBe('Angular');
  });
});
```

In this example, the service method **`getData`** is mocked using an observable to return the mock data.

Question 15: How do you validate form validation logic using Angular testing?

Answer: You can test form validation logic by simulating form inputs and validating their state. The **`TestBed`** environment allows you to directly interact with the form controls and check if they are valid or invalid.

For example:

```
import { ComponentFixture, TestBed } from '@angular/core/testing';
import { ReactiveFormsModule, FormGroup, FormControl, Validators } from '@angular/forms';
import { MyFormComponent } from './my-form.component';
describe('MyFormComponent', () => {
  let fixture: ComponentFixture<MyFormComponent>;
  let component: MyFormComponent;
```

```
  beforeEach(() => {
    TestBed.configureTestingModule({
      imports: [ReactiveFormsModule],
      declarations: [MyFormComponent]
    });
    fixture = TestBed.createComponent(MyFormComponent);
    component = fixture.componentInstance;
  });
  it('should show error when form is invalid', () => {
    component.form = new FormGroup({
      name: new FormControl('', [Validators.required])
    });
    component.form.controls['name'].setValue('');
    fixture.detectChanges();
    expect(component.form.invalid).toBeTrue();
    const errorMessage = fixture.nativeElement.querySelector('.error-message');
    expect(errorMessage).toBeTruthy();
  });
  it('should submit valid form', () => {
    component.form = new FormGroup({
      name: new FormControl('Angular', [Validators.required])
    });
    component.form.controls['name'].setValue('Angular');
    fixture.detectChanges();
    expect(component.form.valid).toBeTrue();
    component.onSubmit();
    expect(component.formSubmitted).toBeTrue();
  });
});
```

In this example, we check if the form is valid, simulate user input, and verify the form's validation state.

End-to-end testing

Question 16: What is a protractor, and why is it deprecated in favor of Playwright or Cypress?

Answer: Protractor is an **end-to-end (E2E)** testing framework for Angular applications. It is built on top of Selenium WebDriver and integrates tightly with Angular's change detection cycle, enabling automatic synchronization with the application's model. However, Protractor is deprecated due to several reasons:

- **Performance**: Selenium WebDriver, the backbone of protractor, is slower compared to newer alternatives like Playwright and Cypress.
- **Modern features**: Playwright and Cypress offer built-in support for modern JavaScript features, automatic waiting, better debugging capabilities, and simpler APIs.
- **Community support**: Protractor's development has slowed down, and the Angular team has officially recommended switching to Playwright or Cypress for future projects due to their active communities and more up-to-date features.

Question 17: How do you write E2E tests using Cypress for an Angular application?

Answer: To write E2E tests with Cypress in an Angular application, you must first install Cypress and then create tests within its framework. Follow the steps in the given example of how to get started with Cypress for an Angular app:

1. Install Cypress using **`npm`**:

   ```
   npm install cypress --save-dev
   ```

2. Add a script to your **`package.json`** to open Cypress:

   ```
   "scripts": {
     "cypress:open": "cypress open"
   }
   ```

3. Create a basic E2E test in Cypress:

   ```
   describe('Angular App', () => {
     it('should load the app and verify title', () => {
       cy.visit('http://localhost:4200');
       cy.contains('Welcome to Angular!');
     });
   });
   ```

4. Run the test:

   ```
   npm run cypress:open
   ```

This test visits the application and checks whether the page contains the text **`Welcome to Angular!`**

Question 18: How do you handle waiting for asynchronous operations in Angular E2E tests?

Answer: In Cypress, waiting for asynchronous operations can be done using built-in commands like **`cy.wait()`**, **`cy.intercept()`**, or implicitly waiting for elements to appear after a change. Cypress automatically waits for elements to be available, so you do not need to manually wait for Angular's change detection.

For example:

```
describe('Async Test', () => {
  it('should wait for API call to complete', () => {
    // Mock the API request
    cy.intercept('GET', '/api/data', { fixture: 'data.json' }).as('getData');

    // Visit the page
    cy.visit('http://localhost:4200');
    // Wait for the API response
    cy.wait('@getData');
    // Verify the data appears
    cy.get('.data-item').should('have.length', 3);
  });
});
```

Here, **`cy.wait('@getData')`** ensures that the test will wait for the GET /api/data request to complete before verifying the results.

Question 19: How do you test Angular authentication and authorization flows in E2E tests?

Answer: In E2E tests, authentication and authorization flows can be tested by mocking the authentication service and verifying that the application behaves as expected for authenticated and unauthenticated users.

Consider the following example:

```
describe('Authentication Flow', () => {
  it('should redirect to login page when user is not authenticated', () => {
    cy.visit('http://localhost:4200/dashboard');
    cy.url().should('include', '/login');
  });
  it('should allow access to protected routes when authenticated', () => {
    // Mock the authentication service to simulate a logged-in user
    cy.intercept('GET', '/api/user', { fixture: 'user.json' }).as('getUser');
    cy.visit('http://localhost:4200/dashboard');
    cy.wait('@getUser');
    cy.url().should('not.include', '/login');
  });
});
```

In this example, the first test ensures that unauthenticated users are redirected to the login page, while the second test checks that authenticated users can access protected routes.

Question 20: What are the best practices for writing maintainable and scalable E2E tests in Angular?

Answer: Here are some best practices for writing maintainable and scalable E2E tests in Angular:

- **Use Cypress or Playwright**: Both are modern and more efficient than older tools like Protractor, offering faster execution and better debugging tools.
- **Modularize tests**: Organize tests into logical groups and separate them by feature. Use **`describe()`** blocks to group related tests together.
- **Leverage page object pattern**: This helps you maintain a clean and **Don't Repeat Yourself** (**DRY**) approach, by abstracting interactions with the UI into separate page object classes or functions.

  An example of the page object pattern is as follows:

  ```
  class LoginPage {
    visit() {
      cy.visit('/login');
    }
    fillUsername(username) {
      cy.get('input[name="username"]').type(username);
    }
    fillPassword(password) {
      cy.get('input[name="password"]').type(password);
    }
    submit() {
      cy.get('button[type="submit"]').click();
    }
  }
  ```
- **Use fixtures for test data**: Store reusable test data in fixtures to avoid hardcoding data in tests.
- **Avoid overuse of cy.wait()**: Prefer waiting for specific elements or API calls to complete, as Cypress automatically waits for elements to be available, reducing the need for explicit waits.

- **Use custom commands**: Cypress allows you to create custom commands to simplify repetitive actions in your tests, improving maintainability.
- **Test edge cases and negative scenarios**: Write tests for edge cases, such as invalid user input or unauthorized access, to ensure the robustness of your application.
- **Run tests continuously**: Integrate your tests into a **continuous integration** (**CI**) pipeline to ensure they are run frequently and issues are caught early.

By following these practices, you can ensure that your E2E tests remain easy to maintain as your application grows and evolves.

Performance, debugging, security-related tests

Question 21: **How do you optimize performance when running large Angular test suites?**

Answer: To optimize performance when running large Angular test suites, follow these steps:

1. **Run tests in parallel**: Utilize test runners like Karma with parallel execution, or leverage CI/CD tools to run tests on multiple nodes concurrently.
2. **Lazy loading of test modules**: Only load modules needed for each specific test. Avoid loading all the modules at once.
3. **Use beforeEach() smartly**: Avoid redundant setups in **`beforeEach()`**. Reuse common setup code where possible.
4. **Test coverage optimization**: Focus on testing core functionality. Skip testing trivial details and use mocks and spies to limit unnecessary overhead.
5. **Use Jasmine's fdescribe()/fit() for selective test execution**: Temporarily focus on smaller groups of tests for debugging or quicker runs.
6. **Remove redundant mocking**: Avoid redundant mocking and spying in the same tests. Mock only what is required for each test case.

Question 22: **How do you test Angular applications for memory leaks using Jest or Cypress?**

Answer: For testing memory leaks in Angular:

- **Jest**: Use jest to test memory leaks by monitoring the number of event listeners and DOM nodes before and after component destruction.

  For example:

  ```
  afterEach(() => {
    const initialCount = performance.memory.usedJSHeapSize;
    // Your component mounting and unmounting logic
    const finalCount = performance.memory.usedJSHeapSize;
    expect(finalCount - initialCount).toBeLessThan(100000); // Allow for small memory
  usage
  });
  ```

- **Cypress**: You can track memory usage indirectly by using **`cy.window()`** to get the window object, and check the memory heap before and after the test runs.

Question 23: **How do you debug failing Angular tests effectively?**

Answer: To debug failing Angular tests effectively, follow these steps:

1. **Enable verbose logging**: Increase verbosity in Jasmine and Karma to get more detailed output on test failures.
2. **Use browser DevTools**: For failing E2E tests in Cypress or Protractor, open the browser's dev tools to inspect console logs, network requests, and application state.

3. **Isolate failing tests**: Use `fdescribe()` or `fit()` to isolate failing tests and focus debugging efforts on them.
4. **Use debugger statements**: Place debugger statements in your code to pause execution and inspect variables during runtime.
5. **Run tests with --watch mode**: This mode in Karma allows you to run tests continuously and catch failures early during development.
6. **Check for timing issues**: Failing tests due to timing can be debugged by increasing waits or using Angular's async utilities like `fakeAsync()` and `tick()`.

Question 24: How does Angular 20 improve test execution speed and debugging support?

Answer: Angular 20 introduces several optimizations:

- **Faster test execution**: By reducing unnecessary computations and improving the `TestBed` setup, Angular 20 enhances test execution speed.
- **Better debugging**: Angular 20 integrates deeper debugging support, such as improved stack traces, better error messages, and enhanced logging.
- **Smarter change detection**: Tests benefit from more intelligent change detection, where unnecessary checks are skipped, speeding up test execution.

Question 25: How do you test Angular server-side rendering (SSR) applications in the latest versions?

Answer: To test SSR applications in Angular:

- **Use Angular universal testing tools**: Angular provides `@angular/platform-server` for SSR testing.
- **Mock HTTP requests**: Use mock data for API calls during SSR tests to ensure server-side rendering behaves correctly.
- **Test rendering on server**: Validate that the application renders the correct markup server-side and matches the client-side rendering output.
- **Run integration tests**: Use tools like Cypress or Jest to simulate user interactions after SSR content is loaded.

Conclusion

Testing is an essential part of Angular application development, ensuring that components, services, directives, and pipes work as expected. By leveraging unit tests, integration tests, and E2E tests, developers can maintain high-quality, robust applications.

Tools like Jasmine, Karma, and Cypress provide powerful capabilities for writing and executing tests efficiently. Additionally, best practices such as test isolation, mocking dependencies, and using fakeAsync() for time-based operations help improve test reliability.

A well-tested Angular application leads to fewer bugs, better maintainability, and a smoother development process.

In the next chapter, we will explore how to integrate Angular Material components into applications, enhancing the UI with pre-built, customizable design elements.

CHAPTER 21
Angular Material

Introduction

Angular Material is a UI component library that provides pre-built, customizable, and accessible components following Google's Material Design principles. It enhances Angular applications with a consistent look and feel, making development faster and more efficient. This chapter explores how to integrate Angular Material into projects, customize themes, and utilize various components to build modern and responsive user interfaces.

Structure

This chapter covers the following topics:

- Understanding Angular Material
- Advanced Angular Material
- Angular Material authentication and authorization

Objectives

By the end of this chapter, you will have a comprehensive understanding of Angular Material and its role in creating modern, responsive, and accessible Angular applications. You will learn how to install and configure Angular Material, apply theming and customization, and effectively use pre-built UI components for forms, navigation, layouts, and data display. Additionally, this chapter will cover implementing authentication and authorization mechanisms using Angular Material components to build secure user interfaces. Finally, you will explore best practices to enhance performance, maintain UI consistency, and improve the overall user experience in your Angular applications.

Understanding Angular Material

Question 1: What is Angular Material?

Answer: Angular Material is a UI component library for Angular applications, developed by the Angular team at *Google*. It provides a set of reusable, accessible, and responsive UI components (for example, buttons, forms, tables) that follow Material Design guidelines, ensuring a consistent and modern user experience. It is built on top of the Angular **component dev kit** (**CDK**) and integrates seamlessly with Angular to speed up development.

For example: Using a basic button from Angular Material:

```
import { MatButtonModule } from '@angular/material/button';
@NgModule({
  imports: [MatButtonModule],
  // ...
})
export class AppModule { }
```

In your component template:

```
<button mat-button color="primary">Click Me</button>
```

This uses the latest styling and accessibility features of Angular Material.

Angular Material works seamlessly with standalone components by importing Material modules into the component's imports array directly. You do not need an NgModule to use Material components in a standalone component. Let us look at how to use Angular Material components in standalone components. To create a standalone component, follow these steps:

1. **Use --standalone flag when generating the component**:

   ```
   ng generate component my-standalone --standalone
   ```

2. **Import Material modules**:

   a. Import Angular Material components (for example, **`MatDialog`**) directly to the imports array:

   ```
   import { MatDialog } from '@angular/material/dialog';
   @Component({
     selector: 'app-my-standalone',
     standalone: true,
     imports: [MatDialog]
   })
   export class MyStandaloneComponent { ... }
   ```

3. **Use Material components**: You can now use Angular Material components like dialogs, buttons, and so on, inside your standalone component.

This way, Angular Material components integrate easily with standalone components for a more modular and flexible application.

Question 2: **How does Angular Material differ from regular Angular?**

Answer: Angular is a full-fledged framework for building web applications, providing core features like components, services, routing, and dependency injection. Angular Material, on the other hand, is a library built on Angular that focuses on UI components and styling, adhering to Material Design. While Angular provides the structure, Angular Material adds pre-designed, themed components to enhance the UI.

For example: A regular Angular might define a component like this:

```
import { Component } from '@angular/core';
@Component({
  selector: 'app-example',
  template: '<button>Click</button>',
})
export class ExampleComponent {}
```

With Angular Material, you enhance it:

```
import { MatButtonModule } from '@angular/material/button';
@NgModule({
  imports: [MatButtonModule],
})
@Component({
  selector: 'app-material-example',
  template: '<button mat-button color="primary">Material Click</button>',
})
export class MaterialExampleComponent {}
```

The material version includes styling, hover effects, and accessibility out of the box.

Question 3: How do you install Angular Material in an Angular project?

Answer: To install Angular Material in an Angular project (using Angular CLI), follow these steps:

1. Ensure you have Angular CLI installed and an Angular project set up.
2. Run the following command to add Angular Material:

   `ng add @angular/material@latest`
3. During installation, you will be prompted to select a prebuilt theme (for example, Indigo-Pink), set up animations, and configure global typography. Choose **Yes** for animations and a theme.
4. After installation, Angular Material, Angular CDK, and Angular Animations are added to your **`package.json`**, and styles are set in **`styles.scss`**.

Refer to the following key points:

- The **`ng add`** command configures Angular Material with best practices, including accessibility and theming.
- For Angular 18+ standalone components (default in later versions), import Material modules directly into components, avoiding NgModules.
- Recent updates (Angular Material 19) improved installation with better tree-shaking and **server-side rendering** (**SSR**) support.

For example: Verifying installation by importing a module:

```
import { MatCardModule } from '@angular/material/card';
@NgModule({
  imports: [MatCardModule],
  // ...
})
export class AppModule { }
In your template:
<mat-card>
  <mat-card-title>Card Title</mat-card-title>
  <mat-card-content>Content here</mat-card-content>
</mat-card>
```

Question 4: What are Angular Material themes? How do you create a custom theme?

Answer: Angular Material themes define the visual style (colors, typography, density) of components. The library provides prebuilt themes (for example, **`indigo-pink`**, **`deeppurple-amber`**), but you can create custom themes for unique designs.

To create a custom theme (latest version):

- Use SCSS to define a custom theme in a file (for example, **custom-theme.scss**):

```
@import '~@angular/material/theming';
$custom-primary: mat-define-palette(mat-blue, 500, 100, 900);
$custom-accent: mat-define-palette(mat-amber, A200, A100, A400);
$custom-warn: mat-define-palette(mat-red, 500);
$custom-theme: mat-light-theme($custom-primary, $custom-accent, $custom-warn);
@include angular-material-theme($custom-theme);
```

- In your **styles.scss**:

```
@import './custom-theme';
```

This creates a light theme. For dark themes or dynamic switching, use mat-dark-theme or Angular's theming APIs.

For example: You can apply the theme to a component as follows:

```
<button mat-button color="custom-primary">Custom Theme Button</button>
```

Question 5: What is a Material Dialog, and how do you use it?

Answer: A Material Dialog (mat-dialog) is a modal window for user interaction, such as forms or confirmations. It is opened programmatically using the **MatDialog** service. For example, to use **MatDialog** with a standalone component in Angular (version 19+), follow these steps:

1. **First, create a standalone dialog component**:

```
import { Component } from '@angular/core';
import { MatDialog } from '@angular/material/dialog';
import { MatButtonModule } from '@angular/material/button';
@Component({
  selector: 'app-dialog',
  template: `<h2 mat-dialog-title>Dialog</h2>
             <button mat-button mat-dialog-close>Close</button>`,
  standalone: true,
  imports: [MatButtonModule]
})
export class DialogComponent {}
```

2. **Now, open the previous dialog in the main component**:

```
import { Component } from '@angular/core';
import { MatDialog } from '@angular/material/dialog';
import { DialogComponent } from './dialog.component';
import { MatButtonModule } from '@angular/material/button';
@Component({
  selector: 'app-root',
  template: `<button mat-button (click)="openDialog()">Open Dialog</button>`,
  standalone: true,
  imports: [MatButtonModule]
})
export class AppComponent {
  constructor(private dialog: MatDialog) {}
```

```
  openDialog() {
    this.dialog.open(DialogComponent);
  }
}
```

The result is that clicking **Open Dialog** opens the dialog.

Consider another example of using **`MatDialog`** with NgModule:

1. **Import MatDialogModule in your module**:

```
import {MatDialogModule} from '@angular/material/dialog';
@NgModule({
  imports: [MatDialogModule],
})
export class AppModule { }
```

2. **Create a dialog component**:

```
import { Component } from '@angular/core';
@Component({
  selector: 'app-dialog',
  template: `<h2 mat-dialog-title>Confirm Action</h2>
             <mat-dialog-content>Are you sure?</mat-dialog-content>
             <mat-dialog-actions>
               <button mat-button [mat-dialog-close]="false">No</button>
               <button mat-button [mat-dialog-close]="true" cdkFocusInitial>Yes</
button>
             </mat-dialog-actions>`,
})
export class DialogComponent {}
```

3. **Now, open a dialog from another component**:

```
import {MatDialog} from '@angular/material/dialog';
constructor(private dialog: MatDialog) {}
openDialog() {
  const dialogRef = this.dialog.open(DialogComponent, {
    width: '250px',
    data: {name:'User' },
  });
  dialogRef.afterClosed().subscribe(result => {
    console.log('Dialog result:', result);
  });
}
```

This uses Angular Material enhanced dialog features, like improved focus trapping and ARIA support.

Question 6: How do you use Angular Material Table (mat-table) with sorting, filtering, and pagination?

Answer: The **`<mat-table>`** component displays data in a tabular format with sorting, filtering, and pagination. Consider the following example:

- **Import required modules**:

```
import { MatTableModule } from '@angular/material/table';
```

```
import { MatSortModule } from '@angular/material/sort';
import { MatPaginatorModule } from '@angular/material/paginator';
import { MatFormFieldModule } from '@angular/material/form-field';
import { MatInputModule } from '@angular/material/input';
@NgModule({
  imports: [MatTableModule, MatSortModule, MatPaginatorModule, MatFormFieldModule, MatInputModule],
})
export class AppModule { }
```

- **Component and template**:

```
import { Component, ViewChild } from '@angular/core';
import { MatTableDataSource } from '@angular/material/table';
import { MatSort } from '@angular/material/sort';
import { MatPaginator } from '@angular/material/paginator';
export interface User {
  name: string;
  email: string;
}
@Component({
  selector: 'app-table',
  template: `
    <mat-form-field>
      <mat-label>Filter</mat-label>
      <input matInput (keyup)="applyFilter($event)" placeholder="Ex. Mia">
    </mat-form-field>
    <table mat-table [dataSource]="dataSource" matSort>
      <ng-container matColumnDef="name">
        <th mat-header-cell *matHeaderCellDef mat-sort-header> Name </th>
        <td mat-cell *matCellDef="let element"> {{element.name}} </td>
      </ng-container>
      <ng-container matColumnDef="email">
        <th mat-header-cell *matHeaderCellDef mat-sort-header> Email </th>
        <td mat-cell *matCellDef="let element"> {{element.email}} </td>
      </ng-container>
      <tr mat-header-row *matHeaderRowDef="displayedColumns"></tr>
      <tr mat-row *matRowDef="let row; columns: displayedColumns;"></tr>
    </table>
    <mat-paginator [pageSizeOptions]="[5, 10, 20]" showFirstLastButtons></mat-paginator>
  `,
})
export class TableComponent {
  displayedColumns: string[] = ['name', 'email'];
  dataSource = new MatTableDataSource<User>([
```

```
    { name: 'Mia', email: 'mia@example.com' },
    { name: 'John', email: 'john@example.com' },
  ]);
  @ViewChild(MatSort) sort: MatSort;
  @ViewChild(MatPaginator) paginator: MatPaginator;
  ngAfterViewInit() {
    this.dataSource.sort = this.sort;
    this.dataSource.paginator = this.paginator;
  }
  applyFilter(event: Event) {
    const filterValue = (event.target as HTMLInputElement).value;
    this.dataSource.filter = filterValue.trim().toLowerCase();
  }
}
```

This example uses Angular Material improved table performance and accessibility.

Question 7: What are Angular Material's best practices for accessibility (a11y)?

Answer: Angular Material emphasizes accessibility with built-in ARIA attributes, keyboard navigation, and screen reader support. Best practices include:

- Use semantic HTML and ARIA roles (for example, **`aria-label`**, **`aria-describedby`**).
- Ensure keyboard navigation works (for example, *Tab*, *Enter*, *Space*).
- Test with screen readers like NVDA or VoiceOver.
- Use **`cdkTrapFocus`** for modal dialogs to trap focus.

For example:

```
<button mat-button aria-label="Close dialog">Close</button>
<mat-form-field>
  <mat-label>Username</mat-label>
  <input matInput aria-describedby="user-desc" placeholder="Username">
  <span id="user-desc">Enter your username</span>
</mat-form-field>
```

Question 8: How do you implement drag-and-drop using Angular Material?

Answer: Use the Angular CDK's drag-and-drop module, which Angular Material builds upon. Refer to the following example:

- **Import DragDropModule**:

  ```
  import { DragDropModule } from '@angular/cdk/drag-drop';
  @NgModule({
    imports: [DragDropModule],
  })
  export class AppModule { }
  ```

- **Component template**:

  ```
  <div cdkDropList class="example-list" (cdkDropListDropped)="drop($event)">
    <div class="example-box" *ngFor="let item of items" cdkDrag>{{item}}</div>
  </div>
  ```

- **Component TS**:

```
import { CdkDragDrop, moveItemInArray } from '@angular/cdk/drag-drop';
@Component({...})
export class DragDropComponent {
  items = ['Item 1', 'Item 2', 'Item 3'];
  drop(event: CdkDragDrop<string[]>) {
    moveItemInArray(this.items, event.previousIndex, event.currentIndex);
  }
}
```

This uses Angular Material drag-and-drop enhancements for smooth animations.

Question 9: **What are Angular Material Steppers?**

Answer: Angular Material Steppers (mat-stepper) guide users through a series of steps, like a wizard or form process.

For example:

```
import { MatStepperModule } from '@angular/material/stepper';
@NgModule({
  imports: [MatStepperModule],
})
@Component({
  template: `
    <mat-horizontal-stepper>
      <mat-step label="Step 1">
        <p>Step 1 content</p>
        <button mat-button matStepperNext>Next</button>
      </mat-step>
      <mat-step label="Step 2">
        <p>Step 2 content</p>
        <button mat-button matStepperPrevious>Back</button>
        <button mat-button matStepperNext>Next</button>
      </mat-step>
      <mat-step label="Step 3">
        <p>Step 3 content</p>
        <button mat-button matStepperPrevious>Back</button>
      </mat-step>
    </mat-horizontal-stepper>
  `,
})
export class StepperComponent {}
```

Question 10: **What is new in Angular Material (latest version)?**

Answer: As for Angular Material:

- **Better performance**: Optimized bundle sizes and lazy loading support.
- **Enhanced accessibility**: New ARIA roles and improved keyboard navigation.

- **Dynamic theming**: Support for runtime theme switching via CSS custom properties.
- **New components**: Updated data grids and form controls with better customization.
- **Improved documentation**: Interactive examples and API explorer.

An example of new dynamic theming is as follows:

```
:host {
  --mdc-theme-primary: #1976d2;
  --mdc-theme-secondary: #f44336;
}
```

Question 11: How do you lazy load Angular Material modules?

Answer: Lazy load Material modules using Angular's **`loadChildren`** in routes.

For example:

```
const routes: Routes = [
  {
    path: 'material',
    loadChildren: () => import('./material.module').then(m => m.MaterialModule),
  },
];
@NgModule({
  imports: [RouterModule.forRoot(routes)],
})
export class AppRoutingModule { }
```

In `material.module.ts`:

```
import { NgModule } from '@angular/core';
import { MatButtonModule } from '@angular/material/button';
@NgModule({
  declarations: [],
  imports: [MatButtonModule],
})
export class MaterialModule {}
```

Question 12: How do you use Angular Material Snackbar (MatSnackBar)?

Answer: **`MatSnackBar`** shows temporary notifications. Refer to the following example:

```
import { MatSnackBar } from '@angular/material/snack-bar';
constructor(private snackBar: MatSnackBar) {}
showSnackBar() {
  this.snackBar.open('Message sent!', 'Close', {
    duration: 3000,
    panelClass: ['custom-snackbar'],
  });
}
```

Question 13: What is the difference between mat-dialog and mat-snack-bar in Angular Material?

Answer: See *Answer 8* for a detailed explanation. **`mat-dialog`** is modal and blocks interaction, while mat-snack-bar is non-modal and temporary.

Question 14: How do you test Angular Material components?

Answer: Use Jasmine or Karma with Angular Material harnesses.

For example:

```
import { TestBed } from '@angular/core/testing';
import { MatButtonHarness } from '@angular/material/button/testing';
import { HarnessLoader } from '@angular/cdk/testing';
describe('ButtonTest', () => {
  let loader: HarnessLoader;
  beforeEach(async () => {
    await TestBed.configureTestingModule({
      imports: [MatButtonModule],
    }).compileComponents();
    loader = TestbedHarnessEnvironment.loader();
  });
  it('should click button', async () => {
    const button = await loader.getHarness(MatButtonHarness);
    await button.click();
    // Assert
  });
});
```

Question 15: Can you integrate Angular Material with other UI libraries or frameworks?

Answer: Yes, but ensure there are no style conflicts. Use Shadow DOM or CSS modules.

Consider an example with Bootstrap:

```
:host ::ng-deep .mat-button {
  margin-right: 10px;
}
```

Question 16: What are some common challenges when using Angular Material, and how do you overcome them?

Answer: Challenges include style overrides and bundle size. Use custom themes and tree-shaking.

Only import needed modules:

```
import { MatButtonModule } from '@angular/material/button';
```

Question 17: How do you handle responsive design with Angular Material?

Answer: Use breakpoints and flexible layouts.

For example:

```
import { BreakpointObserver } from '@angular/cdk/layout';
constructor(private breakpointObserver: BreakpointObserver) {
  this.breakpointObserver.observe(['(max-width: 600px)']).subscribe(result => {
    this.isMobile = result.matches;
  });
}
```

Question 18: How do you debug issues in Angular Material components?

Answer: Use browser DevTools, Angular DevTools, and console logs.

For example: Checking for errors:

```
console.log('Component initialized');
```

Advanced Angular Material

Question 19: How does Angular Material optimize rendering performance?

Answer: Angular Material optimizes rendering performance by:

- **Lazy loading**: It allows the lazy loading of modules (for example, **MatDialog**, **MatTable**), ensuring that only the necessary components are loaded when needed.
- **Change detection strategy**: It uses OnPush change detection for components like **MatTable** to minimize unnecessary DOM updates.

For example:

```
@Component({
  selector: 'app-mat-table',
  changeDetection: ChangeDetectionStrategy.OnPush,
  template: `<mat-table [dataSource]="dataSource"></mat-table>`
})
export class MatTableComponent { ... }
```

Question 20: How do you improve performance in Angular Material tables with large datasets?

Answer: Use virtual scrolling and pagination to manage large datasets:

- **Virtual scrolling**: Renders only the rows that are currently visible in the viewport.
- **Pagination**: Limits the number of rows per page.

For example:

```
<mat-table mat-table [dataSource]="dataSource" matSort>
  <mat-header-row *matHeaderRowDef="displayedColumns"></mat-header-row>
  <mat-row *matRowDef="let row; columns: displayedColumns;"></mat-row>
</mat-table>
<mat-paginator [length]="totalLength" [pageSize]="pageSize"></mat-paginator>
```

Question 21: How does Angular Material handle security vulnerabilities like XSS attacks?

Answer: Angular Material provides built-in sanitization to prevent XSS attacks. Angular automatically escapes potentially dangerous content, ensuring that no user-generated content can execute scripts.

For example:

```
<!-- Angular automatically sanitizes dangerous HTML -->
<p [innerHTML]="userInput"></p>
```

Question 22: What is Angular Material's role in Content Security Policy (CSP) compliance?

Answer: Angular Material follows best practices for CSP compliance by avoiding inline scripts and using external JavaScript files. The components use Angular's built-in sanitization to ensure secure usage of data.

Question 23: How do you optimize Angular Material Dialog (MatDialog) for better performance?

Answer: Angular **Material Dialogs (MatDialog)** are powerful but can impact performance if not optimized, especially on mobile or with frequent opens or closes. Here are the best practices to optimize MatDialog:

- **Lazy load dialogs**: Load dialog components only when needed.
- **Use afterClosed** to avoid keeping unnecessary components in memory.

- **Minimize DOM size**: Keep dialog content lightweight.
- **Disable animations if unnecessary**: Reduce CPU usage on low-end devices.
- **Use OnPush change detection**: Limit unnecessary checks.
- **Debounce opens**: Delay dialog opening to prevent rapid triggers.
- **Reuse instances**: Cache dialog instances to avoid recreation.
- **Profile and test**: Use tools to identify bottlenecks.

For example:

```
const dialogRef = this.dialog.open(MyLazyDialogComponent);
dialogRef.afterClosed().subscribe(result => { ... });
```

Question 24: **How do you secure Angular Material Forms against CSRF attacks?**

Answer: Use HTTP interceptors to automatically include CSRF tokens in requests. Ensure Angular Material forms use proper input sanitization and validation.

For example:

```
@Injectable()
export class CsrfInterceptor implements HttpInterceptor {
  intercept(req: HttpRequest<any>, next: HttpHandler): Observable<HttpEvent<any>> {
    const csrfToken = this.getCsrfToken();
    req = req.clone({ setHeaders: { 'X-CSRF-TOKEN': csrfToken } });
    return next.handle(req);
  }
}
```

Question 25: **How does Angular Material improve SSR performance?**

Answer: Angular Material supports SSR by ensuring components are optimized for both server and client. It reduces the initial load time by pre-rendering components and their styles on the server. Angular Material enhances SSR performance through these strategies:

- **Hydration support**: Ensures fast client-side activation after server rendering.
- **Lazy loading**: Delays loading of Material components until needed.
- **Optimized rendering**: Minimizes DOM manipulation and CSS overhead.
- **Pre-rendered components**: Material components render efficiently on the server with minimal JavaScript.
- **Reduced bundle size**: Tree-shaking and modular imports lessen server load.
- **Accessibility and SEO**: Material components maintain ARIA attributes and semantic HTML for better indexing.

Question 26: **How do you reduce Angular Material bundle size?**

Answer: Reducing the bundle size of Angular Material improves load times and performance, especially on mobiles or slow networks. Here are the best practices to reduce bundle size:

- **Import only needed modules**: Avoid importing the entire library; use specific Material modules.
- **Use tree-shaking**: Ensure unused code is eliminated during build.
- **Lazy load components**: Defer loading of Material components until needed.
- **Minify and compress**: Use production builds with minification.
- **Remove unused styles**: Eliminate unused CSS from themes.
- **Optimize assets**: Use CDN or compress assets like fonts.
- **Lazy load modules**: Load Angular Material components only when necessary.

Question 27: How do you prevent clickjacking attacks in Angular Material apps?

Answer: Clickjacking is an attack where malicious code tricks users into clicking on hidden elements, potentially performing unintended actions. To secure Angular Material apps, use these best practices:

- **Use X-Frame-options header:** Prevent your app from being iframed by unauthorized sites.
- **Implement Content Security Policy (CSP):** Restrict framing and scripting.
- **Frame-busting script:** Add JavaScript to break out of iframes.
- **Secure Material Dialogs:** Ensure Material components like dialogs and buttons are not exploitable in iframes.
- **Test for vulnerabilities:** Regularly check for clickjacking risks.

Question 28: How do you optimize Angular Material performance on mobile devices?

Answer: Mobile devices often have limited processing power, memory, and network bandwidth, so optimizing Angular Material components is crucial. Here are the best practices to optimize performance on mobile:

- **Use Material Design's responsive layouts** with media queries.
- **Minimize DOM size:** Lazy load Material components when necessary.
- **Minimize bundle size:** Load only necessary Material modules.
- **Use lazy loading:** Defer loading of components until needed.
- **Disable animations:** Reduce CPU usage on low-end devices.
- **Leverage virtual scrolling:** Render only visible content for lists or tables.
- **Optimize touch events:** Reduce event listeners for better responsiveness.
- **Responsive design:** Adjust layouts for smaller screens.
- **Profile and test on mobile:** Use device emulators or real devices to identify bottlenecks.

Question 29: What are the differences between MDC-based components and legacy Angular Material components?

Answer: **Material Design Components** (**MDC**) is the new set of components introduced in Angular Material that follow the latest Material Design guidelines, offering improved performance and better accessibility. Legacy components are based on Angular's older rendering approach.

Question 30: How to prevent memory leaks when using Angular Material components?

Answer: To prevent memory leaks:

- **Unsubscribe from observables** using takeUntil or async pipe.
- **Destroy dialogs** and subscriptions properly.

For example:

```
ngOnDestroy() {
  this.subscription.unsubscribe();
}
```

Question 31: How do you enable dark mode in Angular Material dynamically?

Answer: You can enable dark mode dynamically by switching between light and dark themes using Angular's MatSlideToggle to toggle themes.

For example:

```
@Component({
  selector: 'app-theme-toggle',
  template: `<mat-slide-toggle (change)="toggleDarkMode($event.checked)">Dark Mode</mat-
slide-toggle>`
```

```
})
export class ThemeToggleComponent {
  toggleDarkMode(isDark: boolean) {
    document.body.classList.toggle('dark-theme', isDark);
  }
}
```

Question 32: How do you implement role-based authentication in Angular Material UI?

Answer: Use Angular's **Route Guards** to secure routes based on user roles and permissions.

For example:

```
@Injectable({
  providedIn: 'root',
})
export class RoleGuard implements CanActivate {
  constructor(private authService: AuthService) {}
  canActivate(): boolean {
    return this.authService.hasRole('admin');
  }
}
```

Question 33: How do you prevent SQL injection and XSS in Angular Material forms?

Answer: Angular Material forms automatically escape unsafe inputs, and you can use Angular's **form validation** and **input sanitization** to protect against SQL injection and XSS.

Question 34: How do you optimize Angular Material tooltips (matTooltip) for performance?

Answer: Angular Material tooltips are lightweight by default, but performance can be enhanced by minimizing DOM overhead, reducing event listeners, and optimizing rendering.

Here are the best practices:

- **Lazy loading**: Load tooltips only when needed.
- **Debouncing**: Delay tooltip display to reduce unnecessary renders.
- **Minimize DOM impact**: Avoid complex HTML in tooltips.
- **Use OnPush change detection**: Reduce unnecessary checks.
- **Limit event listeners**: Optimize hover and focus events.
- **Disable animations if unnecessary**: Reduce CPU usage.
- **Profile and test**: Use browser tools to identify bottlenecks.

Use **manual activation** of tooltips to reduce unnecessary calculations and renderings.

For example:

```
<button mat-button [matTooltip]="tooltipText" matTooltipPosition="above">Hover me</button>
```

Question 35: What are the best practices for handling large datasets in Angular Material Data Table (MatTable)?

Answer: The best practices for handling large datasets in Angular Material Data Table are:

- **Use virtual scrolling**: It allows for rendering large datasets efficiently and renders only visible rows for large datasets.
- **Use pagination**: It will split large data into manageable chunks and limit visible rows to improve performance.

- **Implement filtering efficiently**: Filter on the client or server side without loading all data.
- **Optimize sorting**: Use server-side sorting for large datasets.
- **Lazy loading**: Fetch data in chunks from the server.
- **Reduce bundle size**: Import only necessary modules.
- **Track changes**: Use trackBy to improve rendering performance.

Some additional tips are as follows:

- **Server-side operations**: For thousands of rows, use server-side filtering, sorting, and pagination to minimize client-side load.
- **Debouncing**: Add debouncing to filter inputs to prevent excessive computations.
- **Performance profiling**: Use Angular DevTools or browser Profiler to check render times.

This approach ensures Angular Material MatTable handles large datasets efficiently in Angular 18+, balancing performance and usability.

Question 36: How can you reduce Angular Material's CSS footprint?

Answer: Minimize CSS by:

- Using Angular's built-in tree-shaking to remove unused styles.
- Lazy loading Material modules to load only necessary styles.

Question 37: How do you secure Angular Material file uploads (MatFileUpload)?

Answer: Ensure proper input sanitization and validate file types and sizes before uploading. Use HTTPS to secure file transfers. As of February 2025, Angular Material itself does not provide a built-in MatFileUpload component. However, based on web resources and community packages like angular-material-fileupload or mat-file-upload, you can secure file uploads in Angular Material by implementing several best practices.

To secure Angular Material File Uploads, follow these steps:

1. **Validate file types and size**: Ensure only allowed file types (for example, PDF, images) and sizes are accepted client-side and server-side.
2. **Use HTTPS**: Always use HTTPS to encrypt data in transit.
3. **Authenticate and authorize**: Require users to be authenticated (for example, via JWT or OAuth) and authorized to upload files.
4. **Sanitize inputs**: Validate and sanitize file metadata to prevent injection attacks.
5. **Secure backend**: Use server-side validation, store files securely (for example, in a private directory), and generate unique filenames.
6. **CSRF protection**: Add CSRF tokens for state-changing requests.
7. **Progress and error handling**: Show upload progress and handle errors securely without exposing sensitive data.

Question 38: How do you implement lazy loading with Angular Material components?

Answer: Lazy loading in Angular delays loading of components, modules, or libraries (like Angular Material) until they are needed, improving initial load time and performance. With Angular Material, you can lazy load entire feature modules, standalone components, or specific Material components. The key steps are:

1. **Use Angular routing for lazy loading**: Define routes to load Material components or modules lazily.
2. **Standalone components or NgModules**: Lazy load either standalone components (preferred in Angular 18+) or traditional NgModules.
3. **Tree-shaking**: Ensure only used Material components are included in the lazy loaded bundle.
4. **Preloading strategies**: Optionally use Angular's preloading strategy for a better user experience.

For example: Lazy loading Angular Material components using NgModules and router:

```
const routes: Routes = [
  {
    path: 'lazy loaded', loadChildren: () => import('./lazy loaded/lazy loaded.module').
then(m => m.LazyLoadedModule)
  }
];
```

Question 39: How does Angular Material handle performance optimizations in animations?

Answer: Angular Material uses **animations** based on the **Angular Animation API**, ensuring smooth transitions with minimal impact on performance. It optimizes animations by using Angular's @angular/animations module, leveraging hardware-accelerated properties like transform and opacity, and implementing features like lazy loading and debouncing. In Angular Material (latest version), it includes animation prefetching, CSS custom properties, and the Web Animations API for better performance. You can disable animations for low-performance scenarios using **`NoopAnimationsModule`**. The key points are:

- Angular Material (latest version) optimizations include lazy loading (animations load only when needed), CSS custom properties for dynamic tweaks, and the Web Animations API for cross-browser efficiency.
- Profile performance using browser DevTools to ensure animations remain smooth, especially on low-end devices.

Question 40: How do you prevent memory leaks when using Angular Material subscriptions?

Answer: Use **takeUntil** or **async pipe** to automatically manage subscriptions and avoid memory leaks.

For example:

```
import { Subject } from 'rxjs';
import { takeUntil } from 'rxjs/operators';
export class MyComponent implements OnInit, OnDestroy {
  private destroy$ = new Subject<void>();
  ngOnInit() {
    this.myService.getData().pipe(takeUntil(this.destroy$)).subscribe(data => { ... });
  }
  ngOnDestroy() {
    this.destroy$.next();
    this.destroy$.complete();
  }
}
```

Conclusion

In this chapter, we explored Angular Material, a powerful UI component library that enhances Angular applications with a consistent, responsive, and accessible design. By leveraging its pre-built components, theming capabilities, and flexible APIs, developers can build modern applications efficiently.

With this, we conclude our discussion on Angular Material and the book itself. Mastering these concepts ensures you can create scalable, high-performance Angular applications. Stay updated with the latest advancements, follow best practices, and keep building great applications!

Index

A

www.ingramcontent.com/pod-product-compliance
Lightning Source LLC
Chambersburg PA
CBHW082128210326
41599CB00031B/5907
* 9 7 8 9 3 6 5 8 9 9 5 2 8 *